For Working with Files

To Do This	Select This		
Create a new page	File	New	Page		
Create a new web	File	New	Web		
Create a new folder	File	New	Folder		
Open page	File	Open Page Or double-click on page in Folder view		CTRL-O
Open web	File	Open Web		
Close web	File	Close Web		
Close (either page or web)	File	Close		CTRL-F4
Save	File	Save		CTRL-S
Save as	File	Save As		
Publish web	File	Publish Web		
Import	File	Import		
Preview in browser	File	Preview in Browser		
Set up page	File	Page Setup		
Set properties	File	Properties		
Select from recent files	File	Recent Files		
Select from recent webs	File	Recent Webs		
Exit	File	Exit		

For Changing Views

To Do This	Select This	Or Click This	Or Press This
Switch to Page view	View	Page		
Switch to Folders view	View	Folders		
Switch to Folder List view	View	Folder List		
Switch to Reports view	View	Reports		
Switch to Navigation view	View	Navigation		
Switch to Hyperlinks view	View	Hyperlinks		
Switch to Reveal Tags view	View	Reveal Tags		CTRL-/
Refresh the screen	View	Refresh		F5

For Working with Tasks

To Do This	Select This	Or Click This
View tasks	View	Tasks	
Add a task	Edit	Tasks	Add Task	
Start a task	Edit	Tasks	Start	
Mark a task as completed	Edit	Tasks	Mark as Completed	
Show task history	Edit	Tasks	Show History	

Instant *FrontPage 2000* Answers ...

For Formatting

To Do This	Select This	Or Click This	Or Press This
Format a position	Format | Position		
Apply Dynamic HTML effects	Format | Dynamic HTML Effects		
Format a style	Format | Style	[A_A icon]	
Format style sheet links	Format | Style Sheet Links		
Format a theme	Format | Theme	[theme icon]	
Apply shared borders	Format | Shared Borders		
Format a page transition	Format | Page Transition	[transition icon]	
Format a background	Format | Background	[background icon]	
Remove formatting	Format | Remove Formatting		CTRL-SHIFT-Z
Set properties	Format | Properties	[properties icon]	ALT-ENTER

For Using Images

To Do This	Select This	Or Click This
Insert a picture from a file	Insert | Picture | From File	[picture icon]
Place text on a picture (requires that picture be converted to GIF)		[A icon]
Switch to Auto Thumbnail view		[thumbnail icon]
Position absolutely	Format | Position	[position icon]
Bring forward		[bring forward icon]
Send backward		[send backward icon]
Create a rectangular hotspot		[rectangle icon]
Create a circular hotspot		[circle icon]
Crop		[crop icon]
Set transparent color		[transparent icon]

For Inserting Items

To Do This	Select This	Or Click This	Or Press This
Insert a break	Insert | Break		
Insert a horizontal line	Insert | Horizontal Line		
Insert the date and time	Insert | Date and Time	[clock icon]	
Insert a symbol	Insert | Symbol	[Ω icon]	
Insert a comment	Insert | Comment	[comment icon]	
Insert a Navigation bar	Insert | Navigation Bar		
Insert a page banner	Insert | Page Banner		
Insert a component	Insert | Component	[component icon]	
Insert a database	Insert | Database		
Insert a form	Insert | Form	[form icon]	
Insert a bookmark	Insert | Bookmark		
Insert a hyperlink	Insert | Hyperlink	[hyperlink icon]	CTRL-K

FrontPage 2000 Answers!

ABOUT THE AUTHOR

Alexis D. Gutzman is co-author of *The HTML 4 Bible*. For the past 13 years she's evolved from being a mainframe programmer, to programming for mid-range computers, to developing multimedia on PCs and Macs, and finally to being a Web developer. She's been developing for the Web since 1993, when Mosaic 1.0 was released. She spent 4 years as Director of the Multimedia Resource Center at the University of Virginia, where she assisted professors in developing digital media for instruction and taught Advanced Web Topics classes, including classes about Cascading Style Sheets, JavaScript, Dynamic HTML, and ColdFusion.

Mrs. Gutzman is president and founder of Over The Web, which provides electronic direct mail services to small businesses and non-profit organizations (www.overtheweb.com). She holds a B.A. in Computer Studies from Northwestern University and a Master in Public Affairs from the Lyndon B. Johnson School of Public Affairs at the University of Texas. She's currently a Technology Project Manager for Value America (www.valueamerica.com). She's also a mother of two and a happy wife of one. Mrs. Gutzman lives in Bethel, CT.

FrontPage 2000 Answers!

Alexis D. Gutzman

Osborne/McGraw-Hill
Berkeley • New York • St. Louis • San Francisco
Auckland • Bogotá • Hamburg • London
Madrid • Mexico City • Milan • Montreal
New Delhi • Panama City • Paris • São Paulo
Singapore • Sydney • Tokyo • Toronto

Osborne/**McGraw-Hill**
2600 Tenth Street
Berkeley, California 94710
U.S.A.

For information on translations or book distributors outside the U.S.A., or to arrange bulk purchase discounts for sales promotions, premiums, or fund-raisers, please contact Osborne/**McGraw-Hill** at the above address.

FrontPage 2000 Answers!

Copyright © 1999 by The McGraw-Hill Companies. All rights reserved. Printed in the United States of America. Except as permitted under the Copyright Act of 1976, no part of this publication may be reproduced or distributed in any form or by any means, or stored in a database or retrieval system, without the prior written permission of the publisher, with the exception that the program listings may be entered, stored, and executed in a computer system, but they may not be reproduced for publication.

1234567890 AGM AGM 90198765432109

ISBN 0-07-212101-7

Publisher
Brandon A. Nordin

Associate Publisher and Editor-in-Chief
Scott Rogers

Acquisitions Editor
Joanne Cuthbertson

Editorial Assistant
Stephane Thomas

Technical Editor
Terrie Solomon

Proofreader
Rhonda Holmes

Indexer
David Heiret

Computer Designer
Jean Butterfield
Gary Corrigan

Illustrator
Robert Hansen
Brian Wells

Series Design
Mickey Galicia

Information has been obtained by Osborne/**McGraw-Hill** from sources believed to be reliable. However, because of the possibility of human or mechanical error by our sources, Osborne/**McGraw-Hill**, or others, Osborne/**McGraw-Hill** does not guarantee the accuracy, adequacy, or completeness of any information and is not responsible for any errors or omissions or the results obtained from use of such information.

For Constantine, Trianna, Marika,

. . . counting my blessings

Contents @ a Glance

1	Top 10 Frequently Asked Questions	xxii
2	Implementing Themes for a Unified Look	16
3	Graphics 101	42
4	Creating an Image Map	82
5	The Art of Navigation—Inside and Outside	96
6	Creating Interesting Tables	126
7	Implementing Cascading Style Sheets (CSS)	156
8	Adding Dynamic HTML (DHTML)	184
9	Integrating FrontPage with Access	202
10	Creating Forms to Collect Data	236
11	Commerce and Security Issues	270
12	Publishing Your Site	294
13	Giving Your Site a Facelift	312
14	Managing Your Web Site	354
	Index	375

Contents

Acknowledgments	*xiii*
Introduction	*xv*

1 Top 10 Frequently Asked Questions . . . . **xxii**
    1. Can I design my own themes? 2
    2. Do I have to have the same navigation buttons in the same place on every page? 5
    3. What are shared borders and are there any browser compatibility issues with regards to using them? 7
    4. Why can't I edit my page in Preview view? 8
    5. Will I cause any problems for FrontPage if I edit the HTML by hand? 8
    6. How can I send the results of a form to an e-mail address? 9
    7. How do I change the text that appears on my navigation buttons? 10
    8. Can I publish my FrontPage 2000 site to a Web server without the server extensions? What will I lose? 11
    9. Do shared borders rely on server extensions, or will they work on Unix servers? 13
    10. What resources are there to learn more about FrontPage 2000? 13

2 Implementing Themes for a Unified Look **16**
    ? Understanding Themes 18
    ? Using Existing Themes 20
    ? Using Active Graphics 22
    ? Using Multiple Themes in Your Web 24
    ? Modifying a Theme 26
    ? Creating New Themes 39
    ? Using Themes vs. Using Style Sheets 40

3	**Graphics 101**	**42**
	? Before You Begin Adding Graphics	44
	? Image Formats	44
	? About Color	50
	? Ways to Use Images on Your Site	53
	? Optimizing Images	74
4	**Creating an Image Map**	**82**
	? Selecting the Right Image	84
	? Defining the Hot Regions	87
	? Browser and Download Issues	93
5	**The Art of Navigation—Inside and Outside**	**96**
	? Site Structure	98
	? Navigation Strategies	101
	? About Files	116
	? Analyzing Your Web	120
6	**Creating Interesting Tables**	**126**
	? When to Use a Table	128
	? Creating a Table	133
	? Table Borders	142
	? Padding, Spacing, and Margins	148
	? Other Text Formatting Options	153
7	**Implementing Cascading Style Sheets (CSS)**	**156**
	? Elements of Style	158
	? Style Sheets	179
	? Cascading	180
	? Applying Style Sheets	181
	? Browser Limitations of Style Sheets	183
8	**Adding Dynamic HTML (DHTML)**	**184**
	? Making Sense of DHTML	186
	? Working with the DHTML Toolbar	188
	? Cool Things DHTML Can Do	191

Contents

9 Integrating FrontPage with Access **202**
- Let's Talk Databases 204
- Databases 205
- Access Databases 207
- Text Files or Other Non-Access Solutions 210
- Mapping Fields (Columns) to Form Fields. 219
- Getting FrontPage to Use Your Access Database .. 223

10 Creating Forms to Collect Data **236**
- Forms 238
- Creating a Form 241

11 Commerce and Security Issues **270**
- Making Sense of Commerce and Security Issues .. 271
- Commerce via "Commercials" 275

12 Publishing Your Site **294**
- The Language of Web Communication 296
- ISP vs. Private Server 297
- Server Software 302
- Unix Servers 305
- Windows NT Servers 307
- File Saves and FTP 308

13 Giving Your Site a Facelift **312**
- Template Overview 314
- Shared Borders 315
- Include Page Component
  and Server-Side Includes 320
- Page Templates 324
- Replacing Text and Graphics Globally 329
- Understanding Elements 338
- Fonts as Elements 341
- Graphic Elements 343
- Layout as an Element 349

14	**Managing Your Web Site**	**354**
	? Common File Extensions	356
	? Importing a Web	357
	? Diagnosing Problems	361
	? Working with Teams	363
	? Final Considerations Before You Publish	372
	Index	**375**

Acknowledgments

No book is the sole work of its author. This book would not have been possible without the invaluable contributions of Debra Weiss. Her design work (www.drwwebdesign.com) is second to none. Without the contributions of Pamela Rice Hahn and Keith Giddeon this book would have been a far inferior work. Terrie Solomon, the technical editor on this book, contributed not only her editorial skills, but her wisdom to make this book what it is.

Carole McClendon, as ever, has been invaluable in bringing all of us together to complete this project.

I'd also like to thank Stephane Thomas, who has the patience of Job, Betsy Manini, and Joanne Cuthbertson of Osborne/**McGraw Hill** for all the long hours spent pulling things together. My thanks also go to Claire Splan, Rhonda Holmes, David Heiret, and all of the graphic artists and paging designers who helped to produce this book.

Thanks to the following people at Stream: Sean McKenna, Patrick Flanagan, Christine Le, Bonnie Brown, Karen Malave, Dan Bedard, Howard Lotis, and Peggy Peterson who kept their keen eyes trained during their review of this book.

Finally, I want to thank my husband, Constantine, and our daughters, two-year old Trianna and seven-month old Marika, for letting me ignore them so that I could finish the book.

Alexis D. Gutzman

Introduction

FrontPage 2000 Answers! turns everything you need to know about FrontPage 2000 into the format that your quest for knowledge begins: a question. Rather than take you through each item on the File menu, then take you through each item on the Edit menu, as if you've never used a Microsoft Windows application (and you don't know what cutting and pasting are), this book answers the questions that real Web developers have about FrontPage. After all, this book was written by real Web developers. We know that no one was born knowing all the tricks; we also know that much of what you need to create an exciting Web site you won't find in any software package! However, when you do need to turn your ideas and plans into ones and zeros, in the form of Web pages, we'll help you figure out how to do it with FrontPage.

THE MAKING OF A WEB DEVELOPER

This book assumes that you know enough to find your way around a Microsoft application. We won't bore you with every little mouse click—that's what those 1000-page books on FrontPage are for. This book should be your handbook for fast answers to real problems. We'll show you the screen you should be seeing, if you've followed our explanation, and we'll tell you what choices to make so that things work as you desire.

Real Web developers aren't made overnight. Most people begin their Web publishing careers by publishing static Web pages with a photo of their cat, their grandmother's dolmades recipe, or their team soccer schedule. The next step is to add navigation to a few pages, and links to cool sites. When that gets dull, perhaps a site redesign is in order with a firm plan for navigating, e-mail links, an image map, and perhaps some type of form that gets e-mailed to the webmaster. Eventually, this same Web developer's pages will contain dynamic HTML, Java applets, and database-driven pages. It's a

continuum. We've been there and we'd like to help you move from where you are to the next step and beyond. FrontPage can help, but that's not all.

ORGANIZATION

Consider the types of tasks you'd like to perform. This book is organized around the kind of tasks that real Web developers want to accomplish.

Chapter 1 covers the top ten most frequently asked questions about FrontPage 2000. This list was culled from support sites all over the web, Microsoft's own site, and the top newsgroup for FrontPage support.

Chapter 2 helps you determine how to develop a single look for your entire site. It covers themes, which are FrontPage's way to make an attractive look a snap. It also touches on style sheets, and shared borders.

Chapter 3 answers all your questions about graphics. It covers both what FrontPage will do, and what you'll need a supplementary graphics editor to do. Everything from the Web-safe palette, to optimizing graphics is in here. Sure, you've heard the terms before, now find out what they mean to you and your site.

Chapter 4 shows you how to create an image map in FrontPage, but more importantly, it helps you determine when an image map might not be the right solution. Sure, image maps are sexy, but is an image map really the best answer for your needs?

Chapter 5 is about mapping your site and improving navigation. We dare you to read through this one and not learn anything. Most of the sites on the Web violate the simple principles in this chapter. Even if you think you know it all, go ahead and test your mettle.

Chapter 6 talks about creating interesting tables. Tables have been around for a while, and you may think you've been there and done that, but are you up on all the latest things you can do with tables with cascading style sheets? Tables are more than just formatting tools. Read this and see what you're missing.

Chapter 7 takes the hype out of cascading style sheets. What are they and what do they mean to you? Are they really too good to be true? This chapter gives you some common sense guidelines as to how and when they're appropriate, as well as clear instructions on how to use them in FrontPage.

Chapter 8 demystifies dynamic HTML. FrontPage makes implementing dynamic HTML a breeze. Read about what you can do and how in this fast-moving chapter.

Chapter 9 unveils the nitty-gritty about Web-database interfaces. This chapter takes you through all the things that your systems administrator thinks you can't handle, all in language you'll find reassuring, with plenty of figures to make sure that you're on the same page as we are. ODBC will be more than an unfriendly acronym when you get done with this chapter. Whether you use Access, SQL server, or something else, you'll learn what you need to open the lines of communication between your Web pages and your database. Plus, your Web site will be reading from a database in real time!

Chapter 10 discusses the other half of Web-database interaction: writing to a database. Before you can do that, however, you need to collect some data. This chapter teaches you everything you need to know about collecting data from your visitors, including privacy issues. It also shows that you can get FrontPage to take care of inserting your data into your database. All without any programming!

Chapter 11 explains Web server security and e-commerce. What are your security options? How does encryption work? For the more fiscal-minded, it's jam-packed with ideas for turning your site into a cash cow.

Chapter 12 talks about publishing your site. FrontPage 2000 offers the option of publishing via HTTP, rather than FTP. What does that mean? Read this chapter and find out!

Chapter 13 helps you cope with the inevitable: aging. Your site will eventually need a face-lift. All those carefully crafted pages will soon look out of date. This chapter gives you tips for a painless face-lift. Don't re-vamp your site without reading it!

Chapter 14 talks about the nuts and bolts of maintaining your site. What kind of information can FrontPage give you to keep your site tuned up? This chapter's full of the kind of things you need to know if you're the guy in charge.

WHAT'S NEW?

This is the question we are most pleased to answer! FrontPage 98 was already a force to be reckoned with, but the new features of FrontPage 2000 make it sure to leave the rest of the pack behind.

Better Looking Sites

Themes   FrontPage's templates for creating impressive page design have been improved. FrontPage now ships with 67, although they don't *all* get installed unless you choose to install them all. Additionally, you can modify the canned themes to make your own statement in a snap!

Dynamic HTML   Of course, FrontPage 98 had dynamic HTML, but now the animation effects work better across browsers. Every Web developer knows that compatibility is key, but hard to achieve. FrontPage's animations work in Navigator 4 just as seamlessly as they do in Internet Explorer 4.

Colors Themes are color-family driven, so it's easy to change the look or your entire site by spinning the color wheel. Custom colors are available everywhere, and you can limit yourself to the web-safe palette.

Pixel-precise Positioning and Layering Thanks to CSS2 implementation, you can put something right where you want it with the confidence that it's going to stay there.

CSS Support Cascading Style Sheets have been more fully implemented throughout FrontPage.

HTML Editing

Source Preservation If you don't get excited about that, you must be new to Web development. For the first time, you can bring code created elsewhere (both HTML and scripts written in complementary languages) into FrontPage without grave reservations. It won't touch the code or the formatting!

HTML editing Right in HTML view, you can edit the HTML by hand, or use the menus or buttons to add HTML.

HTML environment personalization FrontPage will let you change the tag colors, indentation, and tag options. And, when new pages are imported or created, they will automatically have your preferences applied!

Reveal Tags If you're new to HTML and you don't know what the tags behind an element look like, you can use reveal tags to show you the code for an element without leaving the comfort of Normal view.

Database Integration

Database Publishing Save your form data directly to an Access database that FrontPage builds for you, to your existing database, or just send it off as e-mail.

Database Results Wizard You thought you liked it before! Create truly dynamic pages that read database tables in real time without any programming.

Access Database Access Update Access databases right from a Web page, not just the data the Web developer makes available, but the entire database!

Cool Web Things

Office Integration   Add components from Office applications into your Web pages.

Microsoft Script Editor   Edit and debug any scripts you write yourself right in HTML view!

Programmers' Paradise

VBA   Visual Basic for Applications, the same powerful language you've been using to program in Access is now available to extend FrontPage.

DOM   Application, Document, and Web object models allow for the most comprehensive types of scripting.

Design Time Controls   Extend FrontPage with Design Time Controls and Visual InterDev.

And More . . .

FrontPage has added new views, new reports, new groupware and collaboration features; it's also added subwebs and categories to make growing a site even easier. There are so many features that if we list them all, this will end up being a 1000-page book. So . . . let's get to those questions!

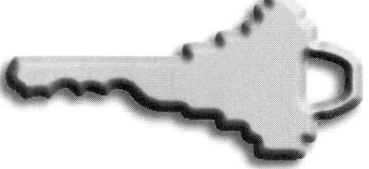

Chapter 1

Top 10 Frequently Asked Questions

- DESIGNING YOUR OWN THEMES 2
- PLACING NAVIGATION BUTTONS 5
- USING SHARED BORDERS WITH DIFFERENT BROWSERS 7
- EDITING YOUR PAGE IN DIFFERENT VIEWS 8
- EDITING HTML BY HAND 8
- SENDING THE RESULTS OF A FORM TO AN E-MAIL ADDRESS 9
- CHANGING THE TEXT ON NAVIGATION BUTTONS 10
- PUBLISH YOUR FRONTPAGE 2000 SITE TO A WEB SERVER WITHOUT SERVER EXTENSIONS 11
- USING SHARED BORDERS WITHOUT SERVER EXTENSIONS 13
- RESOURCES TO LEARN MORE ABOUT FRONTPAGE 2000 13

Top 10 FAQs @ a Glance

FrontPage 2000 adds quite a bit of functionality to the already fully functional FrontPage 98. The most frequently asked question revolve around five areas:

- **Design** Designing your own themes is important, as is placement of navigation buttons, and use and compatibility issues related to shared borders.

- **Interface** FrontPage has three ways to see your work in progress: Normal view, HTML view, and Preview view. You need to understand the difference between the three, so you know what you can change and where you can view it. For example, dynamic HTML effects can't be viewed in Normal view, but have to be viewed in Preview view, and changes can't be made in Preview view, but have to be made in Normal or HTML view. What if you want to make changes to the HTML directly? No problem!

- **How To's** How do you send the results of a form to an e-mail address? How do you change the text that appears on navigation buttons? Read on!

- **Servers** What happens if you publish your site to a server without the FrontPage 2000 server extensions installed? Does the shared borders feature rely on any server or browser release that your visitors might not have installed?

- **Support** An extensive list of online resources, and more brand-new book titles are listed at the end of this chapter. Some of the questions answered in this book inevitably will lead to more questions. Check out these resources for information and support.

Chapter 1 Top 10 Frequently Asked Questions

 1. Can I design my own themes?

Themes are FrontPage's quick and beautiful (as opposed to quick and dirty) way to create a unified look for your entire site. You can edit the Theme Properties in your web by right-clicking anywhere in the background of your web and selecting Theme, as shown in Figure 1-1. You can also get to your Theme properties by way of the menu bar, by selecting Format | Theme.

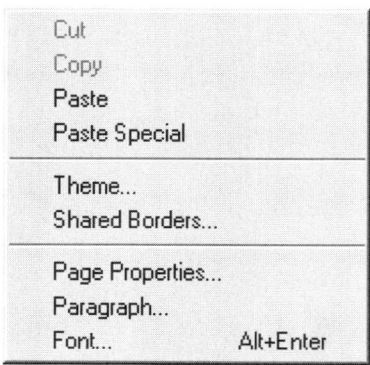

FrontPage ships with 67 themes. By default, during the initial installation only 26 of them load. If you want to load the full assortment of themes, you can either specify that during the installation, or tell FrontPage to go out and get them from the Themes dialog box. To specify during installation, change the settings associated with Additional Themes. It will default to having a yellow 1 on the hard drive icon. When the 1 appears on the icon, click the down arrow to the right of the hard drive icon, and select Run From My Computer, as shown in Figure 1-1.

 Note: *For more extensive information on themes, see Chapter 2.*

While you can perform the steps above either during initial installation or by selecting Add Or Remove Software after Office 2000 is initially installed, you can also tell

Top 10 Frequently Asked Questions

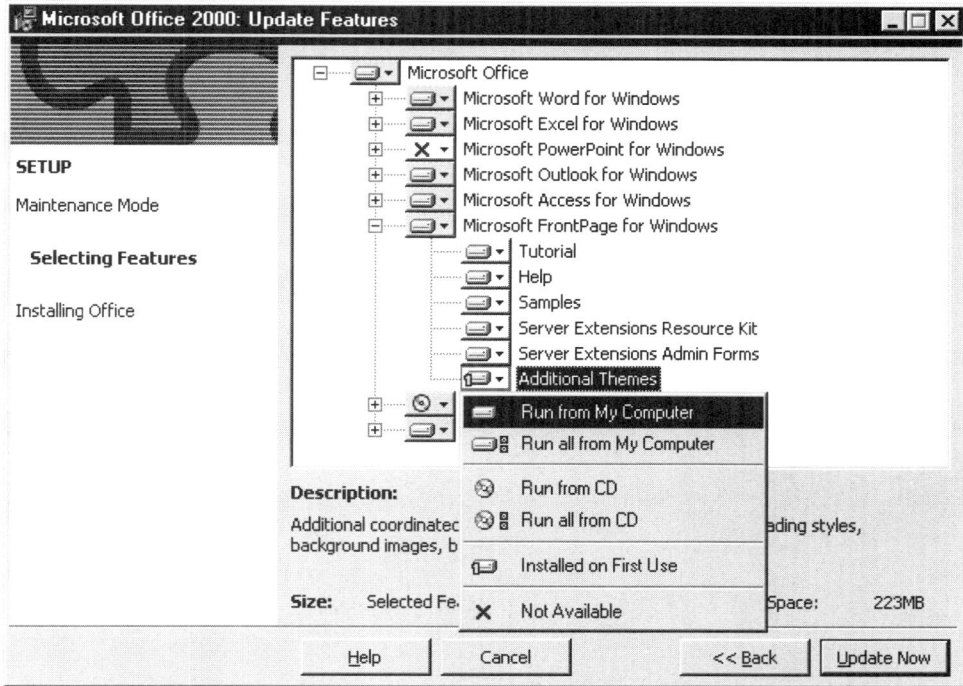

Figure 1-1 Using the FrontPage installation options to install additional themes so you can run them from your computer

FrontPage to go to the CD and get the rest of the themes right from the Themes dialog box.

1. Open the Themes dialog box by right-clicking anywhere in the background of your web and selecting Theme, or by selecting Format | Theme.
2. In the list of themes at the left side of the dialog box shown in Figure 1-2, click Install Additional Themes. You'll see a dialog box asking "Install Additional Themes?" Click Yes.
3. If you don't have the installation CD in your CD drive, a dialog box will ask for it.

 Tip: *The nice thing about adding additional themes from the Themes dialog box is that you don't have to quit FrontPage to do so.*

**Chapter 1** Top 10 Frequently Asked Questions

Click here to expand your library of master themes

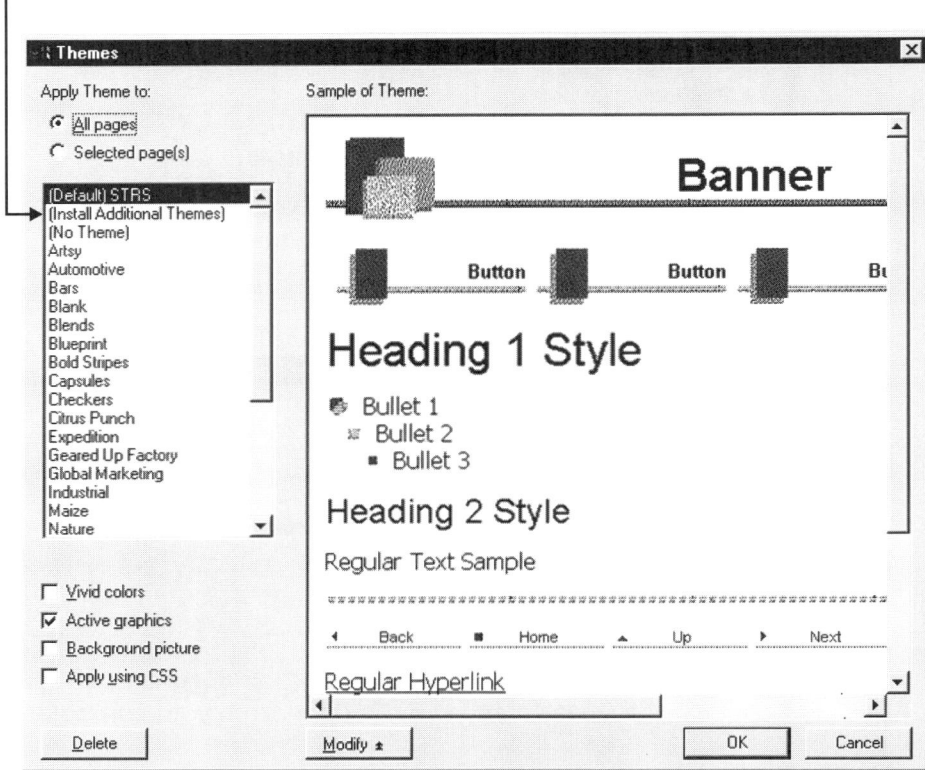

Figure 1-2 Installing additional themes via the Themes dialog box

---

 Note: *Chapter 2 discusses themes in detail. It explains how to modify every part of a theme. Rather than review all the details here, we'll just cover the big picture, and you can flip to Chapter 2 for the specifics.*

To modify a theme, select the theme from the list on the left. The first thing you should do is save the unmodified theme with a new name using the Save As button, so that you don't accidentally make a change to the original theme. After you have a "new" theme with which to work, modify the text, colors, and graphics by clicking the Colors, Graphics, and Text buttons in the Themes dialog box. You can always view your changes right in the preview panel. When you're

Top 10 Frequently Asked Questions

satisfied, click Save, and your changes will be saved in the new theme. Figure 1-3 shows the Themes dialog box when editing a theme.

2. Do I have to have the same navigation buttons in the same place on every page?

Absolutely not. Chances are, you want to have some navigation buttons on all pages, but you probably don't want to have the same buttons in the same places. FrontPage gives you the

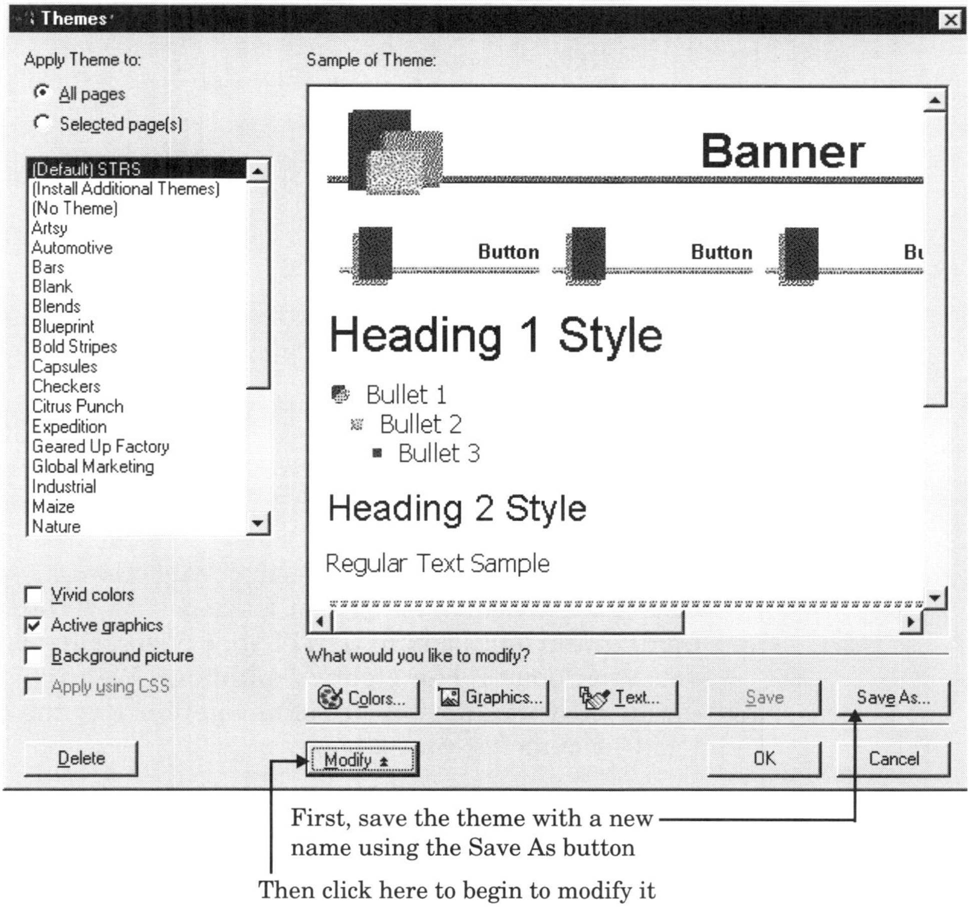

Figure 1-3 Editing a theme

 **Chapter 1** Top 10 Frequently Asked Questions

ability to add navigation buttons anywhere on your site. To add buttons, click Insert | Navigation Bar so that you see the Navigation Bar Properties dialog box, shown here:

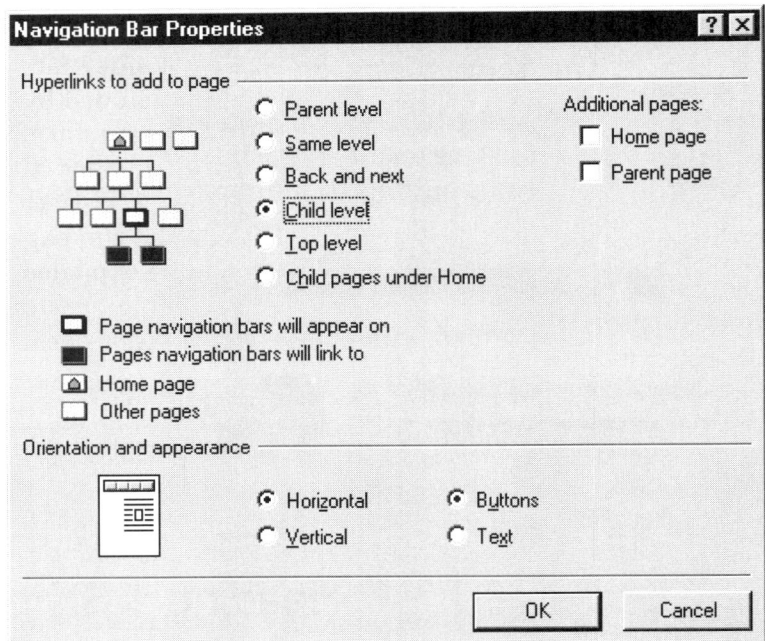

By using shared borders, you can place navigation buttons on the top, left, and bottom of your pages. For some pages—the Home page, for example—it might be more appropriate to have a navigation bar on the page with no shared borders. In addition to giving clear, concise instructions on modifying shared borders and navigation buttons both within the borders and on the main part of your pages, Chapter 2 gives you other pointers for creating a uniform Web site. Chapter 5 discusses general principles of navigation, and the FrontPage tools for mapping your site.

 Note: *Chapter 5 is the place to go for a thorough discussion of approaches to site navigation.*

Top 10 Frequently Asked Questions

 3. What are shared borders and are there any browser compatibility issues with regards to using them?

Shared borders are FrontPage's way of letting you have a common area on every page (or even a subset of pages), while having the work exist in only one place. Because FrontPage uses include files, they are included by the server and will work on any browser. *Include files* are files that contain HTML, but aren't full-fledged pages (they're missing some of the tags that browsers expect). They can be called from full-fledged pages. By the time the page gets to the browser, the shared borders have been exploded into the page, and to the browser it looks like one big page of HTML. There's no way for the browser to know (nor does it care) that it didn't start off as one big page.

 Note: *Chapter 13 covers shared borders in detail.*

FrontPage gives you the option of having shared borders on the top of pages, on the left side of pages, or on the bottom of pages. Additionally, you can turn them on or off by the page or by the web in the Shared Borders dialog box, as shown here:

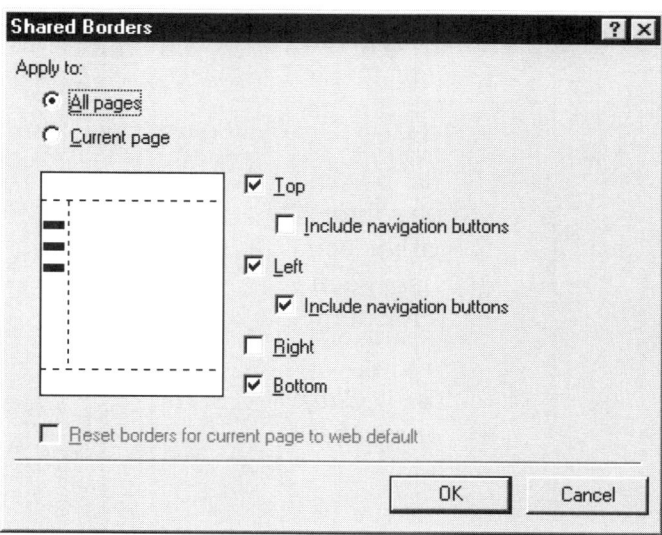

**Chapter 1** Top 10 Frequently Asked Questions

Note: *Chapters 5 and 13 discuss shared borders at length.*

4. Why can't I edit my page in Preview view?

Preview view shows what your page will look like in a browser. You can't edit there because it's just a window to the rendered HTML. To edit the page in a WYSIWYG (what you see is what you get) environment, edit the page in Normal view. To edit the page by diving into the HTML, edit the page in HTML view. You can jump between the three views by pressing CTRL-PAGE UP or CTRL-PAGE DOWN.

5. Will I cause any problems for FrontPage if I edit the HTML by hand?

You won't cause any problems for FrontPage, but you might cause problems for yourself. FrontPage allows you to edit the HTML directly in HTML view, but it doesn't give you any clues if you mangle the HTML or forget to add a closing tag. Of course, you can take a look at the rendered page in Preview view, but that will only give you the view from Internet Explorer. You won't know that Netscape Navigator chokes on a certain type of HTML slip-ups until you hear about it from a dissatisfied visitor (unless your e-mail address is somewhere after the open-table tag, in which case he won't even be able to send you mail telling you about the problem!).

Caution: *If you leave the end-table tag (</TABLE>) off the end of your table, Navigator won't render the table at all, which will give you a big blank page.*

Breaking into the code is nearly unavoidable for advanced Web developers, but be sure to test the results of your editing on multiple browsers to make sure that you didn't inadvertently miss a closing tag.

Top 10 Frequently Asked Questions

6. How can I send the results of a form to an e-mail address?

Once you have a satisfactory form on your page, you can edit the form properties by using FrontPage's Form Properties dialog box. By default, all new forms will have a filename of _private/form_results.txt (that is, in the _private directory, the file will be called form_results.txt). To access the Form Properties dialog box, shown in the following illustration, click on the form in your web, and select Insert | Form | Form Properties. (Note that if you have not selected a form in your web, the option will not be active.)

In addition to providing an e-mail address here, you'll also have to make sure that the Web server is configured to send e-mail; your web server can e-mail the results of a form whether the Web server is on Windows or Unix. If you're not the server administrator, ask him or her to make sure that the Web server is properly configured, then test it out to make sure it's been done right. Within the Form Properties

dialog box, click the Options button. FrontPage will then display the Options for Saving Results of Form dialog box shown in the following illustration. Select the E-mail Results tab of the dialog box.

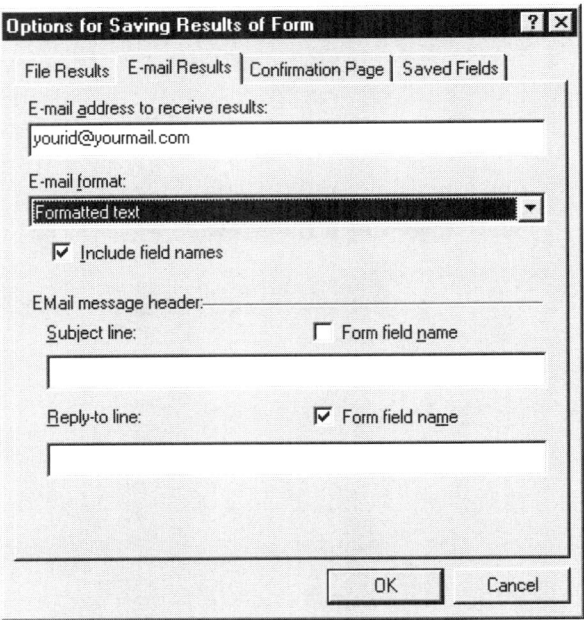

You can also tell FrontPage how to format the e-mail that you receive. You can dictate what you want the subject line to be, in case you want to filter all mail from a form into a specific folder, and what you want the reply-to line to be, in case you want to be able to reply to the e-mail address provided by the visitor either with a personal message or with an auto-generated message.

Note: *Chapters 9 and 10 are all about forms processing. Start there to understand all the fields in a form and your processing options for forms.*

7. How do I change the text that appears on my navigation buttons?

FrontPage is a bit confusing in this respect because it permits you to change what appears to be the name of a page in three

Top 10 Frequently Asked Questions

separate places. The only one that matters is the name of the page in Navigation view. While you can also change the file properties on the file list (or in Folder view), and you can change the title of a page in the page properties from within Page view, only by changing the name of a file in Navigation view can you affect the names that appear on the navigation buttons or text. (See Figure 1-4.)

Tip: *A good rule of thumb for the amount of text that will fit on a button is to look at the text on the mini-page in Navigation view—if it doesn't extend beyond the mini-page, it'll probably fit.*

8. Can I publish my FrontPage 2000 site to a Web server without the server extensions? What will I lose?

You can publish your web to a server with FrontPage 2000 extensions, with FrontPage 98 extensions, or with no extensions. You can even publish your web to a server other than Microsoft Internet Information Server. You will, however, lose some functionality.

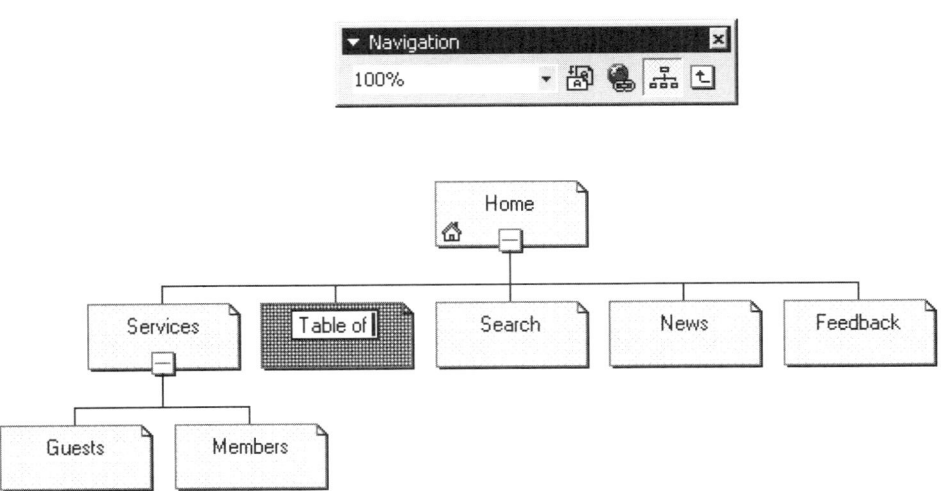

Figure 1-4 Changing the name of a page in Navigation view will change what appears on navigation buttons

Chapter 1 Top 10 Frequently Asked Questions

Your best bet is to tell FrontPage what your server can handle before you create your web so that it doesn't permit you to use functionality that isn't supported by your server. For example, if your server doesn't have the FrontPage 2000 extensions, you won't be able to use the Database Results Wizard. Once you tell FrontPage that you don't have the server extensions, it turns off that option in the Insert menu.

To set server compatibility for your web, select Tools | Page Options, then click on the Compatibility tab. You'll see the dialog box shown here:

Uncheck any boxes for features your server doesn't support. It's also a good idea to find out from your systems administrator which Web server you're publishing to, so you can set that value correctly.

9. Do shared borders rely on server extensions, or will they work on Unix servers?

Shared borders take advantage of include files. Fortunately, all Web servers can process include files without the assistance of any server extensions, regardless of whether they are Unix-based or Windows-based. Include files herald from the days when all Web servers ran on Unix boxes. With the growing popularity of Linux as a network platform, they may again!

10. What resources are there to learn more about FrontPage 2000?

There are lots of great places to look for tips and tricks for FrontPage. They're pretty much all online, but since you're a Web developer, that shouldn't be a handicap. Here's a list of places to start. Many of these sites have links to other sites.

- Microsoft's own FrontPage site: www.microsoft.com/frontpage/
- The Microsoft KnowledgeBase (for thorny technical questions): search.microsoft.com/us/default.asp?MSCOMTB=MS_Search
- About.com, (formerly Miningco.com), a page of links to great FrontPage resources: microsoftsoft.miningco.com/msubFrontPage.htm
- ZDNet.com, a site based on several computer magazines with a plethora of useful articles about many software tools: (search for FrontPage) www.zdnet.com
- Builder.com, great articles about Web tricks using FrontPage and other tools; read what the pros read: www.builder.com/Authoring/
- Dynamic.net, a Web development company that's not afraid of educating the competition; this site is tops for FrontPage resources: dynamicnet.net/support/frontpage.htm

Chapter 1 Top 10 Frequently Asked Questions

- DejaNews.com, a site for reading, posting, and sophisticated searching of newsgroups, including the FrontPage newsgroups:
  www.dejanews.com

- Public Newsgroup, a place to ask your colleagues how they solved a certain problem:
  news://Microsoft.public.frontpage.client

- Here are some of the latest Osborne books on FrontPage that are definitely worth checking out:

    FrontPage 2000: The Complete Reference, by Martin Matthews and Erik Poulsen

    FrontPage 2000 Developer's Guide, by Mike Jennett

    FrontPage 2000 for Busy People, by Christian Crumlish

Chapter 2

Implementing Themes for a Unified Look

Answer Topics!

UNDERSTANDING THEMES 18
- ? What themes are
- ? Why you should use themes
- ? What kinds of things are defined in themes

USING EXISTING THEMES 20
- ? When to choose the theme
- ? Using a pre-fabricated theme

USING ACTIVE GRAPHICS 22
- ? Understanding active graphics
- ? Using active graphics on a server without FrontPage extensions installed
- ? The downside to using active graphics

USING MULTIPLE THEMES IN YOUR WEB 24
- ? Using more than one theme in your web
- ? Creating a new web vs. using more than one theme

MODIFYING A THEME 26
- ? Changing the font of the body
- ? Changing the banner
- ? Changing navigation buttons
- ? Changing the colors of the headings
- ? Removing formatting after colors and fonts are assigned to text without styles
- ? The amount of graphics to use on a page
- ? How FrontPage decides which pages to include as buttons

CREATING NEW THEMES 39
- ? Creating a new theme
- ? Changing a theme you have created

USING THEMES VS. USING STYLE SHEETS 40
- ? Implement a theme with style sheets
- ? How FrontPage formats pages without style sheets
- ? The advantage of using style sheets

Implementing Themes for a Unified Look @ a Glance

Themes are FrontPage's way of giving a distinctive and consistent look to your entire Web site (a.k.a. your web). FrontPage comes packaged with a number of predesigned themes. Users of PowerPoint will find them familiar. In addition to using the pre-fabricated themes as they are, you can modify the existing themes or create entirely new ones. This chapter takes you through the questions that commonly arise when using themes. The questions fall into the following categories:

- **Understanding Themes** answers questions related to what themes are and why you should use them. It also lists all the elements and properties of the elements that themes customize.

- **Using the Existing Themes** shows you how to implement themes as they are installed from the CD, without modifying or altering them in any way.

- **Using Active Graphics** answers questions about the active graphics feature of themes. This clever tool gives your visitors instant feedback in the form of animated buttons as they roll their mouses over your buttons. Can you use it on your site? Read ahead and find out.

- **Using Multiple Themes in Your Web** is something you might be considering. Perhaps you'd like a corporate theme for the main section of your Web site, then a techno-looking theme for the computer downloads section. This section explains how to use more than one theme in your web and why you might want to use this feature.

- **Modifying a Theme** is useful if you're not satisfied with FrontPage's predesigned themes the way they appear on the CD. You can change any property of any element on the page.

- **Creating New Themes** is an extension of the section "Modifying a Theme." You can't actually create a theme from scratch. This section suggests good ways to turn a theme into a completely different one.

Using Themes vs. Using Style Sheets is an interesting discussion. While they both can achieve the same result, there are good reasons to favor one over another under different circumstances. For example, themes work on more browsers, but style sheets load more quickly.

UNDERSTANDING THEMES

What are themes?

FrontPage has many nice features, and the ready availability of themes is one of the most useful.

- Themes are a way of defining the entire look of your web from one location.
- They are an ingenious way of making sure that all the pages have the same look and feel.
- They handle everything from the choice of font for your navigation buttons to the choice of images to be used in your bullets (up to three levels deep).

If you took the time to define every aspect of every element that can appear on every page in your site, you would have taken the time to define a theme. In Figure 2-1, you can see the theme called *cactus*. Each theme has a name that is supposed to be descriptive of the look and feel or atmosphere it creates. However, you can see that the cactus theme looks southwestern, but not particularly cactusy.

Notice that every element on the page harmonizes with every other element. They all look like they were created by the same person on the same day; that's something you can't say about too many Web sites. Because these ready-made themes are uniform in their presentation, they give the final web a look of professionalism, as though designed by a graphic artist. This extra sophistication added to your web can give visitors an impressive sense of your professionalism, too.

Understanding Themes 19

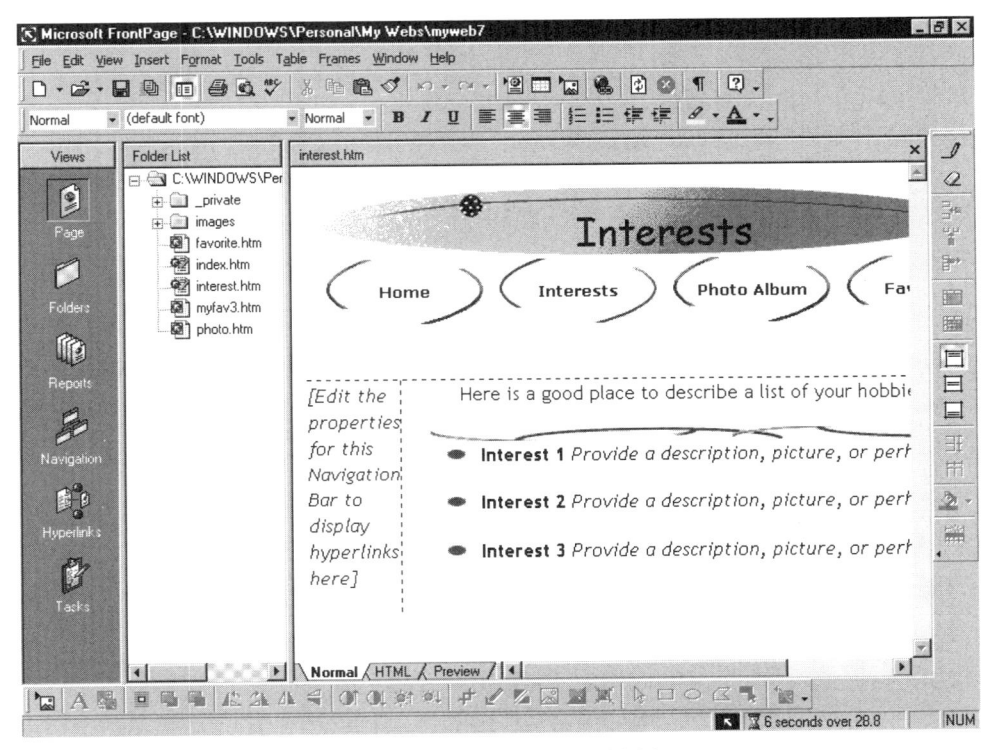

Figure 2-1 The cactus theme in FrontPage 2000

Why use themes?

Themes give you three things that many sites lack:

1. **Logical Navigation** Themes give you consistent, intuitive navigation tools. Many sites fail to provide a logical way to navigate them.

2. **Consistency** When most people start building a Web site, they don't sit down and make a list of all the different types of elements they're planning on using and how they'll handle each one—font choices for each heading, link colors, graphics treatments, footers with copyright statements, order of navigation buttons—they just begin building a page. Then they *try* to remember how they handled it later on when they're working on

their thirtieth page two months later. Themes give you a consistent Web site right out of the box; your fonts look the same from page to page, your buttons are in the same place, your colors don't change, and so on. Consistency is particularly important if your site is developed by a team, as so many corporate sites are.

3. **Ease of Development**   When you work with themes, you don't have to put a lot of energy into deciding how your site is going to look. You only have to worry about the content. Presumably, that's why people come to your site: for what it contains. The pre-fabricated FrontPage themes bring your site up to the solid, professional level that visitors expect. Providing them with good content so they'll want to come back is your job. FrontPage frees you up to do just that.

4. **Ease of Overhaul**   As enamored of your site as you are the day you publish it, you'll soon tire of it. Web trends change. You'll want to completely re-vamp your site every so often to take advantage of the capabilities of the upgraded browsers that the majority of your site visitors are using. With FrontPage themes, you can change your site with only minor page-by-page revision and tweaking.

What kinds of things are defined in themes?

Themes define the default properties of just about every element in your site. Table 2-1 lists all the elements for which you can define properties in a theme. You probably won't use all of these elements, but FrontPage has definitions for them within every theme.

USING EXISTING THEMES

When can I choose the theme?

You can choose a theme at any time. FrontPage is so sure that you'll want to use a theme in your web that it assigns

Element	Properties
Body	Color, Font Face
Hyperlink	Color
Hyperlink (Active)	Color
Hyperlink (Followed)	Color
Heading 1	Color, Font Face
Heading 2	Color, Font Face
Heading 3	Color, Font Face
Heading 4	Color, Font Face
Heading 5	Color, Font Face
Heading 6	Color, Font Face
Banner	Color, Image, Font Face, Font Style, Font Size, Horizontal Alignment of Text, Vertical Alignment of Text
Global Navigation Buttons	Color, Images for both static and dynamic pages, Font Face, Font Style, Font Size, Horizontal Alignment of Text, Vertical Alignment of Text
Horizontal Navigation Buttons	Color, Images for both static and dynamic pages, Font Face, Font Style, Font Size, Horizontal Alignment of Text, Vertical Alignment of Text
Vertical Navigation Buttons	Color, Images for both static and dynamic pages, Font Face, Font Style, Font Size, Horizontal Alignment of Text, Vertical Alignment of Text
Table Border	Color
Background	Color, Image
Bullet List	Image (three sizes of bullets for three levels deep)
Back Button	Images for both static and dynamic pages, Font Face, Font Style, Font Size, Horizontal Alignment of Text, Vertical Alignment of Text
Home Button	Images for both static and dynamic pages, Font Face, Font Style, Font Size, Horizontal Alignment of Text, Vertical Alignment of Text
Next Button	Images for both static and dynamic pages, Font Face, Font Style, Font Size, Horizontal Alignment of Text, Vertical Alignment of Text
Up Button	Images for both static and dynamic pages, Font Face, Font Style, Font Size, Horizontal Alignment of Text, Vertical Alignment of Text
Horizontal Rule	Image

Table 2-1 Theme Elements with Properties to Be Defined and Modified

one for you when you choose to create a new web. If you don't like the theme it chooses, follow these steps to change your theme at any time:

1. Select Format | Themes.
2. Click on the theme you want to use from the scrolling list of themes. Most likely, you won't yet know which one you want to use. That's why FrontPage provides samples to the right of the scrolling list of themes.
3. Select OK.

You'll notice that when you change your theme, it takes a moment to give you back control of the application. FrontPage is busily applying all the features of your new theme to all the pages you've created, or to the default pages that come with the web you've selected.

How do I use a pre-fabricated theme?

The beauty of using a theme is that you don't have to do anything special. Once you select a theme, you'll see it manifested in all the pages you create or edit (if they were created by FrontPage with your web). If you don't like what was selected for you by FrontPage, change it.

USING ACTIVE GRAPHICS

What are active graphics?

Active graphics are what you see when you move your cursor over an image and it changes slightly (jumps out at you or changes color, sometimes with a one-pixel offset). You can tell FrontPage to use active graphics with any theme. The default for most themes is not to use active graphics. Active graphics only apply to *hot* elements of your page—only graphics are active in themes.

1. Select Format | Theme.
2. In the Themes dialog box, click the Active Graphics check box.
3. Click OK.

Can I use active graphics on a server without FrontPage extensions installed?

Active graphics are not server-dependent. The way they work is that when the page is sent from the server to the browser, two sets of graphics are sent for every clickable image on the page. JavaScript is used to tell the browser that when the mouse is over the image, show the alternate image. As long as two different images are provided, this will work. The two images don't need to be identical except for color.

What's the downside to using active graphics?

Download time. If you have a page with navigation buttons (as opposed to just text), make note of the download time in the lower-right corner of the screen, then set the theme to use active graphics. Now, take a look at the download time again. It probably increased.

Note: For a thorough discussion of the relationship between graphics file sizes and download times, see Chapter 3.

Another thing to consider is browser compatibility. If your site is visited a lot by people who are likely to be running version 2 browsers, or older, then JavaScript might not work properly.

Finally, if you're creating graphics yourself to customize your web, you're going to need to create twice as many navigation buttons: one for the button without the mouse over it and one for the button with the mouse over it. Table 2-2 gives you an inventory of the graphics you'll need two of if you choose to use active graphics when customizing your theme.

Graphics Inventory for Creating Themes with Active Graphics
- ✓ Horizontal navigation buttons
- ✓ Vertical navigation buttons
- ✓ Quick Back button
- ✓ Quick Next button
- ✓ Quick Home button
- ✓ Quick Up button

Table 2-2 Use Two of Each of These If You Customize Your Theme Using Active Graphics

USING MULTIPLE THEMES IN YOUR WEB

What if I want more than one theme in my web?

Normally, you'd want your entire site to look the same, but there may be cases when you need to have an entirely different look for part of your site. You can accomplish this design arrangement in one of two ways. If you have a lot of pages to which you need to assign the new theme, then follow these steps:

1. Make sure your folder list is visible. If it's not, either click on the Folder List icon in the toolbar shown here, or select View | Folder List.

   Folder List icon

2. Select the folder at the very top of your list with the web name next to it.
3. Right-click and select New Folder from the list.
4. Give the new folder an appropriate name.
5. Drag each page to which you want to apply the alternate theme into the new folder.
6. Click on the folder name so that it is selected.
7. Choose Format | Theme. In the Themes dialog box, select the new theme you want and make sure you select the radio button for Selected Pages.

   FrontPage will now apply the new theme to all the pages in the new folder. You can either drag the pages back out of the folder by selecting them and then dragging and dropping them on top of the name of the folder they were previously in, or you can just leave them in the new folder. FrontPage takes care of making sure all the links still work, even when you've put pages into a new folder.

Think First, Write Later

Just as few people set out for driving trips to distant cities without looking at a map to decide which highways to take, few Web developers should start creating a Web site without giving more than a passing thought to what that site should contain. A good Web site requires planning. What information do you want to convey? What's the purpose of publishing a site at all? Why will visitors be coming to your site?

One of the downsides of being given so much by FrontPage—product pages, services pages, search pages, and so on—is that it tends to give the impression that your material needs to fit into and fill all those pages. How should your material be organized? Don't rely on FrontPage's structure to guide you.

Carpenters and seamstresses have a saying: "Measure twice, cut once." A slight twist on the adage works for Web developers. Many people waste far too much time designing and re-designing a site because they don't know what they want from their site. Take the time with a good book that covers this topic at length, such as *The HTML 4 Bible* by Bryan Pfaffenberger and Alexis D. Gutzman (IDG Books Worldwide, 1998), and outline the material you want to include. Think of it from the visitor's perspective. What does he or she want to find? Make it easy to find the information that's needed, make the information complete (so the visitor doesn't need to go to five different places on your site to get the complete answer), and organize the material so that it's clear from the moment the visitor arrives on a page that the answer is there. When you've accomplished the above, you'll have a formula for a winning site.

After you've done all that, you are ready to use FrontPage to actually produce the site. Just remember that neither FrontPage nor any other Web development tool are a substitute for good planning.

> ***Caution:*** *New pages that you create and put into the new "alternate theme" folder won't automatically get the new theme. You'll have to tell it again to give the theme to the folder or to those pages as you create them.*

If you only have a few pages that need the new theme, make sure your folder list is visible, as described above, then follow these steps:

1. Click on and select the name of the page for which you want to change the theme.
2. Select Format | Theme. In the Themes dialog box, select the new theme you want and make sure you select the radio button for Selected Pages.

If I want more than one theme in my web, should I create a new web?

Generally not. You should only create a new web if you want a different navigational structure. If you want integrated navigation between the two themes, then stick to one theme and apply it selectively. If you create two separate webs, you will lose much of the convenience of letting FrontPage work for you. Unless the two webs need to sit on two different servers (in which case, they probably should be two different sites), use a single web for a single site.

MODIFYING A THEME

How do I change the font of the body?

You can change the body style, size, color and font *face*. (Font is called font face in HTML. FrontPage calls it *font* in the Properties dialog box. You may also hear font referred to as the typeface. Since fonts have multiple attributes, including size and color, we'll call it the font *face* to distinguish it from those.) To change the font *face* of the body (or of any other text element):

1. Select Format | Theme. FrontPage displays the Themes dialog box.
2. In the Themes dialog box, click the Modify button. FrontPage will display three boxes above the Modify button: Colors, Graphics, and Text.

Modifying a Theme

3. Click the Text button. FrontPage will display the Modify Theme dialog box for changing text, as shown in Figure 2-2.

4. In the Items drop-down list, make sure to select the Body item. (From the same drop-down list, you can also select all the headings to change fonts.)

5. Select the font you'd like from the Font drop-down list.

FrontPage also offers a More Text Styles option at the bottom of the Modify Theme dialog box. Click this option and FrontPage displays the Style dialog box. This is the place to associate fonts with styles (as in cascading style

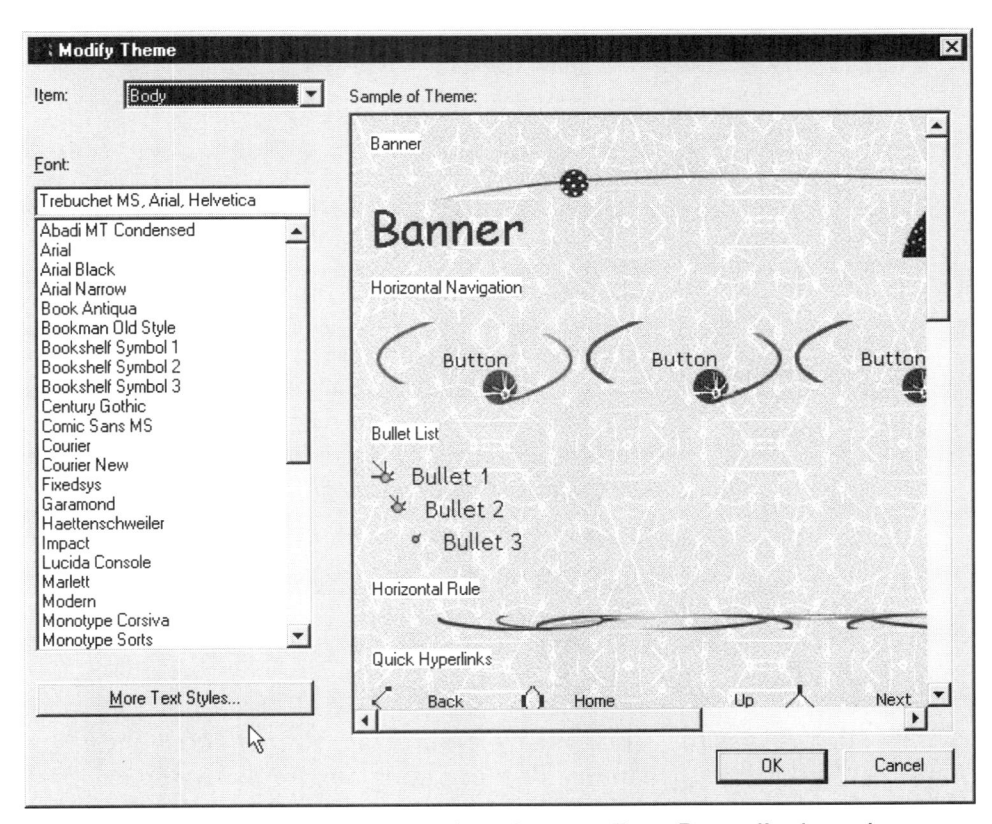

Figure 2-2 When you click the Text button, FrontPage displays the Modify Theme dialog box for changing text

Chapter 2 Implementing Themes for a Unified Look

sheet styles). Refer to Chapter 7 for a thorough discussion of style sheets.

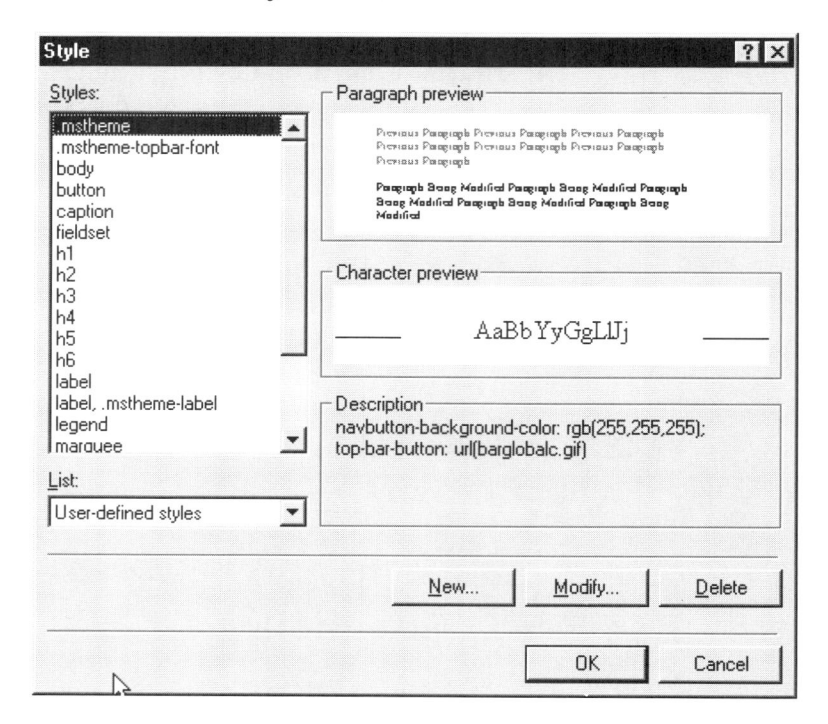

[Figure: Style dialog box showing Styles list (.mstheme, .mstheme-topbar-font, body, button, caption, fieldset, h1–h6, label, label,.mstheme-label, legend, marquee), Paragraph preview, Character preview (AaBbYyGgLlJj), and Description (navbutton-background-color: rgb(255,255,255); top-bar-button: url(barglobalc.gif)), with New, Modify, Delete, OK, and Cancel buttons.]

Remember that if you select an obscure font and your site visitors don't have it on their desktops (Windows 98 has a far wider selection of fonts than Windows 95 or Windows NT), they'll see whatever their default font is set to, which is probably Times Roman.

6. Click OK to close the Modify Theme dialog box.
7. Click OK to close the Theme dialog box.

To change the color, repeat steps 1 and 2 above, then follow these steps:

1. Click the Colors button. FrontPage will display the Modify Theme dialog box for changing colors. It offers three tabbed options pages from which you can change colors: Color Schemes, Color Wheel, and Custom. Click the Custom tab. FrontPage displays the Custom tab, shown in Figure 2-3.

Modifying a Theme

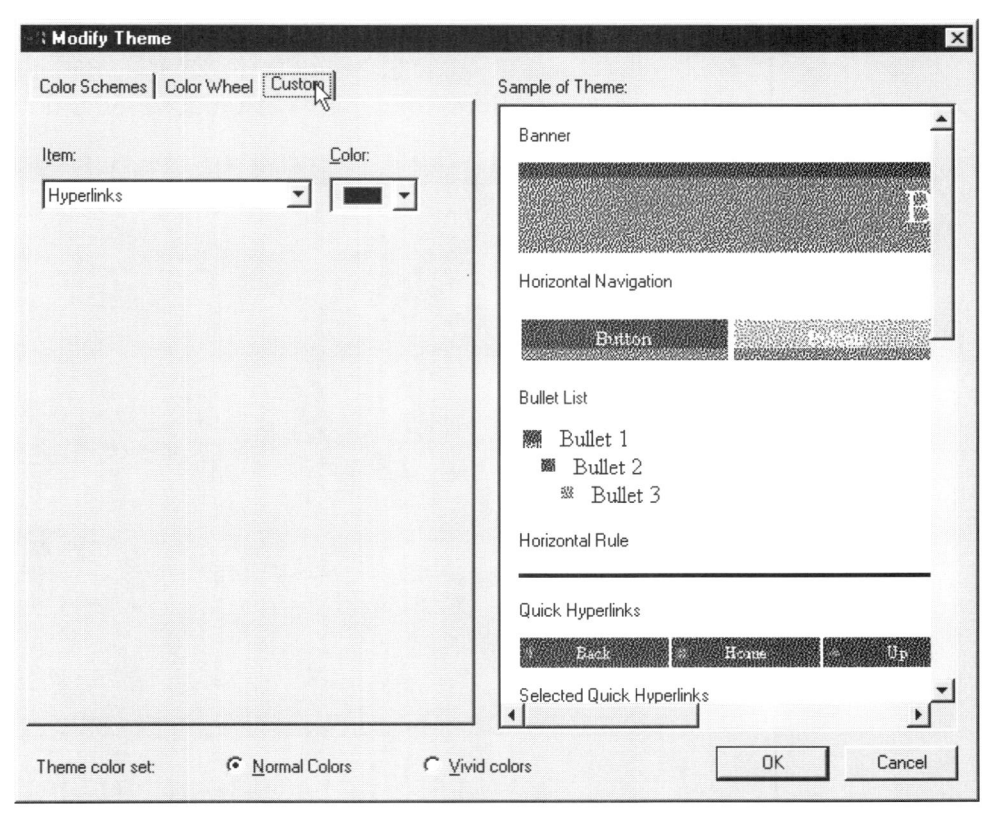

Figure 2-3 Click the Custom tab to see the options

2. From the drop-down items list, select Body so you can modify its color.
3. Click the down arrow in the Color options box. FrontPage displays a small color palette from which to select a color.

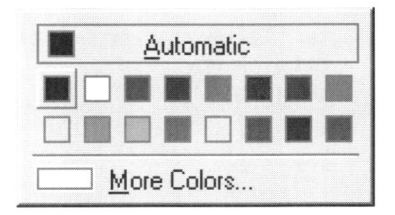

This palette also has a button for selecting more colors. If you click this button, FrontPage displays a More Colors dialog box with a detailed palette.

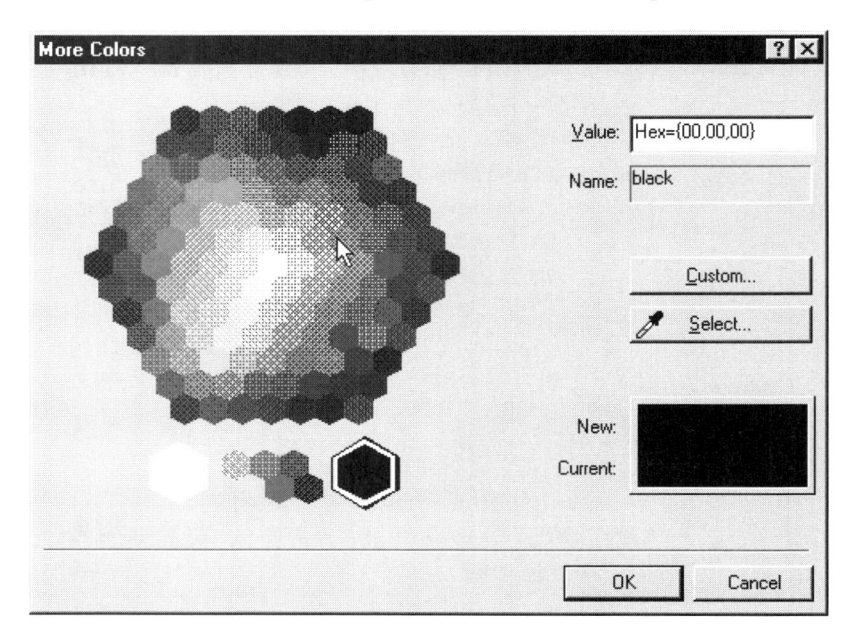

5. If you want to use Vivid Colors for your entire theme, select the radio button option from the Custom tab of the Modify Theme dialog box.

6. You can see samples of your color choices in the Sample of Theme panel on the right of the dialog box.

7. Click OK to close the Modify Theme dialog box.

8. Click OK to close the Themes dialog box.

It will take a moment for your Normal view to reflect your changes.

How do I change the banner?

You can change both the text and the image in your banner. The steps are very similar to those for changing color and text.

1. Select Format | Theme.

2. In the Themes dialog box, click the Modify button. FrontPage will display three buttons above the Modify button: Colors, Graphics, and Text.

3. Click the Graphics buttons. FrontPage will display the Modify Theme dialog box for changing graphics, shown in Figure 2-4.

4. If you want to change the image FrontPage has defined for the banner, choose the Picture tab and select Banner from the Item drop-down menu. Update the Banner image name with the one you want, either by typing in

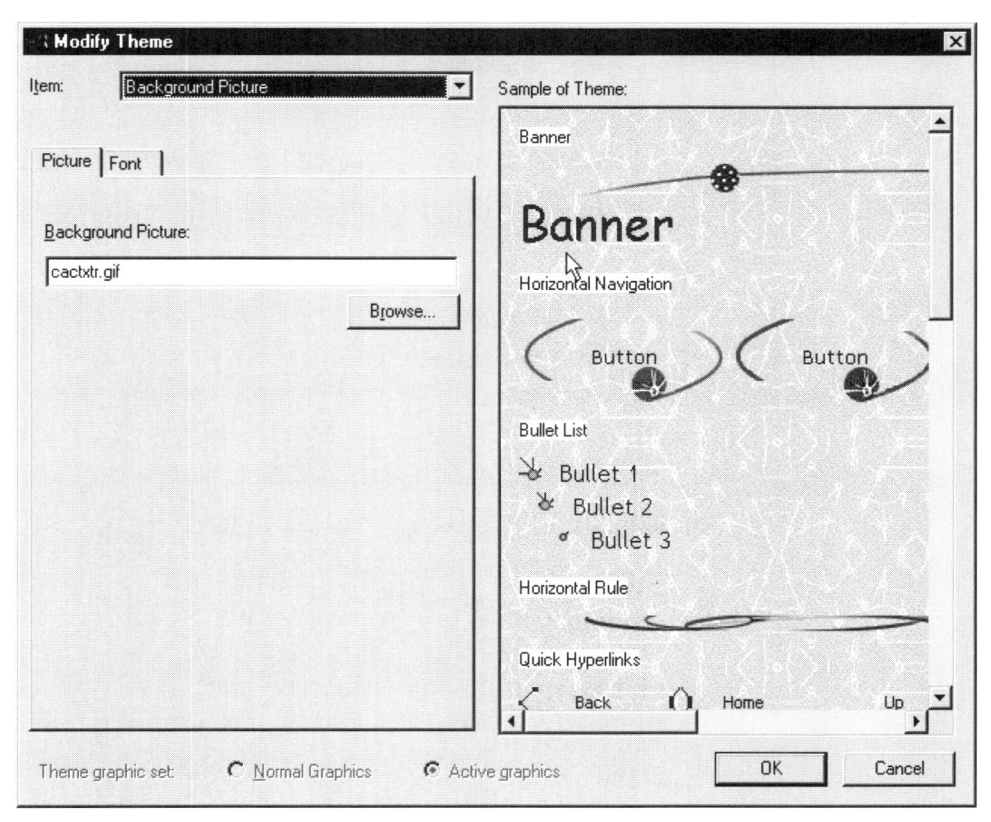

Figure 2-4 If you select Graphics from the Themes dialog box, FrontPage will display the Modify Themes dialog box for changing graphics

Chapter 2 Implementing Themes for a Unified Look

the name, or by using the Browse button. If you select Browse, FrontPage displays the Select Picture dialog box.

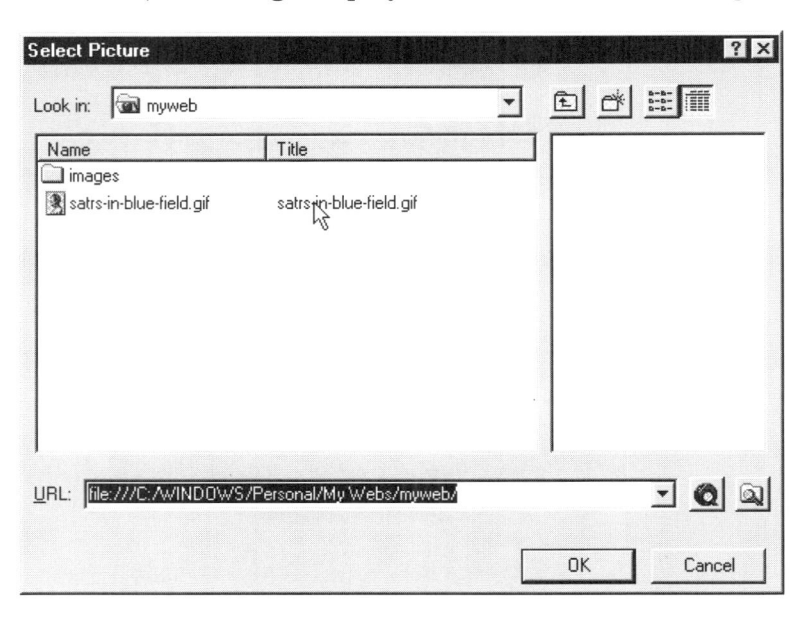

5. The Select Picture dialog box assumes that your image is in your web somewhere. If your image is in your web, find it and click OK. If it's not, then click on the standard browse button in the lower-right corner and find the file on your computer.

6. If you want to change the font for the banner, choose the Font tab, shown in Figure 2-5.
7. From the Font tab, you can select a new font, change the font style (regular, italic, bold, bold italic), change the font size, or change either the horizontal (left, center, right) or vertical (top, middle, bottom) alignments.
8. When you have finished making changes to the banner font, click OK to close the Modify Theme dialog box, and click OK again to close the Themes dialog box. After a few seconds, FrontPage will display the changes to your web.

Modifying a Theme

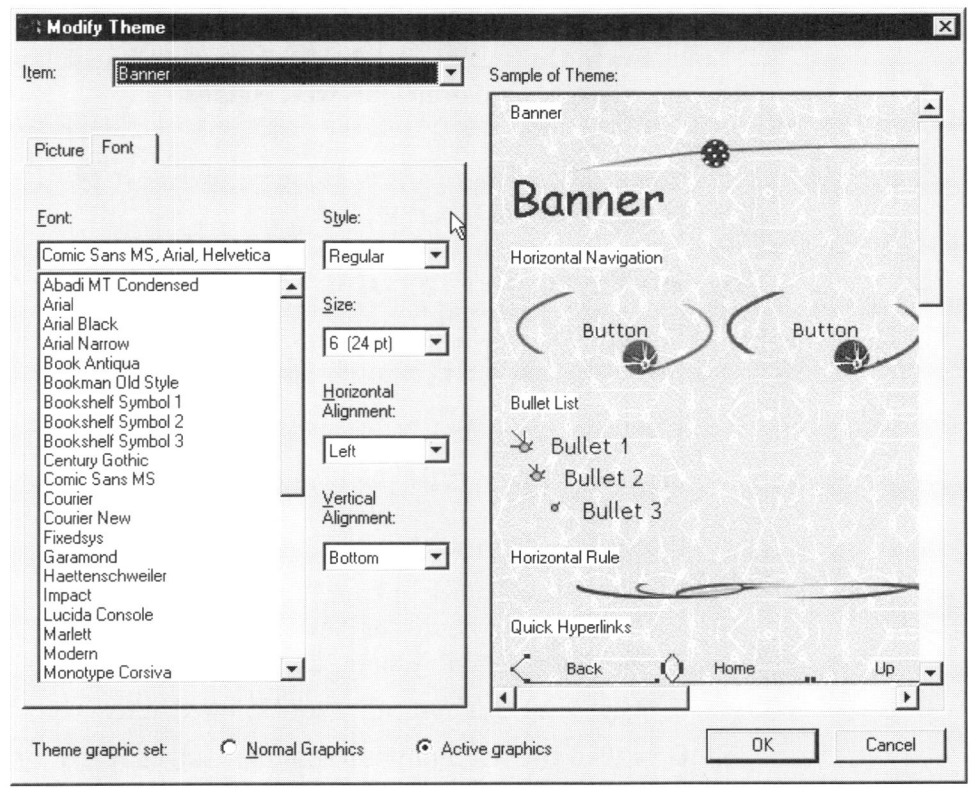

Figure 2-5 With the Font tab's options, you can modify the banner's font in several ways

Do I have to have so many navigation buttons?

No. FrontPage gives you many places where you *can* put navigation buttons, but you probably don't want to take advantage of all of them. You need to decide, based on what you want your Web site to be, where you want to place your navigation tools on your page. FrontPage gives you the option of having text-based navigation tools or navigation buttons or both. You can also choose between vertical and horizontal navigation tools.

Don't let the availability of navigation tools make you think you should use them all. Consider putting the navigation tools within shared borders. Put a navigation bar in the left shared border, then assign the left shared border to every page but the home page. The advantage of using shared borders is that you only have to set them up once, and they'll appear in the same place on every page. Shared borders give you instant consistency between pages.

> *Note:* *Read more about choosing where to put your navigation tools in Chapter 5.*

How do I change the colors of the headings?

To change the color assignment of the headings, follow the same steps used for changing the font color:

1. Select Format | Theme.
2. In the Themes dialog box, click the Modify button. FrontPage will display three buttons above the Modify button: Colors, Graphics, and Text.
3. Click the Colors button. FrontPage will display the Modify Theme dialog box, which offers three tabs: Color Schemes, Color Wheel, and Custom.
4. Click the Custom tab. FrontPage displays the Custom tab.
5. From the drop-down items list, select Heading 1 so that you can modify the color.
6. Click the down arrow at the Color options box. FrontPage displays a small color palette from which you may select the color you want.
7. For more choices, click the Select More Colors option. FrontPage will display a More Colors dialog box with a detailed palette for your color selection.
8. You can see samples of your color choices in the Sample of Theme panel on the right. You can change as many headings as you want.
9. When you're done making changes, click OK to close the Modify Theme dialog box.
10. Click OK to close the Themes dialog box.

Web Development Hazards

Is the most popular site on the Internet the most beautiful one? Clearly not. The most popular sites on the Internet have the best content (or the best-organized links to good content). Content is King. Keep that in mind when you're developing a Web site.

Here are three Web development hazards you'll want to avoid. Heed these and your visitors will keep coming back:

- **Thin Content**   Thin is in, but not when it comes to Web sites. You need to give serious thought to how much material you really have and how it should be organized. Don't fall into the trap of assuming that since FrontPage lets you divide your content (or even encourages you to divide your content) you need to fill the templates. You don't need to use every page that FrontPage provides. Don't leave your visitors asking "Where's the beef?" when they get to your pages.

- **Overly Distributed Content**   Hyperlinks are the way the Web works. Everything is linked to everything else, right? Yes and no. Links are great, but sometimes they're just not appropriate. Don't cut up your pages just because you can or because you're concerned that your visitors will need to scroll to see the entire page. As long as you keep the navigation tools at the top or on the left (FrontPage makes this easy), visitors will know how to get off a page if they don't want to be there. It's safe to assume that visitors know how to scroll. If the material you are presenting is something your Web site's visitors may want to print, by all means, keep it all on one page. If the material naturally goes together, leave it on one page. The key is to base the page on your own material, not to have more pages, or to shoehorn your material into the pages FrontPage provides for your web.

- **Buried Content**   Keep in mind that few Web site visitors have a satisfying experience visiting a Web site where the content is difficult to find. Experts recommend that no destination page should be more than three clicks away. Your site should be intuitively organized. Use your friends as a focus group and see whether they can find things within your site that you tell them are there. Additionally, your Web site should have a good search tool. Navigation buttons should be clear and say what they mean; don't be cutesy. Don't rely on pictures to replace text. The goal is to let the visitors find the content, not to keep them hunting.

Tip: *Use styles rather than just selecting text and changing the color, size, style, and face on a line-by-line basis. You can set the style by highlighting the text you want to set and selecting the style from the Style drop-down box, which is located just under the toolbar, on the left.*

How can I remove formatting if I've already assigned colors and fonts to text without using styles?

If you've assigned colors in the way that you're used to doing in word-processing software—setting font type, style, color, and so on by highlighting the text then making the changes to it on the toolbar, then you have assigned properties at a level where nothing else can override them. Fortunately, FrontPage gives you the ability to strip out all the formatting you've assigned at the text level.

To remove formatting from text:

1. Highlight the text from which you want formatting removed.
2. On the Format menu, hold your cursor over the double down arrow, or click on it to see the menu items that are hidden.
3. Select Remove Formatting.
4. Select the text that needs a new style.
5. From the toolbar, select the style in the Style dialog box.

Unfortunately, you'll have to go through these steps for every item you formatted on every page in your web. You can perform steps 1 through 3 a page at a time by selecting all the text on a page and removing the formatting from it, but you'll have to perform steps 4 and 5 on each element of your page. It's a lot easier to use the built-in styles in the first place.

Do I have to have so many graphics on my page?

You don't have to have *any* graphics on your page. FrontPage does give you the option of having graphical elements for all your navigation buttons, but you can just as easily use

Modifying a Theme 37

navigation tools that don't use graphics. It all depends on
how you want your Web site to look. Don't feel that you have
to use gizmos just because FrontPage makes it easy to do so.
You can create a strictly text-based page using any theme you
like. You can do it either with shared borders, or without. If
you're creating an entire site, you'll probably want to use
shared borders. Instructions for both situations follow.

Note: Chapter 3 discusses graphics at length.

Creating Shared Borders with Navigation Bars Without Graphics

1. If you already have shared borders, skip to step 4.
   If you don't have shared borders, select Format |
   Shared Borders.
2. Indicate whether you want shared borders only on the
   current page (in which case they're not really shared,
   are they?) or on all pages.
3. Select which sides of the page you want the borders on.
   Top and/or left are standard.
4. Double-click on the navigation component of the shared
   border to open up the Navigation Bar Properties dialog
   box, shown in the following illustration.

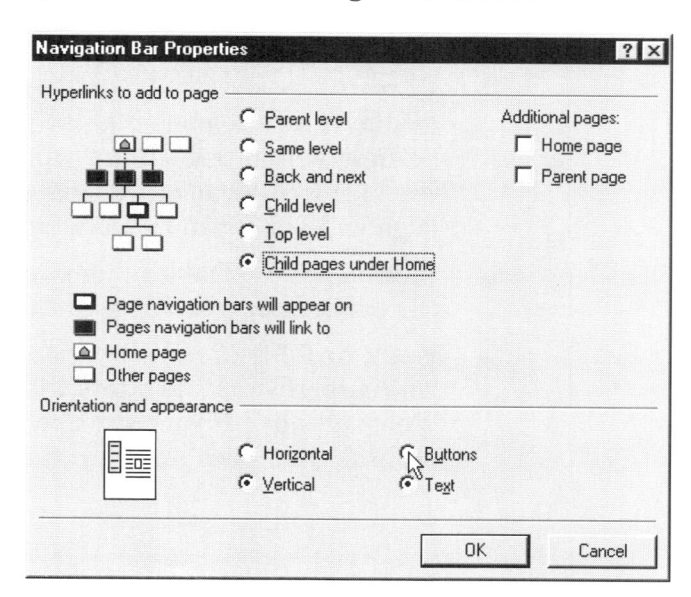

5. Make sure the Orientation and Appearance option is set to Text, not Buttons.
6. Click OK.
7. If you have any other navigation elements in other shared borders, repeat steps 4 through 6 for each of them.

Creating Navigation Bars Outside of Shared Borders Without Graphics

1. Position your cursor where you want to insert the navigation bar, or if you already have a navigation bar, double-click on it to edit its properties and skip to step 3.
2. Select Insert | Navigation Bar.
3. You'll see the Navigation Bar Properties dialog box.
4. Make sure the Orientation and Appearance option is set to Text, not Buttons.
5. Click OK.

How does FrontPage decide which pages to include as buttons?

You can indicate which pages you'd like included in navigation bars (whether they're buttons or text) from the Navigation Bar Properties dialog box. Your choices are:

- **Parent Level** The level above the page which is displayed. If the page displayed is the home page, then nothing will appear in the link. If the page displayed is one of the children of the home page, then only the home page will appear in the navigation list.
- **Same Level** The level of pages on the same level as the existing pages. These are the sibling pages.
- **Back and Next** The previous and subsequent pages in your site, if your site offers this type of navigation (most Web pages do). If your site doesn't lend itself to sequential perusal, then Back and Next buttons wouldn't make sense.

- **Child Level**   The children of the page you are on.
- **Top Level**   For sites with no single home page, the pages at the top level.
- **Child Pages Under Home**   The pages immediately under the home page. This is a very common way to handle navigation.
- **Add the Home Page**   If you haven't already indicated that you want the top level or the parent level of pages as navigation buttons, you can add the home page as one of the navigation buttons.
- **Add the Parent Page**   If you haven't already indicated that you want the parent level as the navigation buttons, then you can add the parent page as one of the navigation buttons.

CREATING NEW THEMES

How do I create a new theme?

Creating a theme is as easy as modifying an existing theme. Follow the instructions under the earlier section "Modifying a Theme," then, instead of saving the changes you've made, click Save As and give the changed theme a new name. You're not limited to the themes or the names that FrontPage provides.

How do I change a theme I've created?

You can change any of the properties of a theme from the Themes dialog box:

1. Select Format | Theme.
2. In the Themes dialog box, click the Modify button. Three buttons will appear above the Modify button: Colors, Graphics, and Text.

3. Click the button for the type of property you want to modify. The Modify Theme dialog box will open.
4. Make your changes.
5. Click OK to close the Modify Theme dialog box.
6. Click OK to close the Themes dialog box.

USING THEMES VS. USING STYLE SHEETS

Should I implement my theme with style sheets?

If you know that visitors will be coming to your site from an intranet where the installed base of browsers is Internet Explorer 4 or above or Netscape Navigator 5 or above, then you can probably use cascading style sheets (CSS) to implement your themes without concern. Otherwise, you're probably better off letting FrontPage implement your themes without CSS.

How does FrontPage format my pages if it doesn't use style sheets?

If you choose not to use style sheets, then FrontPage will modify the HTML elements using properties such as Align and Valign, or using the FONT element. If you can't be sure that your visitors have adequate browsers to have CSS work correctly, then don't go with style sheets—some of your visitors may find your site unattractive.

What's the advantage of using style sheets?

If you know your visitors will be coming to your site with browsers that handle CSS well, then by using style sheets, you'll be giving them smaller pages to download and decreasing load time. All the properties that have to be applied to each individual element can be specified only once in the style sheet, so much of the text of the page (especially those nasty FONT elements) won't be necessary.

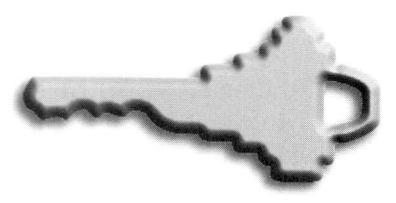

Chapter 3

Graphics 101

Answer Topics!

IMAGE FORMATS 44
- ? Standard formats for images on the Web
- ? When to use GIF and when to use JPEG
- ? The difference between a GIF that's interlaced and one that's not
- ? Why you should care about transparent GIFs
- ? Letting FrontPage make an image transparent for you

ABOUT COLOR 50
- ? Dithering
- ? Anti-aliasing

WAYS TO USE IMAGES ON YOUR SITE 53
- ? Making an image map
- ? Making hotspots on images in FrontPage
- ? Making smaller versions of images that link to bigger ones
- ? Reducing the file size and load time of large images

- ? Finding slow-to-load pages
- ? Making pages load faster
- ? Making a site with images more accessible to the disabled
- ? Resampling vs. resizing an image
- ? Resampling an image in FrontPage
- ? Cropping pictures in FrontPage
- ? Cropping vs. resampling
- ? Reducing the number of colors to make an image smaller
- ? Making an image black and white
- ? Why you shouldn't use HTML to scale an image
- ? Using HTML to scale images to your advantage
- ? Inserting a vertical rule in FrontPage
- ? Making backgrounds using the scale-up trick
- ? Preventing an image from tiling
- ? Viewing pages in different resolutions

- **?** An alternative way to change screen resolution on the fly
- **?** Why breaking up tables makes pages load faster
- **?** Reducing the size of animated GIFs

OPTIMIZING IMAGES 74
- **?** Modifying JPEGs
- **?** Modifying GIFs

- **?** Using colors that are outside the Web-safe palette
- **?** FrontPage tools for manipulating graphics
- **?** Making an image change into something else when the mouse is hovered over it
- **?** Image-swapping via DHTML and using hover buttons without the FrontPage extensions

Graphics 101 @ a Glance

Once you've got your content ready, it's time to enhance your site by adding visual elements that aid the visitor in navigation and illustrate your content. This chapter covers basic information relating to image use on the Web, and offers some great hints and tricks.

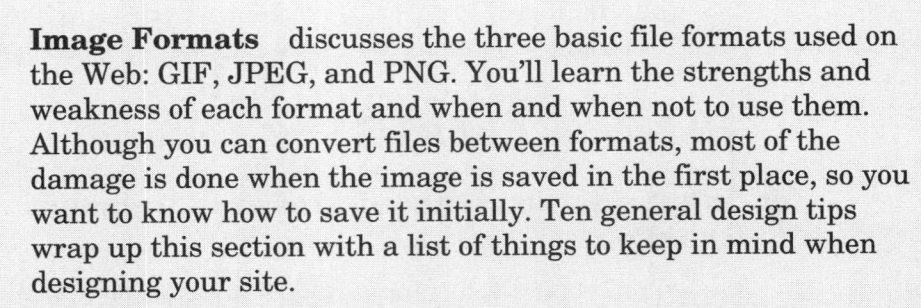

Image Formats discusses the three basic file formats used on the Web: GIF, JPEG, and PNG. You'll learn the strengths and weakness of each format and when and when not to use them. Although you can convert files between formats, most of the damage is done when the image is saved in the first place, so you want to know how to save it initially. Ten general design tips wrap up this section with a list of things to keep in mind when designing your site.

About Color covers how color is handled by the browser, and explains dithering, anti-aliasing, and the Web-safe palette.

Ways to Use Images on Your Site shows you how to make image maps; define hotspots; slice, dice, and reassemble large images; and how to determine the load speed of your pages. Also presented are ten ways to make your pages load faster.

Optimizing Images shows you some tricks for working with existing GIFs and JPEGs.

BEFORE YOU BEGIN ADDING GRAPHICS

In a nutshell, the text should be the meat of your site, and in most cases, the graphics should be an enhancement. Good graphic design can make a site intuitive to navigate, easy to read, and enjoyable to experience. Part of graphic design for the Web is the placement and manipulation of digital images.

There are two standard formats for digital images used on the Web: GIF and JPEG. There's a rather new format too, called PNG. We'll be talking about those in more detail a little bit later.

Graphics should be optimized to have the smallest file size possible. The smaller the files, the faster they load.

Different computers and monitors show color and images differently. It's really difficult to get your site to look exactly the same on all systems, browsers, and platforms. It's next to impossible, really, but that doesn't mean you shouldn't try!

FrontPage offers some basic tools to manipulate your finished images, which we'll be discussing in this chapter. However, if you want to create or modify images, you'll need a separate application such as Image Composer, which comes bundled with FrontPage, or another package like Adobe Photoshop or Macromedia Fireworks.

IMAGE FORMATS

What are the standard formats for images on the Web?

The two main formats are GIF and JPEG, and there's a third one that's new, called PNG.

GIF Graphics Interchange Format. Most color images and backgrounds on the Web are GIF files. This format is best for graphics that use only a few colors. GIF images are limited to 256 colors, which is why GIF isn't the optimum format for color photographs, which can contain millions of colors. GIF was developed in 1987 and purchased by CompuServe, which named it GIF87. Two years later new features such as interlacing, transparency, and animation were added to create the format known as GIF89a. When an image is converted to GIF the color palette is reduced to 256 colors. Colors that fall somewhere between the available 256 are approximated. A photo of a sunset will have striping in the sky because the colors can't be represented. Images of text compress well as GIF, though, because color accuracy is less important than the crispness of the borders.

The standard GIF format allows only 256 colors because of its 8-bit format. GIF is lossless—in other words, it compresses every bit of available picture information. But it doesn't contain information that adjusts its display on various host platforms, which reduces its portability.

JPEG   Joint Photographic Experts Group. This format for color-intensive images was developed by the Joint Photographic Experts Group committee. JPEG compresses graphics of photographic color depth better than competing file formats like GIF, and it retains a high degree of color fidelity. This makes JPEG files smaller and therefore quicker to download. You can choose how much to compress a JPEG file, but since it is a lossy format (meaning that some of the data about the image will be irretrievably lost), the smaller you compress the file, the more color information that will be lost and the more the quality of the image will be diminished. JPEG files can be viewed by a wide range of browsers on both the PC and Mac.

PNG   Portable Network Graphics. The World Wide Web Consortium (WC3) adopted the recommendation for this format in October 1996. Early in the Web's development, patent problems with the Graphics Interchange Format, which culminated in the purchase of GIF by CompuServe, spurred developers to work up a lossless, portable, patent-free replacement for GIF images.

PNG offers true color up to 48 bits. It also offers indexed or palette color, like GIF does, which gives the developer more control over the way colors will actually appear to a viewer. It is lossless, and it uses a non-patented compression algorithm.

Most newer browsers support PNG, and you probably visit Web sites that use it without knowing it. You can check out WC3's test page at http://www.w3.org/Graphics/PNG/Inline-img.html to see if your browser displays PNGs.

FrontPage 2000 supports PNG, as do dozens of graphic development tools, including CorelDRAW, Adobe Illustrator, Macromedia Freehand Graphics Studio, PaintShop Pro, and Visio Technical. Macromedia's Fireworks uses PNG as its native format. As time goes by, PNG is heading towards a true Web image format standard, although at this writing, that's not yet the case.

When should I use GIF and when should I use JPEG?

While GIF is the forerunner of image formats on the Web, JPEG has become the standard format for compressing photographic images. Both GIF and JPEG compress images, but JPEG does a much better job of crunching images with lots of colors, particularly for photos. JPEG's other benefit is color depth—GIFs can have no more than 256 colors, but JPEGs can use a full 24-bit color palette to create millions of colors. The new kid on the block is the PNG format, which handles compression without losing information, can display more colors than a GIF, and can use a 48-bit color palette. The disadvantage of JPEG is that it doesn't do a very good job on text.

Use GIF for images with flat color, line drawings, clip art, or images that don't have millions of color. Remember, GIF can only display 256 colors. Most image editors have a tool to create an "indexed color" image, which is useful when you want to limit the palette of colors used in an image—for example, when you want to use the image in a Web page. Using an indexed color table lets you reduce the file size of an image while maintaining the visual quality that you need. When you index the colors to the Web-safe palette, you can be pretty certain that your visitors will view your images as you intend.

There is a plethora of information on the Web about optimizing images. Some tips and tricks are included in this chapter. Your image editor's documentation probably covers the subject as well. The best rule is to know your audience. If you're creating materials for your corporate intranet, or you know what kind of equipment is being used to view your Web pages, you have more options available.

What's the difference between a GIF that's interlaced and one that's not?

A GIF that's interlaced displays in two "passes" of alternating lines instead of loading them one line at a time. Depending on which graphics viewer or Web browser is being used, interlaced GIFs may produce a "horizontal blind" effect or simply a blurry or blocky image that gradually sharpens. Pages using interlaced GIFs let people see at least the outline of an image sooner; thus the pages often appear to load faster than those with noninterlaced graphics. If a browser doesn't support interlaced images, an image will simply appear as a normal (noninterlaced) GIF

What's a transparent GIF, and why should I care?

An image that's transparent allows the background to show through. When creating the GIF, the designer can designate one color in the image's palette as transparent. When the GIF is displayed, areas using that color reveal whatever is underneath. Transparency is most often applied to a GIF's background color to let the page's own background show through, so that images appear to float on the page. Most modern Web browsers support transparent GIFs.

Can FrontPage make an image transparent for me?

Yes. Remember, though, that you can only make *one* color transparent. If you want several areas in your images to be transparent, make sure they are all the same exact color when you are creating it. When you save the page, FrontPage will convert the image to a GIF, if it wasn't that format already. If it was a JPEG, the file size will probably be bigger, and you may not get the results you want. To designate a color in an image as transparent in FrontPage:

1. In Page view, click on the picture.
2. On the Pictures toolbar located at the bottom of the screen, click the Set Transparent Color tool.
3. Click the color in the picture where you want to make it transparent.

General Design Tips

Good page design is a skill. If you know absolutely nothing about page layout and design, it'll show. If you are attempting to design a site for commercial use, it's probably best to hire a professional. While it doesn't have to be "hard" to create a Web site, it can be hard to do well, just like any endeavor. If you're willing to put in the time and effort, more power to you! Here are our top ten tips to keep in mind.

1. *Think of the underlying design as a hanger.* Once you figure out what the basic design is, everything else "hangs" off it. If you don't have the hanger, you're going to be struggling with each element, and it's going to drive you insane.

   Real Life Example: Check out Colonnade Realty at www.colonnaderealty.com. The designer is Debra Weiss, of drw Design (www.drwwebdesign.com). Here's what she said about it: "I was struggling over the look and feel of this site for quite some time. I wanted it to look elegant, but didn't want the design to get in the way of the functionality. Then, it struck me. When I was visiting the Colonnade offices, I remembered noticing several framed prints of Greek architectural drawings of temples and columns and admiring them. I was able to locate some wonderful digital artwork of this type—floor plans, pillars, columns, and colonnades. This concept became the hanger. Each section of the site has a different column that represents it. One of the page backgrounds is a screened back floor plan. The headline font is Palatino, a classical font. The navigational icons are teeny column tops. The design just snapped into place."

2. *Be consistent.* If you don't remember anything else, remember this. You want your visitors to get around your site intuitively. Keeping elements the same throughout is the way to achieve this. Don't let your basic design fall apart as the visitor gets deeper into your site, which is the mistake made by many, many nice sites. Decide on your page layout structures—it's okay to have different layouts for different levels of your site, as long as you use them in the same way consistently.

3. Use real typographical marks. This is a subtlety, but it makes a subconscious impression on the reader. Most Web browsers display quotation marks like this: "hello." You want this: "hello." You insert real typographical quotes from your keyboard using the ALT key and the numbers from the numeric keypad, with NUM LOCK on. The keyboard combinations are as follows:

   "   ALT-0147
   "   ALT-0148
   '   ALT-0146
   '   ALT-0145

4. *Decide on your colors and fonts and stick with them.* If your colors are navy, burgundy, and cream, don't make your links in green. FrontPage will show you your document's colors along with the palette. If you've chosen well, you'll only need three to five colors for just about every element on your site. Use different font styles sparingly. A good rule of thumb is to pick two font families *at the most*. Use one for your headlines and subheads. Use the other for body copy.

5. *Anti-alias your display fonts.* This is the difference between a professional and non-professional site. See Figure 3-6 later on in this chapter for an example of a first-rate site with anti-aliased fonts.

6. *Be target-aware.* Many sites make the mistake of providing hundreds of links to other sites. It's hard enough to get people to come to your site—why send them away? If you link to other sites, considered targeting your links to open in a new window. That way, visitors can return to your site easily. Opening links in a separate window also solves anomalies that occur when your site has frames and you link to a site that also has frames. If your site uses frames, open up links outside your site inside the frame on your site to keep your visitors with you. Always provide a way for your visitors to "break out" of frames.

7. *People read from left to right, and from top to bottom.* This seems obvious, but inexperienced designers seem to have trouble remembering this. Put your most important elements at the top-left of the page. If you don't grab the reader's attention there,

you're never going to get them to read on. Keep your most important content "above the fold" which is above the point where the visitor has to scroll down.

8. *Think carefully about bells and whistles.* Animations, marquees, DHTML, and so on are all great, *when used in moderation.* Don't pull all your tricks out of the bag and plop them all on one page. If your content isn't good enough to stand alone, rethink it.

9. *White space is good.* Lots of white space is even better. When you perceive a site as "clean-looking" it's probably because there's good use of white space. Spread things out—you don't have to put everything on one page in a giant scroll-a-rama.

10. *Look at your site using the worst conditions possible.* Get a copy of Netscape 2.0. Set your display to 600 × 480, 256 colors. Set your modem down to 14.4 or 28.8 and take a look at every page in your site. If you can't stand it, redesign until it's acceptable. If it looks great under the worst conditions, it'll shine under the best ones.

ABOUT COLOR

What does "dithering" mean?

If a monitor can't show a certain color, dithering will approximate the color by placing pixels in colors that the computer can display close together. To see one example of dithering, look at the comics in your Sunday newspaper. They look like they are in color, but when you look closely, you see that the colors are really little dots with white in between them. When viewed from a distance, your eye fills in the space, and you see them in solid colors. That's dithering. On the Web, if a computer is running in 256-color mode, and it encounters an image with more colors, it attempts to show the colors by mixing together the colors it has. That's dithering, too.

About Color   51

When working with color on the Web (in most cases) you want to avoid dithering, because your computer will sometimes do an awful job of it, rendering your beautiful color image as a horrid mess. That's why the "Web-safe" palette, also known as the "browser-safe" or 216-color palette, was developed.

What's anti-aliasing?

On a computer monitor the unit that displays color is called a *pixel*. A pixel is square. You have probably noticed that when you see non-square shapes, particularly text, on the Web the edges look jagged, rather than smooth. That's because each pixel gets stepped down in a row trying to simulate a curve, and it looks pretty bad. That's where anti-aliasing comes in. When an image is anti-aliased, pixels of washed-out color along the curve are added in. This actually makes text seem a little blurred but, strangely enough, more readable. See Figure 3-1 for a side-by-side comparison.

Chapter 3 Graphics 101

Figure 3-1 The text on the left is not anti-aliased, and in the blow-up you can see the jaggies. The text on the right is anti-aliased, which is done by adding pixels of blended colors which blur or soften the edges, making the text appear smoother

The "Web-Safe" Palette

Macs and PCs each have a standard 256-color palette used to display color on screen. The problem is that the Mac uses one set of colors and the PC uses another set. Therefore, if you create a graphic on a Mac using the standard palette and then view it on a PC, the PC is forced to dither the colors. The same thing happens the other way around.

There are 216 colors which are common to both the Mac and the PC system palettes. So if you use these colors, you're safe: Anybody visiting your Web page with a 256-color Mac or PC *should* (and that's the operative word here) see the same set of colors, with no dithering.

WAYS TO USE IMAGES ON YOUR SITE

I want to have a large image offering sections that visitors can click on sending them to various pages in my site. How do I do this?

This is called an *image map,* and there are a couple of approaches. One way is to draw *hotspots* on a larger image. The hotspots are hyperlinks to other pages. The other is to "cut up" or "slice" your large image into smaller ones, and assemble them back together on the page, and designate hyperlinks for each image.

Note: *For a detailed discussion of image maps, see Chapter 4.*

How do I make hotspots on my image in FrontPage?

Creating a hotspot is as easy as selecting the region you want to make *hot*, then defining the link you want as the destination.

1. In Page view, click the picture.
2. On the Pictures toolbar, click the Hotspot button corresponding to the shape you want: Rectangular, Circular, or Polygon.

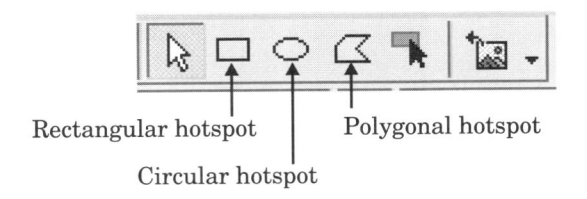

Rectangular hotspot | Polygonal hotspot
Circular hotspot

3. On the graphic, draw the shape you chose. To draw a polygon, click where you want the first corner of the polygon to start, drag to place the next corner of the polygon, click, keep going, and double-click to finish.
4. When you let go of the mouse button, the Create Hyperlink dialog box opens.
5. Specify the destination for the hotspot—in the current web, on your network or hard drive, or on the Internet.

Chapter 3 Graphics 101

6. If you want to create an e-mail message when a site visitor clicks the graphic, click E-Mail. Type the e-mail address where you want the message sent.

Can FrontPage make small versions of my images that link to bigger ones?

Yes, they are called thumbnails and FrontPage has a nice feature called Auto Thumbnail. In Chapter 13, thumbnails are discussed under Graphic Elements.

How can I reduce the file size and load time of large images?

Cut them up into smaller images and use a table to reassemble them. You'll need to do this in an image editor like Image Composer. Use the following steps for slicing your own images.

1. Turn on your image editor's "guides" feature—guides are gridlines you can usually pull down from the rulers to aid in placement. Pull down enough guides from the top to divide an image into horizontal sections, which may be all you need. If you want smaller sections, pull guides from the vertical ruler and divide further. Turn on the Snap to Guidelines feature.

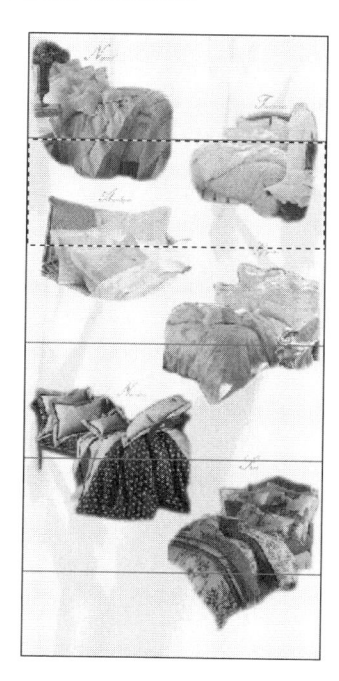

Ways to Use Images on Your Site 55

2. Then, make rectangular selections of your images, snapping to the guidelines. Copy and paste each selection into its own window, because you'll be saving each one as a separate file, as shown in Figure 3-2.

3. Keep a list of the height and width of each image. Save or Export each image to your web's Images Folder.

4. Create a table—make sure the borders are set to 0.

5. Load the images into your table.

6. Click on each image and assign a hyperlink, as shown in Figure 3-3.

Note: Creating images with tables is discussed in detail in Chapter 6.

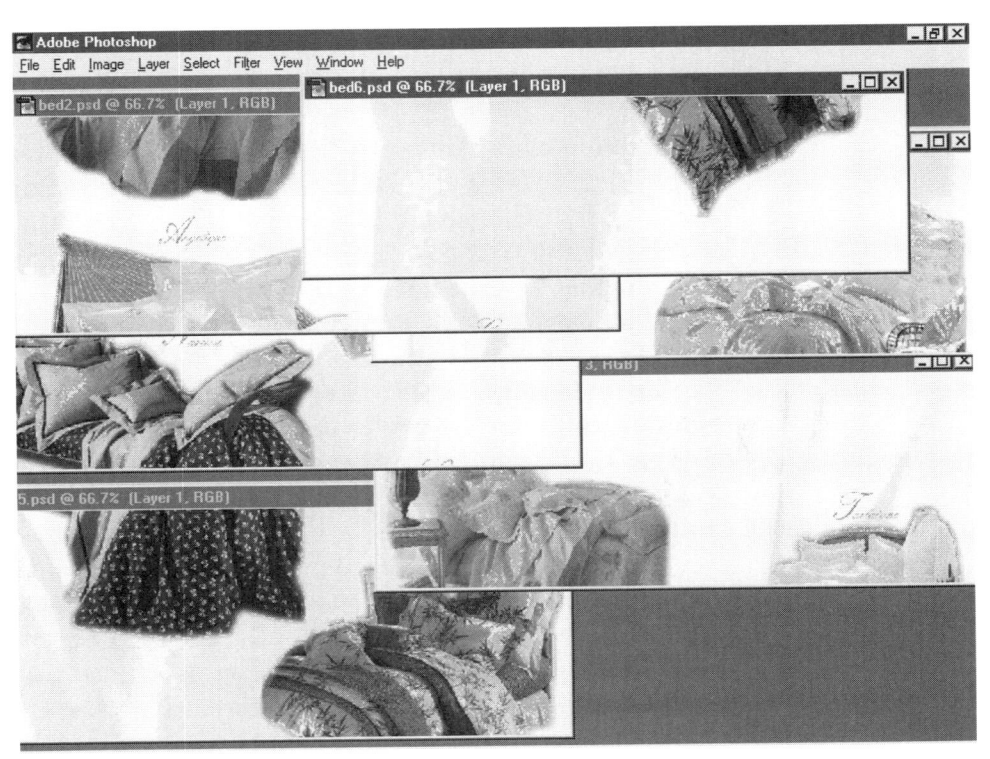

Figure 3-2 Each part of the image must be pasted into its own file

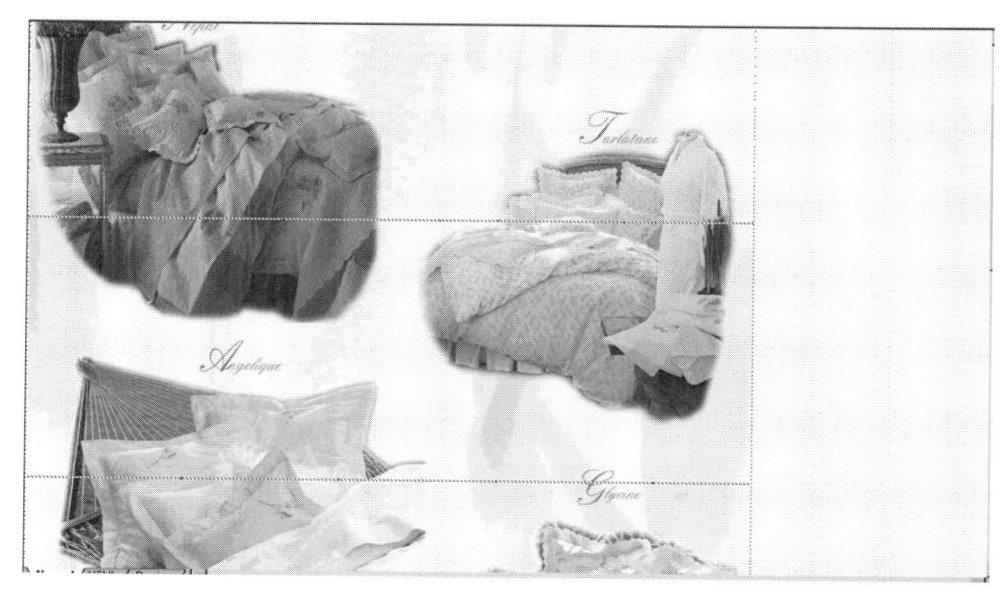

Figure 3-3 The cut up images reassembled into a table

Macromedia's Fireworks offers a feature called the Slice Tool that will do this for you. Load your images, create your slices, add your hyperlinks, and Fireworks will export all the images to the folder of your choice, create a table and the code for reassembly! Figure 3-4 shows Firework's Slice tool in action.

The drawback of a large image is the load time. If an image map contains an image that's large in file size, your visitors may not wait around for it to load. Cutting it up into smaller units may be preferable. However, it's annoying to go to sites that overdo slicing and dicing. Have you ever watched a home page load with a table with lots images and see on the status bar something like "1 of 49 images?" Ick!

Cutting up a large image permits you to optimize each piece individually. When you slice and dice, you can save each part of the whole image individually. You can export the text portions as GIFs, which do justice to text, and export other sections as JPEGs, with a high compression rate.

Ways to Use Images on Your Site

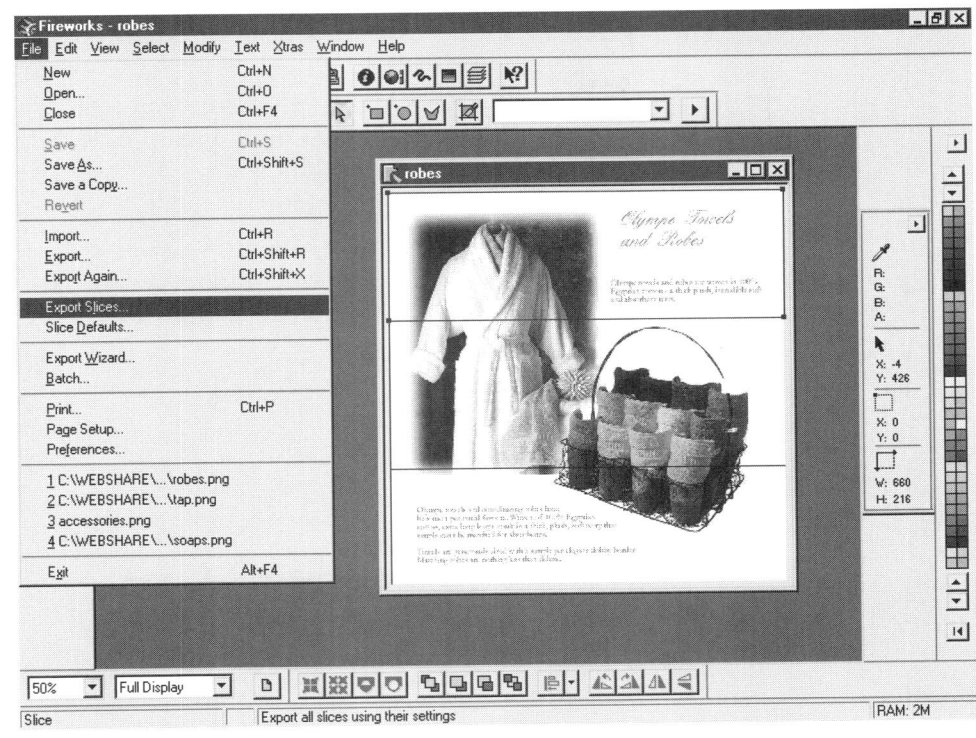

Figure 3-4 Macromedia's Fireworks Slice tool in action

How can I tell if my page will load slowly?

A great new feature of FrontPage is the Reports view. You can set the default speed to what you consider to be slow, and ask FrontPage to tell you which pages match your criteria.

1. Select View | Reports | Site Summary.
   In the Slow Pages row, the Count column lists the number of slow pages in your web. The Description column lists the download time and modem speed used to define a slow page.

2. To view the Slow Pages report, double-click the Slow Pages row, or select View | Reports | Slow Pages.

Chapter 3   Graphics 101

To define the connection speed and the amount of time used to calculate a slow page, click Tools | Options, choose the Reports View tab, and enter new values for the "Slow Pages" Take at Least option and the Assume Connection Speed Of option. Figure 3-5 shows a FrontPage site summary that shows two slow pages and five broken hyperlinks.

How can I make my pages load faster?

Here's a checklist of the top ten actions you want to take on your image, pages, and site before you publish. A detailed discussion of each item in the checklist follows.

Top Ten Ways to Make Your Pages Load Faster
- ✓ Reduce the number of images.
- ✓ Reduce the size of individual images by resampling or cropping.
- ✓ Reduce the number of colors in an image.
- ✓ Consider changing to grayscale.
- ✓ Don't scale the image using HTML.
- ✓ Do scale images with solid colors for color bars.
- ✓ Break up tables.
- ✓ Trim animated GIFs.
- ✓ Reuse elements on each page.
- ✓ Provide a text-only version of your site.

1. REDUCE THE NUMBER OF IMAGES.   This sounds obvious, but if your pages are loading like turtles, you're going to have to consider cutting some elements—usually graphics. Think to yourself, "Is this image really enhancing my message? Is its presence making it easier for my visitors to get around, or understand what I'm trying to say?" If the answer is no, consider getting rid of it. Some designers think that more than four images on a page is too many. Use your own judgment.

2. REDUCE THE SIZE OF INDIVIDUAL IMAGES.   If you don't want to dump some of your images, consider making them smaller. If they are placed well on the page, a

Ways to Use Images on Your Site

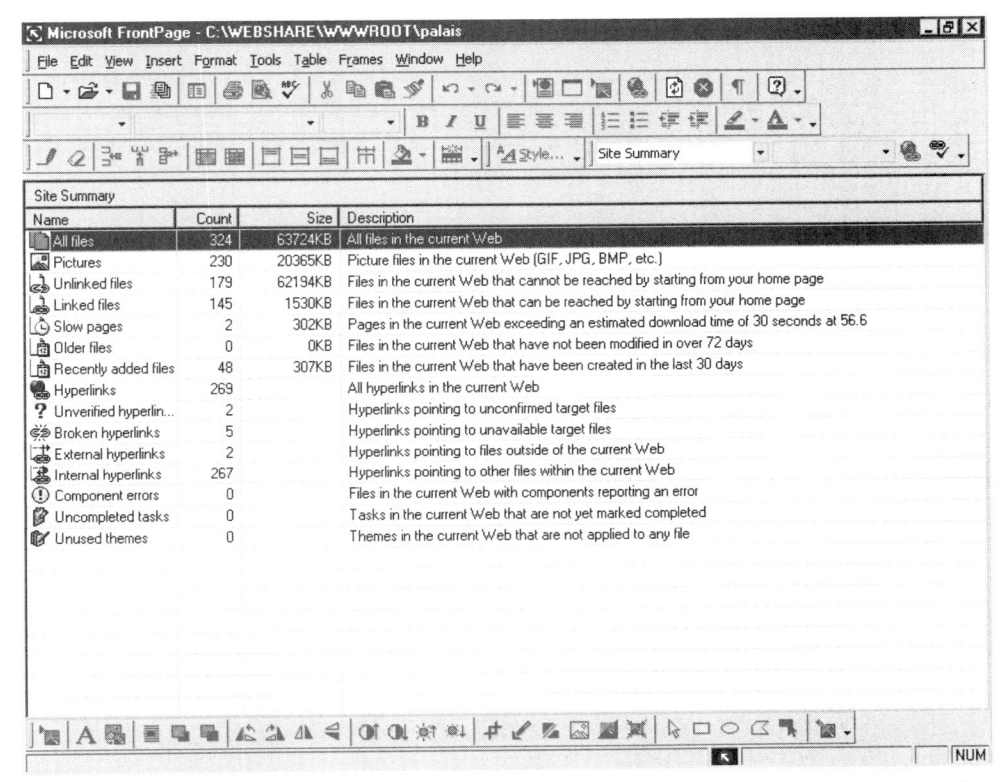

Figure 3-5 A site summary in Reports view shows two slow pages and five broken hyperlinks

little scaling down shouldn't matter, and might make a big difference. Make sure you are *resampling*, not *resizing* from the HTML code!

3. CROP IMAGES. By cropping a picture, you can remove areas of the picture that you don't want to use. Cropping also lets you change the proportions of the picture—for instance, you can crop a picture to be narrower or shorter. Cropping also changes the *focus* of an image. Sometimes cropping makes the picture more interesting and dramatic.

4. CONSIDER CHANGING FROM COLOR MODE TO GRAYSCALE. By removing color information from images, you reduce file size. Sometimes grayscale images give a dramatic and clean look to your site.

5. DON'T SCALE IMAGES USING HTML. Resample your images, don't resize them. If you resize using HTML height and width parameters, then your page will still load the larger images, but will permit the browser to size the graphic to fit the space.

6. DO SCALE IMAGES WITH SOLID COLORS FOR COLOR BARS. It's okay to scale up using HTML height and width parameters. If you want a line that's 100 pixels by 2 pixels, by all means make the actual image 2 × 2 and let the browser stretch it to fit the space.

7. BREAK UP TABLES. The browser populates the page one table at a time. If the entire page is one table, then you'll have to wait for the entire page to load before you see anything.

8. TRIM ANIMATED GIFS. Reduce the size of the animation and the number of frames to achieve a smooth animation without the file size problems.

9. REUSE ELEMENTS ON EACH PAGE. Did you know that every page you browse on the Web is downloaded to your computer? Yep! Every image, every graphic is living on your system! If you use Internet Explorer, take a look at your Temporary Internet Files Folder, located by default in your Windows folder. If you use Netscape, this is located in your Netscape\Users\Cache folder by default. This is why you should do some housekeeping and delete these files on a regular basis; they take up lots of room on your hard drive. Both browsers provide an option for deleting these files.

10. PROVIDE A TEXT-ONLY VERSION OF YOUR SITE. If you really want your site to download quickly, remove all the graphics! Some people have images turned off because they just want the facts. If your site is small, and you have the time, a text-only version might be a nice alternative to offer.

? How can I set up my site to make images more accessible to users who turn off graphics?

If you don't want to provide a text-only version, be sure to include ALT attributes with your images. Most browsers display ALT information in place of images if the visitor has images disabled in his or her browser. By using the ALT attribute, you can give your graphics-disabled visitors some idea of what they're missing. (See Figure 3-6.)

For example, if you had an image of the Statue of Liberty that was 200 pixels high and 350 pixels wide, the <IMG> tag using the ALT attribute might look like this:

```
<IMG src="liberty.gif" height="200"
   width="350" alt="Sunset on Lady Liberty>
```

Another thing to consider is search engines. Search engine robots can't see images, but they can see text. Search engine robots do read ALT tags.

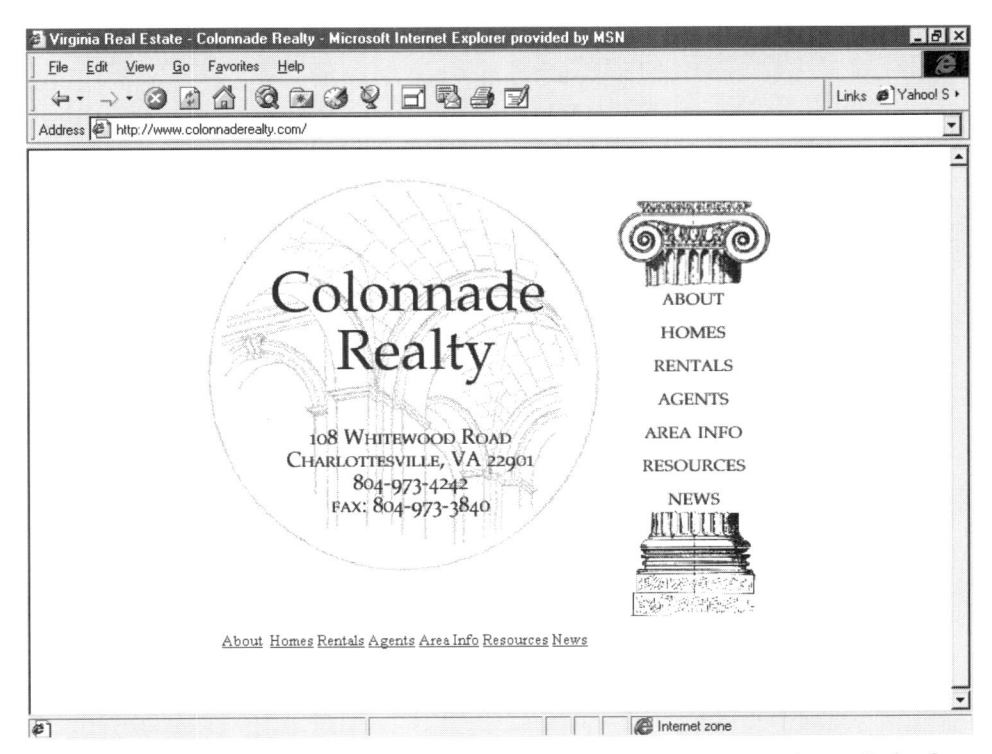

Figure 3-6 Colonnade Realty uses both an image map and text links for navigation

Chapter 3 Graphics 101

You can also use ALT tags to give instructions to your visitors, such as "Click Here to Enter" or "Back to Home Page," which they see while the image is loading and if they hover their mouse over the image once it's loaded.

What's the difference between resampling and resizing an image?

Resampling a picture changes its pixel size to match its current display size. For example, if you *resize* a picture to 50 percent of its original size, the picture *appears* smaller on the page, but the file size is unchanged—resizing a picture only changes the HTML tags that tell the Web browser how to display the picture. But, when you resample the picture, the file size is reduced to match the smaller size.

How can I resample an image in FrontPage?

Before you can resample a picture, you must resize it. To resize:

1. In Page view, right-click the graphic. FrontPage will display the Paste Special drop-down menu. Click on Picture Properties from the shortcut menu, and FrontPage displays the Picture Properties dialog box, shown below. Click on the Appearance tab.

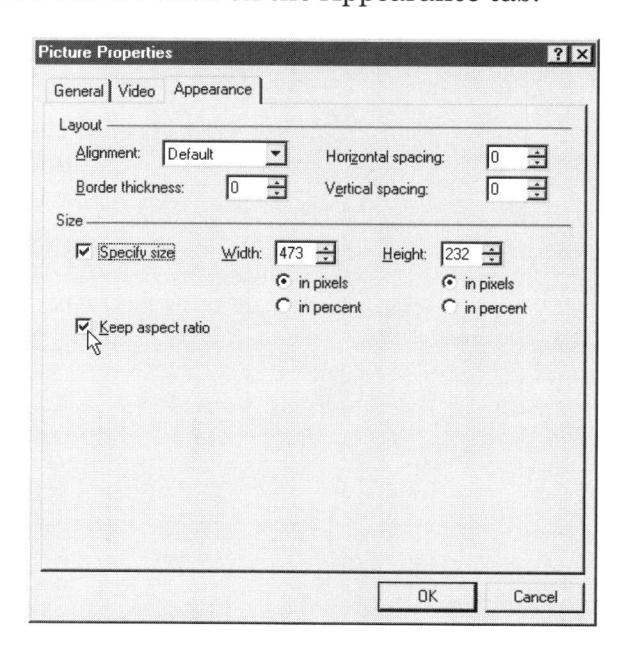

2. Choose the Specify Size check box.

3. If you want to preserve the height/width proportions, select the Keep Aspect Ratio check box. If you select this check box and then enter a pixel value in either the Width or Height box, FrontPage automatically changes the value in the other box to preserve the image proportions.

4. Specify whether you want to change the size in pixels or percentage, and then enter values in the Width and Height boxes.

You can also resize the graphic manually. Select the graphic, and then resize it by clicking and dragging the handles on the graphic. To resize the graphic and preserve its proportions, drag a corner handle. When you drag a side handle, the graphic will be distorted.

To resample:

1. In Page view, select the picture that you have resized.
2. On the Pictures toolbar at FrontPage's bottom, click Resample. FrontPage will resize the picture accordingly.

Can I crop pictures in FrontPage?

Yes. You will need to make sure your Picture toolbar is in sight. Click View | Toolbars | Pictures to display it.

1. In Page view, click on the picture.
2. Click Crop on the Pictures toolbar.
3. By clicking and dragging the handles on the cropping box, resize the box to include the part of the picture that you want to keep. To draw the cropping box manually, click outside the cropping box but inside the picture, and then draw the box. Click Crop again to remove the area outside of the cropping box.

What's the difference between cropping and resampling?

See Figure 3-7. The first vase is the original image. The middle one is cropped, meaning that part of the picture has been removed, in this case, the base. The third vase is resampled to reduce its size. It's the whole image, just smaller.

Why does reducing the number of colors make an image smaller?

GIF images use what's called Indexed Color. As mentioned earlier, a GIF image can display up to 256 colors. However, your image might look great with 128 colors, or 64, or even

Figure 3-7 The difference between cropping and resampling an image

Ways to Use Images on Your Site

8 colors. The fewer colors you use, the smaller your file will be. You reduce colors of an image in your image editor, not in FrontPage.

Figure 3-8 shows the two vases again, and it's impossible to really see when you're not looking at both images in color, but the one on the left has millions of colors. The one on the right has only 16 colors. Surprisingly, the 16-color images looks fine. The only noticeable difference is that the leaves right on top of the planter look a little less green than in the original. And the file size is considerably smaller.

How can I make an image black and white?

In Page view, click the picture. If you want to convert the background picture to black and white, you do not need to

Figure 3-8 Which vase has fewer colors?

Chapter 3 Graphics 101

make a selection. On the Pictures toolbar, located at FrontPage's bottom, click Black and White.

Why shouldn't I use HTML to scale an image? That's the easiest way, right?

No! Using the HTML code to define the height and width of an image only reduces the *display,* not the actual file size. Two things happen if you change the height and width. First, the same big image loads, so you aren't going to reduce the load time. Second, you risk distorting an image if you don't change the height and width proportionately.

How can I use HTML to scale images to my advantage?

Remember, it's not a good idea to scale images *down* using the HTML code, because the file size doesn't change, only the display of the image in the browser. However, there may be times when you might want to use the HTML code to scale a teeny image *up*. Consider the following:

For a colored bar, create an image that's one pixel high and one pixel wide. Import it into your web, and set its properties to the height and width you need. The colored bar is going to take up less space than a corresponding GIF of the same size. Also, a one pixel GIF can be scaled up to various dimensions. And here is a vertical rule!

Hey! A vertical rule! This one is 3 pixels wide

Ways to Use Images on Your Site

❓ I know how to insert a horizontal rule. How can I insert a vertical rule in FrontPage?

It's always been a mystery why there's no tool for vertical rules. However, using the one-pixel trick in the previous answer, you can make vertical rules by laying out your text in a table. Include a skinny column cell between your two columns of text. Insert your pixel, and scale up. Keep increasing the height until the rule is as long as you need.

❓ Can I make backgrounds using the scale-up trick?

Yes! You can also take advantage of *tiling*, which is the automatic repetition of a background image that is smaller than the browser window. You can make a quick page background that's a colored bar running vertically down the left side of the page using this technique:

1. Create an image that's 1,200 pixels wide and 2 pixels high

2. Make a rectangular selection on the leftmost part of the rectangle that's about 100 pixels wide, or however wide you want your border, and 2 pixels high.

3. Fill the selection with color and save as a GIF.

4. Designate the image as the page background and see what happens!

What if an image is tiling in a way I don't want? How can I prevent an image from tiling?

The way to prevent an image from tiling is to make it wider or longer, usually both. On the Web, people view pages at different resolutions, which means that just because the page background doesn't tile on your monitor running at 800 × 600, it might tile at 1,024 × 768 on a 21-inch monitor. Conversely, if you look at the same page on a small monitor running at 640 × 480, you might see something totally different.

Can I see pages in different resolutions in Front Page?

This is a new feature in FrontPage 2000, and it's a handy one.

1. In Page view, open the page you want to preview. Select File | Preview in Browser.
2. Under Window Size, select the resolution you'd like to simulate when you preview the page. The choices displayed reflect the screen resolutions available on your computer.

Is there another way to change screen resolution on the fly?

Yes, and it's a little setting that's enormously useful.

1. From the Windows Start menu, select Settings | Control Panel. Windows displays the Control Panel window.
2. Choose Display. Windows shows you the Display Properties dialog box. Select the Settings tab.

Ways to Use Images on Your Site

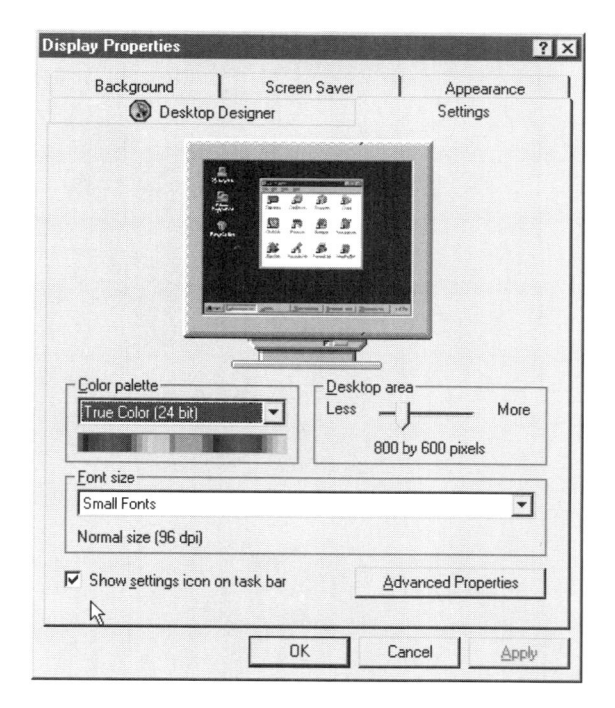

3. Click the Advanced options box. Windows will display a dialog box specific to your video hardware setup.
4. Click in the Show Settings Icon on the Task Bar box.

Tip: *The shortcut for changing your display properties is to right-click on an empty area of your desktop, then choose Properties.*

You'll see a little monitor appear in your tray, near the clock. When you click on it, you'll see all your available settings. Pick one, and everything changes. This is handy for quickly testing how your site will look in different resolutions. You might see more options by using the tray icon than you will in FrontPage.

```
640x480 256 Color
800x600 256 Color
1024x768 256 Color
1152x864 256 Color
1280x1024 256 Color
1600x1200 256 Color

640x480 High Color (16 bit)
800x600 High Color (16 bit)
1024x768 High Color (16 bit)
1280x1024 High Color (16 bit)

  640x480 True Color (24 bit)
✓ 800x600 True Color (24 bit)
  1024x768 True Color (24 bit)

Adjust Display Properties
```

Why will breaking up tables make my pages load faster?

The most common page layout device in HTML is the table. This may change as more people use browsers that support cascading style sheets, but for now, most Web designers use tables to control layout.

Unfortunately, if your page consists of a collection of elements in one large table, the entire page has to download before the browser can start displaying it. To avoid this delay, it's usually a good idea to break a single large table layout into several separate tables, as shown in Figures 3-9a and 3-9b.

Ways to Use Images on Your Site   71

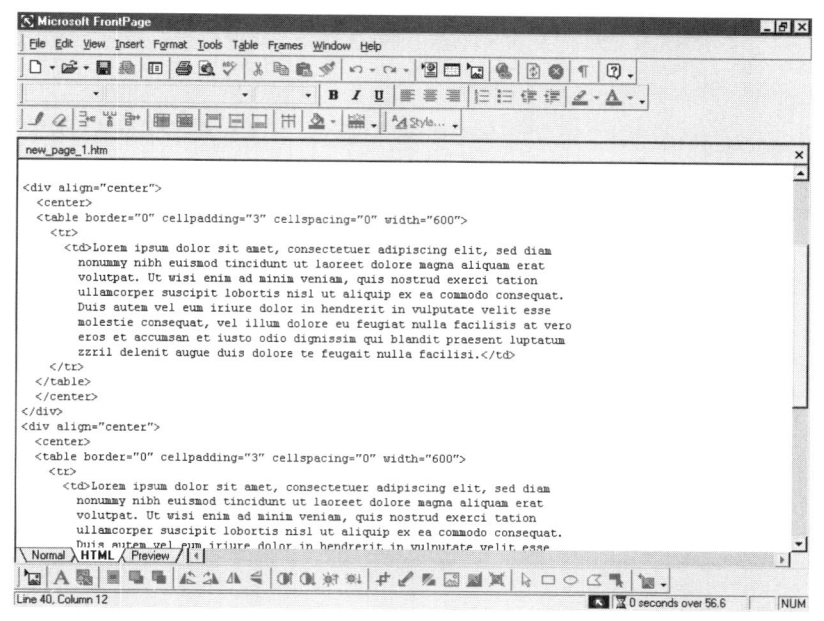

Figure 3-9 (a) The code shows the text is inserted into two separate tables;

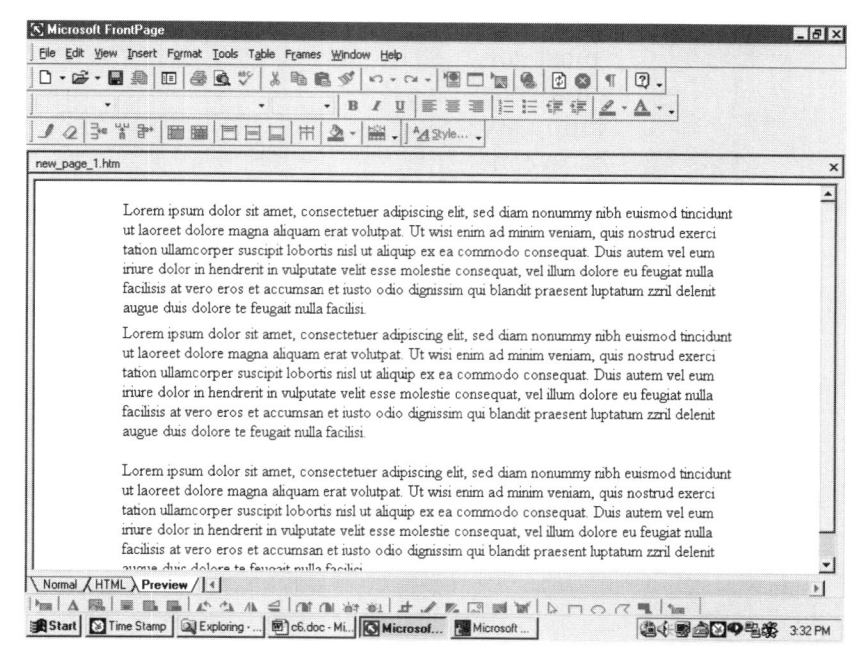

Figure 3-9 (b) The visitor doesn't see the two separate tables, but the browser does

Chapter 3   Graphics 101

❓ How can I reduce the size of my animated GIFs?

Animated GIFs display a series of images—one on top of another—to create the illusion of motion. Depending on how savvy you are at creating it, an animated GIF can be smaller than an equivalent applet or plug-in. But the real advantage is that unlike an applet or plug-in, your browser doesn't need to spend time cranking up the Java Virtual Machine or launching a plug-in application.

The problem is, since an animated GIF is really just a series of regular GIFs strung together, the file can easily mushroom to a gargantuan size. One way to control that mushroom is to start with a single background GIF and then create the animation by placing smaller GIFs on top of the background. Most GIF animation tools support this "leave in place" option, letting you paint a series of smaller GIFs on top of the first instead of using a full-size GIF for each cell. Note how only the images of the eyes change, not the text or background.

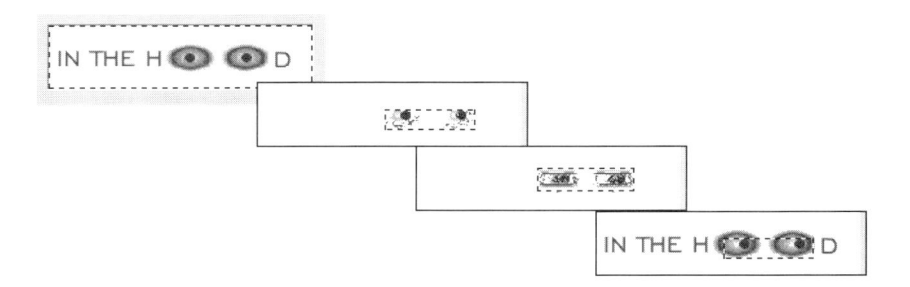

The Internet on Your Hard Drive

In order to speed up your browsing experience, everything you browse on the Net is downloaded to your hard drive. When you go to a page, the browser checks your hard drive and asks itself "Do I already have this?" If so, it doesn't have to download the items again, it just retrieves them from its cache. If not, it transfers them. That's why graphic-intensive pages seem to load slowly the first time you visit a site, and more quickly on subsequent visits.

You can also tell your browser how often to check to see if it's already got the existing graphics. In Internet Explorer 4, this option is located under View | Internet Options | Settings; in IE 5, you have to use the Tools pull-down menu. Select Internet Options and Explorer displays the Internet Options dialog box. The tabs are General, Security, Content, Connections, Programs, and Advanced. If you want to delete or customize the deletion of temporary Internet files, these options are on the General tab. In the middle section of the General tab, select the Settings option. IE5 then displays the Settings dialog box, from which you can customize the deletion of temporary Internet files. In Netscape, check Edit | Preferences | Advanced | Cache. The exact settings may be different on different platforms and different versions of the browser, but they are there.

As a Web designer, you want to use caching to your advantage. Once a visitor goes to your key pages, they pretty much have all the graphics you're offering—the ones that repeat from page to page. Therefore, if you change only a small element, the new ones won't take much time to download.

If you reuse images or parts of images in different places on your site, you can speed downloading by breaking them up. For example, a navigation bar can actually be a series of small GIFs, not one big GIF. This way, only a single small GIF needs to be downloaded to update the toolbar as it changes from page to page.

> The disadvantage? As you slice apart images you'll have to come up with a layout structure (like a table) that will enable you reassemble the pieces. The more pieces, the more complex the structure needed to hold them together.
>
> The nature of the protocols used to send pages over the Web adds another factor. For example, browsers and servers that use older versions of HTTP have to reconnect and retrieve each image separately. This extra overhead means that it might be faster to download a single big image than a number of smaller ones. You should take this into account when determining if the savings from reusing images is worth the effort. Remember, there's no hard and fast rule. Test your pages, and use your best judgment.

TIP: Use your cache as a "storage bin" for images you're working with. For example, say you're a Web designer developing a graphic-intensive site for a client. You create a lot of images while creating the site, and decide to clean out the images folder before delivery. You move a lot of images to the _private folder and delete a bunch. While checking out your site, you're horrified to realize you've deleted an image or two that you need—images that would take forever to re-create from scratch. If you've looked at your site in your browser, check out your cache and there's an excellent chance the file you need is in there. It might be under an unrecognizable name, but look at dates and file sizes for clues.

OPTIMIZING IMAGES

I found a JPEG I liked from a clip art site. I changed it a bit, and resaved it, and now it looks pretty bad. How can I fix it?

You should export an image as a JPEG only once, since at that point you're working with a compressed imitation of the original. The most effective way to edit a JPEG is to modify the original image and then re-export it as a JPEG.

But sometimes that's not an option—you may have lost the original file or never had it to begin with. For example, when you download art from a clip art site, it's often a JPEG. When you're stuck, there are some tricks you can use. With medium to highly compressed JPEGs, or images that have already been resaved, the main problem is eliminating the subtle defects, called *artifacts*, created by JPEG encoding.

One tip is to scale the image down slightly. Assuming your image editor has anti-aliasing, many of the artifacts will go away. If you don't want to scale down the image, you can use filters. Most good image editors list them as *filters* or *effects* in the menus. A Blur or Unsharpen filter can be helpful, especially if it has adjustable settings. Mildly blurring the whole image can make the artifacts less noticeable when the JPEG is re-encoded. Other filters that may work include Despeckle, Reduce Noise, and Remove Dust And Scratches, found in Photoshop and other editors. By cleaning out tiny imperfections, these filters can eliminate JPEG artifacts directly. Experiment to find which one works for your image.

When you're done modifying the image and you're ready to resave the JPEG, be sure to save the image in a true format like PSD or PNG, so that you won't ever have to re-encode it again.

What about modifying GIFs?

When you need to add something to a GIF image it's often difficult to get the precise color you want. Even after adjusting your image editor's color picker to the tone you want, it might give you something unexpected.

This happens because the image editor sticks to the GIF's color palette and you might be trying to choose a color that isn't in the palette. The answer is to open the GIF and change it to true color (RGB). Now you'll have access to any color you want. Reduce/re-index it back to 8-bit or lower so that you can resave it as a GIF.

Even if you don't need to add new colors, watch to see if your alterations remove any colors, especially if you crop the GIF. Since every color removed from the palette helps shrink the file size, take the opportunity to have your image editor recount the colors. Some image editors require you to switch to true color first, but when you return to indexed color, the palette may be smaller.

If you just want to replace one color with another, with the GIF still in indexed color mode, open the palette (look for *palette* or *color table* in your image editor) and click on the color you want to replace. Enter the RGB values for the new color, then close the palette. Every pixel that was in the old color will now be in the new one.

What's a good way to use colors that are outside of the Web-safe palette? I'm having trouble finding the colors I want to use.

Lots of other folks have asked this exact question, and there are options. One way is to take two or three Web-safe colors and use them to mix your own.

The Colormix Web site (www.colormix.com/) does this for you, and best of all it's free! Pick any color, or enter in your own RGB values, and Colormix will match that color using the Web-safe palette and present you with a swatch you can download.

If you want to buy something, consider: BoxTop Software's answer to the problem is ColorSafe (www.boxtopsoft.com). ColorSafe lets you input the numeric RGB values directly, or from three sliders, or as HEX! ColorSafe also reblends on the fly, which gives you immediate feedback and makes tweaking colors a pleasure.

ColorSafe blending allows you to be much more creative in your Web pages, as you are not limited to 216 solid non-dithering colors—you can blend these colors to simulate RGB equivalents for a much larger range of colors. Note that you should use these blends for larger areas of color in your Web graphics, like backgrounds. Also, overlaying anti-aliased text can appear jagged on some blends.

What tools does FrontPage offer for manipulating graphics?

Import a graphic onto your page, and click on it. Activate the Picture toolbar, if it's not available by right-clicking somewhere in an empty area of the toolbar and choosing Picture. The Picture toolbar lives on the bottom of the FrontPage screen by default. You'll see several options if you hover your mouse over the icons.

You can use FrontPage to do some basic things with your graphics, including:

- Flipping and rotating images
- Adding a beveled edge
- Adjusting brightness and contrast
- Washing out an image
- Cropping an image
- Making an image transparent
- Resampling an image

How can I make an image change into something else when the mouse is hovered over it?

Two ways. You can use Dynamic HTML (DHTML), which can be viewed by browsers that support it, or FrontPage's hover buttons, which also require a Java-enabled browser. Both are easy to set up.

To use the DHTML feature, follow these steps:

1. Create two images and import them into your web.
2. Place the first one on your page, and select it.

3. Select Format | Dynamic HTML Effects. FrontPage will display the DHTML options box, which can be used to apply the Swap Picture effect to a button.

```
DHTML Effects
On  Mouse over     ▼   Apply  Swap Picture    ▼   < Choose Settings >   ▼    Remove Effect
                                                  Choose picture...
```

4. In the Choose an Event pull-down option box located on the left side of the DHTML options box, select the Mouse Over option.

5. In the Apply pull-down box in the middle of the DHTML options box, select the Swap Picture option. (That's the only available option.)

6. In the Settings Box located on the right side of the DHTML options box, FrontPage will prompt you to select the second picture.

7. That's it! Save and you're done!

To use the hover button feature with your own images, follow these steps:

1. Create two images, and import into your web. In this case, both images need to be the same height and width.

2. Place your cursor in the spot where you want your button.

3. Select Insert | Component | Hover Button. FrontPage will display the Hover Button Properties dialog box.

4. On the Hover Button Properties dialog box, select the Custom option. FrontPage will display the Custom dialog box.

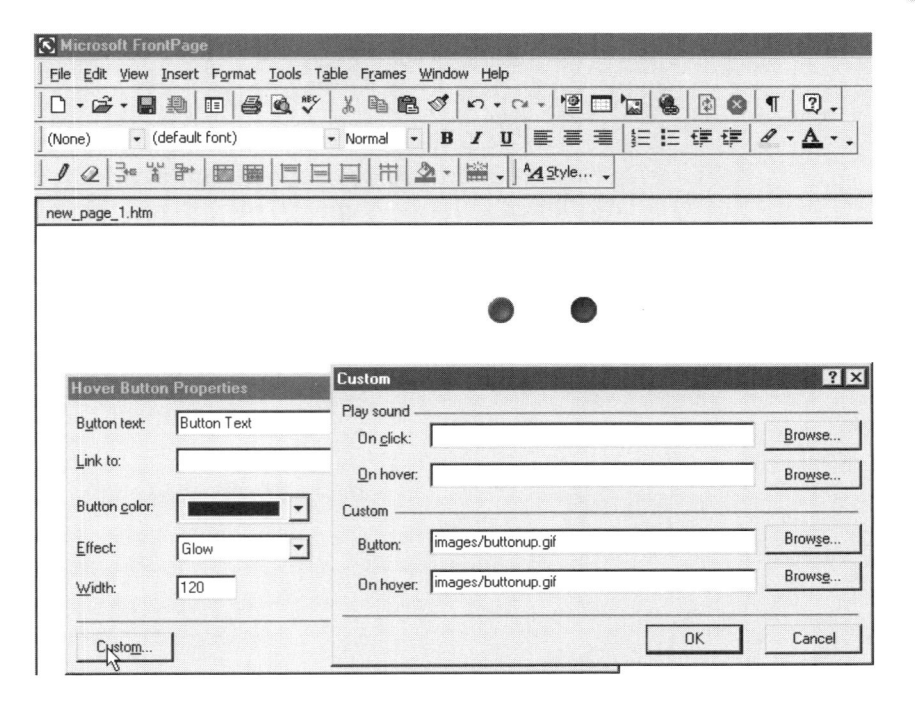

5. In the Custom spaces in the lower half of the dialog box, type in or browse to retrieve the filenames of your two images. Click OK.

6. Define the height and width of your button.

That's it! You must save the page before the preview will work. If you are FTPing the files manually, make sure you transfer over the .class files and the .js file that FrontPage creates. Don't change the directory structure either. Keep the files the way you have them on your web.

Does image swapping via DHTML and hover buttons work without the FrontPage extensions?

Yes, it does. Remember, though, that such effects are dependent on the browser. If you are concerned that your audience is likely to be using old, old browsers, and you're using the buttons for your main navigation, make sure you provide a text alternative, which is a good idea anyway!

Chapter 4

Creating an Image Map

Answer Topics!

SELECTING THE RIGHT IMAGE 84
- Making a good image map
- Using words in addition to images
- Making the entire image hot
- Using text navigation tools for site visitors who have images turned off

DEFINING THE HOT REGIONS 87
- Creating a hotspot
- Associating text with a hotspot
- Viewing all your hotspots at once
- Setting a default hyperlink for the rest of the graphic (other than the hotspots)
- Modifying a hotspot once it's been created

BROWSER AND DOWNLOAD ISSUES 93
- Limitations on using image maps
- Alternatives to using image maps
- Browser support for image maps

Image Maps @ a Glance

Image maps permit you to embed links right into an image so that different parts of the image link to different pages. The image itself is called an *image map*, and each area that can be clicked is called a *hotspot*. The place where each link takes you is referred to as the *destination*. There are so many poorly done image maps on the Web today. Before you jump into image mapping and add an image map to your site, be sure that your image map meets some basic requirements and that an image map is, in fact, the best way to deliver navigation to your visitors.

The following sections discuss how to produce an image map using FrontPage, answer common questions about image maps, and challenge you to use image maps to provide creative solutions to navigation problems.

- **Selecting the Right Image** The most important part of an image map is the *image*. This section gives you pointers and a checklist for deciding whether your image is up to the task. After reading this section, you may even decide that an image map isn't the best way to go.

- **Defining the Hot Regions** How do your visitors know where to click? Does the image in the hot region make clear where the link will take them? This section covers the mechanics of creating the hot regions as well as guidelines for including accompanying text to make the destination of the hot region absolutely clear.

- **Browser and Download Issues** Are there any limitations to using image maps? What alternatives do you have? This section discusses browser and download limitations, as well as suggestions for producing the effect of an image map without using an image map.

SELECTING THE RIGHT IMAGE

What makes a good image map?

A good image map is like a bathroom with the international symbols for a woman and a wheelchair on it. It lets you know exactly what to expect.

An image map has to give crystal clear guidance as to what the visitor will find when he clicks on a hotspot. If you have any doubt about what information your image map conveys, make the information clearer. In the early days of the Web, you'd see many pages using unclear images to link to pages. Visitors who took their chances spent a lot of time hitting the Back button. Table 4-1 shows a checklist to help you create useful and understandable image maps.

The Illusion of an Image map

The effect of an image map is cool: One seamless image with navigation built right in. Images are more visually appealing than boring old text, but the same drawbacks to using images that are discussed at length in Chapter 2, namely download time, apply to image maps. In some applications, the *effect* of an image map can be created in a more efficient manner than an image map. The goal is to create the *illusion* of an image map; the site visitor doesn't care about the mechanics.

The most common method of creating the illusion of an image map without actually creating one is to use a very tight table with images in each cell. Consider those horizontal navigation bars that you see under a banner across the top of many pages. They're usually thin strips of graphics. An image map, right?

Not necessarily. Many sites use a table with a graphic in each cell. Each of the cells is coded as a link, but the entire table isn't a single image, as it appears to be.

Need to make your page load even more quickly? Try using background colors for each cell (either the same color for all cells, or different colors for each cell), then putting text in an interesting font into each cell. Make the text in each cell a hotspot. It looks like a graphic, but it will always load faster than a graphic of equal size.

Selecting the Right Image

Is Your Image Map Web-Worthy?

✓ Does each hot spot of the image map clearly indicate where it links?
✓ Do you have alternate text for each hot spot?
✓ Do you have hot text elsewhere on the page that links to the same destinations?
✓ Is the other hot text on the page on screen at the same time as the image map?
✓ Is the image map the lowest bit depth that the image will stand?
✓ Is the image map as small as possible?
✓ Are the hotspots as large as possible?

Table 4-1 A Checklist for Determining if Your Image Map Is Web-Worthy

Should I use words in addition to images?

Absolutely use words in addition to images. Words are almost always necessary to help meet the three purposes of an image map, which are

- **Functionality** The purpose of an image map is primarily to permit hyperlinks to other pages. This is a navigational tool.

- **Aesthetics** If all you needed was functionality, words would have sufficed. You've chosen to use an image map because you'd like the navigational tool to contribute to the graphic treatment of the page or site. A graphic sets itself apart from text and grabs your attention. You want your navigational tools to do that so they're readily apparent to the visitor.

- **Expediency** Sometimes a picture really is worth a thousand words. An image map on a sports site with a baseball bat linking to the baseball page, a football linking to the football page, and a hockey stick linking to the hockey page is expedient. It should always be that clear and that simple. In most cases, the message you're trying to convey is better communicated with the addition of words.

Chapter 4 Creating an Image Map

❓ What if I want the entire image to be hot?

If you want the entire image to be a single hot spot, then don't use an image map. In that case, all you have to do is make the image a hyperlink. To do that:

1. Click on the image you want to be hot.
2. Click on the Hyperlink tool on the toolbar (shown in the following illustration), select Insert | Hyperlink, or press CTRL-K. Any of these actions will bring up the Create Hyperlink dialog box shown in Figure 4-1.
3. Enter the hyperlink destination in the URL field or use the Web search icon or the browse icon to find the destination page. You can select either a local file (if your web will be published locally), an absolute reference, or a relative reference. If you're using frames, enter the target frame in that field.

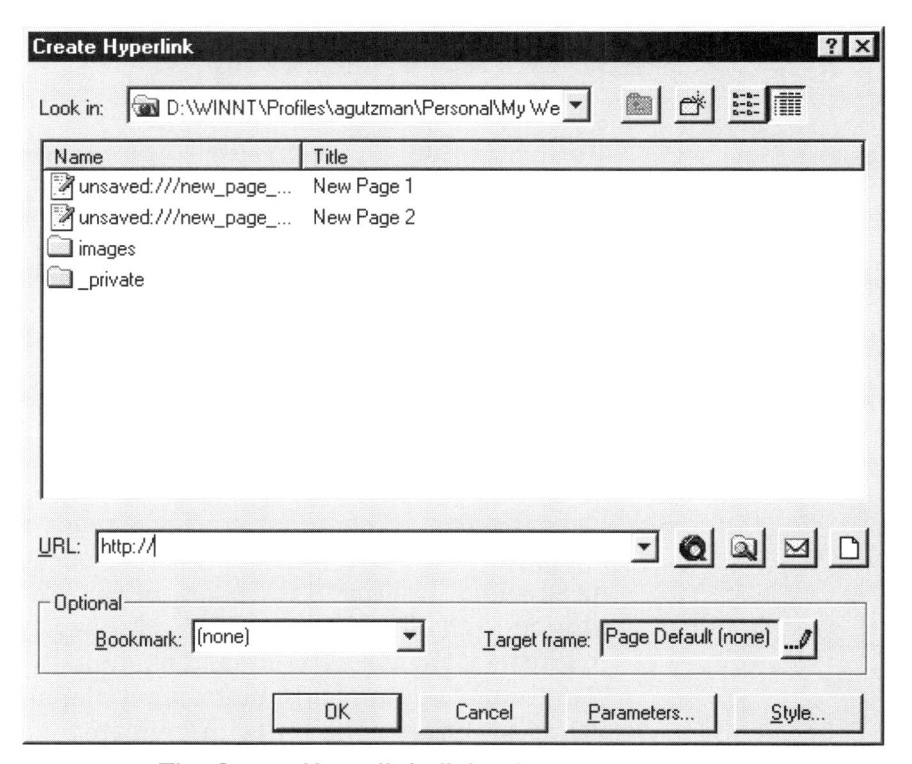

Figure 4-1 The Create Hyperlink dialog box

4. If you're passing CGI parameters through the URL, which you might be doing if you're working with a database, then click on the Parameters button to enter the parameter names and values.

5. When you've defined the destination of the hyperlink and entered any CGI parameters, click OK.

When you switch to Preview mode from Normal mode, you'll notice that when you hold the mouse over the image, the mouse changes from an arrow to a finger. Clicking anywhere on the image will take you to the same destination.

What if site visitors have images turned off?

You absolutely need to have a text-only navigation bar on the screen at all times. Take a look at one of the most visited sites on the Internet: Yahoo. Its navigation bar is entirely text. Pages with lots of graphics take longer to load, put more strain on your servers, and frustrate dial-in visitors with slow connections.

Assume the worst. Assume that your visitors are on slow connections, are impatient, and can't make heads nor tails of your images. Text loads before images, so providing text navigation tools gives them instantly loaded hyperlinks.

DEFINING THE HOT REGIONS

How do I create a hotspot?

In order to create a hotspot, you need to have the image you want to image map already on your page. So, if it's not inserted into your page yet, insert it now.

You create a hotspot by drawing a rectangle, a circle, or a polygon on top of the image, then associating alternate text and a hyperlink with each area you select. Here are the specific steps you need to take:

1. In order to have access to the image mapping tools, you need to turn on the Pictures toolbar so it appears at the bottom of your screen. You can do that by selecting View | Toolbars, then making sure that Pictures is checked.

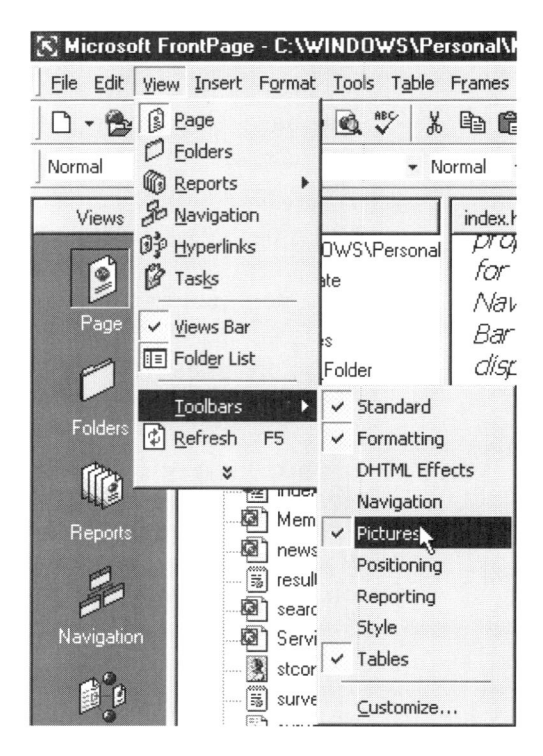

Chapter 4 Creating an Image Map

2. If you haven't selected the image with which you want to work, then the tools on the toolbar will be inactive. Click on the image you want to map to make the tools active, if they're not active already. The following illustration shows the Pictures toolbar.

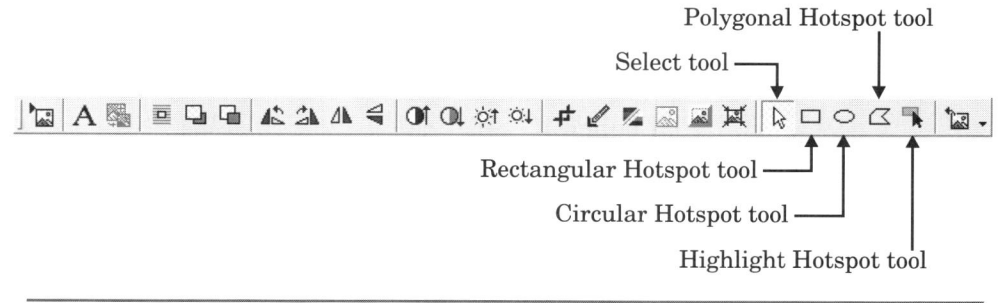

Polygonal Hotspot tool
Select tool
Rectangular Hotspot tool
Circular Hotspot tool
Highlight Hotspot tool

Note: For image-mapping purposes, you only need to concern yourself with the five tools toward the right end of the toolbar (shown in the preceding illustration and detailed next).

Rectangular Hotspot

1. If you'd like to create a rectangular hotspot, click the Rectangular Hotspot tool. You'll notice that your pointer becomes a pencil.

2. Click the place on your image that you'd like to be the upper left-hand corner of the rectangle. While still holding down the mouse button, drag the pencil to the place where you'd like the lower right-hand corner of the rectangle to be. You'll notice that when you're dragging, the outline of a box shows. Let go of the mouse button when you reach the end point of the rectangle.

Circular Hotspot

1. If you'd like to create a circular hotspot, click the Circular Hotspot tool. You'll notice that your pointer becomes a pencil.

2. Click the place on your image that you'd like to be the center of the circle. While still holding down the mouse button, drag the pencil to the place where you'd like the edge of the circle to be. You'll notice that when you're dragging, the outline of a circle shows. Let go of the mouse button when you reach the desired size.

Polygonal Hotspot

1. If you'd like to create an odd-shaped hotspot, neither rectangular nor circular, then click the Polygonal Hotspot tool. You'll notice that your pointer becomes a pencil.

2. Click on any point along the edge of the hotspot you want to create. You'll notice that a line trails behind the pencil from your starting point. Draw an outline of the hotspot you want to create, clicking with the mouse button any time you want to put down a point and change directions. When you get to the starting point (and you need to make sure that you do that), click on the original point.

After You've Drawn Any Kind of Hotspot

1. The Create Hyperlink dialog box appears.
2. Either use the File Manager that is provided to point to the page which you want to be the destination page in your web, or type in the URL of the page you want to link to in the URL field.
3. Click OK.

How do I associate text with a hotspot?

FrontPage doesn't give you a way to add ALT text (alternative text that pops up in a box when you rest your cursor over a hotspot) to image maps. This is unfortunate, but not an insurmountable problem. If you'd like to associate ALT text, then you're going to have to edit your HTML coding by hand. Changes you make to your HTML code in FrontPage won't affect your ability to use FrontPage for everything else. You might have wondered why they made the HTML view an option. This is the reason.

To associate text with a hotspot in your image:

1. Click the HTML view tab at the bottom of the screen, shown in the following illustration.

   HTML view tab

2. Find the HTML for the image map. It should be right at the bottom of the screen, and you should not have to scroll to find it. Also, the HTML for the image you are mapping should be highlighted to make this easier.
3. For each hotspot you've created, there will be an area element. At the end of the last area element you'll find the IMG element for the image you're mapping. All the other area elements will be on their own lines, making editing easier.

> *Note:* Even if you've defined ALT text for the image itself, once you map it, no ALT text will appear for the image unless you assign it individually to each of the hotspots and to the hotspot for the background, if you've assigned a default destination.

4. Right before the closing mark for the area element, add an ALT property and value, as below:

```
<area href="feedback.htm" shape="rect"
   coords="48, 137, 183, 190" alt="Send us your comments">
```

In this example, the words "Send us your comments" will appear when the visitor holds his or her mouse over the rectangle defined in this hotspot. When he or she clicks on the area, it'll link to the feedback page. The words between the word "alt" and the close-quotes were typed by hand in the HTML view; FrontPage doesn't give you the option of creating ALT text where you'd expect it—in the Create Hyperlink or Edit Hyperlink dialog boxes.

> *Note:* If you later decide to delete a hotspot for which you've added ALT text, FrontPage will know to delete the ALT text as well.

Can I see all my hotspots at once when I'm creating them?

To see all your hotspots at once, click the Highlight Hotspots tool on the Pictures toolbar. What this does is make the image itself disappear and only shows the hotspots. If any of your hotspots are selected when you click this tool, those hotspots will appear as solid black. Unselected hotspots will show up only as outlines. To unhighlight your hotspots and make the image visible again, click the Highlight Hotspots tool again.

Chapter 4 Creating an Image Map

? Can I set a default hyperlink for the rest of the graphic (other than the hotspots)?

You can set a default hyperlink for the graphic (to link to if none of the hotspots is selected) from the Image Properties dialog box. Follow these steps:

1. Click on the image to select it, but not on the part of the image that is part of a hotspot.
2. Right-click and select Picture Properties (or press ALT-ENTER, or select Format | Properties).
3. Insert a destination in the Default Hyperlink Location field either by typing it by hand, or by clicking the Browse button and pointing to the destination page.
4. Click OK.

? How do I modify a hotspot once I've created it?

1. Double-click anywhere within the hotspot. You might have to click the image once to see the outlines of all the hotspots, or click the image and then select the Highlight Hotspots tool to see only the hotspots.
2. You'll see the Edit Hyperlink dialog box, as shown in the following illustration.

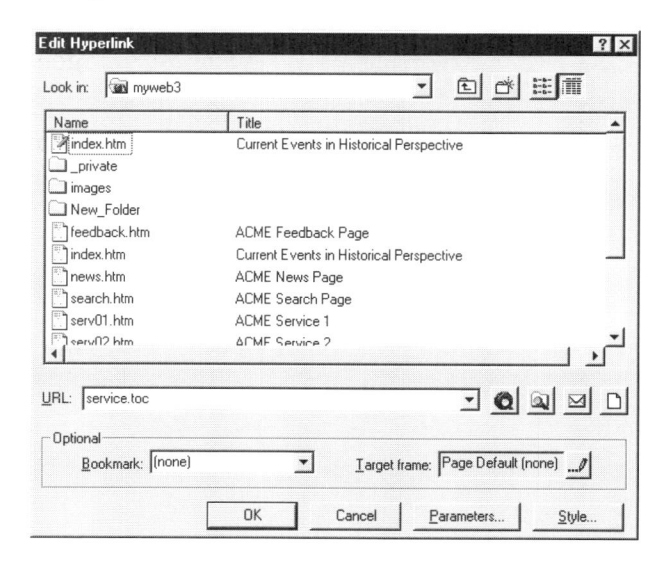

3. Make any changes you need to make to the destination URL, the target frame, or the parameters from this dialog box.

***

Tip: *You can't modify the ALT text of a hotspot from the Edit Hyperlink dialog box. You need to go into HTML view and make that change by hand.*

BROWSER AND DOWNLOAD ISSUES

Are there any limitations on using image maps?

Image maps will work on Version 2.0 browsers and above, so there really are no functional limitations to using image maps. The real image map limitation is download time for graphics. If you send a screen-size image map to your visitors, the download time will probably be unacceptable. You can accomplish the same thing using smaller images positioned strategically in a table with borders turned off and the background color set appropriately.

Think creatively about how to create the effect of an image map without actually using an image map. If you really do need to use an image map, reduce the bit depth, increase the compression, and reduce the dimensions of the image as much as you can without sacrificing its ability to communicate where each link goes.

***

Note: *For more information about bit depth and compression, see Chapter 3, which discusses graphics at length.*

What are the alternatives to using image maps?

If you don't want to use an image map, you have options, such as text, text in a table, graphic images of text in a table, or graphic images in a table.

Text

Since an image map is nothing more than a fancy navigation tool, consider using the original navigation tool: hypertext. You can simply mark the text you want as a hyperlink.

1. Highlight the words that link to the first destination.
2. Click the Hyperlink icon, select Insert | Hyperlink, or press CTRL-K.
3. Enter the destination in the URL box.
4. Click OK.
5. Repeat these steps for each set of words that link to a different destination.

Tip: If you want to create a standard navigation bar that links to parallel pages in your site (siblings, parents, children of the home page, and so on) then use the Insert Navigation Bar feature, rather than doing it all by hand. That way if you re-arrange your pages, the navigation bar automatically reflects your design changes. Chapter 5 discusses navigation and navigation bars at length.

Text in a Table

If you want your text to go across the page (a horizontal layout) or down the side of the page (a vertical layout), format it using a table. To make it look especially nice, set the background colors of the cells or use a small image tiled as the background image in the cells. Turn cell and table borders off so that the borders don't compete with the text. Don't forget to make your text hyperlinks.

Graphic Images of Text in a Table

If you're not happy with the fact that text always displays as pixelated, take your text into your favorite image-editing software and anti-alias it against the right background color. Crop each image to the right size for the cell and assign an image of text to each cell. Finally, make each image a hyperlink. Again, be sure to turn borders off or it will ruin the effect.

Graphic Images in a Table

If you're convinced that you need images instead of (or in addition to) text as part of your navigation tool, and you don't want to use an image map, create your images with a table in mind. Put each image into a cell and assign a hyperlink to each image.

What levels of browsers support image maps?

Image maps are supported by Internet Explorer, Mosaic, and Netscape 2 browsers. Incompatibility is no reason to avoid using image maps.

Chapter 5

The Art of Navigation—Inside and Outside

Answer Topics!

SITE STRUCTURE 98

- ? Things to think about before you begin creating your site
- ? Designing your site map
- ? Understanding storyboards
- ? Organizing information

NAVIGATION STRATEGIES 101

- ? How navigation determines your site map
- ? Why some sites don't have a home page
- ? Using shared borders with navigation buttons
- ? Other navigation concerns
- ? Generating a Table of Contents
- ? Creating a site map
- ? Navigation using frames

ABOUT FILES 116

- ? Organizing files
- ? Organizing a complex site with subareas and graphics that are only current for a certain period of time
- ? Understanding filenames

ANALYZING YOUR WEB 120

- ? What a Site Summary report shows
- ? How to see a list of broken hyperlinks
- ? How to tell if pages will load slowly
- ? How FrontPage's own components can be broken
- ? How to see the publishing status of files
- ? Why some files wouldn't be published, and how to tell FrontPage to not publish a file

The Art of Navigation @ a Glance

Most Web sites are not designed to be a one-time project. Since "shelf space" isn't a problem, and nobody has to worry about the cost of four-color printing, most of the information contained on a Web site can stay around for quite some time. In fact, the best Web sites are living, growing entities, constantly changing, updating, and archiving content.

For those of us who are charged with the task of maintaining these "living", growing entities, the way a site is set up and organized is key. Changing and updating web content can either be sheer drudgery or a no-brainer. This chapter discusses strategies you can employ to keep all that under control, and takes a look at the tools FrontPage offers to help you.

The core of any Web site is its structure and navigation. If visitors can't easily get around, they will quickly get frustrated and leave. Intuitive navigation is tricky to create, and requires a lot of planning beforehand. This chapter discusses some useful strategies to keep in mind while in the design and development phases of your site. These are the main sections covered in this chapter:

- **Site Structure** offers some ideas on how to set up a site from scratch, including making a site map, storyboarding, and organizing information.

- **Navigation Strategies** explains how FrontPage uses levels to determine navigation and gives you nine great tips regarding navigation design.

- **About Files** discusses setting up subareas for complex content and establishing file-naming conventions.

- **Analyzing Your Web** shows you the reporting tools you can use to monitor and manage your web.

SITE STRUCTURE

What are some things to think about before I begin creating my site?

If you're lucky enough to be at this stage, instead of having to play catch-up later, or worse, inheriting someone else's mess, consider yourself ahead of the game! The best advice is:

Plan your site BEFORE creating it.

Your contractor can't remodel your house unless he or she has a working set of plans from the architect. The plans determine which walls will be knocked down, how much wood needs to be purchased, and which subcontractors, such as plumbers, carpenters, and so on, are going to be needed to complete the job. What's in the plan will ultimately determine the cost of the project. If you suddenly decide you have to have a hot tub out on the deck, the plans have to be redrawn, additional supplies purchased, and the cost refigured.

The exact same concept applies to creating a Web site. The blueprints are called the "site map." The site map shows the skeletal structure of the site, similar to an outline. It should show the hierarchy of pages—in other words, what's going to go where. If you are doing a site for clients, insist that they provide you with one, or, if you're organizing their materials, create a map, and make them sign off on it before you begin creating the site.

If you are bidding on a job, the map is the key that determines the scope and ultimate cost of the project. Say you bid the job based on 12 pages. You can pretty closely figure how long it might take to complete the tasks involved, if you know from the map that each page is going to have the same navigational elements, one graphic per page, and five paragraphs of text. If, however, halfway through the project the clients decide that they just have to have a discussion group, a search page, and a members-only section, you have to be ready to make a new map and refigure the cost of the job. One approach, if you're basing the cost of the project as a flat fee rather than hourly, is to add a "not to exceed" cost into your contract. This way, if the clients expand the scope of the project when you're well into it, you don't have to have unpleasant discussions about the increased cost, because you've added a cushion to cover just this type of thing.

What should my site map look like?

It doesn't have to be super-fancy. It's a working document that keeps you on track during the design and development phase. It can be a simple outline created in Word, or it can be a flow chart, or even similar to a table of contents. Just make sure you do it! (See Figure 5-1.)

You can also make some diagrams to show how information is going to flow through the back end to the visitor. A web designer I know tells the story of trying to explain to her clients how her employees could enter information into a web-based form that would manipulate a database running on the server that would in turn display dynamically created pages to web visitors. As the clients' eyes started to glaze over, the designer turned over a paper plate, drew boxes representing the form, the server, the database, and the Web browser. Then she wrote the words "magic here"

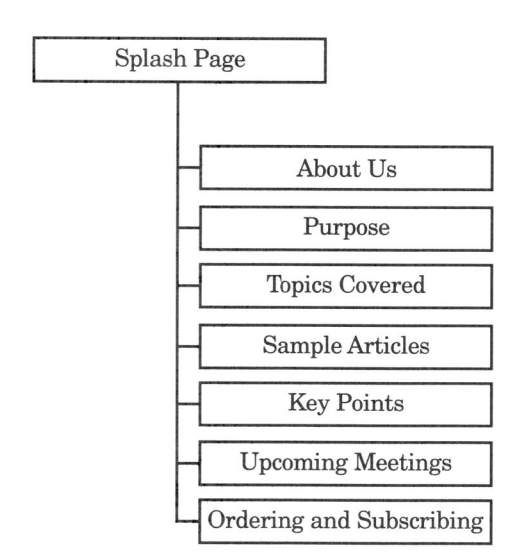

Prostate Forum Site Map

```
Splash Page
    ├── About Us
    ├── Purpose
    ├── Topics Covered
    ├── Sample Articles
    ├── Key Points
    ├── Upcoming Meetings
    └── Ordering and Subscribing
```

Figure 5-1 Site map for the Prostate Forum

What's a storyboard?

Storyboarding is another technique for planning out something before creating it. Storyboarding comes from the film industry, where each shot may be sketched beforehand, sometimes in great detail showing exactly what the camera will see.

For web design, a storyboard can be a sheet of paper with squares marked off for each page, providing a thumbnail view of the site. Graphic elements are denoted, as well as navigational structure. Storyboards are a great way to figure out what you're going to need before you create anything, and they really help you stay focused and on track during the design phase.

How should I think about organizing information?

First, determine what kind of site you're designing. Is this an informational site or an entertainment site? Is it graphic-intensive or text-intensive? Is it fun and casual in tone or more serious and sophisticated? This assessment will help determine content priorities.

This might sound obvious, but put your most important items first. If your site is informational or promotional, your visitors are going to want to take a look at what you've got to offer (your product) right away. They might not be as interested in your company's history, who's on your board of directors, or what your building looks like as you are!

Don't overwhelm with too many choices. This might sound obvious as well, but many big companies make this mistake. Take Fox Sports for example. As you can see in Figure 5-2, there's so much packed into the front page that you don't know where to go first. As a contrast, The Gap does a great job on their front page, shown in Figure 5-3. The navigation goes across the top—it's the first thing you see on the page. The pictures of their spring specials are big, and they haven't cluttered up the site sections with a lot of text. A good rule of thumb is to include no more than ten items in a menu.

Figure 5-2 Fox Sports has so much happening on the front page, where do you go?

NAVIGATION STRATEGIES

What about navigation? Doesn't that determine my site map?

Yes, it does. Your site structure is based on navigation. Each page in your site has to have a way in and a way out. Where each page lives in your structure establishes your navigation. Keep in mind, though, that while you might think of the pages as being optimally viewed in a certain order, your visitors may have different ideas. Your goal is to have your visitors intuitively grasp your site's structure, so they can figure out where they are in the hierarchy of your pages and can cruise your site without getting confused.

Chapter 5 The Art of Navigation—Inside and Outside

Figure 5-3 The Gap, on the other hand does a great job with their uncluttered front page

One of the most frequent complaints about FrontPage is: *"I can't figure out how to make the navigation bars and buttons work. I can't figure out all that parent-child level stuff."* If you're muttering that, you don't grasp your site's structure, and neither will your visitors! If you're not comfortable with parent-child concept, maybe it's easier to think up/down. Is the visitor moving up or down in your hierarchy? The "same level" concept can be thought of as side-to-side. In other words, look at the outline, the hierarchy, the map, whatever it is that defines your structure to determine *which direction* the visitor is moving through the site. That defines your navigational setup.

Let's look at Figure 5-1 again, the site map for The Prostate Forum. We can see at a glance there are only two levels—the parent level in this case is a "splash" page. The splash page doesn't really count as anything, as the viewer sees it only one time—the first time he or she comes to the site. It will have a splashy graphic on it to set the mood and tone for the site. It's the front door. The child level consists of all the pages off the splash (home) page. The site map makes it very easy to create the pages for the site, which have been done in Navigation view, as was done for the Prostate Forum material shown here:

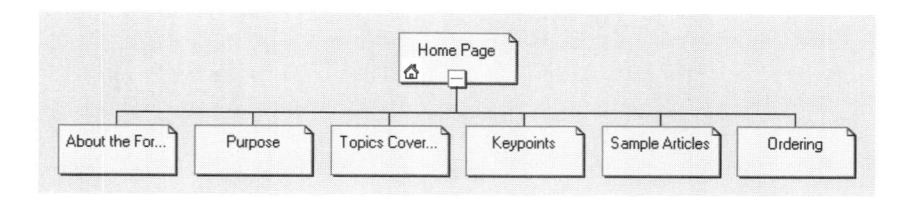

![Site map diagram showing Home Page at top with six child pages below: About the For..., Purpose, Topics Cover..., Keypoints, Sample Articles, Ordering]

Figure 5-4 shows FrontPage's Navigation Bar Properties dialog box, the place where you set the navigation for your site. In this example, the navigational setup for the left shared border is set for Same Level, to show links to every page that's on the same level on our map, which in this case, is every page on the site. In other words, when the visitor is moving, he or she is moving *side to side* through the site, not up or down.

Do all sites need home pages?

No. In some cases it makes more sense to have every page accessible from every other page, resulting in what's called *side-to-side global navigation.* In very small sites, it can be annoying to force navigation into the *hub-and-spoke* system of navigation in which the visitor has to return to the home page after viewing each page in order to go to the next one. If you have a very large site, with lots of different levels, it's good to have a central or "home" page that takes the viewer back to the "beginning," which serves as a table of contents. For smaller sites, though, it's not always necessary.

Chapter 5 The Art of Navigation—Inside and Outside

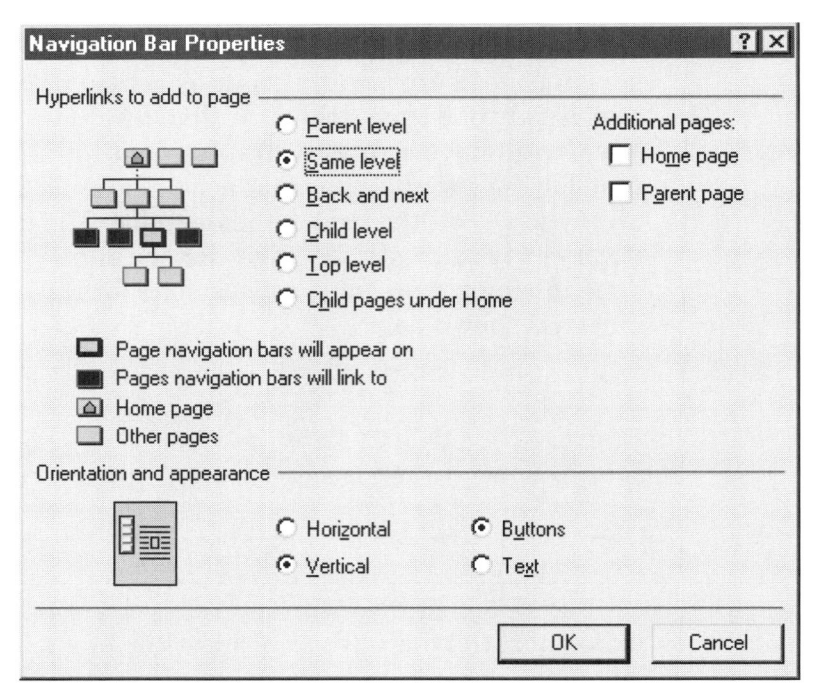

Figure 5-4 Navigational setup for the Prostate Forum

I'm using a left shared border for my navigation, and the buttons don't say what I think they should. What am I doing wrong?

This is where most folks run into trouble. Remember, shared borders are common to *every* page in your web. Depending on how your structure is set up, every page might not have a "child" or every page might not fit into the navigational structure you've chosen in the shared border. To get around this, follow these steps:

1. Disable Shared Borders from the pages that aren't working the way you want. First, right-click on the page

on which you want to work. FrontPage will display the Format drop-down menu. Select Shared Borders. FrontPage will display the Shared Borders dialog box, shown here:

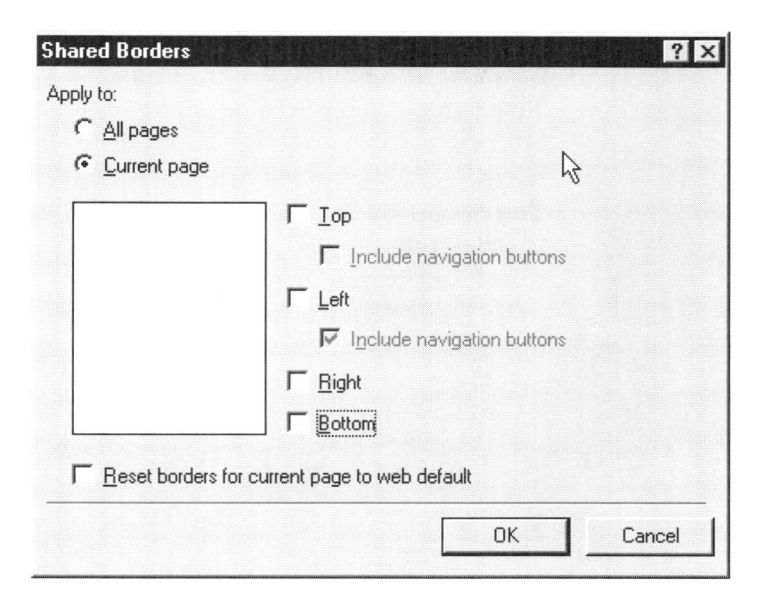

2. Select Apply to Current Page, and deselect the shared border containing the current navigation.

3. Return to Page view, and click on the page where you want the navigation bar to appear. Choose Insert | Navigation Bar to display the Navigation Bar Properties dialog box shown in Figure 5-4. Now you can set your level, set your horizontal or vertical orientation, and choose text or buttons. Click OK when you are finished.

Tip: *If your navigation is going down the left side of the page where the shared border normally is, you might want to create a two-column table and insert the navigation bar in the left cell.*

? What can I do to allow for smoother navigation throughout my site?

Here are nine tips that may help.

TIP 1: OFFER MULTIPLE WAYS IN AND OUT. As you now know, each page should have a way in and a way out. There doesn't have to be just one way, though. Think about offering multiple navigational approaches. You might offer Here, Next, and Back buttons to move to the next logical page. You might offer a Top button that jumps back to the top of the page so the user doesn't have to scroll. Think about offering a "related pages" area at the bottom of a page that points to pages the visitor might also want to see. (See Figure 5-5: www.archipelago.org.)

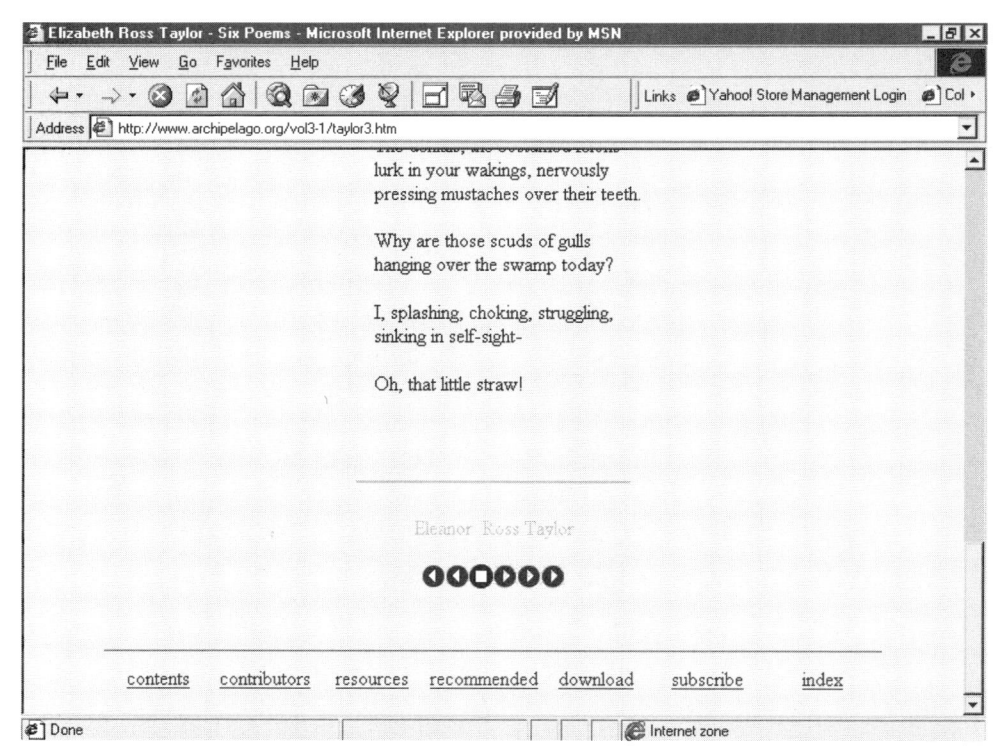

Figure 5-5 The Archipelago Web site features a series of poems using an intuitive graphic navigation technique. The page shown is page 3 of 6 pages

TIP 2: INCLUDE TEXT LINKS. If you have your navigational elements set as graphic images, do include text links as well. Why? Some people have images turned off. Some people are visually impaired and use special text synthesizing browsers that read to them; these browsers can read the text and the alt tags associated with the text, but not the images. Search engines can't read graphics, but they can read text. Text loads faster. You can work the text in with the design. (See Figure 5-6: www.colonnaderealty.com.)

TIP 3: WRITE TEXT LINKS THAT MAKE SENSE. While you might be tempted to be clever with your text links, if you have to explain what they mean to the viewer, rethink your concept! That Patchwork Place (www.patchwork.com) is an example. This is a very good Web site for its niche audience of quiltmakers, but as you can see from looking at the

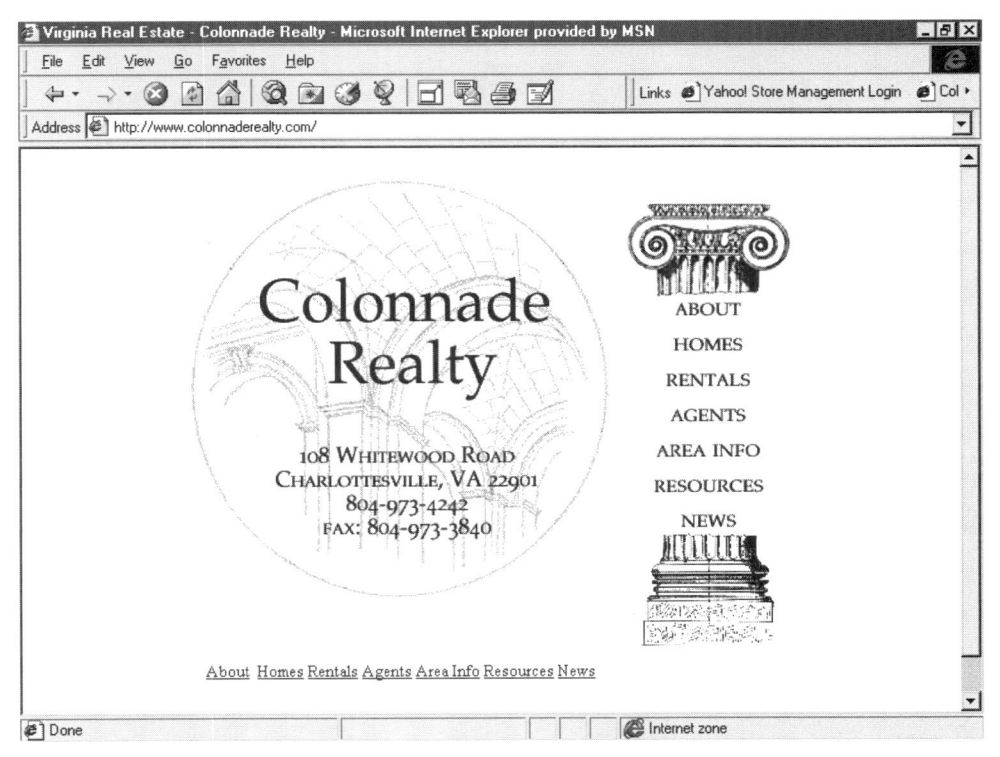

Figure 5-6 The Colonnade Realty site uses both an image map and text links for navigation

screenshot in Figure 5-7, they've taken up most of the front page explaining how the site is organized. They have the "Library," the "Office," the "Rec Room," and the "Kitchen" as the site's main areas. If you've missed this part, when you get further into the site, you have no idea what those links at the bottom of all pages are pointing to. It might have been simpler to create links like "Books and Tools," "Classes and Tours," "Ordering Information," and "Books in Progress." Less creative, but more useful.

TIP 4: MAKE NAVIGATIONAL ICONS THAT REALLY ARE ICONS! How do people recognize icons? A discussion about graphic symbolism could be a book in itself, so we're

Figure 5-7 That Patchwork Place gives too much screen real estate away explaining their site structure

only going to touch on a few basic concepts here. There are three types of symbols:

- **Iconographs**   Literal representations of things translated in a two-dimensional plane. A stick figure of a man is an iconograph. A circle with lines radiating out from it is an iconograph of the sun.
- **Ideagraphs**   Visual representations of abstract ideas—things we can't see. A picture of a heart to represent love or the skull and crossbones to represent danger are examples of ideagraphs.
- **Mnemonic Symbols**   Symbols that trigger a feeling or memory of something you've previously learned. Examples of mnemonic symbols would be an American flag waving in the wind, which might trigger feelings of patriotism in Americans. Company logos are mnemonic symbols too, which is why companies spend so much money to create the perfect one. When you're in a foreign country, struggling with the currency and the weird food, and you see McDonald's golden arches, how do you feel? A hyperlink, by the way, is also a mnemonic symbol. Web surfers quickly learn that underlined text is a signal that something happens when it's clicked on.

When you're designing a navigational interface and deciding the kinds of images to use as symbols, it's probably unwise to try to devise your own mnemonic symbols. For these to work well, it takes an extensive amount of exposure and learning.

Interface elements need to be either explicit, like iconographs, or metaphorical, like ideagraphs to work in the practical world. If the viewer can't grasp the meaning of your symbols instantly, use text instead. Remember, the Web is a global medium. Symbols that Americans take for granted might make no sense to people in other parts of the world. (See Figure 5-8: www.volkswagen.com.)

Chapter 5 The Art of Navigation—Inside and Outside

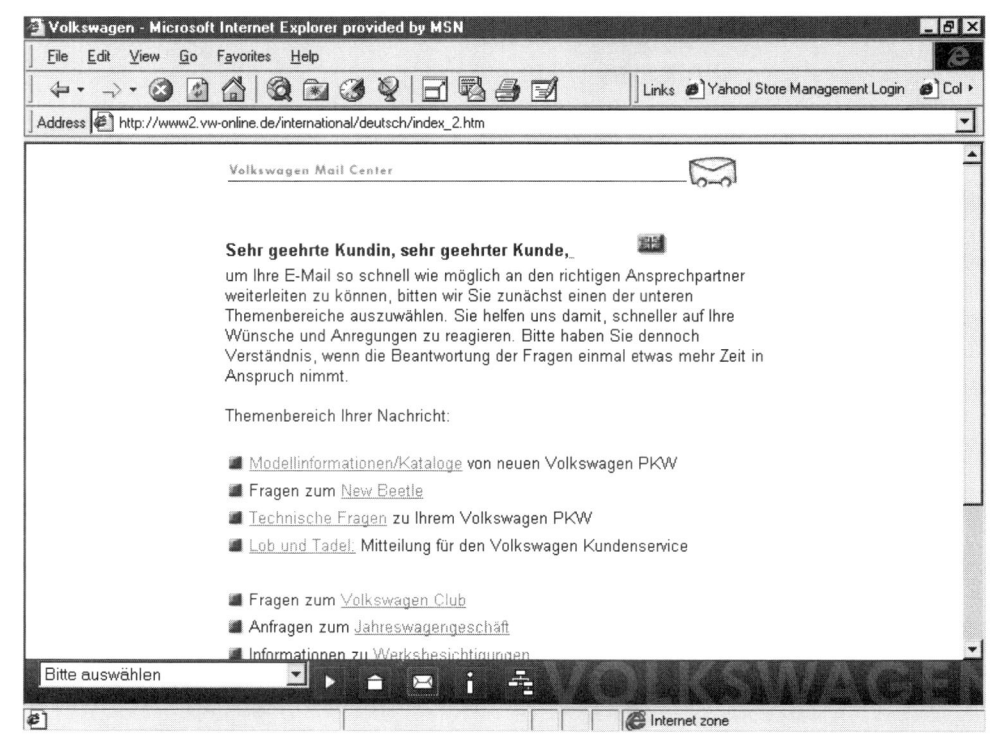

Figure 5-8 This version of the Volkswagen site is in German, but the symbols are so good that just about anyone can figure them out

TIP 5: USE ALT TAGS. If you use graphics for navigation, use the ALT tag to put your images in context. You can insert ALT tags by right-clicking on an image, then selecting Picture Properties, and adding text under Alternate Representations. Viewers see the ALT tags before the image loads, and users who have graphics turned off will get an idea of what they're not seeing. Search engines see ALT text, too.

TIP 6: HELP PEOPLE FIGURE OUT WHERE THEY ARE. When you enter a house, you usually go in through the front door—you don't climb in through a side window. On the Web, you might not have that luxury. A visitor may enter your site through any page if they come via a search engine. Pick a random page in your site. Can you figure out where you are? If not, rethink your navigation.

Navigation Strategies

Here are some tips to help orient people who come to your Web site:

- **Establish your identity.** This can be achieved by putting your company name on every page, or in the title of every page, or through using your company logo on each page.

- **Show your hierarchy on your pages.** You can show, via text, how the visitor arrived. Value America (**www.valueamerica.com**) is a great example. When you get to a page, the navigation at the top shows you how you got there. (See Figure 5-9.)

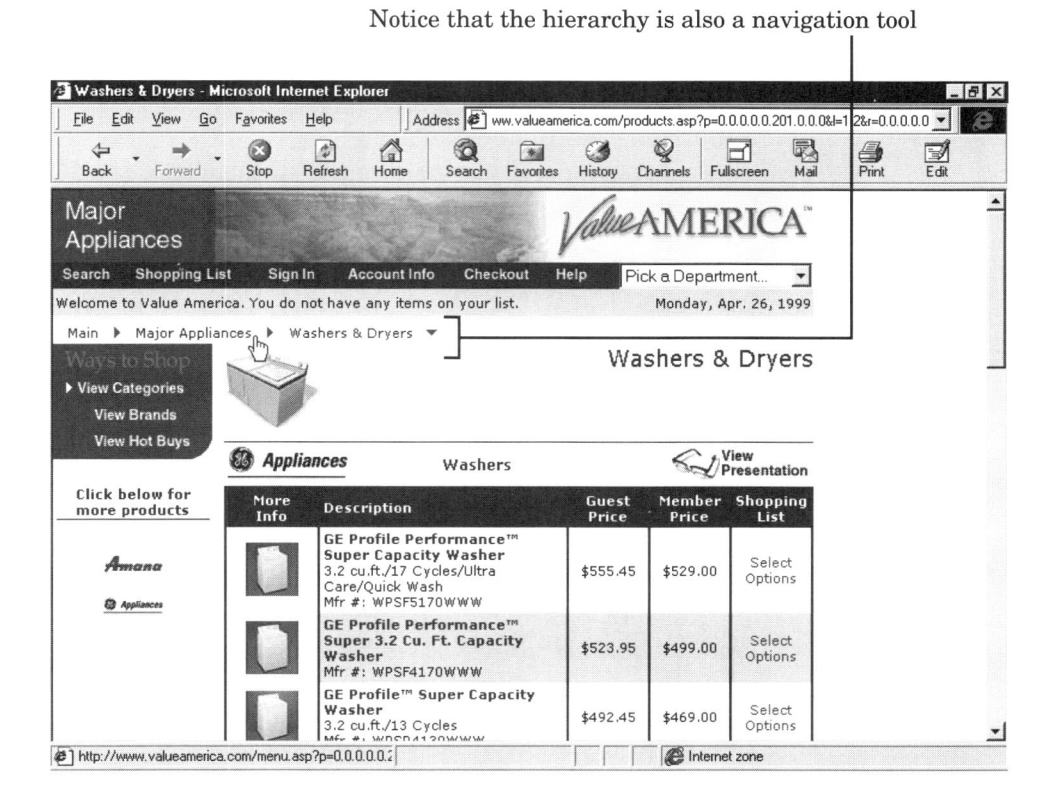

Notice that the hierarchy is also a navigation tool

Figure 5-9 Value America's site is a great example of showing hierarchy and having it be navigable.

TIP 7: PROVIDE SUPPLEMENTAL NAVIGATION.
Supplemental, or remote, navigational elements give users a non-hierarchical way to look at your site. These are just fancy terms for a table of contents, an index, or a site map. A table of contents is good because it's familiar—most people know how to use a table of contents.

TIP 8: USE EMBEDDED LINKS SPARINGLY. Isn't it annoying when you're watching your favorite TV show, and your significant other wants to chat about his or her day? It's the same thing with embedded links. Sometimes you're reading a web page and suddenly some text is underlined and you don't know where you might end up or even why you should follow it.

Here's an example: I recently had a baby. Where's this link going to go? To a picture of the baby? A video of the birth? A newsgroup for new mothers? A better link would be: I recently had a baby. Want to see her? Or: I recently had a baby, and I hang out at Parent Soup.

In summary, if you're going to distract the reader away from your text via an embedded link, do so wisely.

TIP 9: LET VISITORS KNOW WHEN THEY'RE LEAVING YOUR SITE. Usually, the idea is to have such compelling content that visitors can get all the information they're seeking at your site. That's the idea, but most sites provide supplemental links to related sites the visitor might be interested in checking out. It's rather jarring to click on a link, and see the entire design and site navigation change, because you didn't know you were leaving the current site. Think about adding a little disclaimer near your external links informing visitors that they are leaving your site.

Another approach is to open external links in a separate window, which can work well sometimes. But this can also be confusing because there's no way to use the browser's Back button to get back to your site, and, if the second window opens full screen, the visitor might not realize a second window has opened. Another thing to think about is if you have lots of external links and they all open in separate windows, it is highly likely that the whole procedure will annoy your visitor.

Can FrontPage generate a table of contents for me?

Yes, FrontPage can generate a table of contents for you. Here's how:

1. In Page view, position the insertion point where you want to create a table of contents.

2. From FrontPage's main menu, select Insert | Component | Table of Contents. FrontPage displays the Table of Contents Properties dialog box, shown here:

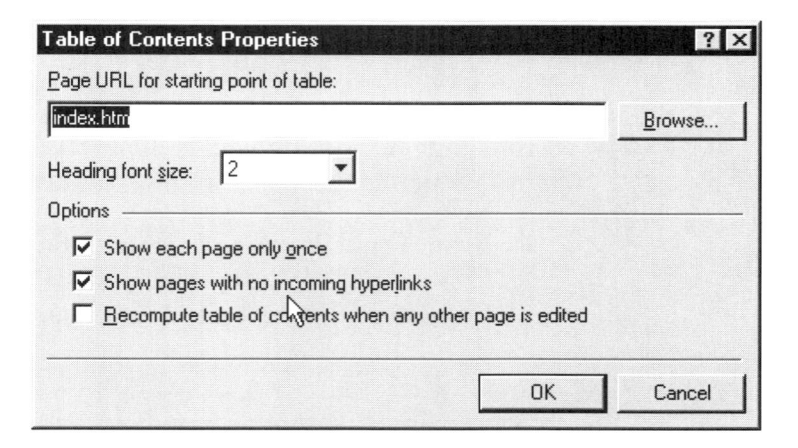

3. In the Page URL for Starting Point of Table box, type the name of the page to use as the starting point for the table of contents, or click Browse to find the page. The starting point determines which pages are outer-most in the table of contents. Pages pointed to by hyperlinks on the starting page will be indented one level in.

4. In the Heading Font Size box, select the paragraph style for starting the table of contents. To exclude the starting page from the table of contents, click None. You'd choose this if the starting point of the table of contents is the same page on which you're creating the table, for example, index.htm.

5. If your web includes pages pointed to by multiple hyperlinks and you want the table of contents to list each page only once, select the Show Each Page Only Once check box.

6. To include pages not pointed to by any hyperlinks in your web, select the Show Pages With No Incoming Hyperlinks check box.

7. To automatically recalculate the table of contents whenever any page in your web is edited, select the Recompute Table of Contents When Any Other Page Is Edited check box.

8. Click OK to close the dialog box.

Can FrontPage create a site map for me?

Sort of. If you've categorized all your files, you can generate what FrontPage calls a site map, but your visitors may not agree! Here's how to create a "sort of" site map with FrontPage, assuming you've done all the categorization work, which is discussed in more detail later in this chapter:

1. From FrontPage's main menu, Select Insert | Components | Categories. FrontPage will display the Categories Property dialog box, shown here:

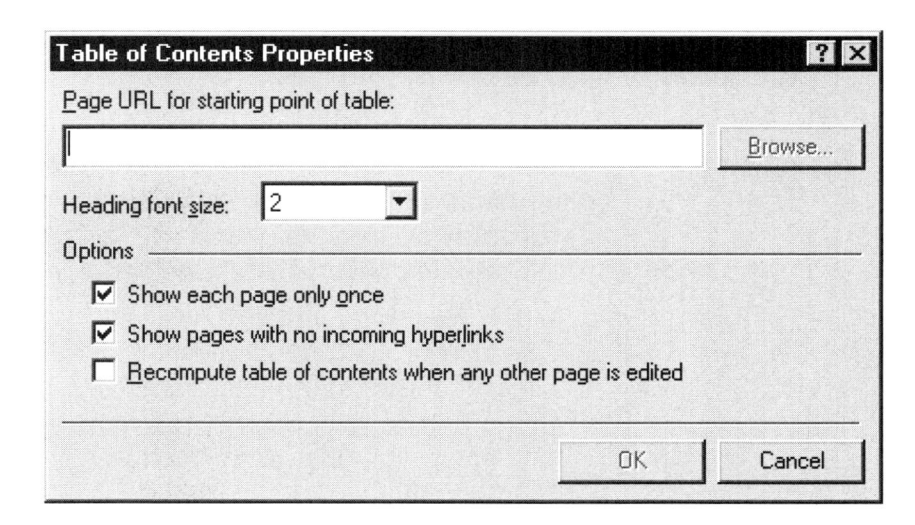

2. In the Choose Categories To List Pages By list, select the check box of the appropriate category.

3. In the Sort Pages By box, click Document Title to sort the list alphabetically by title, or click Date Last Modified to sort the list by file dates.

Repeat these steps for each category list that you want to include on your site map. You can arrange the category lists on your site map page by placing them in tables. Your site map will be updated automatically whenever you add files to or remove files from a category.

What about frames? Why is there no detailed discussion about navigation using frames?

FrontPage does a nice job of defining and working with frames. Even though frames have gotten much better since the dinosaur age of 1996, the reasons people came up with to loathe and avoid frames are still valid today. The URL in the "Address" or "Location" window refers to the first level of the frameset, not the individual frame the visitor comes to after a few clicks, making it difficult to figure out where the heck you are. Frames can break URLs, which means they can also complicate bookmarks, confuse search engines, and render the browser's Back button useless. Framesets can also take longer to load and can be more difficult to print. Oftentimes, a frame's navigation bar takes up too much screen space, annoying those of us not lucky enough to own enormous, high-quality monitors.

I've seen sites I like that use frames. If you use frames, test extensively. From a design standpoint, the only time I like frames is when they are used for navigation and are borderless, which means the number of navigational links is small, so no scrolling is required.

ABOUT FILES

How should I organize my files?

When you create a new, empty web in FrontPage, by default you have three areas:

1. The root web folder
2. The images folder
3. The _private folder

Put your main .html files in the root. Put your graphics in the images folder. Put stuff you don't want visitors to see in the _private folder. This task is easy enough to maintain if your site is fairly small.

My site is more complex. I have subareas. I have graphics that are only current for a certain period of time. How do I organize a site like this?

Make subfolders off the root folder. Put all the files that have something in common in separate folders. You can also create image folders inside your subfolders, and keep the graphics common to those particular files in there. The Archipelago Web site at www.archipelago.org is a perfect example. The site is a literary magazine, published quarterly. Each issue has a volume number and issue number. The first issue was Volume 1, Number 1. The second issue was Volume 1, Number 2. The second year started with Volume 2, Number 1, and so on. There are files that are common to every issue, which are off the root folder. Everything else is contained in its own subfolder for that volume. Each issue that has graphics has its own images folder associated with that volume. Take a look at www.archipelago.org's folder list in Folder view in Figure 5-10.

About Files

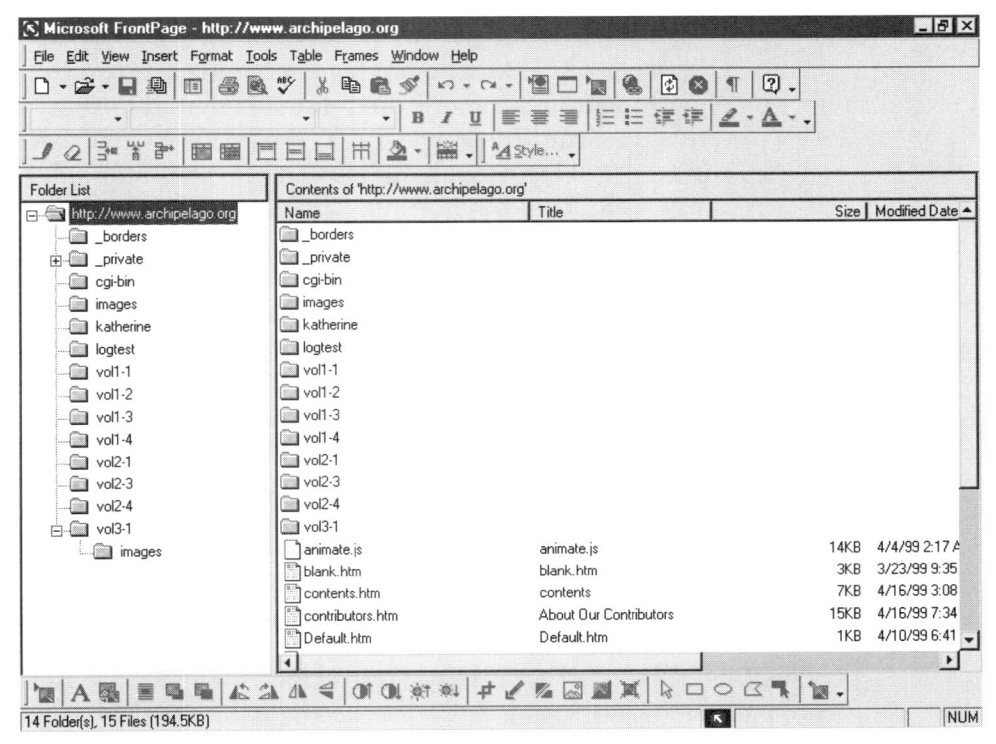

Figure 5-10 Folder view for www.archipelago.org. Each issue of the magazine has its own subfolder which contains a subfolder of images

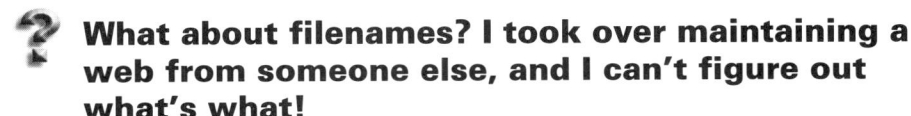

❓ What about filenames? I took over maintaining a web from someone else, and I can't figure out what's what!

If you're working on a large, complex web, and especially if you're working with a team, be sure to establish clear file-naming conventions. The Virginia 2020 Web site (www.virginia.edu/virginia2020) is an excellent example. (This is also a prime example of how to divide your web into mini-webs.) Let's take a look at the structure, shown in

Chapter 5 The Art of Navigation—Inside and Outside

Figure 5-11 and how the page looks on the Web, as shown in Figure 5-12. This web has five sections. There's the main (parent) navigation off the home page, and four subsites: Fine Arts, International Activities, Public Outreach, and Science and Technology. Each subsite has its own subfolder, home page, and local navigation. The web uses two different page templates: one for the home page, which serves as the table of contents for each area (level 1), and one template for the actual content (level 2). Each section has identical navigation going down the left side of the page—Documents, Progress Reports, Meeting, People, and so on.

The file-naming convention enables us to see at a glance how each file fits into the structure. Any level 1 document off the home page begins with h1. Any level 2 document begins with h2. The filename continues with the name of the section in which it lives—h1meetings.htm, h1docs.htm, and so on.

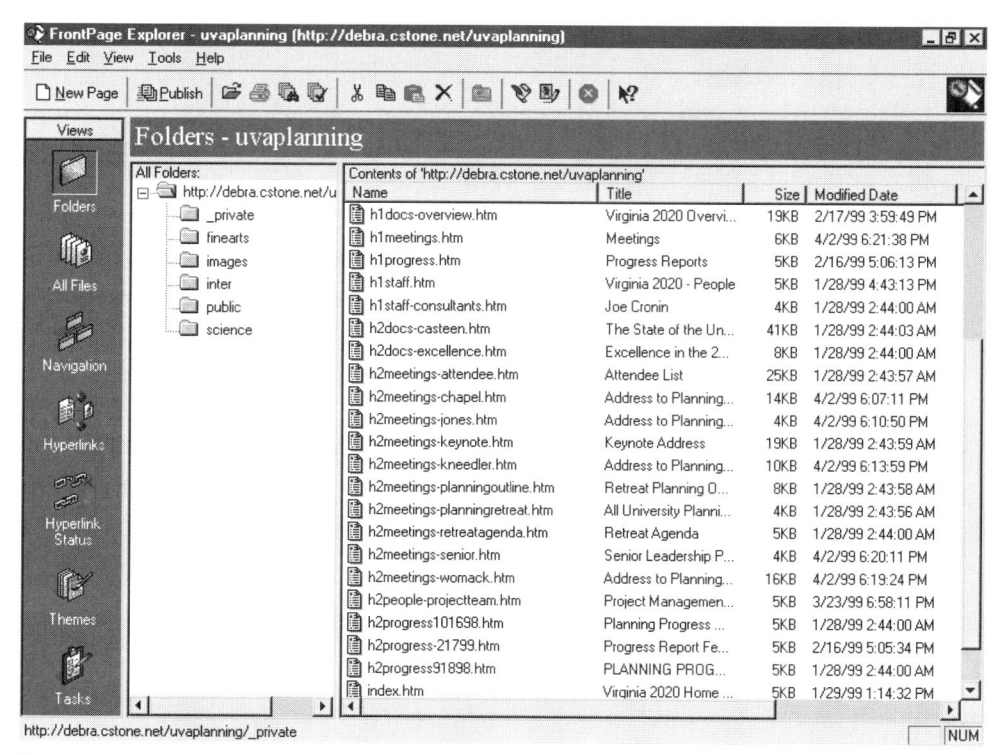

Figure 5-11 The Virginia 2020 web's file structure shows the naming convention

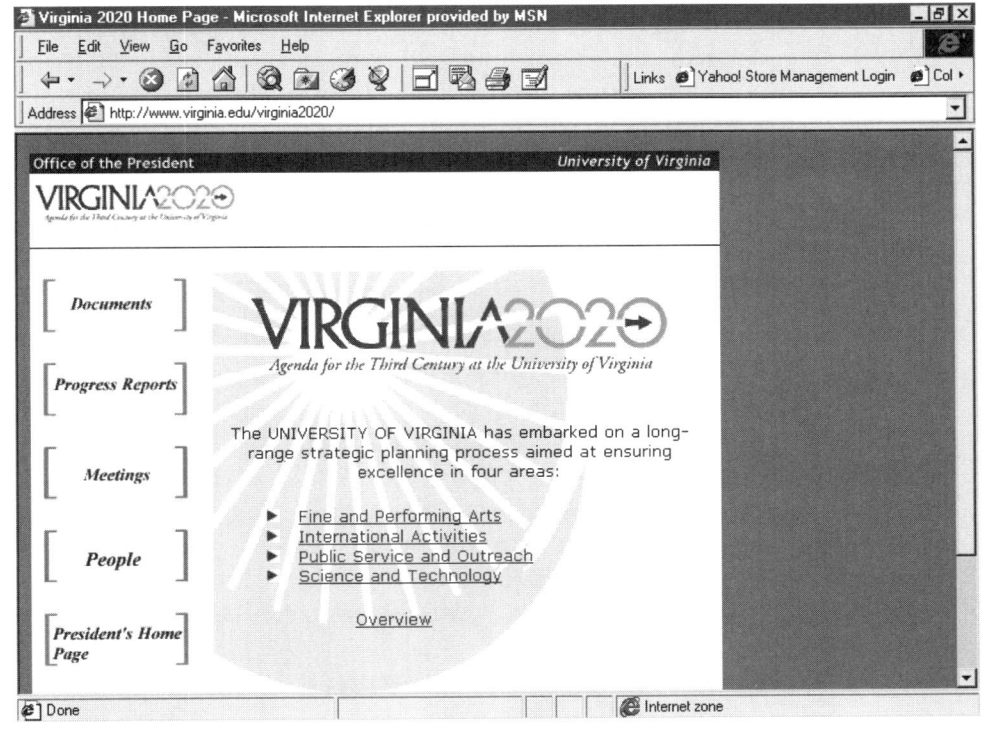

Figure 5-12 How the Virginia 2020 web looks to the visitor

Any documents on the second level are named h2meetings-description.htm, h2docs-description.htm, and so on. Therefore, we can look at any file, and see by its name exactly where it lives in the structure.

The file-naming convention also continues with all the graphics, too. The buttons going down the side are images. Anything that's a button begins with the letter "b." The Documents button is named bdocuments.gif. The Meetings button is named bmeetings.gif. This particular web uses Java code for rollovers on the buttons, which start out blue, but turn green on the rollover, so there are two sets of images for each button—a blue one and a green one. Those images are called bdocumentsg.gif ("g" for "green") and bmeetingsg.gif.

This sort of file-naming convention was quite helpful after the design phase was complete and the clients took over the maintenance of this web. It helps them keep things consistent, and is enormously helpful with routine updates, corrections, and deletions because they don't have to open scads of files just to see what they are.

The best advice is to establish a file-naming convention that works for you, and stick with it! Insist that everyone on your web team use the established file-naming convention and you'll all be a lot happier.

ANALYZING YOUR WEB

What will I see in a Site Summary report?

The Site Summary is just that—an overview of the contents of your web. You'll see how many files, pictures, sounds, and so on you have; which tasks are incomplete; the number of broken links; the pages that will load slowly; and other tidbits that will interest you. Think of it as a quick inventory of your web. The Site Summary should alert you to some obvious problems—particularly broken links and component errors.

To see a Site Summary (shown in Figure 5-13), select View | Reports | Site Summary.

How do I see a list of broken hyperlinks?

Broken links are probably the number one annoying thing about the Web. If your visitors click on links that go nowhere, it's a sure bet they will assume that whoever maintains the Web site is an idiot, or at the very least, not on the ball. Don't let that happen. FrontPage makes it easy to detect and repair broken links.

In the Site Summary report (select View | Reports | Site Summary), double-click the Broken Hyperlinks row to display the Broken Hyperlinks report. Or, from FrontPage's main menu, select View | Reports | Broken Hyperlinks, as shown here:

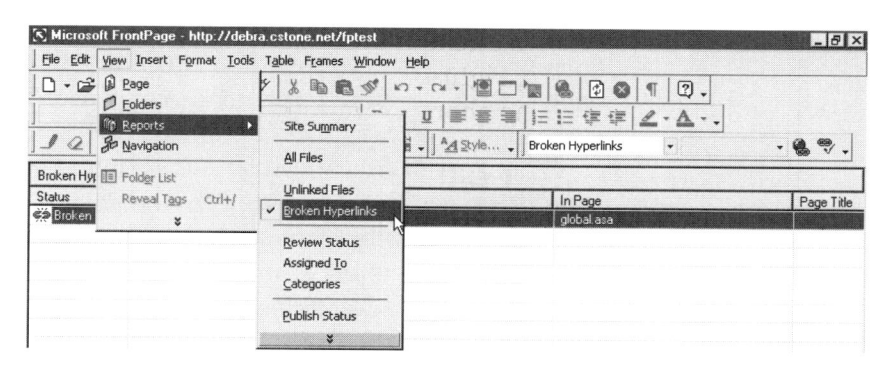

Analyzing Your Web

[Screenshot of Microsoft FrontPage showing a Site Summary report with columns Name, Count, Size, and Description. Rows include: All files (64, 119KB), Pictures (41, 70KB), Unlinked files (63, 117KB), Linked files (1, 1KB), Slow pages (0, 0KB), Older files (3, 13KB), Recently added files (64, 119KB), Hyperlinks (13), Unverified hyperlin... (0), Broken hyperlinks (1), External hyperlinks (1), Internal hyperlinks (12), Component errors (0), Uncompleted tasks (2), Unused themes (0).]

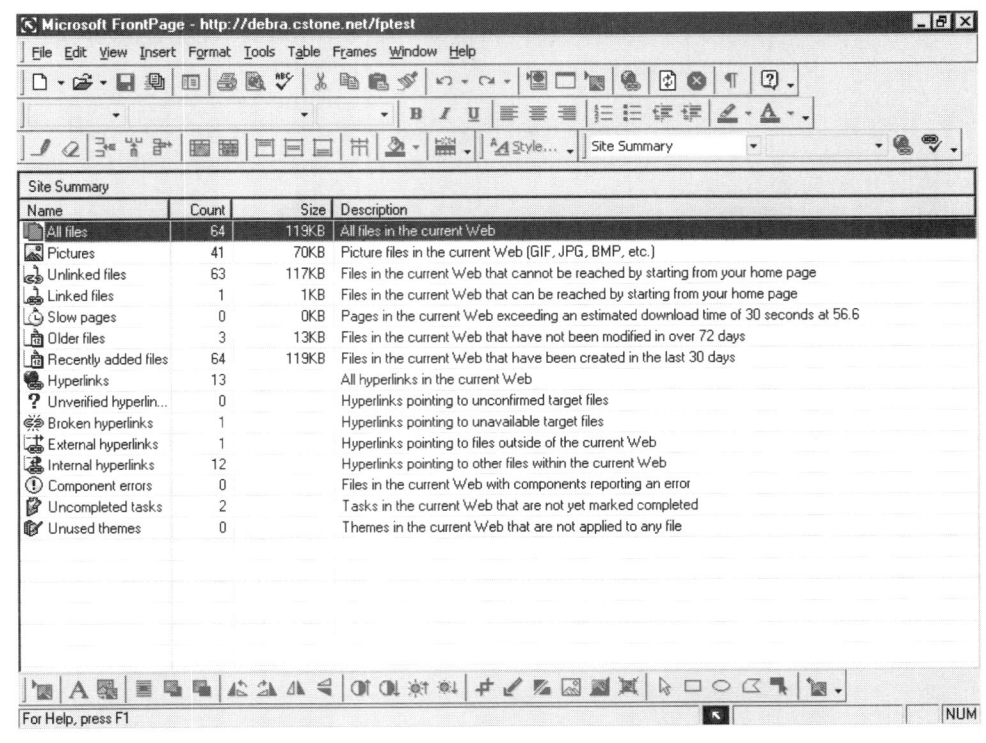

Figure 5-13 This Site Summary report shows there's one broken hyperlink, and two uncompleted tasks

From this report, you can perform any of the following tasks:

- To repair a broken link, double-click a hyperlink to open and edit it, and apply the change to selected pages or all pages in which that hyperlink appears.

- To edit a page, right-click the hyperlink and choose Edit Page.

- To add a task to the hyperlink and assign someone to fix it, right-click the hyperlink and then click Add Task on the shortcut menu.

How can I tell if my pages will load slowly?

Set the default speed you assume the majority of your visitors will be using. You tell FrontPage what you consider

Chapter 5 The Art of Navigation—Inside and Outside

to be slow, and ask FrontPage to tell you which pages match your criteria:

1. From FrontPage's main menu, select View | Reports | Site Summary. FrontPage will display the Site Summary table, shown in Figure 5-14.

   In the Slow Pages row, the Count column lists the number of slow pages in your web. The Description column lists the download time and modem speed used to define a slow page.

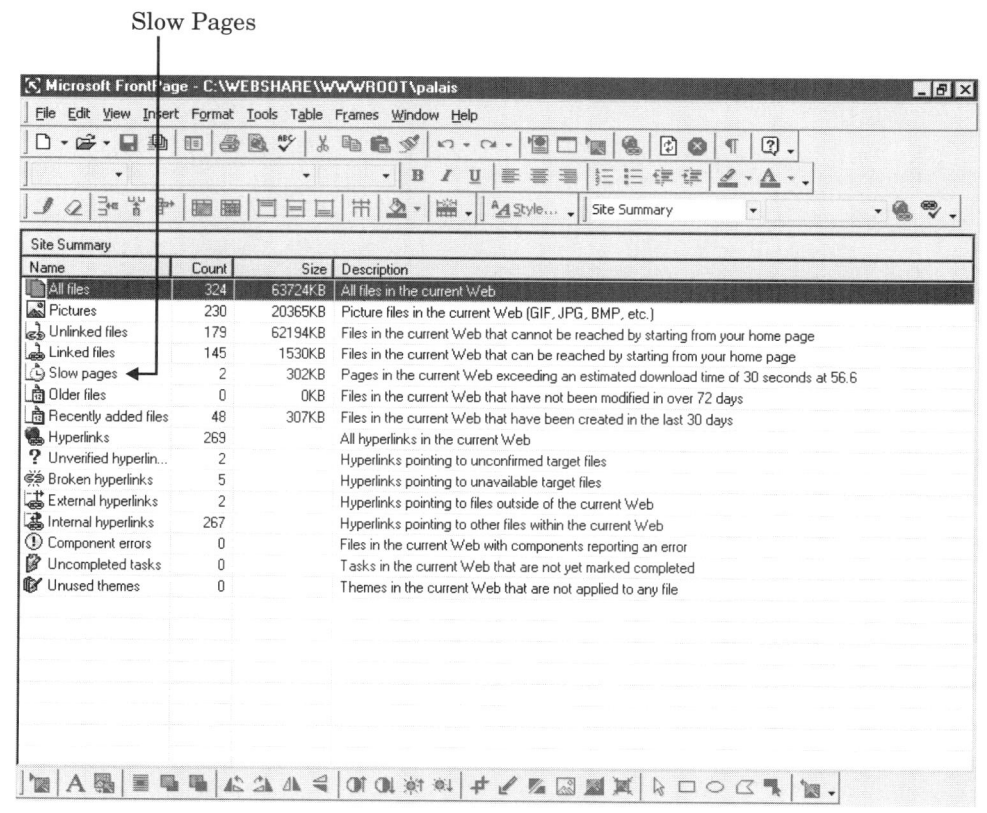

Figure 5-14 The site summary shows two slow pages

2. To view the Slow Pages report, double-click the Slow Pages row, or select View | Reports | Slow Pages.

To define the connection speed and the amount of time used to calculate a slow page, select Tools | Options. FrontPage will display the Options dialog box. Select the Reports View tab and enter new values for the "Slow Pages" Take At Least check box and the Assume Connection Speed Of check box, as shown here:

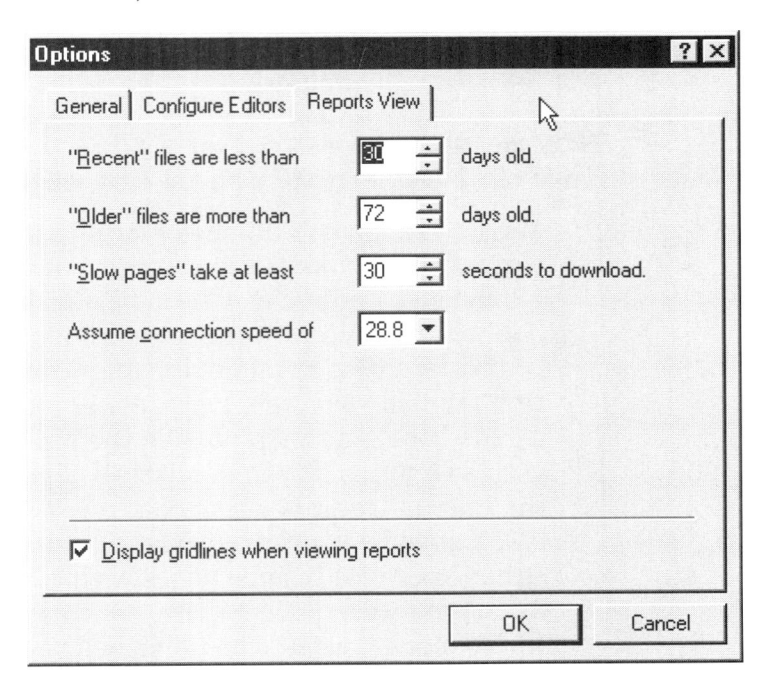

How can FrontPage's own components be broken? I bought it because I know zilch about programming, and want FrontPage to do the work for me.

FrontPage is pretty smart, but you're ultimately in control. FrontPage can only do what you tell it to do. If something's broken, it's most likely your fault. In other words, it's the dreaded case of "operator error." What can break? Say you delete a bunch of pages. Say you tell the Table of Contents to start from a page that's not there anymore. Broken! Maybe you try to "fix" some code in HTML view that validates a form. Kablooey! Perhaps the Database Wizard doesn't work because you've defined a Web server that doesn't have the Front Page extensions installed. Bye-bye!

How do I see the publishing status of my files?

By default, all files are marked for publishing unless you change it. From FrontPage's main menu, select View | Reports | Publish Status.

Why wouldn't I want some files to be published? How do I tell FrontPage to not publish a file?

Maybe you haven't finished editing some pages but you want to publish your web. You can prevent the page from being published by marking it "Don't Publish." When you want to publish the file, mark the page "Publish."

Certain files should not be published again after you first publish your web. For example, you create a web with a guestbook, and then publish the web. Later, you update your web pages. If you publish all of your files, including the file that records guestbook information, you will save a blank guestbook over the existing one, losing all the entries! Other examples include pages with a hit counter and discussion webs.

To mark a page to be published or to prevent it from being published, follow these steps:

1. From FrontPage's main menu, select View | Reports | Publish Status.

2. Select one or more files and right-click them to access the shortcut menu. Choose Properties and then select the Workgroup tab from the tabbed Properties dialog box, as shown here:

Analyzing Your Web

[Screenshot of index.htm Properties dialog, Workgroup tab]

3. Do one of the following:

- To prevent a file from being published, click to select Exclude This File When Publishing the Rest of the Web.

- To mark a file for publishing, clear the Exclude This File When Publishing the Rest of the Web check box.

Tip: *A quick way to get to the Workgroup tab is to right-click on the name of a page in the Publish Status report, then select Properties | Workgroup.*

Chapter 6

Creating Interesting Tables

Answer Topics!

WHEN TO USE A TABLE 128
- ? When to use a table
- ? Why you shouldn't use tables to format text
- ? Why FrontPage uses tables to format text

CREATING A TABLE 133
- ? Creating a table
- ? Creating a table using existing text
- ? Converting a table to text
- ? Formatting a table once it's created
- ? The best way to format a table

TABLE BORDERS 142
- ? The properties for table formatting
- ? Setting table borders
- ? Alternatives to using style sheets

- ? Enabling all the table border choices

PADDING, SPACING, AND MARGINS 148
- ? Eliminating extra cell spacing
- ? Creating a table with borders on only some sides
- ? Creating a table with only some internal borders
- ? Creating tables with colored rows or columns
- ? Increasing cell padding to avoid crowding

OTHER TEXT FORMATTING OPTIONS 153
- ? Changing the color of the text in a table
- ? Aligning text within the cells

Creating Interesting Tables @ A Glance

- **When to Use a Table**   HTML has never really lent itself to beautiful formatting. In early versions of HTML, the only way to format blocks or columns of text was with tables. The HTML formatting required was ugly—very ugly. In fact, it was so ugly that many Web developers, people who often considered themselves *hackers,* started to turn to the early crop of Web-development tools, including FrontPage. These packages used tables to force the text on Web pages into the formatting that people had come to expect from document-layout packages that were used to create paper brochures. After all, most pages in the early days of the Web were nothing more than electronic brochures.

- **Creating Tables**   FrontPage lets you create pretty much any kind of table you can imagine! Having a cell span rows or columns is no problem at all. If you already have text, it's easy enough to draw a table around the text, or create the table based on tabs or other punctuation in the text. The table tools built into FrontPage make table creation a snap.

- **Table Borders**   HTML gives you quite a number of options when defining table borders. You can create tables without any borders at all. You can create sunken or raised tables. You can create tables with dashed borders, or with only internal borders. In order to do the most sophisticated designs, you need to use style sheets. FrontPage can make it quite painless if you know what you want to do.

- **Padding, Spacing, and Margins**   Part of making a beautiful table is selectively deciding which sides of the table will have borders. Some tables look nice with only internal borders. Some look nice with only vertical lines between columns. In order to define specific borders, you need first to understand what cell padding and spacing are. This section will start with the basics and move on to the fancy stuff.

- **Other Text Formatting Options**   Other things you can do with text include setting the color, and aligning it within the cells. This section will help you do just that.

WHEN TO USE A TABLE

When should I use a table?

Use a table when you want aligned text or when you want to create a low-bandwidth graphic, not when you want to lay out text or text and graphics in a certain way on your page. When you want to specify the layout of text or text and graphics, you should use *Cascading Style Sheets (CSS)*.

Note: *Chapter 7 covers implementing CSS in FrontPage in depth. If you really like it, check out the official home of CSS information: http://www.htmlhelp.com/reference/CSS.*

A table is great for aligning text or numbers. You can also use tables to pass nicely formatted text with colored backgrounds without having to send large, slow-to-load graphics across the Internet. Consider one of the very best examples I've found of using tables to create a stunning visual effect without sending any graphics on a Web site, the Cineville Web site shown in Figure 6-1.

The most common reason for using tables is to align text with either text or numbers over a number of lines. Figure 6-2 shows an example of using a table to align text in columns with other text, so that the section headlines on the left side of the screen are parallel to the body text to which they relate.

Another example of table use is shown in Figure 6-3, which is a train schedule for the Metropolitan Transit Authority of New York. This is the classic table format. As you've seen from these three examples, there are a number of ways to format tables other than the basic table borders you see in Figure 6-3. The easiest way to arrange text in columns is by using FrontPage's table features. If you want to arrange text around graphics or other elements, use style sheets instead.

When to Use a Table 129

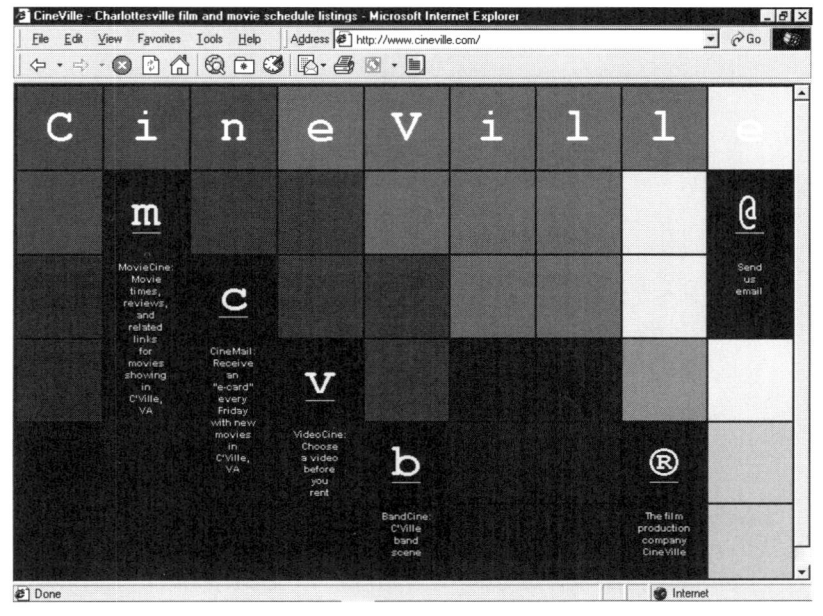

Figure 6-1 The Cineville Web site uses tables with colored cells to create a graphic effect without any graphics

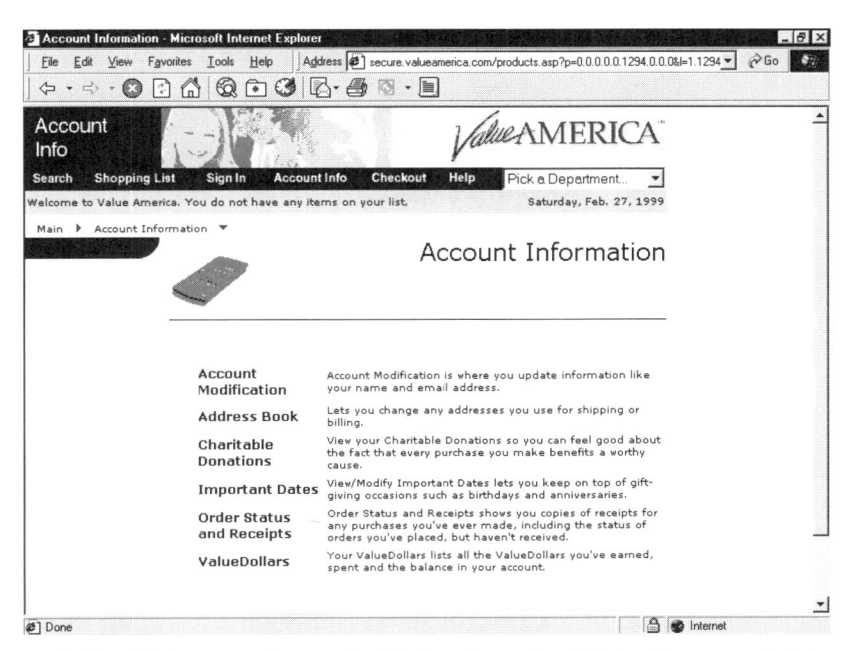

Figure 6-2 This page, from the Value America Web site, uses tables to line up the headings on the left with the descriptions on the right

Chapter 6 Creating Interesting Tables

Figure 6-3 The train schedule on this Web page uses classic table borders

Why not use tables to format text?

There are three excellent reasons not to use tables to format text.

- **You don't have to** There was a time when tables were the only way to format text to look nice on a page—that is to say, to look any way other than each paragraph being a block of text the width of the screen—but that's no longer the case. With CSS, you can format your text as specifically as you want without being locked into the format required by tables.

- **It increases download time** When you format a page with tables, each row has a definition in HTML, then each cell has its own definition. The consequence of these definitions is that every additional cell makes the page a bit bigger. Even though HTML is just text, the more of it there is, the longer the download time of the page will be.

- **It complicates maintenance** Since each row and each cell has its own mark-up, when you move text around on your page you end up with lengthy, messy HTML. Even if you can stand the increased download time, your HTML is a mess.

Doesn't FrontPage use tables to format text?

Yes it does. By default, the *themes* in FrontPage rely on tables. There's a really good reason for this, though. Despite all my preaching about not using tables to format text, the reality is that, to accommodate the browsers that are currently in use, you can't rely entirely on style sheets. The fact is that only Internet Explorer 4 and above support style sheets adequately. Netscape Navigator 4 supports some features of style sheets, but not always consistently with the specifications of the World-Wide Web Consortium (W3C). Internet Explorer 3 supports some features of style sheets, but not enough to build a site. Navigator 3 doesn't support any features.

So, then, unless you know your target audience will be visiting your site from Internet Explorer 4 or 5, you're basically stuck using tables (or frames and tables) to format your pages. If you're building your site for an intranet, in which case you know what's installed on the desktops of your users, or if your site appeals to programmers or to those who are technically savvy (those who are most likely to have upgraded their browsers to Version 4 or 5 software), then you're probably safe using CSS for formatting. Otherwise, stick with the table formatting that FrontPage provides.

Tip: *You can't test too much. There are many, many inconsistencies between the two major browsers. If you don't know for an absolute fact which browsers your visitors will be using, you should absolutely test on Internet Explorer 3, 4, 5, Netscape Navigator 3, 4, and 4.5, and AOL 3 and 4. If somehow, something as seemingly unimportant as the end-table element (</TABLE>) is missing from your page, your entire table won't show up on Navigator! Never assume; always test.*

Anatomy of a Table

You can't really format your table until you understand the anatomy of a table. The following illustration shows you where you're creating space when you increase the cell padding (inside the cell) as opposed to increasing the cell spacing (between cells or between the outside of a cell and the inside of the border).

Anatomy of a Table

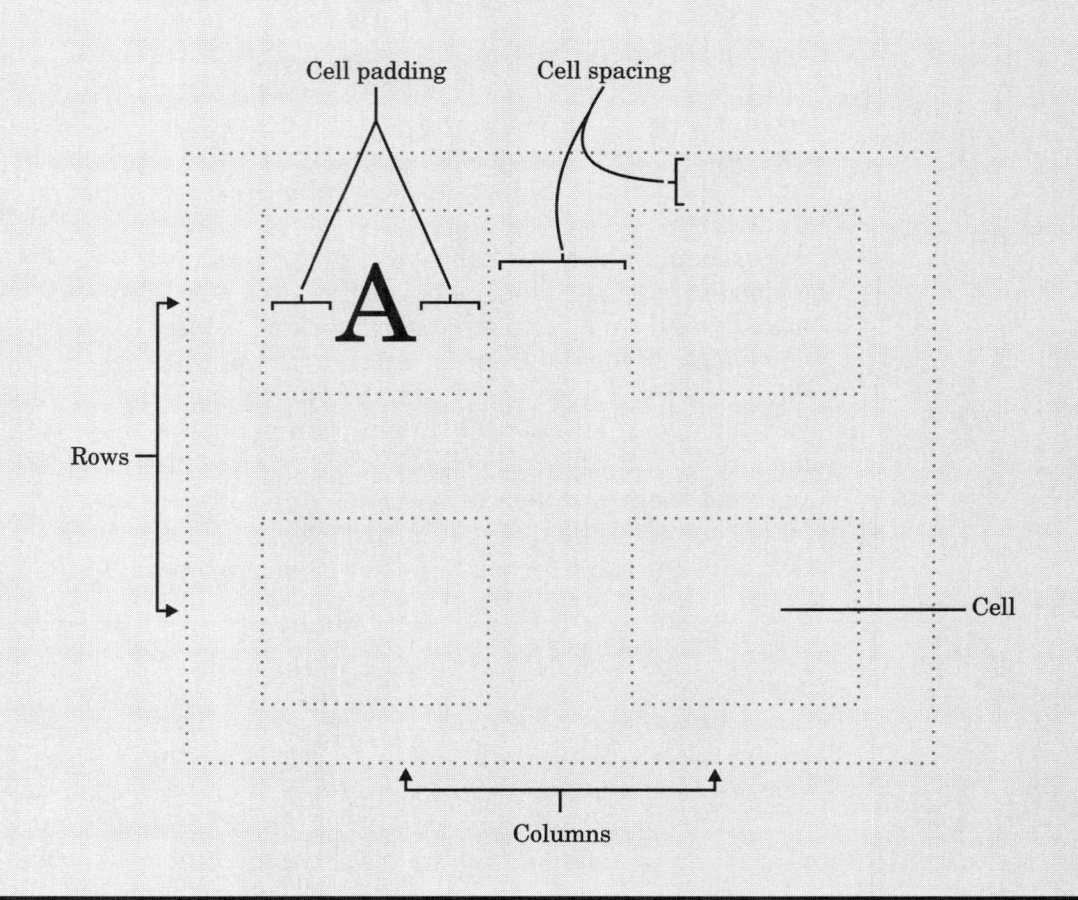

CREATING A TABLE

How do I create a table?

You have three choices for creating a table in FrontPage. Use the Table menu, use the Table Insert tool, or draw a table with the Draw Table tool.

The Table Menu

If you're familiar with Microsoft Word, you'll appreciate the ability to create a table using the Table menu, with a subset of the options that appear on the Word Table menu.

1. Select Table | Insert | Table. You'll see the Insert Table dialog box shown here.

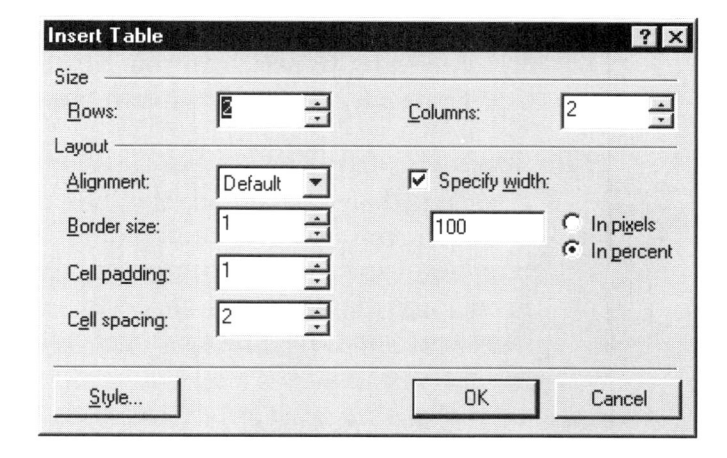

2. Set the number of rows and columns.

3. You can also set the alignment of the table—that is, where you want it to appear on the page—to Left, Right, Center, or Justify, or leave it set to Default. Default alignment means no alignment. The result of not aligning the table is that the table will inherit the alignment that you've defined for the page (see the following sidebar, "Inheritance"). In most cases, having no alignment is the same thing as left alignment.

Chapter 6 Creating Interesting Tables

> ***Tip:*** *Leave table alignment set to the default until you are done formatting your table. When you have your table the way you want it, modify the Table Properties to set the alignment to something other than default. FrontPage is a bit quirky in permitting you to select a table with your cursor if you have defined both the table's alignment and float to be right. The float property indicates to the browser that, if it can, it should try to fill in the space next to the table, image, or text with whatever follows the table, image, or text. It tells the browser to float the table, image, or text off to one side. If you can't select a table, you'll have trouble making changes to either cell or table properties, and thus you'll have trouble formatting the table to your satisfaction.*

4. You can also set the border width (called Border Size in the dialog box), the cell padding, and the cell spacing. Anything you set here you can change later in the Table Properties dialog box, which has additional options as well.

The Insert Table Tool

If you'd rather, you can use the Insert Table tool on the toolbar. When you use the Insert Table tool, you highlight the number of rows and columns you want in your table, then FrontPage inserts a standard table with those dimensions wherever you have placed your cursor. This method saves you a few clicks.

The Draw Table Tool

The Draw Table tool is located on the Tables toolbar. All of the options on the Table menu are also on the Tables toolbar. You can view the Tables toolbar either by selecting View | Toolbars | Tables or by selecting Table | Draw Table. Either way, you get a free-floating toolbar. If you desire, you can drag it to the top of your screen and have it anchored above, below, or to the side of one of the toolbars you already have open.

Inheritance

Inheritance is a profound concept in the world of computers. It is the idea that if an object doesn't have a value specifically defined for a property, that object *inherits* the value of that property for the next larger object. It's basically the trickle-down theory of object definition. HTML calls these objects *block-level elements* as opposed to *inline elements*. Inline elements can't have other elements within them (in theory). Inline elements are things like boldface and italics. Block-level elements are things like paragraphs, tables, and the body of the page.

You should take advantage of inheritance by defining the rule at the highest level, then defining exceptions to the levels at which they're necessary. This makes maintenance of a page or site much easier. For example, if you define the page to have red text, then you don't need to define each paragraph to have red text. Each paragraph and table will inherit the text color from the page. If you do define each paragraph to have red text, then it will be much more work later to change the properties of all the paragraphs, rather than just changing the properties of the page, and have all the paragraphs *inherit* the text color from the page. If you want only one paragraph to have black text, then define the text color to be red at the page level, and define the text color to be black only at the paragraph level. (For more on inheritance, see Chapter 7.)

Tip: *Drag your Tables toolbar to the right side of the screen; that's the least-utilized real estate on most screens. It will anchor itself there and become part of the background. Free-floating toolbars can obscure part of the page that you need to view.*

Chapter 6 Creating Interesting Tables

To create a table using the Draw Table tool:

1. Position your cursor (while it's still just a pointer) where you want the table, and click.
2. Click the Draw Table tool on the Tables toolbar.
3. Your cursor will change into a pencil. Click where you want the upper-left corner of the table to be, then drag your cursor to the right and down until you have a box the size that you want the entire table to be. Release the mouse button. There doesn't need to be enough room on your page for the table. FrontPage will move everything below it out of the way for you.
4. While still using the Draw Table tool, draw in rows and columns where you want them. Neither your rows nor your columns need to go from one end of the table to the other. In Figure 6-4, the part of the table holding the stars was drawn first, then the rows for the stripes were drawn (otherwise, the Erase tool would have to be used a lot).
5. If you find you need some columns to span rows or some rows to span columns, or both, click the Eraser tool and erase the lines you don't want.

If you want to create another table within the one you've already created, you can use the Draw tool to do that, too.

Tip: *The Draw Table tool gives you the most precise control over your table rows and columns of any of the table-creation methods listed above. Unless you don't care how big the columns are or you want them to be of uniform width, use the Draw Table tool. Specifically, if you want to create a table like the one in Figure 6-4, nothing is faster than the Draw Table tool.*

Caution: *FrontPage tools and menus only let you nest tables two deep. If you want to nest more than that, you'll need to dig into the HTML.*

Creating a Table 137

Figure 6-4 This flag will load in a jiffy because the rows are made of table cells with colored backgrounds and the stars are a tiled version of a graphic of just four stars

Can I create a table using the text I've already entered?

Yes. To convert text to a table:

1. Select the text you want in the table.
2. Selecting Table | Convert | Text to Table. You'll get the Convert Text to Table dialog box, as shown here.

3. Indicate how you want the text formatted in the table. If it's a tab-delimited table that you've already created, then select Tabs. If you want it all in one cell, select None.
4. Click OK.

Can I take text out of a table without losing all the formatting?

You will almost certainly lose some of the formatting. The following illustration shows a table that needs to be converted to text.

Pizza Prices by City			
Chicago	$12.95	$16.95	$18.95
Austin	$9.95	$11.95	$13.95

If you need to convert a table to text, follow these steps.

1. Select the table or the part of the table you want to convert to text
2. Select Table | Convert | Table to text.

This option won't give you a way to maintain your columns. If you have more than one column, it will put the text from the first column first, then from the next second, and so on. The following illustration shows how the example table looks when it is converted to text.

Pizza Prices by City

Chicago

$12.95

$16.95

$18.95

Austin

$9.95

$11.95

$13.95

What can I do to format my table once I've created it?

You have many, many options. In fact, you have so many formatting options that you'll want to plan ahead so you know what to do when. Otherwise, you'll end up doing the same type of formatting over and over, every time you make changes to the structure.

Briefly, you can set the borders, the background, the padding within each cell, and the spacing between cells. The types of things you can do to a table include setting properties related to the border: width, color, and type (dashed lines, solid, sunken, and so on). You can also set background colors for cells or the entire table, and background images for cells or one for the entire table (see the following sidebar, "Creating Graphics with Tables"). Finally, you can decide how you want the cells to relate to each other, and how you want the text and graphics in the cells to be aligned.

Creating Graphics with Tables

Now, why would anyone want to create graphics with tables? Speed! Speed considerations are critical in page design. If your page takes too long to load, it won't matter how nice it looks. If your page takes more than 20 seconds to load, you'll lose half your visitors. Can you afford that?

Creating graphics with tables isn't difficult—it just requires a little bit of forethought. It's no different than anything else related to good design: You have to see what you want to create in your head before you can make it on the screen.

The Web sites shown in Figures 6-1 and 6-4 use tables to create graphics that load in a jiffy. The Cineville Web site is a *full-page graphic*. If you wanted to create a full-page image map, it would take minutes to load over a 28.8Kbps modem. The Cineville site loads in three seconds over a 28.8Kbps modem! In the case of the American flag image, there is a background image in the first cell—the one that spans seven rows—that has four stars in it. By allowing the browser to *tile* the image, the field of stars is created from an image that's only 1,097 bytes. That's fewer bytes than the number of characters used on this page. It would take the image of the American flag, on a page by itself, one second to load.

Another very nice feature of FrontPage, one that makes it an excellent tool even if it isn't the only tool you use to develop Web sites, is the Load-Time Monitor, which tells you how long the page will take to load:

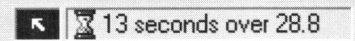

⌛ 13 seconds over 28.8

You can even set the connection speed that it uses in calculating the load time by right-clicking the Load-Time Monitor, then selecting a different speed. The default speed is 28.8Kbps. If you're building an intranet site, where you have reasonable confidence that the visitors to the site have direct connections to the Internet, then you can change the speed appropriately; otherwise, assume you're dealing with visitors with 28.8Kbps modems.

Another commonly used trick to send small graphics that produce the effect of a larger graphic is demonstrated in the following steps:

1. Create the image you want to see on the page, such as the one shown here:

2. Create a one-cell table the same size as the image.

3. Using the Draw Table tool, cut up the table so that the part of the image that isn't a solid color is in its own cell, as shown below. Your cells will both be clear, but we'll fix that later on.

Creating a Table   141

4. Set the background color of the cell (or cells) that map to the solid-colored part of the image to the solid color used in the image, as shown here:.

5. Cut the image into pieces, so that the part of the image that isn't solid is the size of the new cell you created for it in step 3. You won't need to use the part of the image that's a solid color.

6. Set the background image for the cell that isn't solid-colored to be the image part you created in step 5.

Note: See Chapter 4 for a complete description of image maps and how you make them in FrontPage.

What's the best way to format a table?

Assuming you're using the Draw Table tool, which gives you the most flexibility in creating a table, here's the best sequence for formatting tables:

1. Create the table the size you want. If you're going to have it float to the left or right of text or an image, make sure it fits.

2. Create columns and rows in the table to meet your needs in both number of columns and rows and sizes of each.

3. If you need to erase any lines, that is to say, if any of your columns need to span multiple rows, or if your rows

need to span multiple columns, take care of that now with the Eraser tool.

4. Set the properties for the table as a whole: border width, border type, border colors, cell spacing, cell padding, background image, and background color.

5. Set the properties for any cells that need it. Where appropriate, define the properties at the table level (taking advantage of inheritance), and only define properties at the cell level for any cells that need different values than those of the table.

Tip: Take a look at the changes you've made to your table through the Table Properties dialog box before you click OK. The Table Properties dialog box has a button labeled Apply. Click Apply to see your changes while you work.

TABLE BORDERS

What are the properties that I need to know for table formatting?

To understand the properties that you'll use in the various table formatting dialog boxes, take a look at Table 6-1.

Tip: If you don't want the table to re-size itself when your visitor resizes the browser, use pixels rather than a percentage when setting height and width for a table. If you use pixels and the screen is sized smaller than the table, then the entire table won't be displayed at once and the visitor will have to scroll to see all of it.

Table Borders

Property	Description
Border Width	Also called *Border* or *Border Size* by FrontPage. This value is the number of pixels you'd like the border, however you define it, to be painted. If you set it to zero, none of the other border properties will matter. In fact, if you set border width to zero, all of the other border properties should be grayed out.
Border Color	The color of the border.
Border Color Dark	If the border has dimension, this is the color that will be used to represent the border in shadow.
Border Color Light	If the border has dimension, this is the color that will be used to represent the border in the light.
Border Style	How the outside border of the table is represented: solid, dashed, double, groove, ridge, inset, outset.
Background Color	The color inside all the cells of the table, between the cells, and between the cells and the border.
Background Image	The image that fills all the cells, the space between the cells, and the space between the cells and the border.
Cell padding	The space between the cells and the space between the cells and the border.
Cell Spacing	The space between the internal cell walls and the contents of the cell.
Alignment	Where the table appears on the page: default, left, right, center, or justify.
Float	Whether the table is permitted to have another object flow into the space to the left or to the right of it. For example, if you want a table on a page with text to the left of it, you must set the float to right to allow the text to flow to its left.
Height	The height of the table either in pixels or as a percentage of the visible part of the page.
Width	The width of the table either in pixels or as a percentage of the visible part of the page.

Table 6-1   Table Properties

Chapter 6 Creating Interesting Tables

How do I set table borders?

In order to set table borders, you must be in Normal view. Put your cursor anywhere in the table and right-click. You'll get the following Table Properties dialog box.

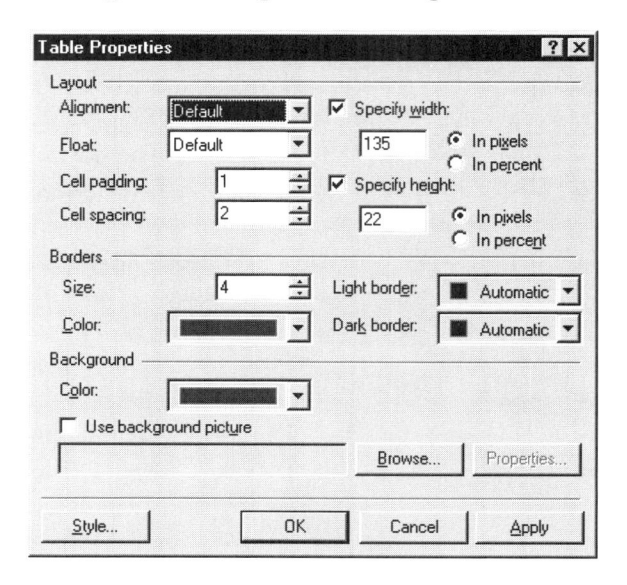

In this dialog box, you can set the very basic table qualities: border size, color, light color, dark color. To create a truly interesting table, click the Style button to bring up the Modify Style dialog box.

This dialog box shows you any styles you already have defined for this object. In the example here, I've defined a border-style of Groove. You can see that it also gives an example of what you've defined. If you want to define classes, this is the place to do so. Classes are groups of elements that are all supposed to look the same.

Note: *If you don't know what classes are, flip to Chapter 7 to read all about them.*

Click the Format button, then click Border to bring up the Border and Shading dialog box.

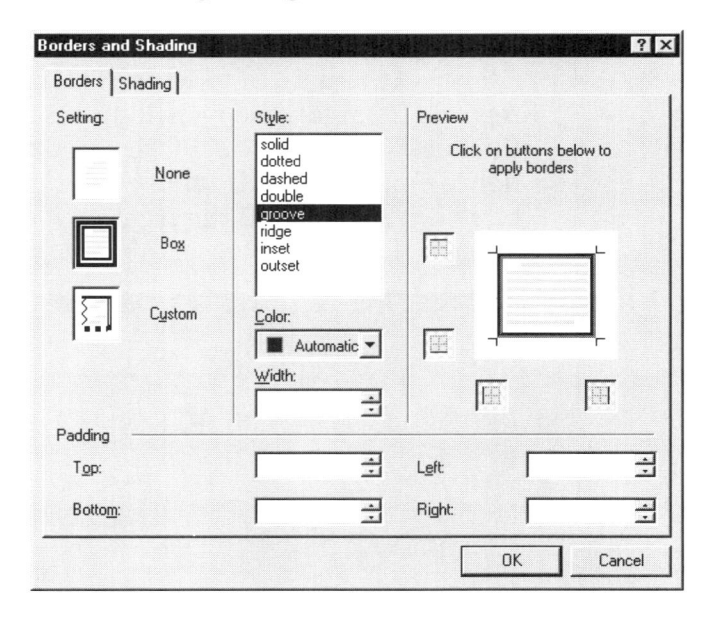

If you use Word much, this box should look familiar. The only thing missing from this dialog box is the ability to turn on or off internal borders—that is, lines between cells. You can do that by setting the properties for groups of cells (rows or columns) or for individual cells in the Cell Properties dialog box (described later in this chapter). For a while, HTML lagged in support for formatting tables. CSS 1, the original version of style sheets, released by the W3C in April 1997, didn't even support style sheets for tables. CSS 2 does support tables, but it isn't supported by most of the browsers.

Tip: *Before you get too wrapped up with how beautifully CSS 2 tables format within FrontPage, test a table in some of the other browsers that your visitors might be using and make sure that if your visitors can't see your wonderful creation, what they do get is at least acceptable.*

What choices do I have if I don't use style sheets?

If you decide not to use style sheets, you still have some flexibility in defining your table, but your borders will be the simple borders shown, in Figures 6-3 and 6-7. Frankly borders are only part of the formula for an interesting table. The other things you can change—cell spacing, cell colors, and alignment—all contribute to a successful table.

If you are limited to what HTML itself can offer with regards to tables, then you'll have to change your border thickness or colors to achieve a reasonably attractive table. In figure 6-5, the default table border creates the illusion of the table being raised off the page. If you want to create the illusion that the table is sunken, assign a darker color to the

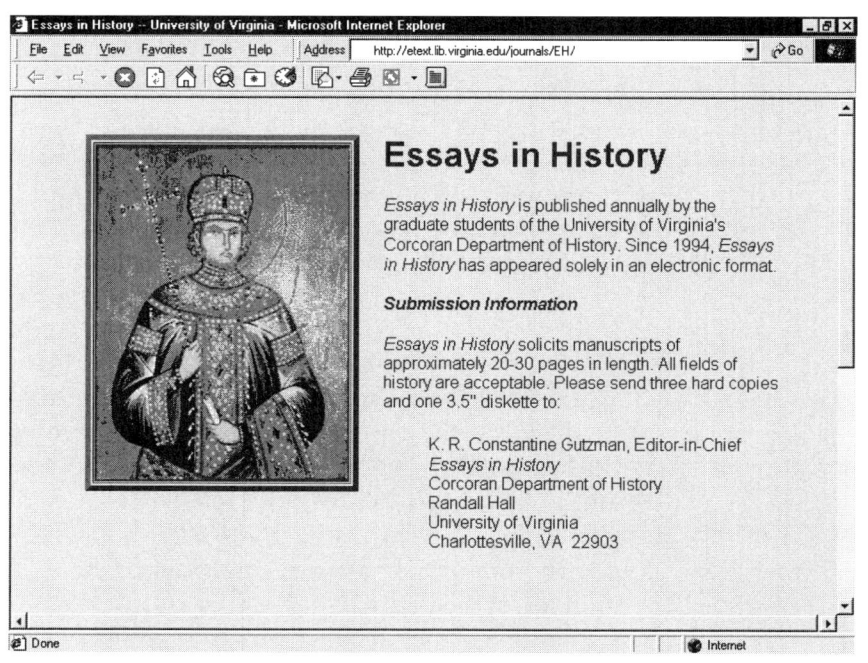

Figure 6-5 This page looks particularly nice in color because the light and dark border colors and the text color coordinate with colors in the image. You can see that the thicker border, while simple, works

Dark Border property and a lighter color to the Light Border property.

> ***Tip:*** *The best way to avoid getting carried away using formatting options that won't be seen in many browsers is to set the Compatibility in the Page Options dialog box, which you can access from the Tools menu. For most Web sites, you'll want to make sure that anything you create is compatible with both Internet Explorer and Netscape Navigator and for Version 3 browsers or later. Chapter 7 discusses browser compatibility with respect to style sheets and Dynamic HTML.*

Why can't I see all the table border choices?

There are two reasons why you might not see all the choices in the Table Properties dialog box. The simplest cause of having many of the table border properties grayed out is having the border size set to zero. Start by checking that.

If that's not the cause of your problem, take a look at how you have compatibility set.

1. Select Tools | Page Options. FrontPage will display the Page Options dialog box.
2. Click on the Compatibility tab, shown here.

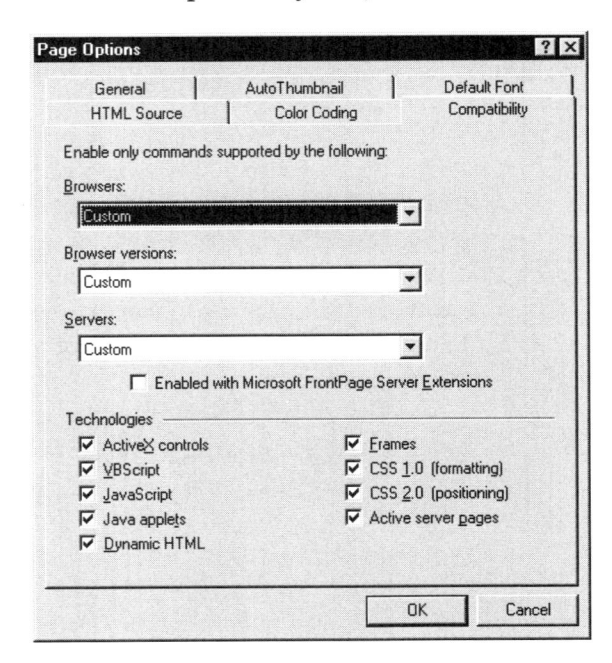

3. To what value is Browsers set? To get the maximum number of options on your Table Properties dialog box, set it to Custom.

4. To what value is Browser Versions set? To get the maximum number of options on your Table Properties dialog box, set it to Custom.

5. All the check boxes in the lower half of the screen should be checked now, with the possible exception of Active Server Pages, which won't be checked if you have the Servers box set to Apache.

PADDING, SPACING, AND MARGINS

Why is there space between my cells? How do I make the table look like a standard table created on a word-processor?

In HTML the cells and the table are different elements. Cells reside in tables, but they have different properties. What you want to do is eliminate the cell spacing. By setting cell spacing to zero, the borders of the first cell will touch the borders of the second cell. You can set cell spacing to zero in the Table Properties dialog box.

How do I create a table with borders on only some of the sides?

In order to create a table with only partial borders, such as only on the top and bottom, you'll need to go into the Table Properties dialog box, which you can do either by right-clicking anywhere in your table or by placing your cursor in the table, then selecting Table | Properties | Table. From the Table Properties dialog box, select Style, then select Format, then select Border.

In the Borders and Shading dialog box, there are two tabs named, not surprisingly, Borders and Shading. The following illustration shows the Borders tab. Here you can set the type of border you'd like: none, a box, or some combination of four sides. You need to indicate the style of border you want from the list shown. You can set the width here or in the Table Properties box. It doesn't matter where you set it because what you set here will reflect itself in the Table Properties dialog box.

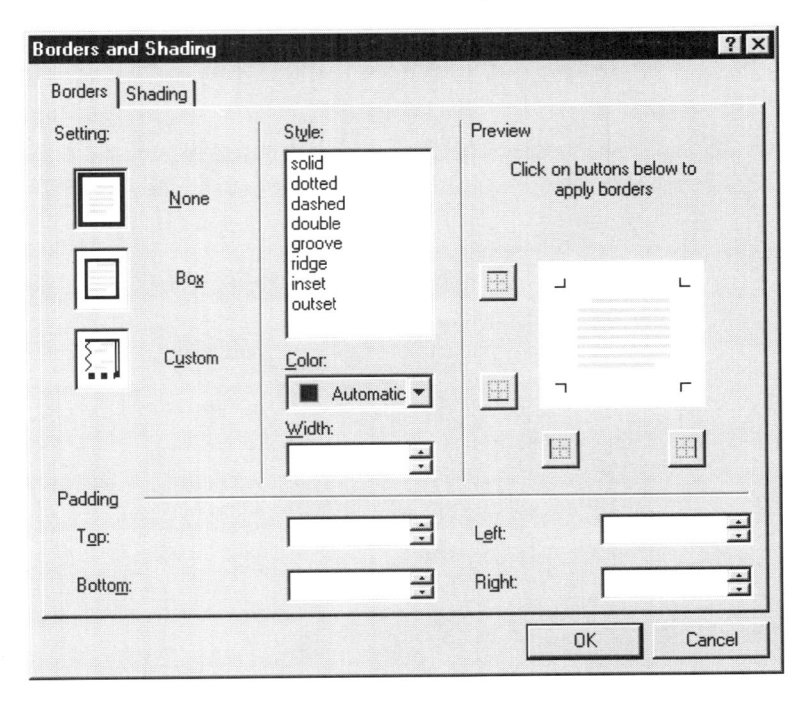

To create a table with unusual or non-standard borders, select the Custom Setting, then on the right in the Preview panel, select the sides on which you want borders. The Preview panel is misnamed because you can't really preview what your table is going to look like; all you can do is see which sides will have borders.

How do I create a table with only some of the internal borders?

Borders between cells are called *rules*. If you want to create a table with only vertical rules so that you have only

150 Chapter 6 Creating Interesting Tables

columns, like the table shown in the following illustration, follow these steps:

	Pizza Prices by City		
City	Small	Medium	Large
Chicago	$12.95	$16.95	$18.95
Austin	$9.95	$11.95	$13.95

1. Highlight the column you want to format, or highlight the entire table if you want vertical borders between every column.

2. Open the Cell Properties dialog box by either right-clicking, pressing ALT-ENTER, or selecting Table | Properties | Cell, as shown next:

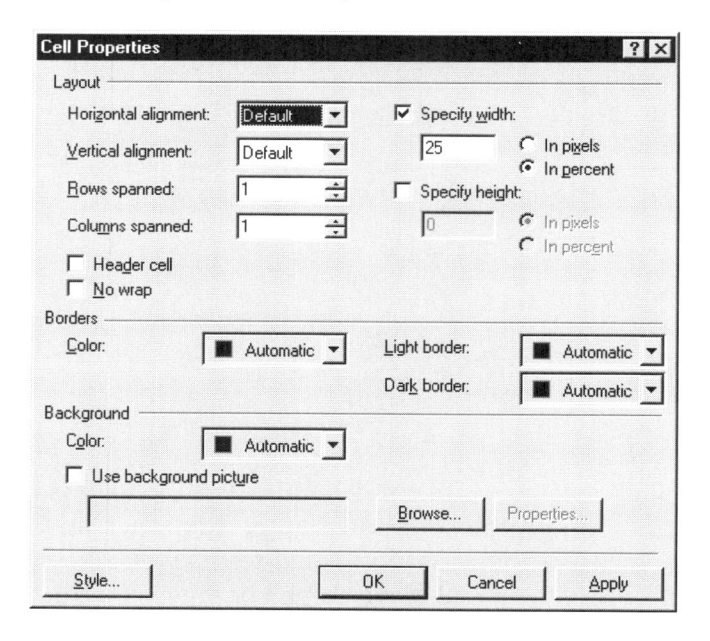

3. Click the Style button and FrontPage displays the Modify Style dialog box

4. Click the Format button. FrontPage displays a drop-down menu, from which you select Border. FrontPage then displays the Borders and Shading dialog box, as shown in the following illustration.

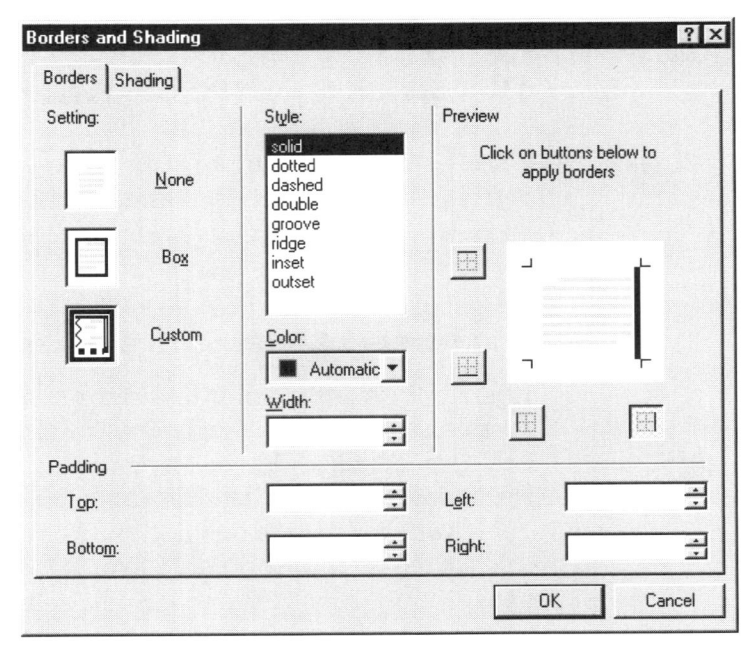

[Screenshot of the Borders and Shading dialog box, Borders tab, showing Setting (None, Box, Custom), Style list (solid, dotted, dashed, double, groove, ridge, inset, outset), Color, Width, Preview, and Padding (Top, Bottom, Left, Right) fields with OK and Cancel buttons.]

5. Click Custom, then in the Preview section of the dialog box select only the right side, only the left side, or both the right and left sides.

6. Choose a style of border or let it default to solid.

7. Choose a color.

Caution: *FrontPage won't let you define a different color for the rules of two adjacent cells if the cell spacing for the table is set to zero.*

8. Specify a border width. If you select both left and right side borders, and in the Table Properties dialog box you set the cell spacing to zero, then the rules will actually be twice as wide as you expect. Remember, each cell has its own border; even if you press them up against one another, you are defining borders for both cells.

9. Click OK to close the Borders and Shading dialog box.

10. Click OK to close the Modify Styles dialog box.
11. Click OK to close the Cell Properties dialog box.

Tip: When defining rules for adjacent columns or rows, define a border on only one side. This will help you avoid the problem of having a double rule, and you won't have strange borders if cell spacing is set to something other then zero.

How do I create tables with colored rows or columns?

If you only want to color one row or column (or cell, for that matter), highlight the cells you want to color and go into the Cell Properties dialog box by right-clicking and choosing Cell Properties from the list. Set the background color you want.

If you want some but not all the cells in a table to be one color, then go into the Table Properties dialog box and set the background color you want. Next, select the few cells that will be colored differently and set the second background color from the Cell Properties dialog box.

Caution: When you set the background color of a table, the cells as well as the cell spacing take on that color. If you truly only want cells to have the color you've selected, and you need to have cell spacing (that is to say, you need to have it set to greater than zero), then you should set the table background color to affect only the cell spacing color, and set the cells' color from the Cell Properties dialog box.

My table seems awfully crowded. What can I do?

Try increasing your cell padding. *Cell padding* is the space between the cell walls and whatever you've put inside the cell. Increasing cell padding is an easy way to add white space in your table, either between the contents of cells and the borders, if you have borders, or between the contents of adjacent cells.

FrontPage lets you define cell padding for the entire table in the Table Properties box. To define cell padding for individual cells or groups of cells, follow these steps (many of which are identical to the steps you used to create a table with only columns):

1. Highlight the cell or cells you want to modify.
2. Open the Cell Properties dialog box.
3. Click the Style button. FrontPage displays the Modify Style dialog box.
4. Click the Format button. FrontPage then displays a drop-down menu, from which you select Border. FrontPage displays the Borders and Shading dialog box.
5. In the lower half of the Border tab, set the cell padding for the left, right, top, and bottom of cells. You may find that if you have borders turned off, setting the padding on only one side provides the white space you need.

OTHER TEXT FORMATTING OPTIONS

How do I change the color of the text in my table?

There are two ways to do this. You can either use the traditional method of highlighting the text whose color you want to change, selecting Format | Font, and then setting the font color, or you can assign the values at the table or cell level. More browsers can see the text color properly if you use the first method and set the color from the Font dialog box.

If you're a purist and you really want to use style sheets, follow these steps to set the text color in cells or a table. The page will load faster if you use this method than if you assign text color in the traditional method, but unless the table is huge, the difference in load time will be small.

1. Open the Cell Properties dialog box.
2. Click the Style button. FrontPage displays the Modify Style dialog box.
3. Click the Format button. FrontPage displays a drop-down menu, from which you select Border. FrontPage displays the Borders and Shading dialog box.

4. To set the text color, change the Foreground Color.
5. Notice that you can also change the Background Color from the Borders and Shading dialog box.

Caution: Text color for cells set through the traditional method overrides the Foreground Color property of table settings.

What choices do I have for aligning text within the cells?

You can align the text within a cell both vertically and horizontally. Horizontally, you can select from left, center, right, or justified (like a book with flush left and flush right margins). Vertically, you can choose from top, middle, and bottom. You can make all these decisions right on the Cell Properties dialog box, without even needing style sheets.

Chapter 7

Implementing Cascading Style Sheets (CSS)

Answer Topics!

- **ELEMENTS OF STYLE 158**
  - ? What a style is
  - ? What styles look like
  - ? The difference between headings (H1, H2, H3) and styles
  - ? What can be defined in a style
  - ? Which elements take styles
  - ? Which attributes of an element can be changed
  - ? Changing the attributes of an element

- **STYLE SHEETS 179**
  - ? What style sheets are
  - ? Why styles are put in a sheet
  - ? Using styles in places other than style sheets
  - ? Publishing the style sheet with your web

- **CASCADING 180**
  - ? Understanding cascading
  - ? Overriding styles in a style sheet
  - ? Overriding styles on a page

- **APPLYING STYLE SHEETS 181**
  - ? Applying styles to elements
  - ? Applying styles at the web level
  - ? Elements that can be modified with style sheets
  - ? Applying styles to tables

- **BROWSER LIMITATIONS OF STYLE SHEETS 183**
  - ? Reasons not to use style sheets
  - ? Browsers that support style sheets

Implementing Cascading Style Sheets @ a Glance

Cascading style sheets are the coolest thing to hit the Web since colored text. Style sheets allow you to define the way you want an element on your page to look in one place, then have every instance of that element take on the look instantly. If you change the definition in only one place, every instance of that element changes to match the style you've defined. If you want to define another style for only one or a few instances of an element (say, all headings are blue and 14 pt, but one is red and 14 pt), then you can do that, too. In fact, you can set the style for an element for the entire site, then set the style for instances of that element, and even set styles just for a specific element.

FrontPage makes implementing styles a breeze. If you've ever seen a style sheet, you know that while they're not rocket science, they're not exactly a natural language. Once you understand how style sheets work, you can start to apply them to your web, your pages, and specific elements on a page.

- **Elements of Style** This section explains what styles are and what they mean to your web site. It also gives you an idea of the extent to which you can use styles to modify the attributes of elements on your pages.

- **Style Sheets** This section explains how you can take advantage of style sheets to change the look of a single element across all the pages in your site.

- **Cascading** Because you can put style definitions in more than one place, the browser needs to understand the rules and the weights associated with each area of your web in which you can define styles. This section explains how cascading works.

- **Applying Style Sheets** This section explains how FrontPage can help you apply style sheets in your web to text elements, images, and tables.

- **Browser Limitations of Style Sheets** Every silver lining has a gray cloud. As powerful as style sheets are, they're not fully implemented in every browser. This section explains the browser limitations of style sheets.

ELEMENTS OF STYLE

What is a style?

A style is the way something is rendered on a browser, the way it appears on the screen. Microsoft Word takes advantage of styles. You might not use them, though. Have you ever noticed the word "Normal" in the upper-left corner of your screen, just under the standard toolbar? (See Figure 7-1) That's where you indicate the style you want to use for the text you're typing. In the drop-down box that says "Body Text," you can also see the entire list of styles included in the normal template. Click on the drop-down arrow, and you will see other defined styles including Heading 1, Heading 2, Normal,

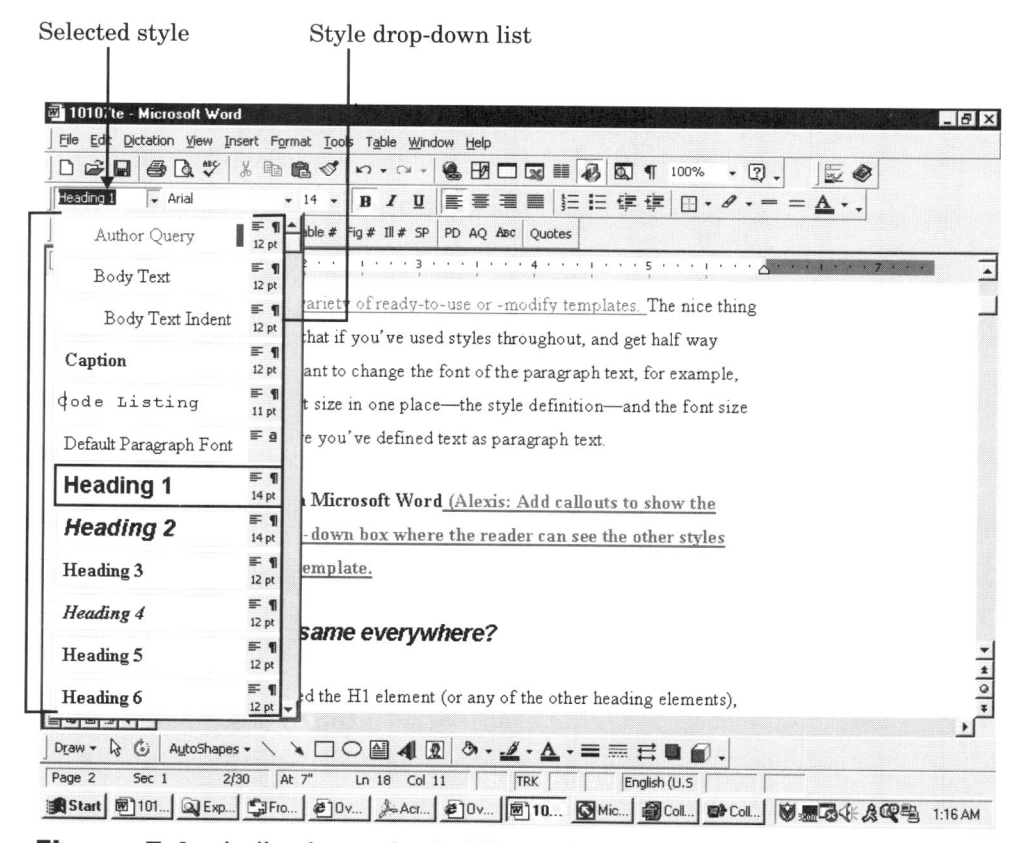

Figure 7-1 Indicating styles in Microsoft Word

and Default Paragraph Font. A collection of defined styles shared in a document section or entire document is called a *template*. You can see a collection of Word's predefined templates by accessing the File drop-down list, and clicking on New. FrontPage displays the New File dialog box; click on the Templates tab to see Word's variety of ready-to-use-or-modify templates. The nice thing about using styles in Word is that if you've used styles throughout and decide halfway through your document that you want to change the font of the paragraph text, for example, you just need to adjust the font size in one place—the style definition—and the font size change takes effect everywhere you've defined text as paragraph text.

Do styles look the same everywhere?

No. If you've ever used the H1 element (or any of the other heading elements), you know that headings render differently on different browsers and on different monitors. If you have used the heading elements in HTML, then you've already been using styles.

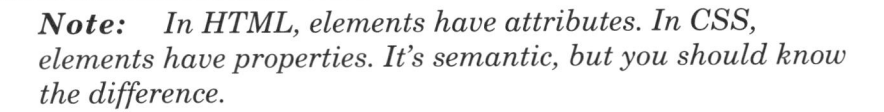

Note: In HTML, elements have attributes. In CSS, elements have properties. It's semantic, but you should know the difference.

Aren't headings (H1, H2, H3) styles?

Heading elements are styles for which properties have already been defined. When your browser comes across the <H1> (Heading 1) tag in HTML, it has a very specific idea of how to render it. It knows what type size to use, what typeface to use, and what color type to use.

When you use style sheets, you can continue to use H1 and other heading elements as they are, although they will be rendered differently from desktop to desktop, or you can define more specifically how you want these (and other) elements to appear in style sheets, giving you far more assurance that your page will render the same way everywhere.

> **Caution:** Style sheets only work on the newest browsers: Internet Explorer 3 and 4 and Netscape Navigator 4. Be sure to test anything you create using style sheets on both Navigator and Internet Explorer to make sure you get the results you expect. Research shows that visitors will be using, and Web sites will have to support, Version 4 browsers until 2003. Most Web visitors are very reluctant to upgrade their browsers, despite the fact that the upgrades are free, because they don't want to hassle with the enormous files and possible problems this could cause on their already working systems. Don't assume visitors have the newest browsers.

What can I define in a style?

It all depends on the element that the style modifies. If you are defining a style for text, you can usually modify the typeface including its color, size, letter spacing, and alignment, provided you use one of the "safe" fonts commonly supported by the most popular versions of the major browsers. You can get this list of "safe" fonts from W3C (the World-Wide Web Consortium) and from a sidebar about fonts in Chapter 13.

If you are defining a style for an image, then you will be able to define the horizontal alignment, the vertical alignment, whether text is allowed to flow around it, and what the borders, if any, look like.

Which elements take styles?

All of the elements shown in Table 7-1 take styles.

Element	Description
(A) Anchor	Indicates how text hyperlinks are displayed. Can be refined to indicate how text hyperlinks look both before they've been visited and after, and how they look when they are being clicked.
(ABBR) Abbreviation	Allows you to define the way an abbreviation of a term is displayed. Unless you define a style for it, it will render exactly as regular body text displays on your page. This element is infrequently used.

Table 7-1 Elements That Take Styles

Elements of Style

Element	Description
(ACRONYM) Acronym	Marks an acronym. Most browsers render anything marked this way as regular text. You can change the way the element renders by defining a style for it.
(ADDRESS) Address	Indicates an address on the page, but it will render exactly as other body text renders unless you define a style for it.
(APPLET) Applet	Allows you to insert Java applets into your page. You can change the attributes on everything related to applets, from the text that displays if the applet can't run to the alignment of the applet itself.
(AREA) Area	Allows you to define all the standard attributes for areas. This element is quite rare. You'd have to insert it by hand, if you wanted to use it.
(B) Bold	Allows you to define attributes for boldface text. Horrifyingly, you can define a style for the bold element that's not even bolded. The bold element is one of the very few styles that renders the same way on every monitor.
(BASE) Base	Part of the Head element; nothing displays as a result of its presence or absence.
(BASEFONT) Basefont	Use of this element is discouraged. Web designers used to use it to set the font for the page; today, Web designers use the Font element to set the font, or better yet, they use a style sheet to set the font.
(BGSOUND) Background Sound	Allows you to set a background sound for your page. You can set attributes for this style, but I'm not sure why you'd want to set attributes for this style.
(BIG) Big	Makes the font size bigger. This element is new to HTML.
(BLINK) Blink	Makes text blink. Use this element sparingly, if at all.
(BLOCKQUOTE) Blockquote	Sets apart a block of text from both the left and right margins. Using style sheets, you can specify anything special you want to about this element, including how much it indents from both sides and whether there are borders around it.
(BODY) Body	The mother of all elements, literally. What you define for the body is reflected in all elements that the body contains, and that's everything you see on a page, unless you specifically change that attribute at the element level. This is the ideal place to set the typeface, type size, type color, and so on, for all text on the page. This is also where you can define margins for the entire page.

Table 7-1 Elements That Take Styles *(continued)*

> ***Tip:*** *If you need to format text as something other than bold, don't modify the BOLD element, but create a new class of either bold or some element, or, better yet, use the Span (SPAN) or Div (DIV) elements to do the formatting.*

Element	Description
(BR) Break	The equivalent of a hard return on a word processor. Believe it or not, you can modify this element.
(BUTTON) Button	Allows you to insert a graphic in place of the standard gray Submit button. The button element is relatively new to HTML.
(CAPTION) Caption	Allows you to set a caption for a table.
(CENTER) Center	Allows you to center text. While you can set properties for this one, I'm not sure why you'd want to. Using the CENTER element is discouraged, anyway. You should set the attribute of the element you want to center to have centered alignment instead.
(CITE) Citation	Indicates that text is a citation. Most browsers don't show this any differently, but the ones that do render it as italics.
(CODE) Code	Renders text in a monospaced font (in which all characters, regardless of width, occupy the same amount of space) such as Courier. Use of this element is discouraged. Use the PRE element instead.
(COL) Column	Defines how a specific column in a table should look. The column definition needs to come at the top of the table, before any rows are defined.
(DD) Definition Data	Works in conjunction with two other elements: Definition Term (DT) and Definition List (DL). First, you must define a definition list, then each word in the list is marked as a definition term, then the actual definition of each term is marked as definition data. These elements render differently from browser to browser, with most simply not recognizing the elements at all. If you're going to have a lot of definitions on your site, you might want to take advantage of these elements, rather than using other elements to format terms and definitions.
(DEL) Deleted Text	Allows you to note revisions in text by marking the text that was deleted as deleted text. Most browsers that support this will render the text with a strikethrough. This is useful for showing the progress of legal contracts or a document with several reviewers.
(DFN) Definition	Works outside the framework of definition lists. You can use it to mark a definition, but it won't render any differently than other text on most browsers.
(DIR) Direction	Permits you to render some text as right-to-left, rather than left-to-right. This can be useful for foreign languages, but there can be other font-related issues with foreign languages.

Table 7-1 Elements That Take Styles *(continued)*

Note: *See Chapter 13 for detailed information about fonts.*

Elements of Style

Element	Description
(DIV) Division	Suppose you wanted a paragraph followed by a blockquote, a bulleted list, and then another paragraph, all formatted with a yellow background. You could either set the background color on each of those four elements, or you could set it once by wrapping them all into a DIV element with the background color set to yellow and allow inheritance to take care of passing that information onto those elements (see the sidebar, "Inheritance").
(DL) Definition List	Works just like an ordered list (OL) or an unnumbered list (UL) in that by itself it does nothing, but each item in the list—marked as a definition term—is affected by the attributes of the definition list.
(DT) Definition Term	Takes definition data; exists within a definition list.
(EM) Emphasis	Usually renders as bold, but you can define how you want this element to render in a style sheet.
(EMBED) Embed	This element was formerly used for many types of embedded multimedia, such as audio files. Use the OBJECT tag, which is more generic, instead.
(FIELDSET) Fieldset	Allows you to group fields in forms and format them as a group—for example, putting a box around a group of radio buttons. This new element is only supported in the very latest browsers.
(FONT) Font	Formats elements if you don't use style sheets. Try to stay away from this element because you can't make changes to it at a macro level if you want to revamp your site later.
(FORM) Form	The shell in which all form elements must be defined. You don't see anything on the screen when you define a FORM element, but without it, depending on the browser, either the Form fields won't render at all, or the Submit button won't take any action.
(FRAME) Frame	Allows you to define the frames that will be defined within the frameset of your page.
(H1, H2, H3, H4, H5, H6) Headings	H1 is the largest heading you can display; H6 is the smallest, unless you define them otherwise (which I would discourage).

Table 7-1 Elements That Take Styles *(continued)*

> *Tip:* Just because an element is legal doesn't mean it will work on any given browser. When using elements that are newer, check to see how they render on a variety of browsers, including the two most recent non-beta versions of Netscape Navigator, Internet Explorer, and AOL.

Chapter 7 Implementing Cascading Style Sheets (CSS)

Element	Description
(HEAD) Head	The part of the page that stores the title (which appears at the very top of your browser), and the meta data (data about data which describes your page so that search engines can index it better).
(HR) Horizontal Rule	Helps to break up your page without requiring any graphics. By changing the width, color, length, and justification of this element, you can spice up your page without impairing load time.
(HTML) HyperText Markup Language	Contains the entire page, whether the page is a head and a frameset, or a head and a body.
(I) Italics	Permits you to italicize text on your page. You probably don't want to change how italics render.
(IFRAME) Internal Frame	Allows you to create a frame within the body of the page, rather than in a frameset.
(IMG) Image	Displays images. By modifying the style, you can change the alignment, padding, border color, border width, and border style.
(INPUT) Input	Form fields are all defined with the INPUT element. You can specify which type of Form field you want by selecting a value for the Type property (text, check box, radio, and so on).
(INS) Insertion	The other half of the Insertion-Deletion pair. If you enter text as part of an insertion element, it will appear underlined in browsers that support this element.
(ISINDEX) Isindex	Use of this element is discouraged. Once upon a time, it was used to create single-line text forms that resided in the head of the page. Use the FORM element, instead.
(KBD) Keyboard	Indicates keystrokes, which appear as a fixed-width font. Use the PRE element instead.
(LABEL) Label	Allows you to group a Form field and the text associated with the Form field so that (as in most desktop applications), when you click on the text associated with the Form field, such as a radio button, the cursor moves to that field.
(LAYER) Layer	The alternative to using the z-axis to dictate which elements go in front of which other elements. This element only works on certain versions of Netscape Navigator. It's use isn't recommended.
(LEGEND) Legend	Provides a title for fields grouped with the FIELDSET element.

Table 7-1 Elements That Take Styles *(continued)*

Note: To see how to create animated text, see Chapter 3.

Elements of Style

Element	Description
(LI) List Item	Marks items in an ordered list (which uses the OL element) or an unordered list (which uses the UL element). You can change the indentation of list items by changing their styles.
(LINK) Link	Used to dictate the relationship between this page and other pages on the site. It's part of the head, thus isn't displayed. This element hasn't caught on.
(MAP) Map	Allows you to create an image map. You place the definitions of the hotspots inside this element.
(MARQUEE) Marquee	Displays scrolling text. Don't use this element, because only Internet Explorer can render it. There are better ways to display scrolling text, such as client-side JavaScript.
(MENU) Menu	Creates a single-column list. Use the PRE element instead.
(META) Meta	Allows you to provide information about your page to search engines and other indexing programs. Since META tags are in the head, they don't render on the page.
(NOBR) No Break	Prevents a line from wrapping.
(NOEMBED) No Embed	Tells the page what to render if the multimedia element that was embedded can't load for whatever reason.
(NOFRAMES) No Frames	Used to create the page that will be seen by visitors to your site who don't have frame-enabled browsers. It's the substitute for the BODY element when you use a frameset.
(OBJECT) Object	Used to embed multimedia into your page.
(OL) Ordered List	One of the elements that holds list items (LI). You can format the numbering system and the starting number using style sheets.
(OPTGROUP) Option Group	Allows you to have subgroups in select lists in forms. This is not widely supported, so use with caution.
(OPTION) Option	Allows you to put items into a select list in a form. Each item on the select list must have its own OPTION element. The entire list of elements must be within the select element.
(P) Paragraph	Used to define a paragraph. With style sheets you can create indentation (or a hanging indent) for a paragraph, something never before possible without the use of images. You have a tremendous amount of flexibility in how you define paragraphs (margins, borders, line height, and more) with style sheets.

Table 7-1 Elements That Take Styles *(continued)*

Note: For more information about image mapping, see Chapter 4.

Element	Description
(S) Strikethrough	Creates a strikethrough effect. Use the DEL element instead.
(SAMP) Sample Output	Creates text that's displayed with a fixed-width font. Use of this element is discouraged. Use the PRE element instead.
(SCRIPT) Script	Where you put client-side scripts (such as JavaScript), if you use any. This element can go in either the head or the body.
(SELECT) Select	Used to create select lists. For no obvious reason, FrontPage refers to a select list as a drop-down menu. Each item you want in your list must have its own OPTION element.
(SMALL) Small	Decreases the font size.
(SPAN) Span	The minor league version of the DIV element. The DIV element can format across larger elements, like paragraphs, blockquotes, and lists. The SPAN element can only format within one of these elements.
(STRIKETHROUGH) Strikethrough	Creates a strikethrough effect. As with the S element, its use is discouraged. Use the DEL element instead.
(STRONG) Strong	Usually displays as bold. You can change this with style sheets.
(STYLE) Style	Contains or points to style sheets.
(SUB) Subscript	Permits you to display subscripted characters.
(SUP) Superscript	Permits you to display superscripted characters.
(TABLE) Table	Doesn't display anything by itself, but it's required in order to display tables. All the table elements (TR, TD, COLUMN, COLGROUP, and so on) need to reside within this element.
(TBODY) Table Body	Permits you to define rows of your table as being the body of the table (not to be confused with the BODY element). Right now it doesn't render any differently with this element, but there are plans to combine the use of the TBODY, THEAD, and TFOOT elements to permit you to print a multipage table with the header and footer printed on each page.
(TD) Table Data	Defines each cell of a table.

Table 7-1 Elements That Take Styles *(continued)*

> *Note:* To read about select lists and forms, turn to Chapter 10.

Elements of Style

Element	Description
(TEXTAREA) Text Area	A field for free-form text entry. It is usually displayed as a multiline box. The TEXTAREA field must reside in the FORM element.
(TFOOT) Table Footer	Doesn't do anything special yet. See "Table Body" above.
(TH) Table Header Cell	Creates a cell with special formatting to indicate that it's a header. All TH elements must reside in a TR element.
(THEAD) Table Header	Not to be confused with the TH element, this element is part of the threesome including TBODY and TFOOT. See "Table Body" for a description of its planned use.
(TITLE) Title	The only element in the head that is displayed on the page. The title of the page displays at the very top of your browser. You really can't change the formatting of this element.
(TR) Table Row	Holds the TD or TH elements and must reside within a TABLE element.
(TT) Teletype	Formats a fixed-width font. Use of this element is discouraged. Use the PRE element instead.
(U) Underline	Underlines text. Use of this element is really discouraged because underlined text is usually a hyperlink.
(UL) Unordered List	Creates a bulleted list. Bullet items must go into LI elements, but you can define formatting for the entire list at the UL level.
(VAR) Variable	Was used to mark a variable in a computer program. Its use is discouraged in favor of the PRE element.

Table 7-1 Elements That Take Styles *(continued)*

> ***Note:*** *For a thorough treatment of HTML in all its glory and all the nitty-gritty of style sheets, get* The HTML 4 Bible *by Bryan Pfaffenberger and Alexis D. Gutzman, published by IDG Books Worldwide, 1998.*

Where can I find out which attributes of an element I can change?

FrontPage permits you to change any attributes of any element. This means that you can change the typeface of the Paragraph element, the List element, and the Blockquote element. You can also change the typeface of the Horizontal Rule element, which is silly, since the horizontal rule has no text.

Inheritance (revisited)

Inheritance is the way that style definitions trickle down from bigger container elements, such as a page or a paragraph, to smaller elements, such as text or a heading. If you define the text color to be blue at the body level, then all text on the page will be blue, unless you define the text color at a lower level (such as the element level) to be a different color. If you want all text to be blue and one heading to be green, rather than define the text color to be blue for all text-based elements (headings, paragraphs, blockquotes, and so on) and defining the color for that one heading to be green, simply define the default color for all text to be blue at the body level and then set the color of that one heading to be green as an exception right at the heading, or in a class for green headings.

If you take advantage of inheritance, you'll not only save yourself a lot of time formatting, but you'll also make site face-lifts much less tedious. As much as possible, define styles at the highest level at which they apply and let inheritance do the work for you. (See the boxed text in Chapter 6 for more information on Inheritance.)

To make any changes to styles, you need to go into the Style dialog box, as shown in Figure 7-2. You can get to the Style dialog box by selecting Format | Style.

How can I change the properties of an element?

Before you start changing the style of an element, you need to make some decisions about the extent to which you want all instances of that element changed. If you want all instances of an element changed (say, all paragraphs should be indented one centimeter), then you simply need to modify the style for the Paragraph element. If you want only some paragraphs to have the new style, then you'll want to create a new class of paragraphs (so that only paragraphs within that class will have a one-centimeter indent).

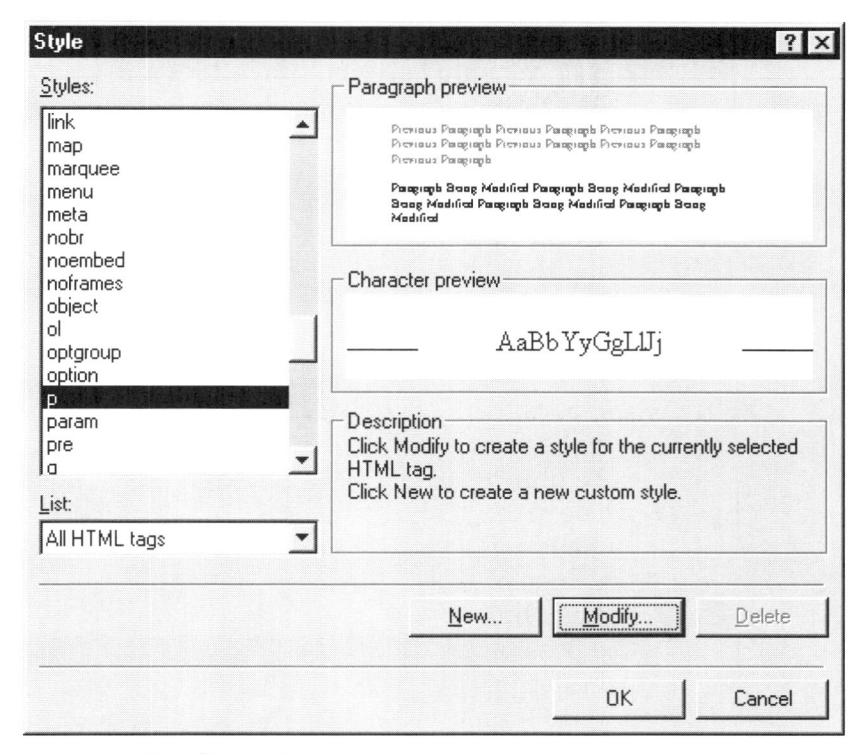

Figure 7-2   The Style dialog box

Modifying a Style for an Element

Follow these steps:

1. Select Format | Style to bring up the Style dialog box, shown in Figure 7-2.

2. Select the element whose style you want to modify from the list shown. If the List drop-down box is empty, then you probably only have User-defined styles showing, make sure the List's drop-down box shows the selection "All HTML tags."

3. Click the Modify button to change the way all instances of this element are formatted.

4. You'll see the Modify Style dialog box. Click the Format button, then select from among Font, Paragraph, Border, Numbering, and Position.

5. If you want to change the way text appears and the relationship between the letters and each other and the letters and the baseline, select Font. You'll see the Font dialog box with the Font tab selected, as shown in Figure 7-3. Here you can change the font, style, size, color, and effects. Make your changes now. You can see the changes you make in the Preview panel. When you're satisfied, click OK.

Note: In order for the font you select to display properly, it has to be installed on the computer of the visitor to your site. For this reason, it's better to stick to a standard font, such as Helvetica or Times Roman, rather than selecting an obscure font such as Batang or Copperplate Gothic Bold.

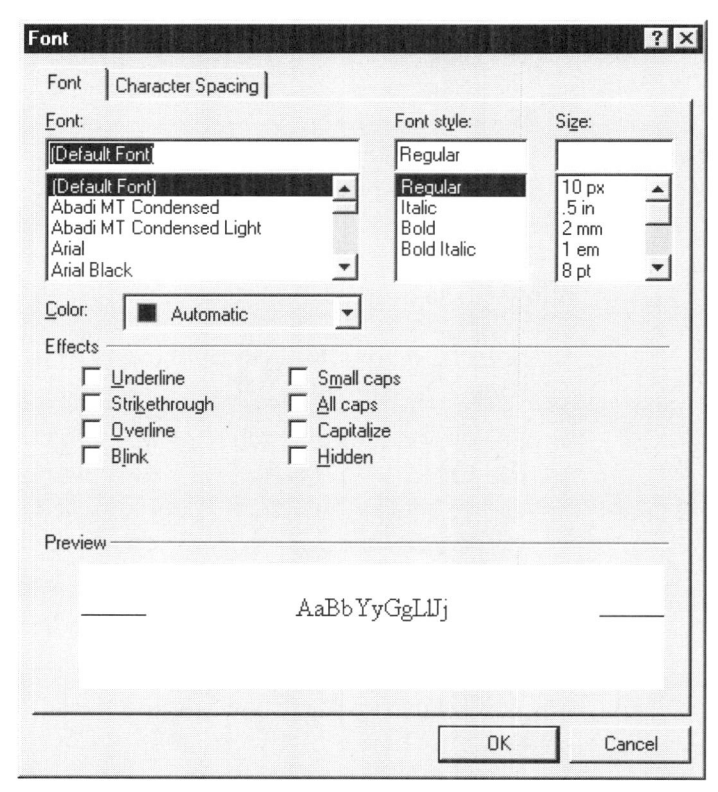

Figure 7-3 The Font tab of the Font dialog box

6. Select the Character Spacing tab, and you'll see the dialog box shown in Figure 7-4. Here you can change the spacing of the letters within and between words, and the position of the letters with respect to the baseline. FrontPage makes this very easy because you can see how your changes are going to look before you commit to them. The Preview panel is a real time-saver. Click OK when you're satisfied. The Font dialog box will disappear and your new selections will be implemented.

Even if you're not modifying the style for text, if you want to indicate that the element being modified needs to be aligned, then you should go into the Paragraph dialog box to align it, which you can do by right-clicking on the text and selecting Paragraph from the shortcut menu. This solution is not very intuitive. All choices for *paragraph* formatting appear in

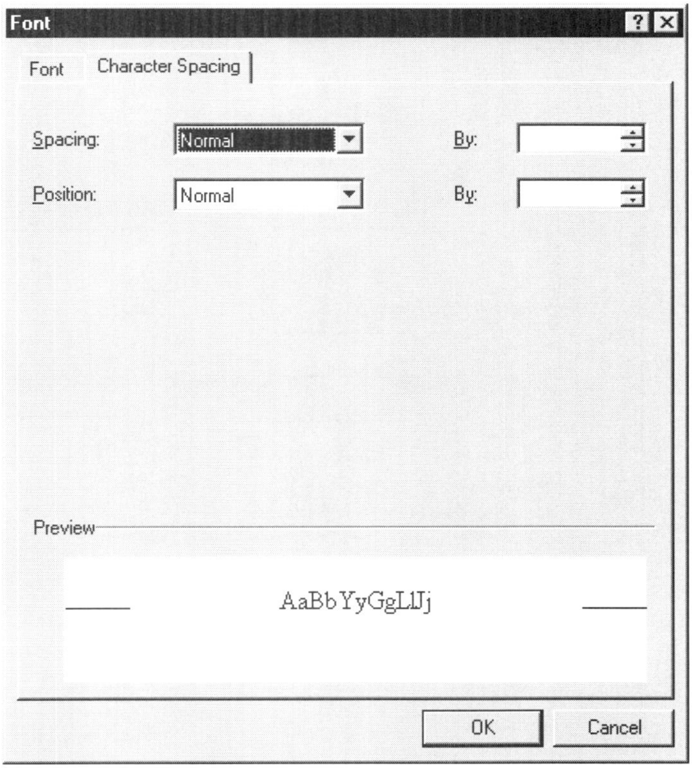

Figure 7-4 The Character Spacing tab of the Font dialog box

the Indents and Spacing tab, as shown in Figure 7-5. You can change the alignment as well as the indentation for the entire paragraph, indentation on either the left or right side, and indentation for the first line. You can also change the spacing between lines, and above and below the paragraph (or table, image, blockquote, or any other element that stands on its own). The spacing above and below the paragraph is usually referred to as the top and bottom margin. Again, the Preview panel is invaluable when formatting a paragraph because the labels on these choices aren't at all clear or intuitive. Click OK when you're satisfied, and the Paragraph dialog box disappears.

Note: *The only way to indent the first line of a paragraph is through style sheets.*

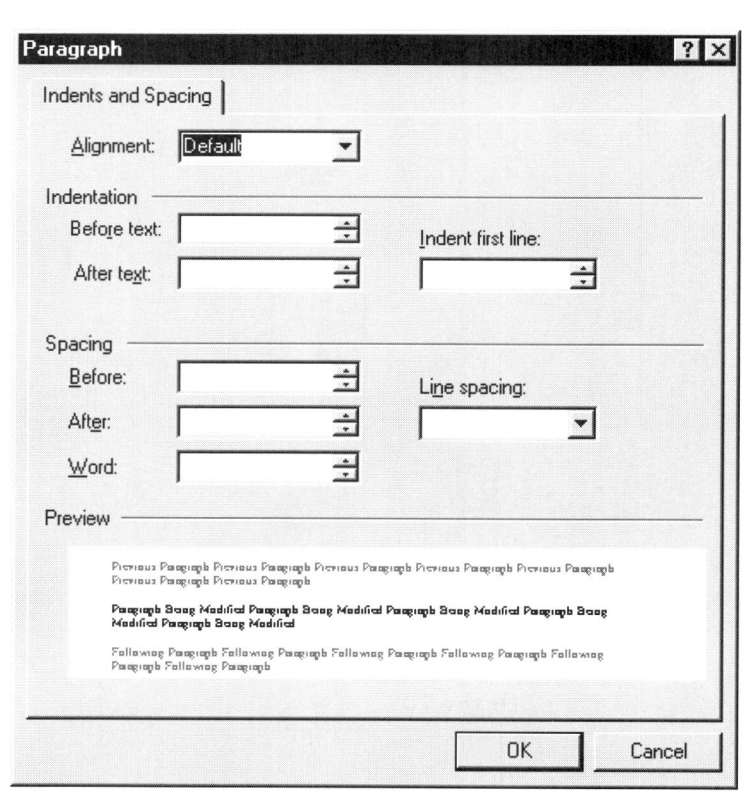

Figure 7-5 The Indents and Spacing tab of the Paragraph dialog box

Changing Border Characteristics

You can also change the characteristics of borders and their shading through FrontPage's formatting options. To change borders and shading, select Format | Borders and Shading to display the Borders and Shading Dialog box.

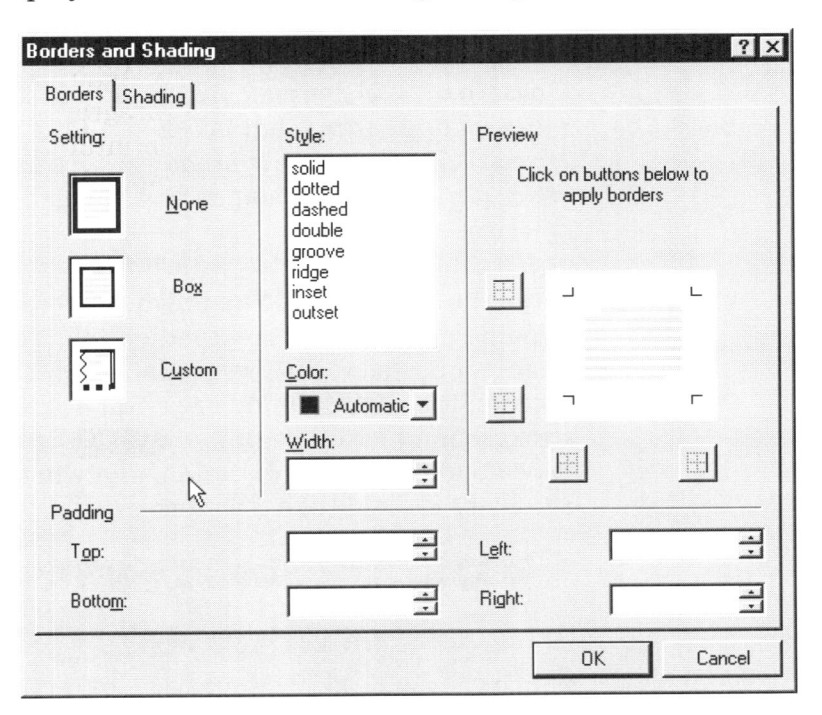

> *Note:* *You can also access the Borders and Shading dialog box from the Modify Style dialog box. To do so, select Format | Styles to display the Style dialog box, shown in Figure 7-2. Click the Modify button to display the Modify Style dialog box (shown in Figure 7-6). From the Modify Style dialog box, you can click the Format button. FrontPage displays a drop-down list of elements; select the one you would like to change. Select Borders from the list, and FrontPage displays the Borders tab of the Borders and Shading dialog box.*

With the Borders tab, you can change *whether* a border appears as well as *how* it appears, including its style, color, and width. The Preview panel is helpful in seeing what you're getting. You can also change the padding for any element.

The *padding* is the space between an element and the border, if there is one. The *margin* is the space between the border, if there is one, and the outside of the margin of the next element. If you define both one centimeter of padding and a one-centimeter margin, but no border, you'll get two centimeters of white space around your element.

Caution: In general, you usually want to define either margins or padding, but not both unless the border is visible. If you define both, you'll probably have twice as much white space around the element as you thought you had requested.

Changing Shading Characteristics

From the Borders and Shading dialog box, you can also change shading options with the Shading tab. You can change the background color, the foreground color, the background picture, the vertical and horizontal positions at which the background picture begins, whether the background picture repeats and in which direction, and whether the attachment scrolls or is fixed (like a watermark).

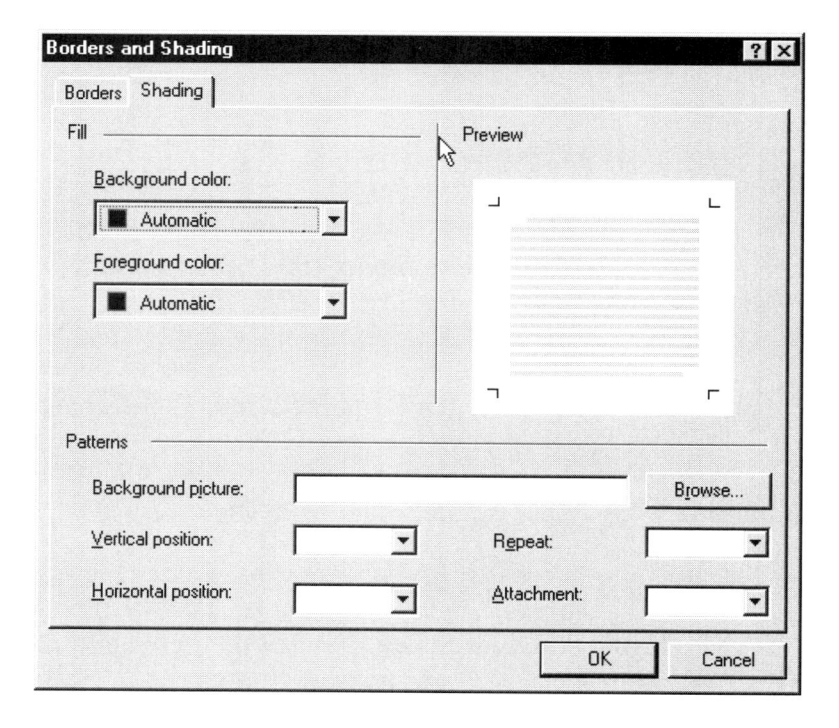

Changing List Options

To change the formatting of ordered or unordered lists, you have two ways to access the Bullets and Numbering dialog box. One way is to select Numbering from the Modify Style dialog box. FrontPage will display the Picture Bullets tab of the Bullets and Numbering dialog box. A second way to access the Picture Bullets tab of the Bullets and Numbering dialog box is to select Format | Bullets and Numbering.

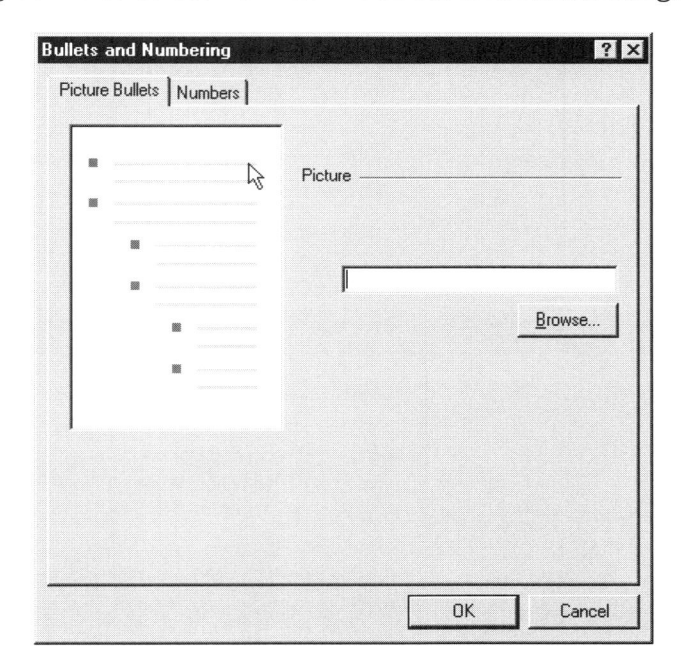

If you would like to use a graphic in place of the standard bullet choices, select the image you want to use. FrontPage knows to replace the bullet with the image you've chosen.

Tip: *If you want to have different images for different levels of bullets, you need to assign the images to different classes and then apply the classes to the appropriate levels of lists.*

From the Bullets and Numbering dialog box, you can also select from three styles of plain bullets. If you prefer, you can select one of them from the Plain Bullets tab, as shown here.

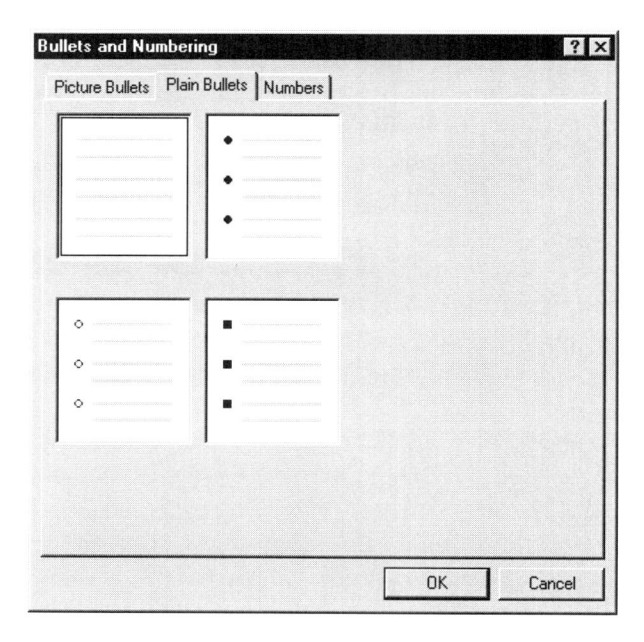

From the Bullets and Numbering dialog box, you can also select from five choices of numbering styles for your ordered lists, as shown here.

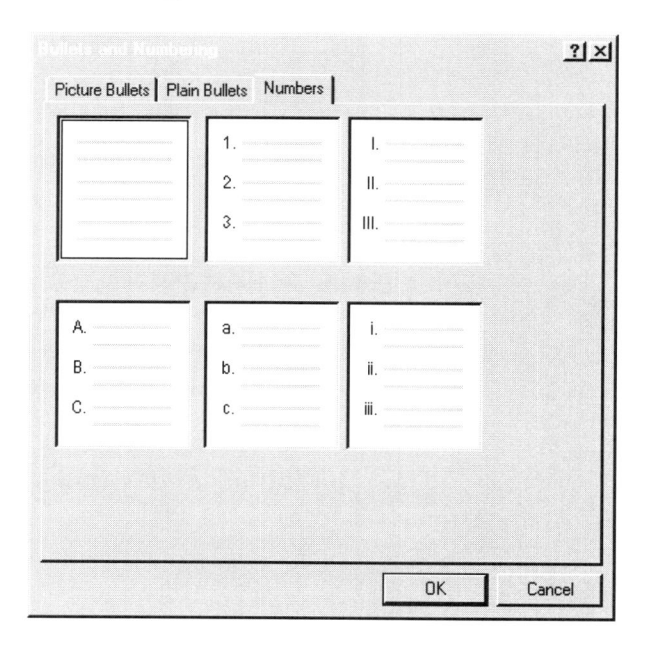

Changing an Element's Position

In addition to selecting *how* an element appears on a Web page, you can also select *where* exactly on the page you would like it to appear. (As a general caution, you shouldn't set this selection for all instances of an element unless you want them all on top of each other.) If you want to layer items on the page using the *z*-axis or if you want to define how text wraps around another element, bring up the Position dialog box by selecting Position from the Format Button on the Modify Style dialog box or by selecting Format | Position from the main menu.

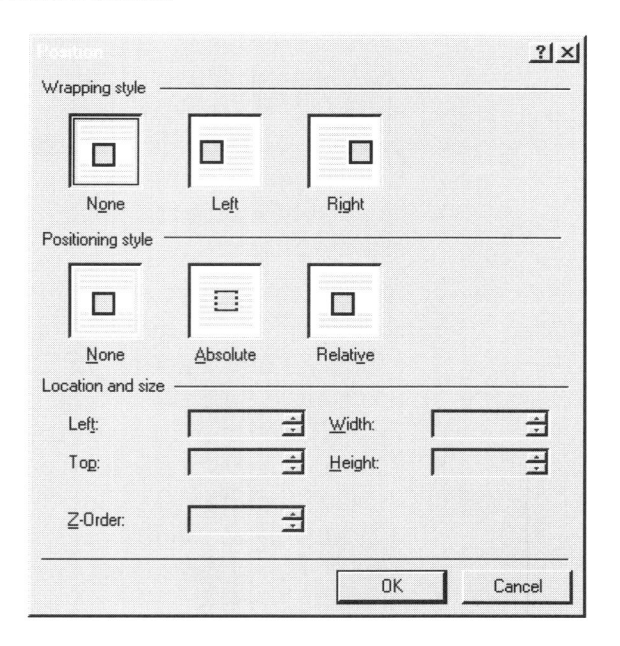

You can define how text will wrap around another element by selecting either None, Left, or Right. You can also define the Positioning style. If you select either Absolute or Relative, you can enter the distance you want the element to be from either the top of the page or another element. If you leave Positioning set to None, the page will put the element wherever it would naturally fall, given the other styles defined.

***

Note: *Before Style Sheets, there was no way to absolutely position an element on the page. This is an exciting development.*

Creating a New Class of an Element

To create a new class of an element, follow these steps:

1. From FrontPage's main menu, select Format | Styles. FrontPage displays the Style dialog box.

2. Click New on the Style dialog box. FrontPage displays the New Style dialog box.

3. In the Name window at the top of the New Style dialog box, give your new style a descriptive name. If you want your new style to work only with a certain element, such as indentation that applies only to paragraphs, then make sure the name you select begins with the name of the element, followed by a period, then the name of the class (for example, **p.indent**). If you want your new style to work with all elements to which it can be applied, then enter only the style name, such as **green**, and you can apply it later to paragraphs, block quotes, headings, or anything else.

4. At the bottom-left corner of the New Style dialog box, click the Format button. FrontPage displays these options: Font, Paragraph, Border, Numbering, and Position. Select the type of element you want to create. FrontPage then displays the appropriate dialog box. If you refer back to the instructions for modifying each of these elements that appears earlier in this chapter, you will be able to modify each element to create a new one with the new name you provided at the top of the New Style dialog box.

5. To modify the style later, you'll need to change the value of List on the Style dialog box from All HTML Tags to User-Defined Styles to see it in the list.

Tip: *Create multiple classes of an element with easily remembered selectors, such as indent and no-indent. That way, you can give more than one look to an element without having to make the style definitions every time you create an instance of an element that's different from the norm, and you won't forget which style does what.*

STYLE SHEETS

What is a style sheet?

A style sheet is a list of rules that a browser should use when rendering your page. A browser will ignore any rules it doesn't understand. You define the rules through the Style dialog box. Then you indicate when you design your page which classes of styles should be applied to which elements. The style sheet must be located on the Web server for this to work.

Why put the styles in a sheet?

For easy modification. The easiest way to give a site a face-lift is to take a site that has a certain style sheet and swap it out for another style sheet. Since all formatting is defined in the style sheet, all the formatting can be changed easily.

Where else can I put a style?

You can actually put styles in three places: in the style sheet, in the style element in the head of your page, and in the element itself. Generally, you want to put styles in the sheet. If you're using a style sheet and need to override one or more styles for your page, you can define the override or additional styles in the style element in the head of your page. Since those styles are defined at a lower level, the browser will automatically give them greater weight and use them instead of the ones in the sheet. It will, however, use the styles in the sheet that aren't overridden by the styles in the style element.

If you need even more specific control over the style of an element, you can put the style directly into an element. This is discouraged because there's just as much maintenance with this as there is with the Font element. Revisions have to be made at the lowest level. If you do put a style into the element, that style will have greater weight for that element than the styles defined either in the style element or in the style sheet.

In a Class by Itself

Styles can either be defined for elements or for classes of elements. A class is a subdivision of an element. What are the classes of an element? Whatever you want them to be. When you create a class, you give it a name and you define the style. When you apply a class to an instance of an element, the element takes on the formatting of the class. Inheritance also comes into play, though, because the element in the class you've created will inherit any formatting from an element that isn't specifically overridden in the class style definition.

Here's an example to help clarify this: You want most of your H2 headings to be blue and italicized, but you want just a few to be green. If you define your standard H2 heading to be blue and italicized and create a class called H2.green, then any H2 headings you mark as having a class of green will be green and italicized. They'll take the green from the class and the italics from the H2 style definition. This is Inheritance at work again.

Does my sheet get published with my web?

Yes. You don't need to do anything special to make sure this happens. FrontPage takes care of it for you.

CASCADING

What are cascades?

Cascading is the term for the way styles are applied, based on the relative weights they accrue by being "closer" to the element. Styles in the sheet are the most distant; they carry the lowest weight. Styles in the style element are less distant; they out-rank styles in the sheet, and they inherit anything they don't override from the styles in the sheet. Styles at the element level have even higher ranking than styles in the style element, and they inherit anything they don't override.

How can I override the styles in my sheet?

You can override the styles in your sheet by putting styles into the style element in the head of your page. Remember, anything you don't override from the style sheet will be inherited by the elements on your page.

How can I override the styles on my page (in the style element)?

If you apply styles at the element level, you will override the styles on your page in the style element. Try to avoid defining styles at that level, though, because maintenance will be particularly painful.

APPLYING STYLE SHEETS

How can I apply styles to elements?

Styles for elements are automatically applied to the elements when you attach a style sheet to a page. If you want to select a class from a style sheet, you need to use the Modify Style dialog box, as shown in Figure 7-6. You can get to the Modify

Figure 7-6 The Modify Style dialog box for applying styles to elements

Style dialog box from any Properties dialog box. Usually, in the lower-left corner of any Properties dialog box there will be a Style button. By clicking the button, you can tell the element which class to apply.

If you still want to apply a style directly to an instance of this element, even though you know it's a bad idea, you can do so by clicking the Format button in the Modify Style dialog box. Then you can format the element exactly as you would a new style sheet definition.

What if I've already applied styles at the element level, but now want them to be at the web level?

Great idea! Even though this seems like a bad time to do this, since your site is already so big, remember that your site will only grow and doing it later will only be more time-consuming. You will have to go back through and remove element-level definitions because the Format | Remove Formatting option doesn't touch styles.

What elements can be modified with style sheets?

Every element in the body of your page can be modified with style sheets. As you can see from the list of elements in Table 7-1, you'd be hard-pressed to find something you can't modify. In general, you can modify headings, paragraphs, blockquotes, tables, images, horizontal rules, and lists.

What about tables? Can I apply styles to tables?

Until recently, tables weren't supported by style sheets, but now you can apply styles to tables. With tables you can modify padding, borders, margins, cell spacing, cell padding, internal rules, background colors of cells, text color within cells, and the background color of the table, for starters.

BROWSER LIMITATIONS OF STYLE SHEETS

Are there any reasons why I shouldn't use style sheets?

Despite the World-Wide Web Consortium's (W3C) most ardent efforts to get all browser makers to comply with their standards, different browsers implement style sheets differently. You can't guarantee that all visitors will see exactly what you see unless they're running the same browser on the same platform on which you developed your site.

Which browsers support style sheets?

That's actually a trick question. Style sheets began to be supported with Internet Explorer 3. Netscape Navigator 3 didn't support them at all. But since the number of things you can change with style sheets has increased since Version 3 and 4 browsers were released, neither of them support all features of cascading style sheets (CSS). The simple answer to this question is that Netscape Navigator 3 and below, and Internet Explorer 2 don't support CSS at all. Later versions of both of these browsers do support CSS to some degree, but not fully and not identically.

Chapter 8

Adding Dynamic HTML (DHTML)

Answer Topics!

- **MAKING SENSE OF DHTML 186**
  - ? What DHTML is
  - ? What makes a DHTML-enhanced Web page different
  - ? How DHTML enhancements are different

- **WORKING WITH THE DHTML TOOLBAR 188**
  - ? Adding the DHTML toolbar
  - ? Moving the DHTML toolbar
  - ? Using the DHTML toolbar
  - ? Accessing DHTML items in FrontPage menus
  - ? How to tell if a DHTML element has been added to an object
  - ? Displaying a DHTML event

- **COOL THINGS DHTML CAN DO 191**
  - ? Swapping one picture for another within a Web page body
  - ? What the Page Transition options are
  - ? Copying DHTML effects from one page element to another
  - ? Removing DHTML effects
  - ? Adding font effects to a hyperlink
  - ? Creating DHTML effects for a hyperlink image
  - ? Creating a collapsible outline

Dynamic HTML @ a Glance

Dynamic HTML (DHTML) is the marketing term for the suite of technologies that enable interesting effects on a page without any server-side interaction. The magic of DHTML is that for the first time you can get the browser page to re-draw itself—either to make space to expand a table of contents or to show a fish swimming through posts—without any extra toll on the server or any special plug-in required on the browser. Before DHTML, the page could only be drawn once based on the data sent from the server. DHTML moves processing off the server onto the browser, where most computers have far more processing power than they are using anyway.

DHTML relies on cascading style sheets (CSS), the document object model (DOM), and JavaScript. Fortunately, with FrontPage you don't need to know or remember any of that! With DHTML, you can add enhancements to your Web page such as text that arrives on or flies off the page a word at a time, links that change color or size, or fancy transition effects between the pages on your site.

Here's what's covered in this chapter on DHTML:

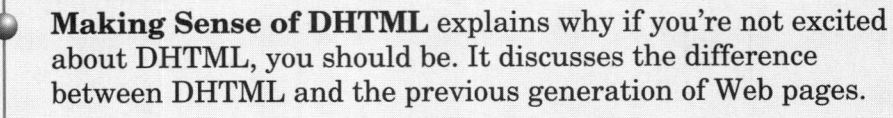

- **Making Sense of DHTML** explains why if you're not excited about DHTML, you should be. It discusses the difference between DHTML and the previous generation of Web pages.

- **Working with the DHTML Toolbar** talks about how the toolbar works and what you can do with it.

- **Cool Things DHTML Can Do** takes you through a few of the most common DHTML tricks you might want your page to do, including swapping pictures on mouse rollover and creating a collapsible outline on your page.

MAKING SENSE OF DHTML

What is DHTML?

Dynamic HTML is actually a group of technologies designed to work together to create and display interactive Web pages. The use of the document object model (DOM) is what allows page developers to access and program a Web page's elements. In other words, because the DOM treats each page element as an object, changes can be made to a page without the need to redraw the entire document.

Dynamic HTML doesn't define an entirely new set of tags or attributes, it makes those tags and attributes totally programmable. In simpler terms, Dynamic HTML is all about control.

DHTML can be *event-driven*. This means that actions on a page can be initiated by the actions of the visitor—for example, text that changes color or an image that leaps out at you or a button that makes a sound when you roll the mouse over it.

Caution: *DHTML won't work consistently on all browsers. Be sure to test anything you create using suggestions in this chapter on both Netscape Navigator and Internet Explorer to make sure you get the results you expect.*

What makes DHTML-enhanced Web pages different?

Before DHTML, Web pages were static. Once the page loaded into a browser, changes couldn't be made to it until the browser went back to the server to download more information. That can be very time-consuming, because it requires the data to travel across the network. In many cases, the inability to do simple changes also took up valuable "real estate" on your page. One such example you'll learn in this chapter is that by using DHTML enhancements, menus and table of contents options can be hidden until the visitor needs them. FrontPage's Dynamic HTML effects make adding such embellishments to your Web pages quick and easy. To access FrontPage's Dynamic HTML effects, select Format | Dynamic HTML Effects.

? How are DHTML enhancements different?

Before Dynamic HTML, Web page designers often had to weigh the appeal of interactivity and custom graphics necessary to attract visitors against the increased download time for those visitors. Dynamic HTML changes all of that because with it, pages can be enhanced so visitors are able to begin scanning the page while it loads, and, once the page is done loading, many page modifications can now be completed "on the client."

That means that page changes can be done in response to visitor actions, such as moving a mouse across some text—the page doesn't have to return to the server to retrieve information in order to complete such a change.

The DOM

The document object model (DOM) is an architectural construct. It's a way of accessing every object on the page by name, or by reference if the object doesn't have a name or you don't know the name. What actually permits you to take action on these objects is JavaScript.

Before the DOM, there was no way to script most objects on your page, but with the DOM, you can call objects by name and take actions on the properties of those objects. For example, an unordered list is an object. The DOM has a name for a given unordered list. The list itself also has properties. One of the properties is the bullet type. Using the DOM, you can refer to the bullet type property of an unordered list. You can't *do* anything to the property, but you can refer to it. That, in itself, is revolutionary!

The downside of the DOM is implementation. Of course, Netscape and Microsoft didn't both do it the same way which means that your scripts need to know which browser is looking at the page before they can refer to the elements properly. Fortunately, FrontPage takes care of this by producing scripts that refer to elements in both browsers properly. Because of this discrepancy in implementation, it's especially good to test your work in both browsers.

WORKING WITH THE DHTML TOOLBAR

How do I add the DHTML toolbar?

The DHTML Effects toolbar is available from the Format menu. You can also select it by selecting View | Toolbars and clicking on DHTML Effects. FrontPage displays the DHTML toolbar. If nothing is selected on your page, the entire toolbar is grayed out. Once you select something, the On drop-down list becomes active. Once you make a selection there, the Apply drop-down list becomes active. After you select something from the list, the Settings list becomes active.

The events listed in the On and Apply drop-down lists will change depending on the type of page element you select. What appears in the place of <Choose Settings> will depend on the element you select and on what choice you made in the Apply drop-down list.

How can I move the DHTML toolbar?

Odds are you won't want the DHTML toolbar to remain in what initially is its default position—the middle of your Normal page view. Not to worry. Moving it to a more convenient location is a snap. Double-click on the title bar and FrontPage moves it automatically, placing it just below the Formatting toolbar toward the top of the page with your other toolbars. Otherwise, you can drag and drop it, if you prefer, to move it to another position.

How do I use the DHTML toolbar?

Select the text or image to which you wish to apply a DHTML effect. Next, you need to choose an event—that action that will trigger the DHTML effect. To choose an event, click the down arrow in the On drop-down list to display a menu of the options available to you for the element you've selected

- Click starts the event after a single click of the left mouse button.
- Double Click starts the event after a double-click of the left mouse button.

Working with the DHTML Toolbar

- Mouse Over triggers the event whenever the mouse pointer touches the object.
- Page Load activates the event whenever the visitor either loads or exits the page.

The illustration below shows the settings available to you for adding dynamic effects to the formatting of text on a mouse over event.

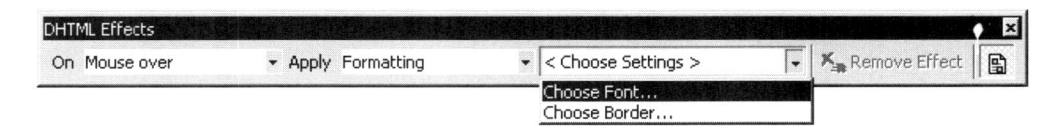

What do I do if I can't access the DHTML items in the FrontPage menus?

If the DHTML menu items are dim, or unavailable, it means that DHTML has been disabled on that page. To enable DHTML, select Tools | Page Options. Click on the Compatibility tab and click to place a check mark in the Dynamic HTML box, as shown in Figure 8-1.

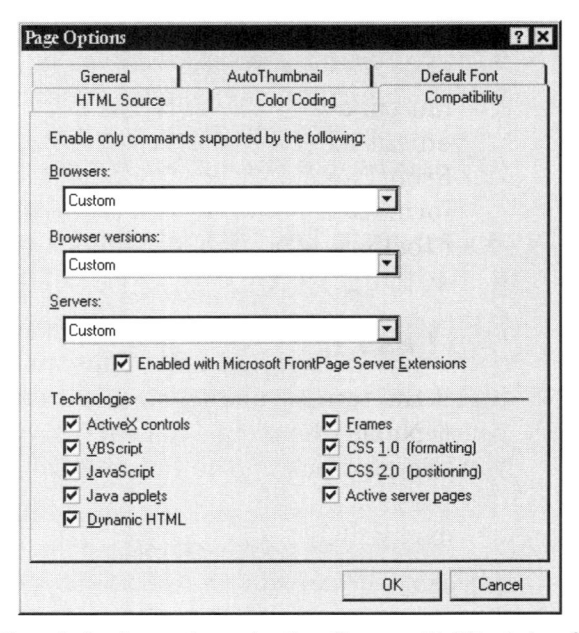

Figure 8-1 The default settings in the Compatibility tab of the Page Options dialog box

Chapter 8 Adding Dynamic HTML (DHTML)

> *Note:* You only want to enable the check box if you have reason to believe that a lot of your visitors are using Internet Explorer 4 or above, or Netscape Navigator 4 or above, as their Web browsers. You also need to be sure to test your site in Internet Explorer 3 or Netscape 3 to make sure what those with older browsers will see is acceptable, since they won't see any dynamic effects.

Is there a way to tell if a DHTML element has been added to an object?

Yes. With your page on the Normal tab in Page view and with the DHTML toolbar enabled, you can turn on highlighting beneath page elements that use DHTML animations or effects. FrontPage puts a box around the affected text or item and adds the highlighting so you can either see which page elements use DHTML animation or effects or verify that you've applied those effects in the way you intended. When you have the toolbar open, the default is for this feature to be active. To make it active, if it's not already, click on the Highlight DHTML Effects, which is the last little box in the DHTML Effects toolbar.

> *Tip:* For those times when you've forgotten which effect you've applied to an element, you can view the details about an effect by pointing at the element. The effect you've applied will appear in a pop-up box just above your mouse pointer.

Once I apply a DHTML event to an object on my page, nothing different seems to happen. Why not?

DHTML effects aren't displayed in Normal view because that's your editing screen. (Can you imagine trying to edit text that changes shape, size, or color, or even all three every time you get the mouse near it?) To see your page in action, you need to click on the Preview tab in Page view.

JavaScript

JavaScript is what makes your DHTML pages *do things*. Using JavaScript, you can change the attributes of the elements that the DOM lets you access. Fortunately, you don't need to write any JavaScript of your own. If you do want to edit JavaScript in the FrontPage HTML view, then you need to modify your options to permit it:

1. Select Tools | Options | Configure Editors, then click Add to add a new entry for JavaScript.
2. Provide the File type of .js, then type in JavaScript for the Editor name, and find the FrontPage application, Frontpg.exe, on your computer by using the Browse button.
3. Click OK when you're done.

Now FrontPage will let you edit JavaScript, if you have a mind to.

COOL THINGS DHTML CAN DO

How can I swap one picture for another within a Web page?

When you want to swap pictures—to show "before" and "after" results, the front and rear views of a home in a real estate listing, or a baby boy by himself and then being held by his big sister—the first thing you need to know is that the pictures must be the same size (or at least have the same proportions). Otherwise, one of the images will be stretched or squashed. Add the first picture and position it on your page, click on the picture to select it, then use the DHTML Effects toolbar to take the following actions:

1. Click the down arrow in the On drop-down list to view your options for actions and select Click.

2. Click the down arrow in the Apply drop-down list to display your actions and select Swap Picture.

3. From the Settings drop-down list, pick Swap picture.

4. From the Picture Select File dialog box, pick your alternative image and click OK.

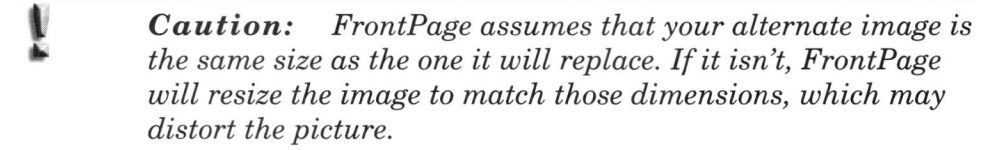

Caution: *FrontPage assumes that your alternate image is the same size as the one it will replace. If it isn't, FrontPage will resize the image to match those dimensions, which may distort the picture.*

How can I allow a visitor action to remove something from the page?

You can add a touch of whimsy to a Web page by having an image or text fly off of the page once the visitor applies a designated action. This is sometimes referred to as *animating an object.* To do this, first select the image or text, then:

1. From the On drop-down list, select Click or Double Click.

2. From the Apply drop-down list, select Fly Out.

3. From the settings drop-down list, select one of the actions, as shown in the illustration below:

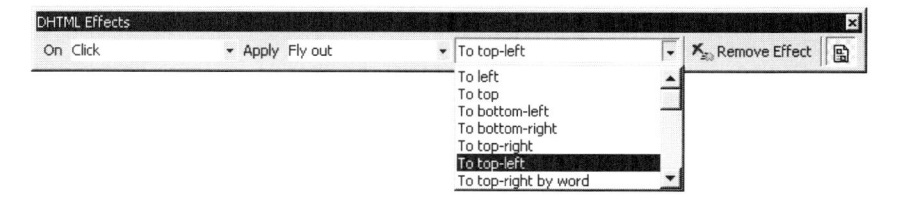

How do I change the font in text when the visitor points to it?

To allow a visitor action to alter formatting, follow these steps:

1. Select the text to which you wish to apply the effect.

2. From the On drop-down list, select Mouse Over.

Cool Things DHTML Can Do

3. From Apply drop-down list, select Formatting.
4. From the Settings drop-down list, select Choose Font, then pick your Font, Font Style, Font Size, Color, and Font Effects from the Font dialog box.

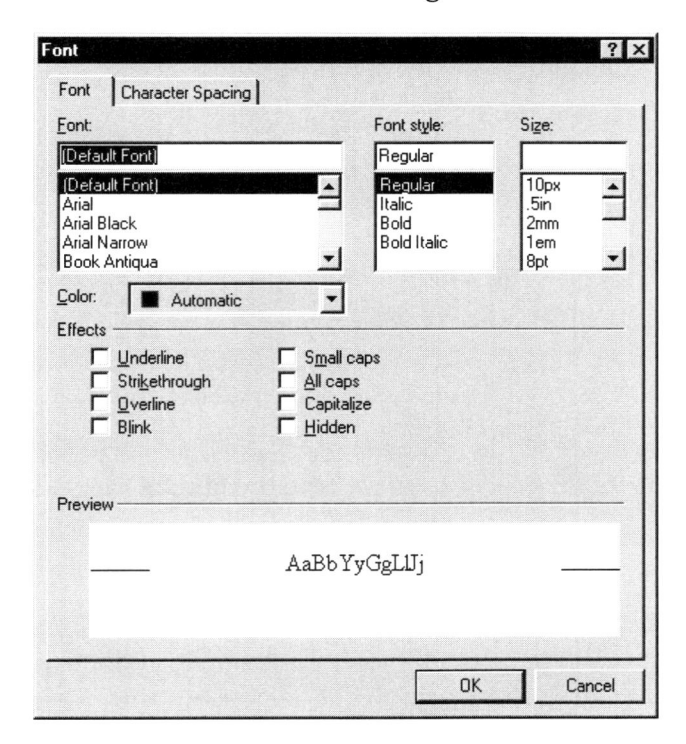

How do I automatically add a border and some shading to text?

You can emphasize text by adding a border and shading to it. To do so, follow these steps:

1. Select the text to which you wish to apply the effect.
2. From the On drop-down list, select Click, Double Click, or Mouse Over.
3. From the Apply drop-down list, select Formatting.
4. From the Settings drop-down list, select Choose Borders.
5. Select your border choice from the Borders tab in the Borders and Shading dialog box

Chapter 8 Adding Dynamic HTML (DHTML)

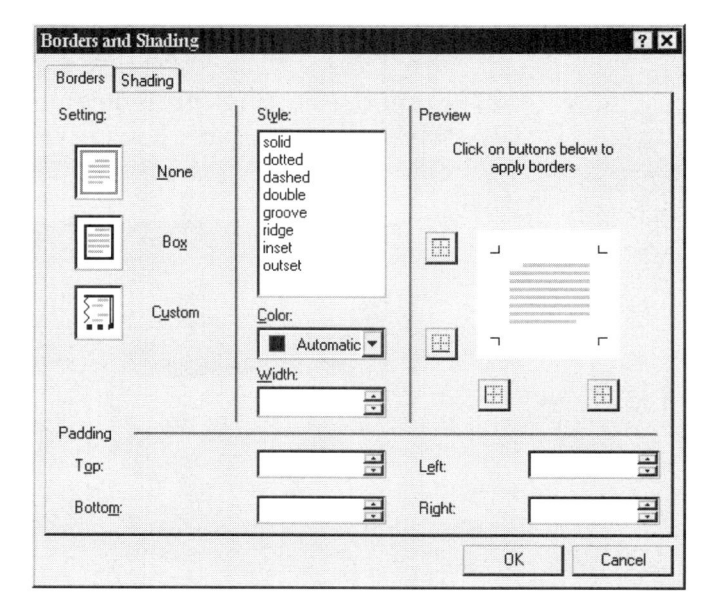

6. In the Preview pane on the right, select the sides of the text on which you'd like to see borders.

7. In the Padding section, add any desired cell padding to the Top, Bottom, Left, and Right.

8. To add any desired cell shading, click on the Shading tab, and select your shading.

> Since I'm also a trivia nut (undefeated family champion—I also occasionally brag), I can't resist mentioning the fact that the same fascination hackers had for coding followed them in their pursuit of cheap food. When they weren't feeding the system, they were feeding them-selves Chinese food.

Note: Don't get carried away with formatting text based on mouse rollovers. The effect is only good when it's used in moderation. Used in excess, it is very annoying. Just because you can apply a certain effect, doesn't mean that you should!

What are the Page Transition options?

You can add some flash to your Web page by selecting Format | Page Transition. FrontPage will display the Page Transitions dialog box.

Cool Things DHTML Can Do

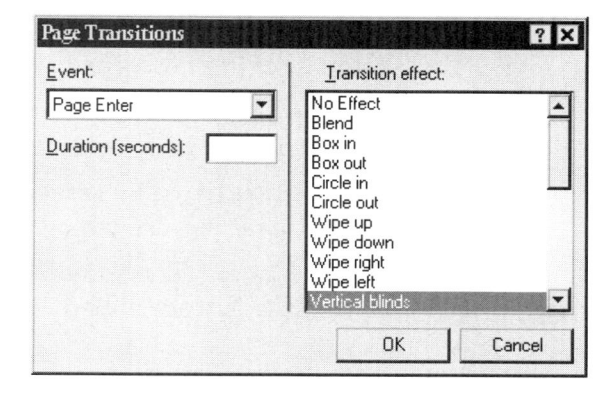

From the Page Transitions dialog box, your choices are:

Event:

- **Page Enter**   Applies a transition to the page on the way into the browser window.
- **Page Exit**   Applies a transition to the page on the way out of the browser window.
- **Site Enter**   Applies a transition to the page when you enter the site.
- **Site Exit**   Applies a transition to the page on the way out of the site.

Duration (seconds): <1-30>

Transition effect:

- **No Effect**   No transition.
- **Blend**   The page blends into the previous page from the top to the bottom.
- **Box In**   The page shrinks to a box in the center of your screen. Better for page or site exits.
- **Box Out**   The page expands from a box in the center of your screen. Better for page or site entrances.
- **Circle In**   Same as Box In with a circle.
- **Circle Out**   Same as Box Out with a circle.

- **Wipe Up** The screen fills in from the bottom to the top as if it were wiped.
- **Wipe Down** The screen fills in from the top to the bottom as if it were wiped.
- **Wipe Right** The screen fills in from the left to the right as if it were wiped.
- **Wipe Left** The screen fills in from the right to the left as if it were wiped.

Tip: *Do your visitors a favor and don't try to use one transition on entering a page and another one on exiting the page for every page in the site or they'll collide! Less is definitely more when it comes to transitions.*

- **Vertical Blinds** The screen is cut into vertical bars, which fade from the current page into the next page (or from the previous page into the current page).
- **Horizontal Blinds** The screen is cut into horizontal bars, which fade from the current page into the next page (or from the previous page into the current page).
- **Checkerboard Across** The new page checkerboards across the old page.
- **Checkerboard Down** The new page checkerboards down the old page.
- **Random Dissolve** The screen appears (or disappears) as random dots on top of (or from) the other page.
- **Split Vertical In** The new page loads from either side until the two halves meet in the middle.
- **Split Vertical Out** The screen splits down the middle to reveal a new page.
- **Split Horizontal In** Same as Split Vertical In but horizontally.

- **Split Horizontal Out** Same as Split Vertical Out but horizontally.
- **Strips Left Down** The page loads as if it were in strips from the top left.
- **Strips Left Up** The page loads as if it were in strips from the bottom left.
- **Strips Right Down** Same as Strips Left Down, but from the right.
- **Strips Right Up** Same as Strips Left Up, but from the right.
- **Random Bars Horizontal** The page loads as horizontal bars, randomly.
- **Random Bars Vertical** The page loads as vertical bars, randomly.
- **Random** The page loads with a random transition.

Tip: *Sometimes the best way to know which DHTML effect will be most effective is to experiment. You can even apply more than one effect to most elements if you wish. Do a little trial and error testing until you achieve results that you like.*

Is there an easy way to copy DHTML effects from one page element to another?

You can use the Format Painter to copy DHTML effects from one page element to another. Select the element whose effect you wish to copy, click the Format Painter icon on the toolbar, and then click on the page element to which you want to apply the DHTML effect.

How can I remove an effect from a page element?

To remove an effect, select the element, then, click the Remove Effect button on the DHTML Effects toolbar.

Chapter 8 Adding Dynamic HTML (DHTML)

How do I add font effects to a hyperlink?

One way to design your hyperlinks is to have them take up a bit less space by being in a smaller font until a visitor runs the mouse across them. By adding a "rollover" effect to a hyperlink so that the font changes color, size, style, or all of these properties, you can grab a visitor's attention. To modify the hyperlinks on a Web page, follow these steps:

1. In Normal view, either select Format | Background or right-click on the page and click Page Properties on the shortcut menu. FrontPage then displays the Page Properties dialog box. Select the Background tab.

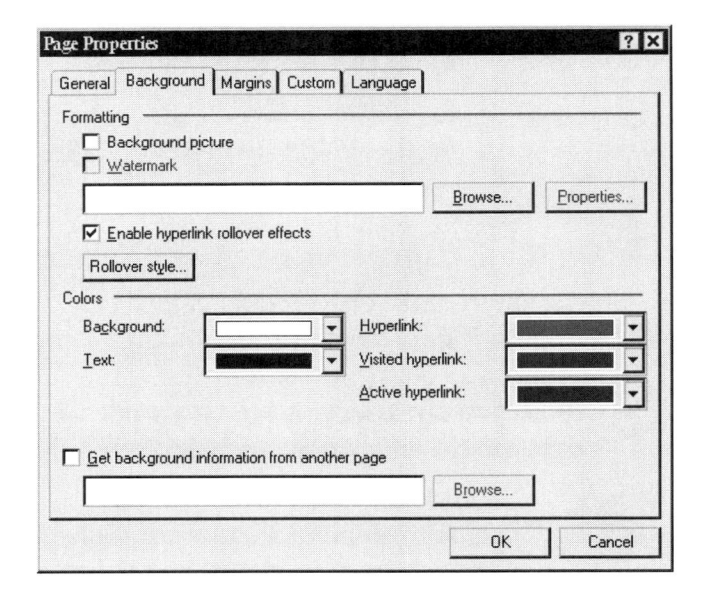

2. Under Formatting, select the Enable Hyperlink Rollover Effects check box.

3. Click the Rollover Style button to bring up the Font dialog box. Select the Font tab.

Cool Things DHTML Can Do

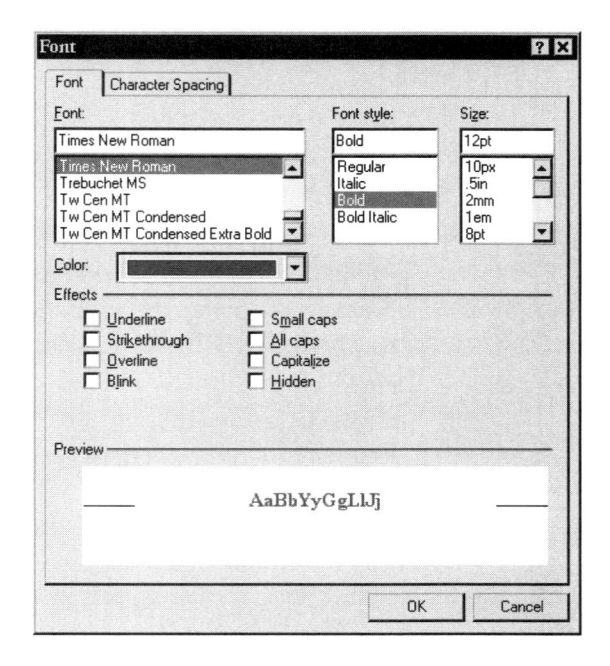

4. From here you can pick your Font, Font Style, Size, Color, and, Effects. Format the font as you want it to look when the mouse is over it. You can see how it will look in the Preview pane.

5. Click OK to apply the changes.

Caution: *Rollover effects cannot be added to a hyperlink if the Web page uses a theme.*

How do I create DHTML effects for hyperlink images?

You can create an animation-style effect by applying the Swap Picture option to image hyperlinks. To do so:

1. Select the picture to swap.
2. In the On drop-down list on the DHTML Effects toolbar, select the Mouse Over option.

3. From the Apply drop-down list on the DHTML Effects toolbar, select Swap Picture (the only option). When you select the Swap Picture option, FrontPage places the option <Choose Settings> in the Settings drop-down list to the immediate right of the Apply drop-down list.

4. From the newly displayed Settings drop-down list, select Choose Picture, which is the only option. When you select this option, FrontPage displays the Picture dialog box, from which you may select the picture you want to swap.

5. If you are uncertain of which picture you want to select, click on the icon of the file folder with the magnifying glass over it (in the lower-right of the Picture dialog box). FrontPage then displays the Select File dialog box. Make your selection and click OK to apply.

Note: *If you have a theme with active graphics, then your theme is already using the hyperlink rollover you just learned above.*

How do I create a collapsible outline?

Collapsible outlines are popular. And, they're easy to do. To create a collapsible list, do the following:

1. Create a bulleted or numbered list.

2. Select the list items you want to collapse and click the Increase Indent button on the Formatting toolbar two times. (This will indent the secondary list items below the top list item and allow you to apply a different bullet or number style to those items.)

3. Select the indented list items and right-click to display the List Properties dialog box.

Cool Things DHTML Can Do

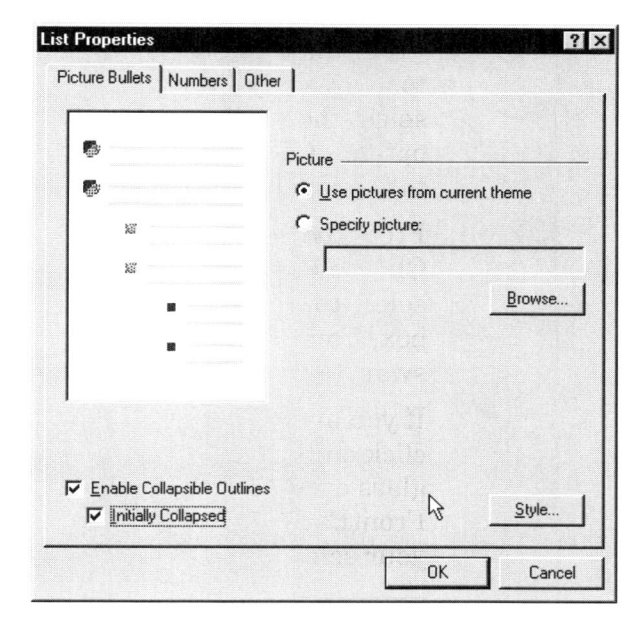

4. Click the Enable Collapsible Outlines check box.
5. Next, click the Initially Collapsed check box to make it active. Clicking this check box ensures that all of your lists will start out collapsed.
6. Click OK.

Repeat steps 1-6 to apply the collapsed list formatting to any remaining list items.

Chapter 9

Integrating FrontPage with Access

Answer Topics!

DATABASES 205
- Relational databases
- Creating a relational database
- The fastest way to create a database
- Letting FrontPage do it for you

ACCESS DATABASES 207
- Adding a table to your database
- Seeing how you've defined the fields (columns) in a table

TEXT FILES OR OTHER NON-ACCESS SOLUTIONS 210
- Writing results to a text file
- Using a different database
- What to do if your database resides on another machine

MAPPING FIELDS (COLUMNS) TO FORM FIELDS 219
- Form fields that are available on a Web page
- Defining a field for a text input box
- Defining a field for a check box
- Defining a field for radio buttons
- Defining a field for a drop-down menu or a list
- Defining a field for a scrolling text box
- Making it clear to Access that all fields aren't required

GETTING FRONTPAGE TO USE YOUR ACCESS DATABASE 223
- Telling the web to use your database
- Writing data to your database
- Getting data from your database into a web page

Integrating FrontPage with Access @ a Glance

Creating dynamic Web sites has never been easier. Before you get too excited, though, realize that nothing in this chapter will work unless your Web server is Microsoft's Internet Information Server (IIS) with the FrontPage 2000 extensions installed. So, if IIS is your Web server, then proceed with enthusiasm.

Creating a dynamic Web site has two parts: getting data and displaying data. This chapter focuses on displaying data from a database. Chapter 10 focuses on the form fields required to accept data from the Web.

- **Databases** This section will help you understand what a database is and how it holds your data. You'll learn how to create an efficient database. You'll even learn the very coolest feature of FrontPage 2000—it can create a database on-the-fly based on the fields in your form.

- **Access Databases** In this section you'll get a short course in Access.

- **Text Files or Other Non-Access Solutions** If you're not ready to use a database and think a text file will be an adequate method of storing your data, or if your database isn't Access, that's okay, too. Read this section to answer your other database-related questions.

- **Mapping Fields (Columns) to Form Fields** You may already have a form design in mind, since you probably already have an idea which questions you want to have answered. In this section we'll talk about how each type of form field (discussed in detail in Chapter 10) maps to a database field.

- **Getting FrontPage to Use Your Access Database** Finally, we'll talk about how FrontPage makes it easy to include data from your database in a Web page using the Database Results Wizard.

LET'S TALK DATABASES

Databases are a way to organize data with things in common. Databases are an ideal way to store data that fits a particular pattern. For example, if you have many sets of answers to the same survey, then you can store them in a database with each complete set of answers becoming a *row* in a table, and the answer to each question making up a *column*.

In order to understand the language of databases, you need to know the vocabulary:

- **Database**   A place to store multiple tables of data with relationships defined between tables, and indexes on each table allowing quick access to the data within tables.

- **Table**   A repository for data, which is added by the row, and has columns in common. A table will usually have a key and indexed fields.

- **Row**   A data entry in a table. The answers to all the questions on a form submitted by one individual visitor would populate a row.

- **Column (or field)**   A placeholder for data in every row. The answer to a single question for every row in the table would reside in the same column or field.

- **Key**   A way to uniquely identify a row within a table. A key can be data that exists, such as social security number, or data that is created when the row is added, such as a record ID.

- **Index**   The way a table maintains quick access to a particular row in a table. Indexing is usually automatic with a key, but can be assigned by you to other non-key fields.

- **Relationships**   Fields in two or more different tables in common such that the combining of those two or more records provide complete information about a single record.

- **Relational Database**   A database with no redundant data. All redundant data is moved into a new table, with shared keys.

DATABASES

What is a relational database?

A relational database is basically the *platonic form* of databases. Ideally, all databases are relational. A relational database is special because there's no redundant data. Redundant data is bad because the more copies of data that exist, the more chances there are for one or more copy of the data to be wrong or become out of date.

Consider a database that stores information about a sales transaction. Two kinds of data one must always provide when shopping online are *billing address* and *shipping address*. A good database designer will put the address information into a separate table from the rest of the transaction information. Then, in place of the billing information, the transaction table would have just the keys of the entry or entries in the address table. The address table, would have one or two entries, depending on whether the billing and shipping addresses were the same or different. Figure 9-1 makes this relationship clearer.

Do I need to create a relational database?

No, but it's not a bad idea. In Figure 9-1, if you had let the visitor key his address data twice, he'd be annoyed, and he'd be more likely to make a typing error. Using relational design makes your database smaller, although it can make it slower, if you tend to reconstruct the real data often enough. If you only use the address data in the context of the transaction, then it's not as necessary to pull it aside into its own table.

Generally speaking, the more places the data appears, the more likely you are to have one copy of that data that's wrong or out of date. If you have multiple copies of data, then when you do updates, you'll need to keep track of all the copies and make sure they all get updated. If you're not careful with your updates, you can wreak havoc on your data. Take, for example, an insurance company that keeps address data in one too many places. Suppose someone covered by the company called to update the address on his auto insurance.

Chapter 9 Integrating FrontPage with Access

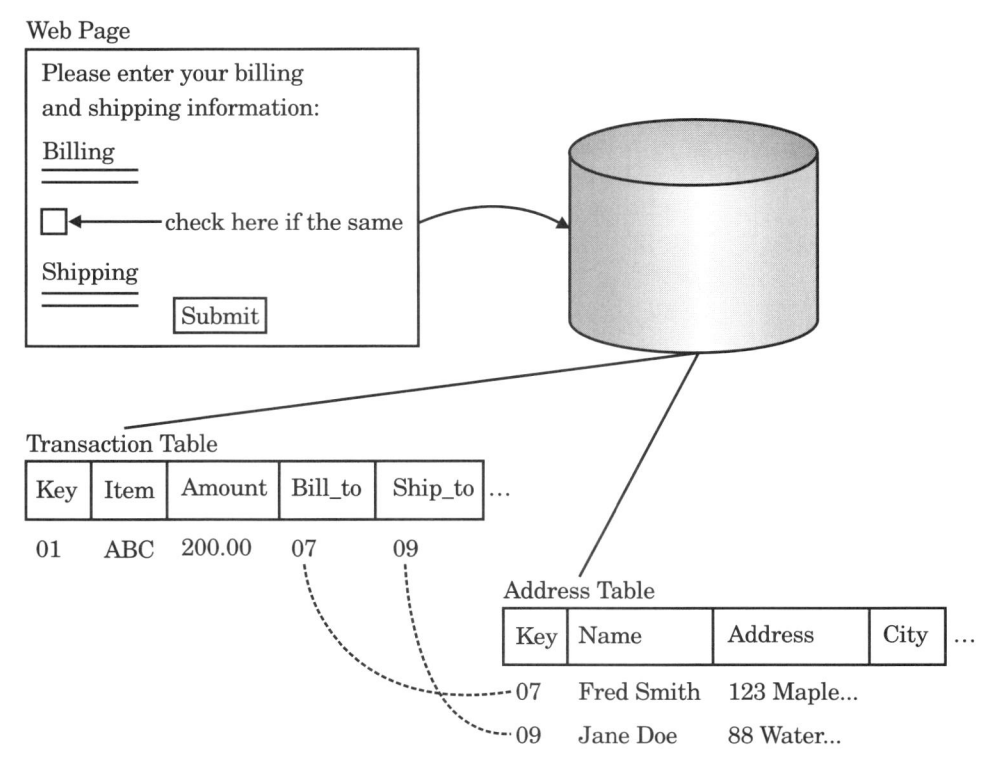

Figure 9-1 Storing data in a relational database

The address could be corrected in one table so that the bill comes to the right address, but because not all tables or fields were updated, he could still be insured for having his car at the wrong address, which might be in an entirely different state with entirely different rates.

What's the fastest way to create a database?

The fastest way to create a database is to let FrontPage do it for you! If you are working in a web and are publishing to a Web server with FrontPage 2000 server extensions installed (and you have the Compatibility dialog box set to Custom server), then once you've set up a form (which is discussed in the next chapter) and edit the form properties, you'll have the option of letting FrontPage create a database on the fly for you! Once you let FrontPage create an Access database for you, you'll still need to know a thing or two about Access databases, if you ever want to change your form.

How can FrontPage create a database for me?

Words cannot express how cool this feature is! And it's twice that easy! Just follow these steps:

1. For a form you've created as part of a web (either by hand or by using the Form Wizard), click anywhere inside the form.

2. Right-click and select Form Properties. If Send To Database is grayed out, close the dialog box, select Tools | Options and open up the Compatibility tab of the Options dialog box, and then change the Web server to Custom, making sure that all the boxes below are checked. Return to the Form Properties dialog box, Send To Database should no longer be grayed out.

3. Click the Send To Database radio button, and click OK.

4. Agree to edit your settings, since you've not set them yet and FrontPage will tell you they're set incorrectly.

5. Click the Create Database button. Agree to let FrontPage put it into the fpdb folder.

6. To save your form data into your new database, follow the directions under the question, "How do I write data to my database?," later in this chapter.

ACCESS DATABASES

How do I add a table to my database?

If you've used the wizard to create your database, then the first thing you'll see when you start your database is a fancy *switchboard* screen with access to all the things that the wizard includes. If you let FrontPage create your database, or if you started with a blank database, then you can skip step 1, because the Database window will already be open. Otherwise, start here:

1. If you want to add a table, you'll need to open up the database page for the database. To do that, click on the drop-down Window menu from Access's main menu, and select Contacts: Database (where *Contacts* is the name you've given to your database).

2. Select the Tables object, and choose Create Table in Design View (Figure 9-1 shows this selection). Access then displays the Table Design View with an open table.

3. Add the field names in the Field Names column. For each field, you need to define the data type. Data types are described in detail later in this chapter. In the lower pane, you can dictate the details of how a field is defined. You can see that our modified field is defined as Date/Time, with the format being Short Date.

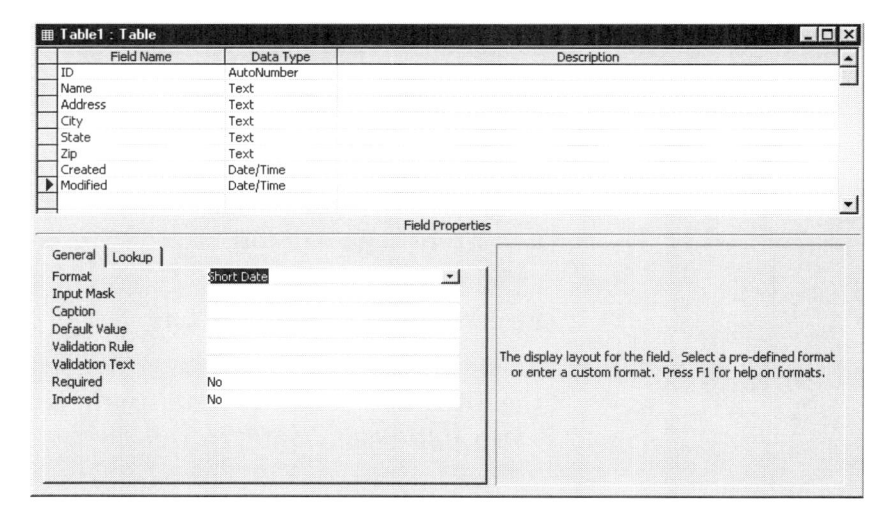

4. When you're done defining fields, click on the floppy disk icon in Access's main toolbar to save your table. Access will ask you to name your table. If you haven't defined a key, Access will ask you to create one. Unless you have no intention of ever accessing any record individually, agree to let Access create a key for you. You'll recall that a *key* is a unique identifier of a record.

How can I see how I've defined the fields (columns) in a table?

With your database open, from Access's main menu select Tools | Analyze | Documenter. Access then displays the Documenter dialog box, as shown in the following illustration. If you can't access this feature, you'll need to re-run the Installation tool and choose to have all the features of Access installed. If disk space is an issue, you won't be able to view your complete table definitions.

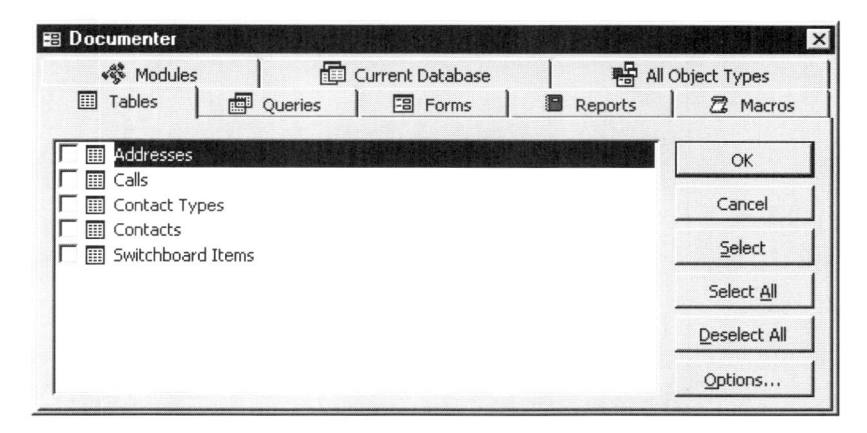

In the Documenter dialog box, select the Tables tab. Then check the boxes next to any tables you want to document (refer to the preceding illustration). Unless you click Options, you'll probably get far more information than you need, so click Options, and you'll get the Print Table Definition dialog box.

In most cases of database use, all you need is the minimum information: field names, data types, and sizes. Click OK to set the options. Access closes the Print Table Definition dialog box and the Documenter dialog box is visible again.

Click OK on the Documenter to create your report. This report will give you all the field definitions in one place, which will be handy when you're creating your forms and your results tables in this and the next chapters.

Note: You can only have one report open at a time.

TEXT FILES OR OTHER NON-ACCESS SOLUTIONS

Can I write my results to a text file?

You can write your results to a text file, but you can't show results from your text file on a Web page. If you want to show the data you've collected, you need to use an ODBC-compliant database.

Text Files or Other Non-Access Solutions 211

ODBC

Open Database Connectivity (ODBC) has made getting at data within a database relatively easy. ODBC allows a program to speak to it in its friendly language, then it converts the commands into the specific language that the database understands. No matter how many upgrades the database goes through, as long as it remains ODBC-compliant, your program will still be able to talk to it.

Before ODBC, if you wanted your program to talk to a database, you had to find out the commands that that database understood, and then write them. If the commands of the database changed, you had to change all your programs. If you had to migrate to a bigger database, you had to change all your programs to send and receive the commands of the new database. OBDC makes migration between databases and communication with databases much easier.

Access, SQL Server, Oracle, and Sybase are all ODBC-compliant. Check to see whether your database program is too. If it is, it's basically interchangeable with any of the other ODBC-compliant programs from the perspective of the program or the Web page.

Can I use a different database?

As long as your database is ODBC-compliant and on a server that's accessible to your Web server via the Internet, you can use any database you choose. The instructions later in the chapter address how to use an Access database that's part of your Web. If you'd like to use another database that meets the requirements of being ODBC-compliant and is accessible via the Internet, then follow the instructions immediately following this paragraph to get FrontPage to connect to it. Since these instructions are a tad more complex, they've been broken up into sections. Your systems administrator might be able to help you out with any issues that arise that are specific to your local installation. Network configuration can complicate things significantly. The instructions below assume the least complex network configuration and no firewall. If you have problems, consult a networking book such as Osborne's *Windows NT Troubleshooting*, by Kathy Ivens, 1998 (ISBN: 0-07-882471-0).

The Configuration

ODBC permits you to have your database reside on the same physical machine as the Web server, or on another machine to which the Web server can connect. To further complicate matters, you can be developing your web on the same machine as the Web server, or on your own machine. Figure 9-2 shows three possible configurations you might have for deployment of a Web site with a database back-end.

There are actually four possible scenarios:

1. Development and deployment on the same physical machine
2. Development and deployment on different physical machines with the database residing on the Web server
3. Development and deployment on different physical machines with the database residing on its own machine
4. Development and deployment on different physical machines with the database on the deployment machine

It would be difficult to imagine a business reason for the last scenario, scenario 4, so it's not included in Figure 9-2.

The Connection

If you're going to develop and deploy on the same machine, chances are the database will reside there as well. If so, then you need only create a single ODBC entry so that both FrontPage and the Web server can find the database. If the database does reside on another machine on the network, you still need only define one ODBC entry, but you'll have to make sure that you have a network connection to the drive on which the database resides.

If you're working with Scenarios 2, 3, or 4, then you need to create two different ODBC connections: one on your FrontPage development machine, and one on your Web server. Both of them should point to the same database, wherever it resides. Two of the most common databases to

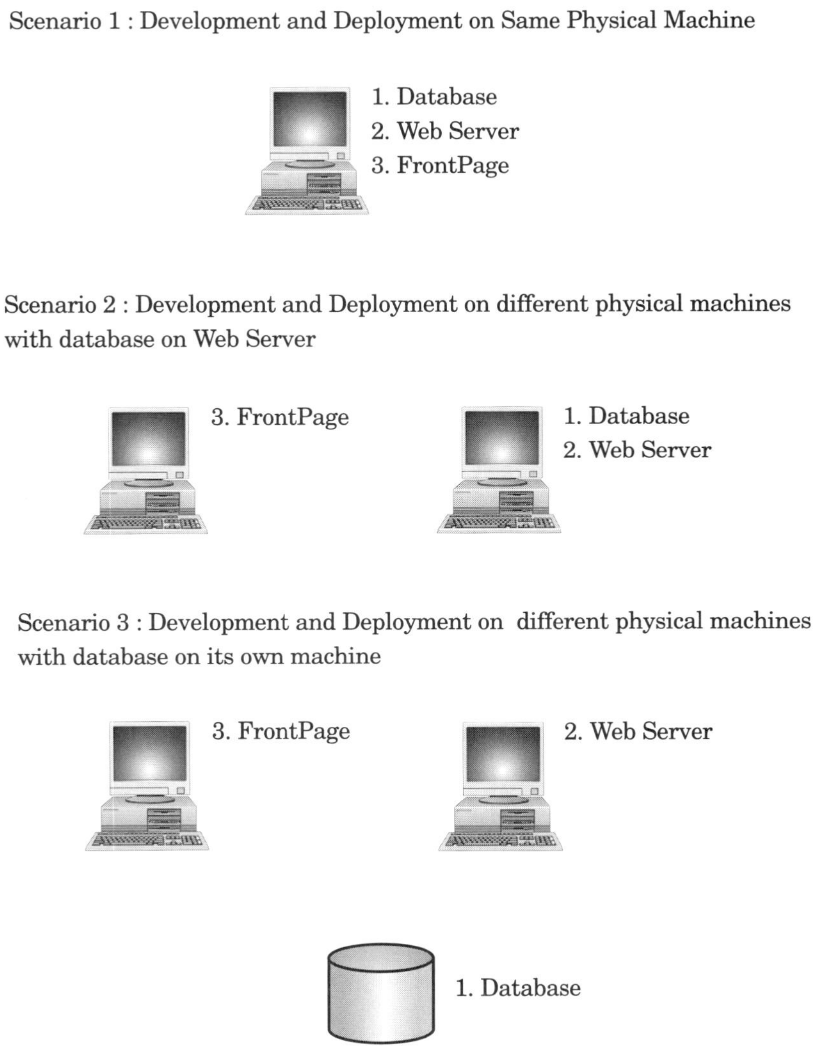

Text Files or Other Non-Access Solutions

Scenario 1 : Development and Deployment on Same Physical Machine

1. Database
2. Web Server
3. FrontPage

Scenario 2 : Development and Deployment on different physical machines with database on Web Server

3. FrontPage

1. Database
2. Web Server

Scenario 3 : Development and Deployment on different physical machines with database on its own machine

3. FrontPage

2. Web Server

1. Database

Figure 9-2 Three possible configurations for deployment of a Web site with a database back-end

which you're likely to connect are SQL Server and Access. Instructions for creating ODBC entries for both follow.

SQL SERVER To create an ODBC connection for a SQL Server database, follow these steps:

Chapter 9 Integrating FrontPage with Access

1. Open your Windows Control Panel by clicking on the Start menu. Then select Settings | Control Panel. Windows will display the open Control Panel.

2. Double-click ODBC Data Sources. (Your system may call it something slightly different.) When you double-click the ODBC Data Sources option, Windows displays the tabbed ODBC Data Source Administrator.

3. Click on the Drivers tab (see the following illustration), and make sure that the driver for the database to which you're planning to connect is on the list. If it's not, see if it came with the database and install the appropriate driver. You might also find an ODBC driver for the database on the Web site of the database manufacturer.

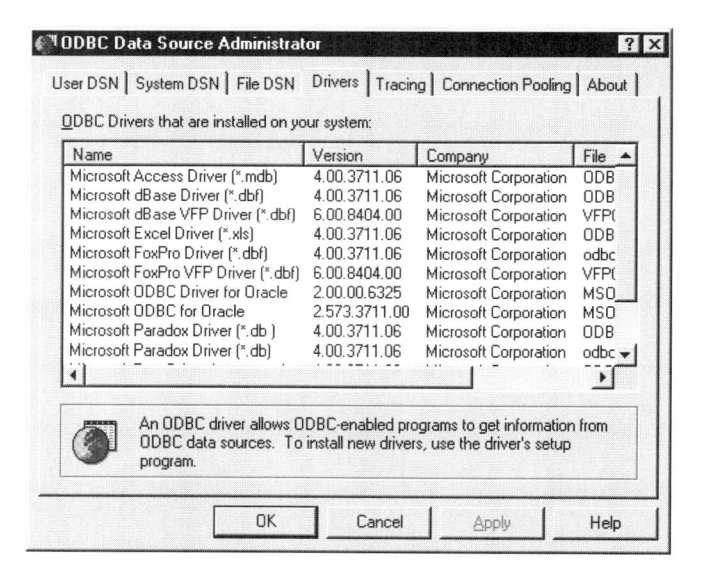

4. Still working in the tabbed ODBC Data Source dialog box, click on the System DSN tab (see the following illustration). The System DSN tab is where you will see the ODBC entry for the database you'd like to access, once you've created it. Chances are your list will be empty. This list has three entries.

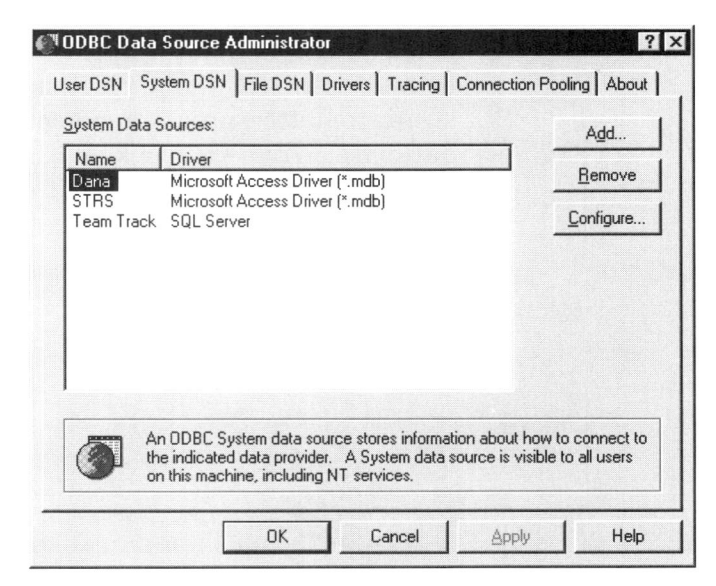

Text Files or Other Non-Access Solutions   215

[ODBC Data Source Administrator dialog, System DSN tab showing Dana, STRS, and Team Track data sources]

5. Click Add to create your ODBC entry, and Windows will display the Create New Data Source dialog box (as shown in the following illustration). In this example, you can see we've elected to create an entry for a SQL server database.

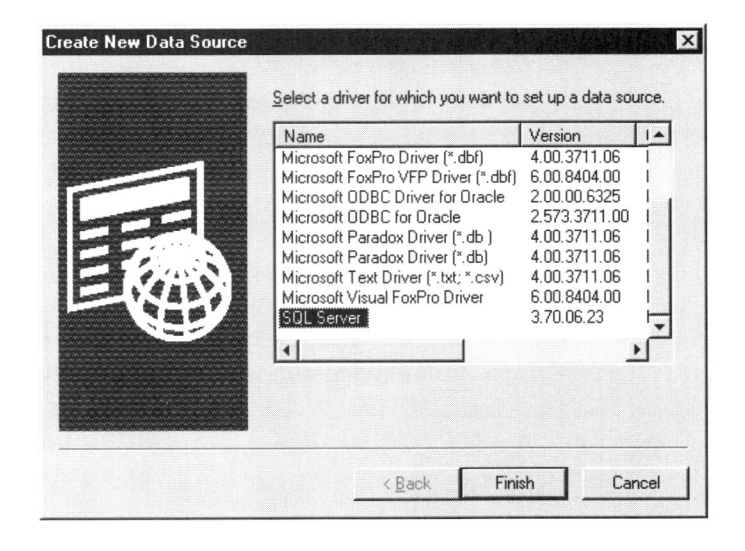

[Create New Data Source dialog box with SQL Server driver selected from list of available drivers]

Chapter 9 Integrating FrontPage with Access

6. Click on the database driver you'd like to use to connect to your database. Click Finish (which is not a very accurate button name) to name and identify the database. When you click on Finish, Windows displays the Create a New Data Source to SQL Server dialog box (as shown in the following illustration).

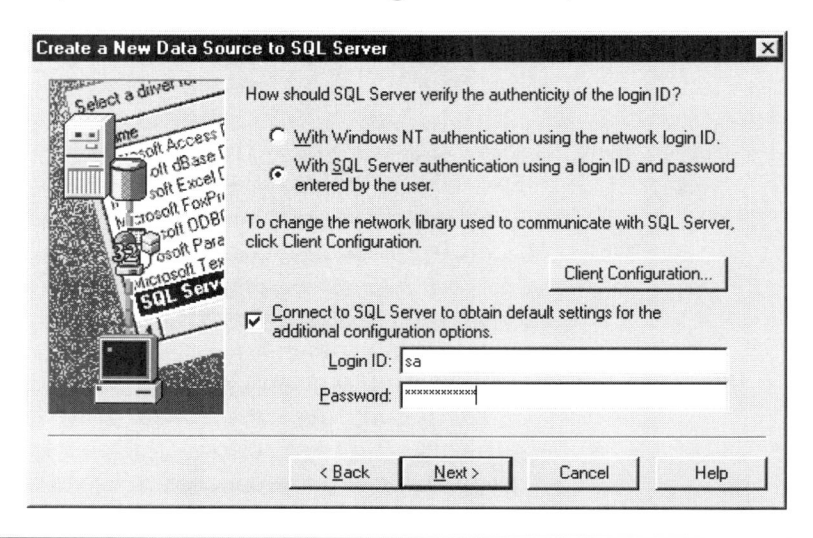

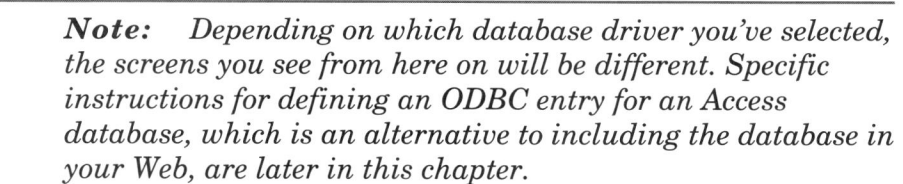

Note: Depending on which database driver you've selected, the screens you see from here on will be different. Specific instructions for defining an ODBC entry for an Access database, which is an alternative to including the database in your Web, are later in this chapter.

7. Give your database connection a short name, a meaningful description, and identify the name of the SQL server on which your database resides. Your SQL server must be on your network. Click Next. Define authentication and provide a login and password.

Note: More than one database can reside on a single SQL server. You'll indicate which database you want to use later.

8. You must now provide security information for the database. Do you want to use NT authentication? If so, however you signed into Windows is how you will

connect to the database. Do you have a special ID and password for your SQL server? We chose the latter. Click Next.

9. Now you can indicate which database (if there is more than one) on the SQL server you'd like to use. Click Next.

10. We'll go with the defaults and click Next. Windows displays the SQL Server ODBC Data Source Test screen.

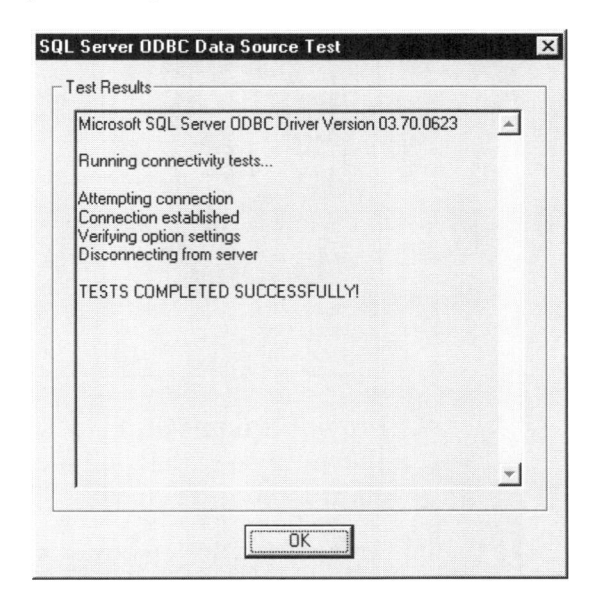

Finally, you're done answering questions. You can test your ODBC connection to make sure it works by clicking Test Data Source. If you did everything right in all of the previous steps, you'll see the screen shown above. If you do not get this screen, try again or consult a network administrator to get configuration information. You might have to change some of the defaults we left alone. If your connection works, click OK, then OK again (or you'll lose all your work).

Now you should see the list of connections in the System DSN tab with your connection on the list.

ACCESS Fortunately, connecting to an Access database, either on the local machine or a remote machine, is far less complex than connecting to a SQL server.

Chapter 9 Integrating FrontPage with Access

1. Follow steps 1 through 4 as defined above for connecting to a SQL server.
2. Click Add to create your Access ODBC entry. Select the Access driver and click Finish.

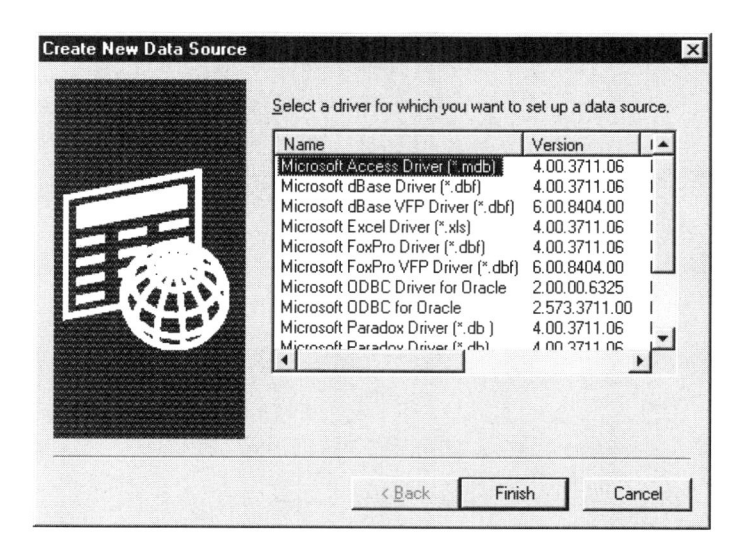

3. Provide a name and a description for your database (as shown in the following illustration), then click Select to point to your database.

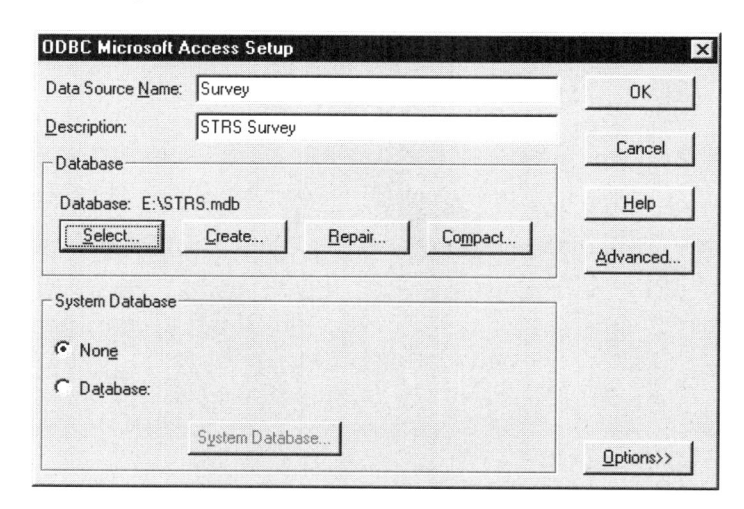

4. Locate the Access database. You need to be able to connect to it either locally, or through a mapped drive. (Chapter 12 explains how to map a drive to a remote computer, if you don't already know how to do that and if your Access database resides on a remote computer.) Click OK. Then click OK again to complete the ODBC definition.

5. You'll be returned to the System DSN tab of the ODBC Administrator. Your database is now on the list.

What if my database resides on another machine?

If your database resides on another machine, then you simply need to create an ODBC entry for your database. In order for your ODBC entry to work, the database must be on a computer that's on a network your computer can reach. Complete details for defining ODBC entries are provided in the previous section of this chapter, under the question *"Can I use a different database?"*

MAPPING FIELDS (COLUMNS) TO FORM FIELDS

What form fields are available on a Web page?

You've seen lots of forms on lots of Web pages. You have an idea of what types of questions you want to ask, but you don't necessarily know how form fields map to database field or vice versa. This section will help you understand how Web form fields should be defined in your database. Figure 9-3 shows all the form fields available for use on a Web page.

How should I define a field for a text input box?

A text input box, also referred to as a *one-line text box*, maps to a text field in Access. In both the form and the database, you can define the maximum length of text you want to permit a visitor to enter. In FrontPage, you can set validation rules that specify both a minimum and a maximum length.

Chapter 9 Integrating FrontPage with Access

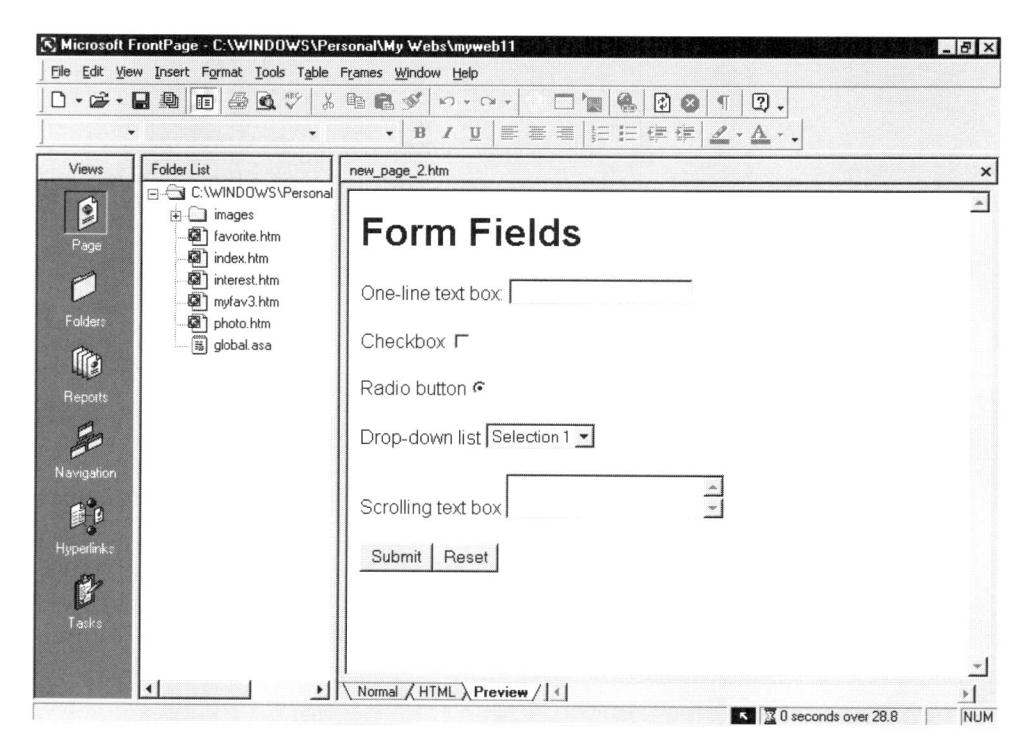

Figure 9-3 Web form fields

Note: *Validating form results is discussed in detail in Chapter 10.*

How should I define a field for a check box?

The most common way is to define the field as a Yes/No field (known as *Boolean* by computer programmers). The Web server sends only a Yes or a No to your database unless you assign a value to the checked state; this is discussed in more detail in Chapter 10. Since you can only send a value when the check box is checked, it's difficult to imagine why you would want to define it any other way in the database.

How should I define a field for radio buttons?

In most cases, your best bet will be to use a text field for answers to radio buttons. If the caption of the radio button differs from the value you send to the server, and the value you send to the server is a number, then you can use a small numerical field, rather than a text field. Small numerical fields, such as Byte, which holds numbers 0-255, are more efficient, faster to process, and take up less space than text fields. It's also faster to perform calculations on numerical fields than it is to perform calculations on text fields. Consider the form in Figure 9-4. By scoring the values of the radio buttons with the values 5 through 1, determining the average response is much easier than if the same results were stored as text answers.

Figure 9-4 The answers to these questions will be easier to tally if the values sent to the database are numeric, rather than text

Chapter 9 Integrating FrontPage with Access

? How should I define a field for a drop-down menu or a list?

Data from a drop-down menu can be either text or numeric. This means that you can use a text field or a numeric field. Even if the values that appear in the drop-down menu are text, you can configure FrontPage to send numeric data to the database so that the field definitions in Access will be numeric. However, you need to be sure that the data you receive into the database is meaningful. If numbers wouldn't be meaningful, then send text to the database, store it as text, and perform processes on it as text.

? How should I define a field for a scrolling text box?

Access provides a field called Memo for text data that's longer than 255 characters. You'll definitely want to use the Memo field for scrolling text boxes. The only problem with the Memo field is that you can't perform any kind of processing on it. All you can do with a Memo field is report its results.

? Access gives me an error if the visitor doesn't complete all the fields. How can I make it so that all my fields aren't required?

When you create a new field in Design view in Access, the default is that the field isn't required. However, the default is also that zero-length isn't permitted. Even though just above that, the property called Required is set to No, the Allow Zero Length property is also set to No. This means that if you try to send an empty—that is to say, zero-length—field to the database, it will return an error to the server. If your database is going to collect data from the Web, be sure to change the value of Allow Zero Length from No to Yes, so you won't continue to have this problem.

GETTING FRONTPAGE TO USE YOUR ACCESS DATABASE

How do I tell the web to use my database?

First of all, you need to be sure that your Page Settings are set such that FrontPage knows that the server on which you're publishing the web is Microsoft Internet Information Server, or another server which supports Active Server Pages (ASP).

Adjust Your Page Settings

To adjust page settings, follow these steps:

1. From FrontPage's main menu, select Tools | Page Options. FrontPage will display the Page Options dialog box. Click on the Compatibility tab, shown here, to set the server information.

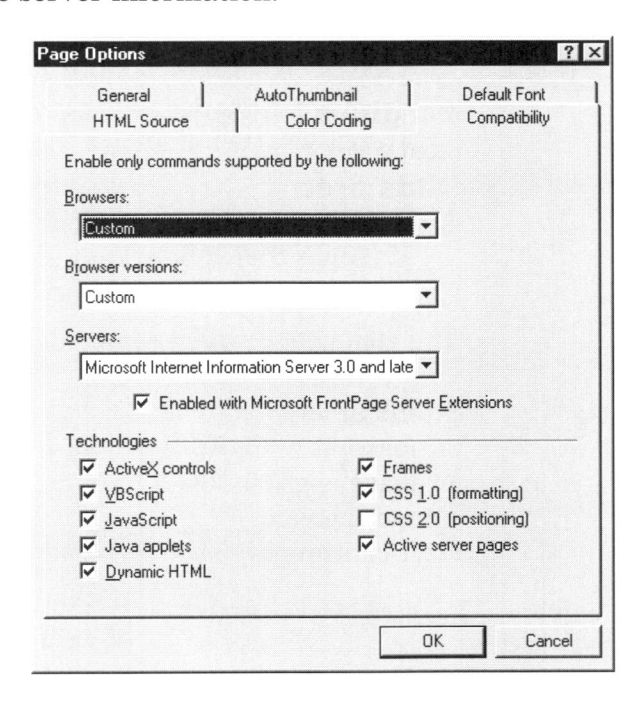

2. Make sure the Servers drop-down list is set to Microsoft Internet Information Server 3.0 and Later. If you don't have this option set, nothing else in the remainder of the

Chapter 9 Integrating FrontPage with Access

chapter will work for you. If the FrontPage extensions are installed on the server, then check the check box next to that option. In order to use FrontPage's full database capabilities, you'll need to publish to a server with the extensions installed.

3. Click OK.

Tell your web to use a database

Now, you need to tell your web to use a database. If the database is an Access database that you'd like to include in the web (meaning that you don't need to get at it through Access directly), then follow these steps:

1. Select FrontPage's Folders view, and then select File | Import. FrontPage will display the Import dialog box.

Note: *In order for the Import command to appear in black on your File menu, you must be in a web, and you must be in Folders view. You can't import a database into a page.*

2. From the Import dialog box, select the Add File option. FrontPage then displays the Add File to Import List dialog box.

3. Find the database on your hard drive in the familiar File Manager dialog box. Your selected database should now appear on the list of files to be imported.

4. Click OK. FrontPage will display the Add Database Connection dialog box as shown in the following illustration. FrontPage will prompt you for the name for your database connection. FrontPage will create an ODBC connection for you.

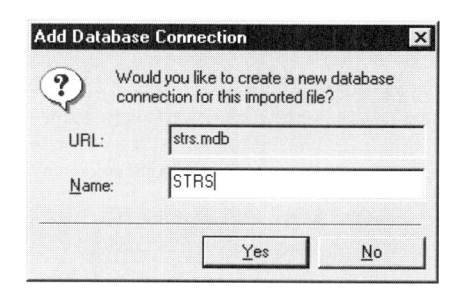

Getting FrontPage to Use Your Access Database   225

5. Finally, FrontPage will display a window that asks you if you want to store the database in a FPDB folder. Click Yes.

If your database is one you either can't or don't want to import into FrontPage, then create your ODBC connection, as explained previously in this chapter in the question *"Can I use a different database?"*

Tell FrontPage About Your Database

Now, follow these instructions to provide FrontPage with information about your database:

1. On FrontPage's main menu select Tools | Web Settings. FrontPage will display the Web Settings dialog box. Select the Database tab.

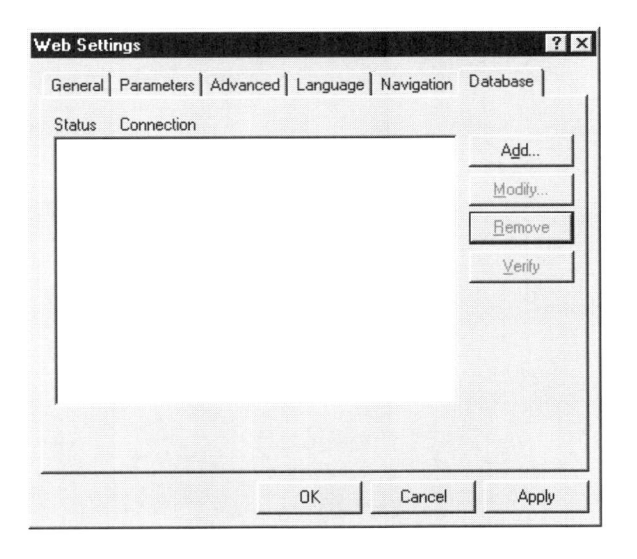

2. If you have any database connections defined, such as an Access database you've imported, they'll be listed here. To add a new connection, click Add. You'll see the New Database Connection dialog box.

Chapter 9 Integrating FrontPage with Access

3. Click on System Data Source On Web Server to indicate that you want to use an ODBC connection. Then click Browse to view all the ODBC connections defined for the computer on which you're working. When you click Browse, FrontPage displays the System Data Source On Web Server window. Notice that the computer on which these screens were captured had four ODBC entries.

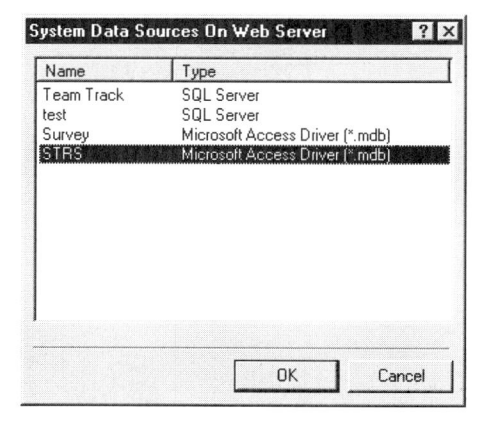

4. Once you select an ODBC connection, FrontPage will redisplay the New Database Connection dialog box, where you can give the connection a name, and then click OK.

5. When you click OK, FrontPage redisplays the Database tab with your ODBC connection listed in it. Now, you're ready to start working with your database in FrontPage.

Getting FrontPage to Use Your Access Database

? How do I write data to my database?

You might need to read ahead a bit in Chapter 10 to understand all of the answer to this question. In order to write to a database, you need to have a form created. Ideally, your form field names will perfectly match the field names in the database. Once you have your form created, you have the database connection defined in your web, and you have your Compatibility Options set to use Microsoft Internet Information Server, you're ready to tell FrontPage that you want the data from your form saved into your database.

1. On your form page, right-click somewhere where there are neither fields nor text within the form. FrontPage will display the shortcut menu. Select Form Properties, and FrontPage will display the Form Properties dialog box.

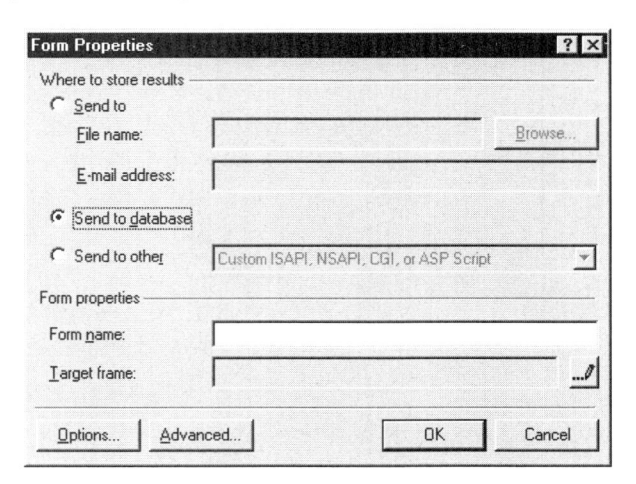

2. Click the Send to Database radio button, and then click OK. FrontPage will then display a warning message that says your settings are invalid, and asks whether you want to edit them now. Click Yes to edit them now.

3. When you click Yes to edit your settings, FrontPage displays the Options for Saving Results to Database dialog box.

Chapter 9 Integrating FrontPage with Access

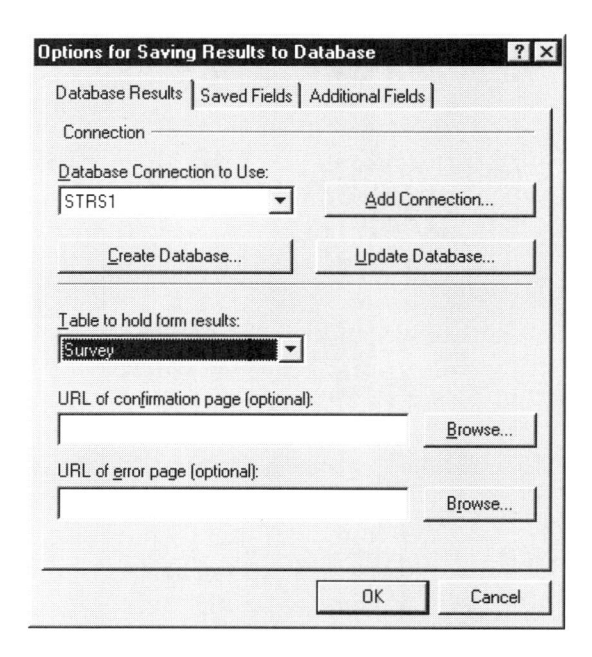

4. In the Database Results tab, you'll see that FrontPage has assumed you want to use the connection you've defined above. If that's inaccurate, either add another one, create a new database, or update the database. In any case, make sure that the database connection you want to use is visible in that drop-down menu.

5. Next, you need to indicate in which table of the database you want to store your results. Most databases have more than one table. Select the table you want to use.

6. If you'd like to display a confirmation page, point to it using the Browse button. Also point to an error page (if you've created one for that), so that visitors will see something informative if their data can't get into the database for any reason.

7. Click on the Saved Fields tab to show the list of fields you're collecting in your form (see the following illustration). For each field that you've collected data,

Getting FrontPage to Use Your Access Database

you need to decide where you want that data to go in your database. One field at a time:

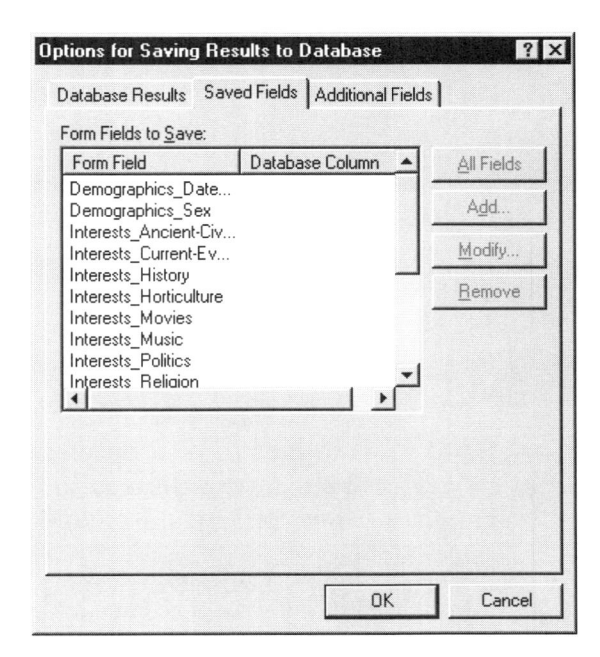

a) Click on the form field name.

b) Click Modify, which will bring up a small dialog box that lets you map one form field to one database field.

c) Select the correct database field name (column) from the drop-down list.

d) Click OK.

8. Click on the Additional Fields tab to see what other information the Web server can collect for you. These additional fields are shown in the following illustration. If you want any of these other types of data collected, none of which require the visitor to take any action, then map them to fields in your database as you did for the Saved Fields above.

[Screenshot of "Options for Saving Results to Database" dialog, Additional Fields tab, listing Browser type, Remote computer na..., Timestamp, User name.]

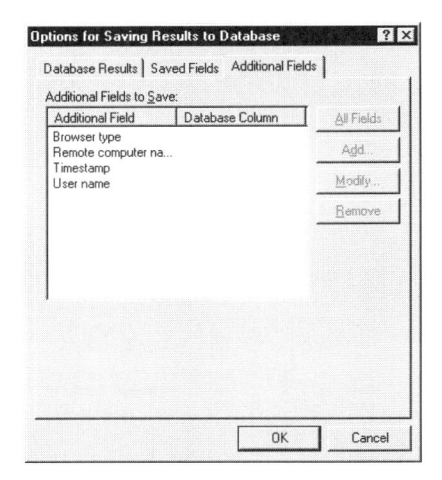

When you're satisfied that all your form fields are mapped to your database fields correctly, click OK. Your form will need to have an extension of .asp to work properly. Rename it now.

Tip: *If you've failed to map any fields that are defined in your database, you'll receive an error message. Every field in your database table must map to something on your form. Not everything on your form must map to something in your database.*

Note: *You must publish your web to your Web server with FrontPage extensions installed in order for this to work.*

How do I get data from my database into a Web page?

This is slightly easier than getting data from a Web form into a database. You'll use the Database Results Wizard.

Note: *As with much else in this chapter, the Database Results Wizard will only work if you have selected Tools | Options and set to use the Microsoft Internet Information Server on the Compatibility tab of the Options dialog box.*

1. Create a new page.
2. Click on the body of the page, and then select Insert | Database | Results. (If the Database option isn't listed in the drop-down menu, click the double down-arrows on

Getting FrontPage to Use Your Access Database

the menu to reveal more menu items. If your Database option on the Insert menu is grayed out, check the Server setting on the Compatibility tab of the Options dialog box, which you can reach from the Tools menu.) FrontPage will begin the Database Results Wizard.

3. The illustration below shows the first of five steps in the wizard. Click Use an Existing Database Connection, and select the connection from the list. Click Next to display the second step of the wizard.

4. In the second step, select your record source, which is the table or query from which you want the data pulled.

If you want to create a custom query, click Edit to do so now. Click Next to move to the next step of the wizard.

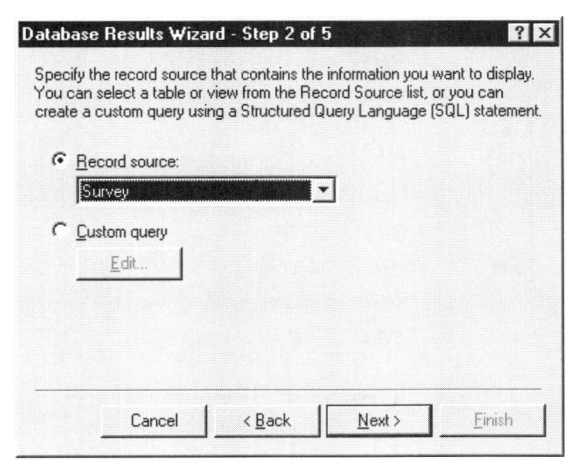

5. In step 3 of 5 in the wizard you can dictate which fields will and won't be displayed. By default, all fields in your

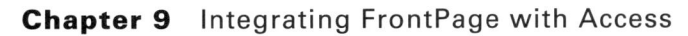

table will be displayed. To change the default setting, click Edit. You'll see the Displayed Fields dialog box.

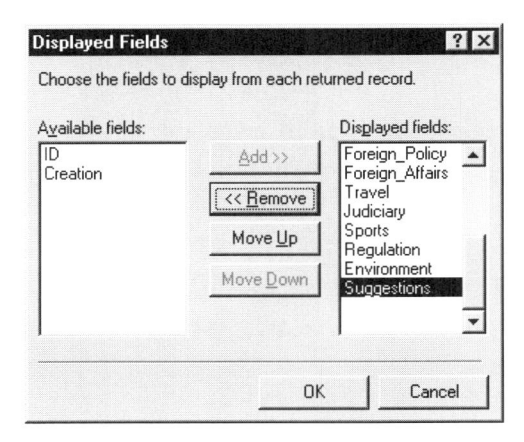

6. Click on any of the fields in the right column, then click Remove to remove them from the list of fields that will be displayed. In the preceding illustration, you can see that we've decided that the record ID and the creation date don't need to be displayed. Click OK.

7. If you want to limit the records that are displayed by filtering the results, or you want the results to be sorted, click More Options. FrontPage will display the More Options dialog box.

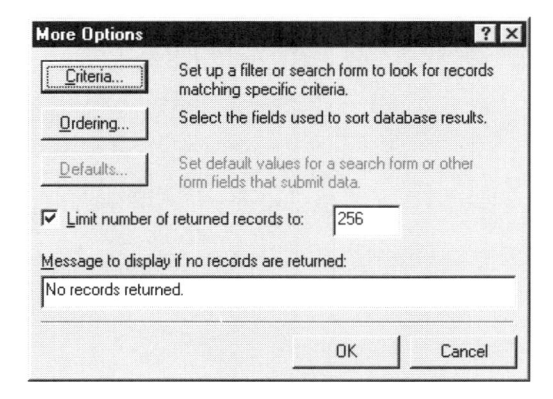

8. Click the Ordering button and FrontPage will display the Ordering dialog box. We decided to display records in ascending order by sex. To add fields to the sort order, click on them in the left-hand column, then click Add.

You can also move them up or down in order by clicking on them in the right-hand column, then clicking Move Up or Move Down. Finally, to change the sort order from ascending to descending, click the yellow arrow to the left of the field in the right-hand column. Click OK when you're satisfied with the sort order. FrontPage removes the Ordering dialog box and redisplays the screen for step 3 of the Database Results Wizard.

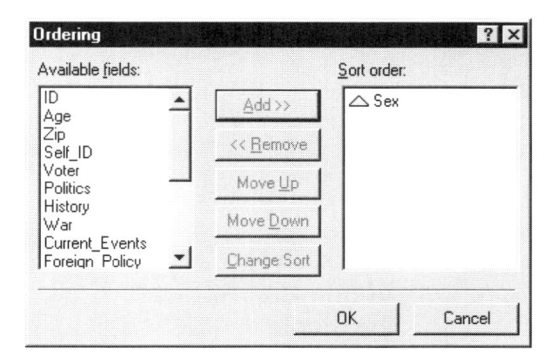

9. Next, let's filter the results. In the wizard's step 3 screen, click the Criteria button. FrontPage will display the Criteria dialog box. Click Add to add criteria.

10. To create a criterion, select a field name, select a comparison, then enter the value in the value field. Click OK.

11. Here is the final criteria list. The results of only respondents to our survey who indicated they were Republicans, Moderates, or Democrats will be displayed. Click OK to save your criteria. Click OK again to move onto the next step.

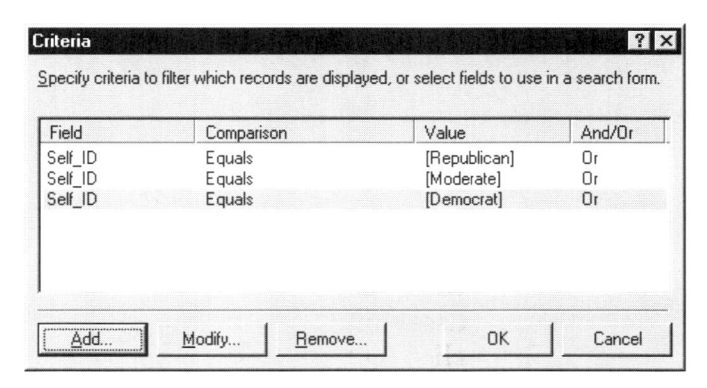

12. Step 4 of the wizard lets you decide how you want the output formatted. Here we've left the default settings. We can always come back and change this later through the wizard. Click OK.

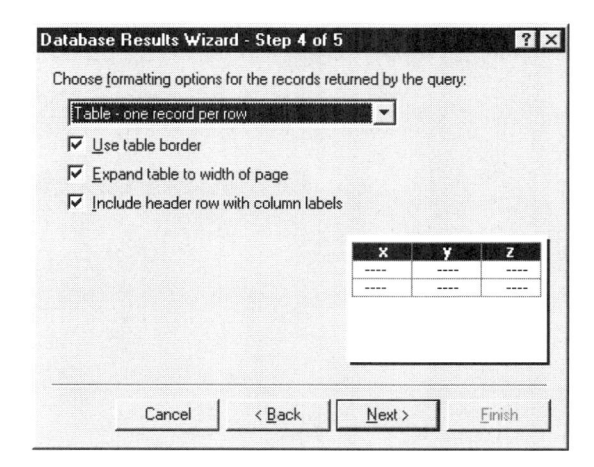

13. Step 5 of the wizard lets you group results and add an optional Search feature. Again, we've left the default settings. Click Finish.

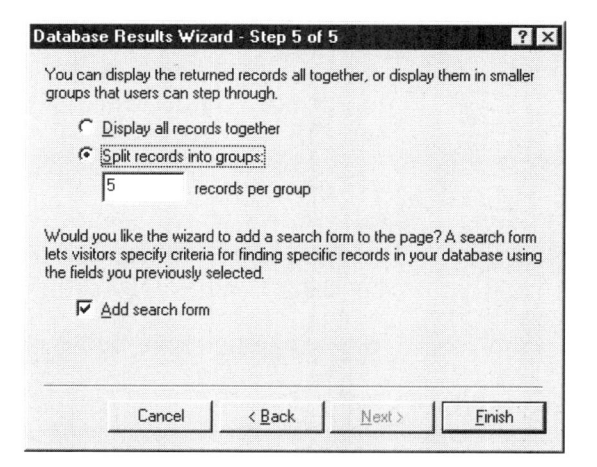

Tip: *If you find that you don't really like what you're getting, you can go back into the wizard by right-clicking somewhere in your results form, then selecting Database Results Properties.*

Getting FrontPage to Use Your Access Database

Figure 9-5 shows how your page will look in Design view. Don't try to modify too much of this by hand. If you need to make changes, go back into the Database Results Wizard and make the changes there. Let FrontPage do the work for you. If you later add or remove fields from your database, you'll need to modify the Database Results Wizard to reflect that.

> *Note:* None of this will work until you publish your web to a server with Microsoft's IIS running on it.

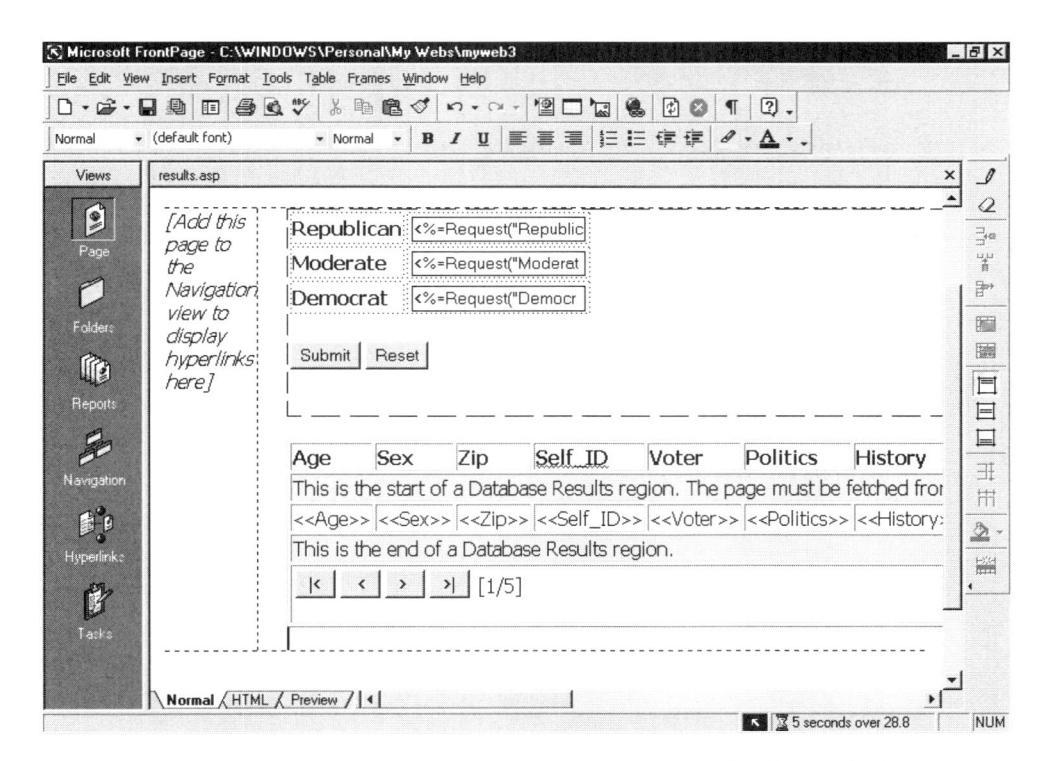

Figure 9-5 The page created by the Database Results Wizard, shown in Design view

Chapter 10

Creating Forms to Collect Data

Answer Topics!

● **FORMS** 238

- ? How forms processing works
- ? What a form is
- ? The components of a form
- ? Where forms processing takes place
- ? Storing the data you collect
- ? Getting people to give you their data

● **CREATING A FORM** 241

- ? Creating a form using the Form Page Wizard
- ? Asking for text data (such as a name)
- ? Keeping visitors from entering garbage
- ? Validating data for a text-input field
- ? Asking a multiple-choice question
- ? Asking for more than one of many choices
- ? Asking a Yes/No question
- ? Collecting answers to open-ended questions
- ? Adding a field after you've left the wizard

Creating Forms to Collect Data @ a Glance

The ability to collect data from site visitors and process it on a server has been available to Web developers since version 2 browsers became available. The three components of forms processing are: the form, the data, and the CGI (common gateway interface) script. This chapter will talk about the form and the data. Chapter 9 talks about integrating FrontPage with Access, which is the easiest form of CGI, and which FrontPage makes available to you without any programming.

FrontPage makes creating a form a breeze. You basically have two choices for creating a form in FrontPage. You can use the Form Page Wizard, or you can create a form and then insert each field individually into the form. Most likely, you'll end up using a combination of the two. You'll use the Form Page Wizard to create the majority of your form. Then, after doing so, you'll realize that you left out a field or two, and have to go back in and surgically insert the new field or fields.

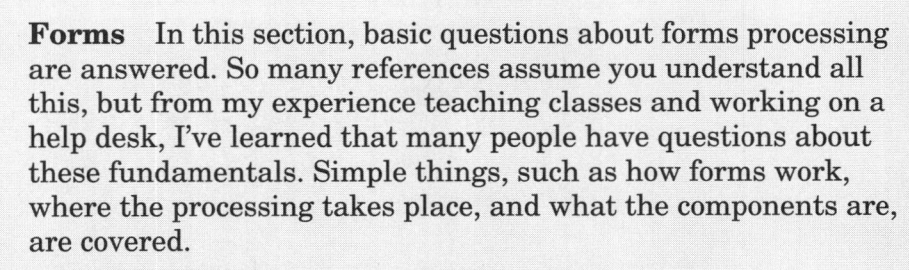

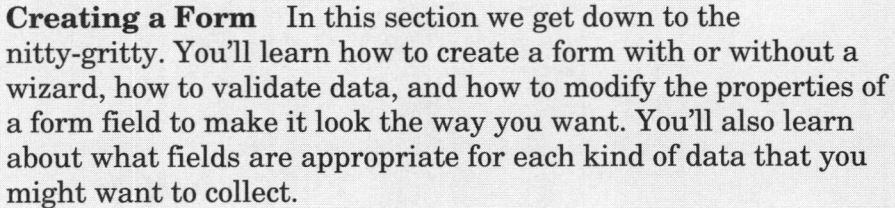

- **Forms** In this section, basic questions about forms processing are answered. So many references assume you understand all this, but from my experience teaching classes and working on a help desk, I've learned that many people have questions about these fundamentals. Simple things, such as how forms work, where the processing takes place, and what the components are, are covered.

- **Creating a Form** In this section we get down to the nitty-gritty. You'll learn how to create a form with or without a wizard, how to validate data, and how to modify the properties of a form field to make it look the way you want. You'll also learn about what fields are appropriate for each kind of data that you might want to collect.

FORMS

How does forms processing work?

The simplest way to understand how the browser interacts with the server to get forms data processed is to see a diagram. Figure 10-1 shows the sequence of events and where each event takes place.

1. The browser loads the form, which is served from the Web server.
2. The visitor completes the form (on his own desktop).
3. The visitor clicks the Submit button.
4. Data is sent back to the Web server as a series of name-value pairs.
5. The server processes and stores data either in a database or in a text file.
6. The server sends some type of confirmation page back to the visitor to confirm that the data was accepted.

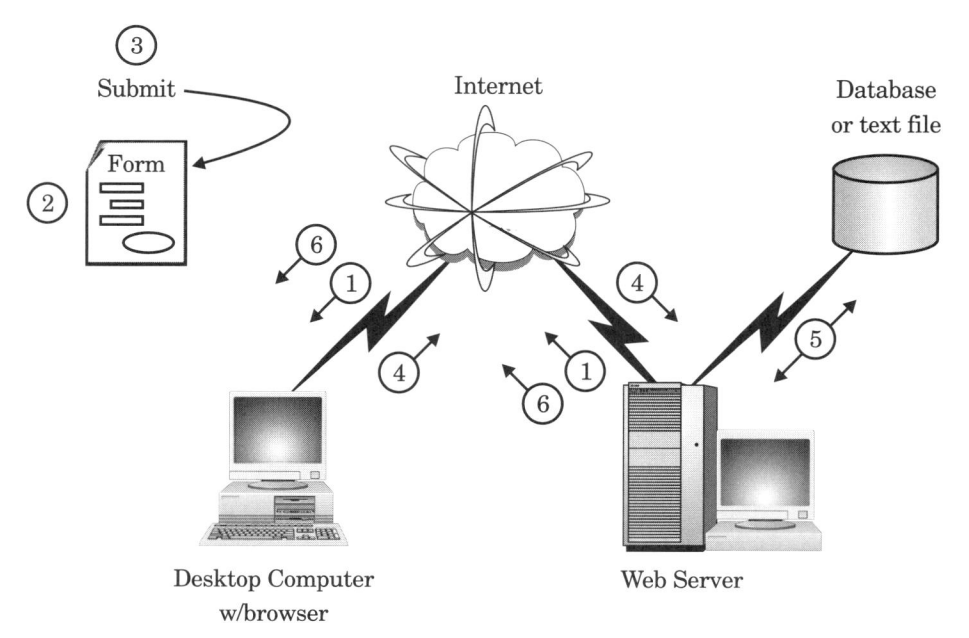

Figure 10-1 Forms processing

This chapter will focus on step 1, creating the form which the Web server serves.

What is a form?

A *form* is a part of an HTML page where fields are displayed for the user to enter his or her own data. The form requires only an action (instructions to the server as to what to do with the data), a method of passing the data to the server, a Submit button, and fields. Fields can be any of the following items (as you'll see later, in Figure 10-2):

- **Text input fields**, where the visitor might type his or her name.
- **Check boxes**, which allow the visitor to answer a Yes/No question, with a check mark meaning Yes.
- **Radio buttons**, permitting the visitor to select one from a short list of options. Usually, with radio buttons, one is checked when the page loads so some data will be returned to the server.
- **Drop-down lists**, which give the visitor the chance to select one or more options from a list.
- **Text areas**, which allow the visitor a place to enter free-form text, such as suggestions.

What are the components of a form?

The components of a form are fields and a Submit button. You can also include a Reset button, but it's not required. Even though a form only requires these minimum components, you can and should include instructions to the visitor as to how you want each field completed. Field labels or captions aren't tied to fields in HTML, but you need to think in terms of providing adequate instructions to your visitors so they understand what kind of data you want from them.

Where does forms processing take place?

Forms processing takes place on the Web server. When the visitor clicks the Submit button, field names and data values are sent to the server.

If the *method* is set to "get," then the data is attached to the end of the URL and looks like this:

```
?field1=alexis&field2=gutzman&field3=virginia
```

If the *method* is set to "post," then the data is sent to the server like this:

```
field1=alexis
field2=gutzman
field3=virginia
```

In this example, there must have been only three fields on the page: field1, field2, and field3. The visitor completed them with the values "alexis," "gutzman," and "virginia." It's impossible in this example to know what type of data was requested and whether it was requested in a text input field, a drop-down list, or a text area. You don't even know if any of the responses were part of a check box or the result of clicking a radio button.

Tip: *Use meaningful field names in your forms so that you know which data was sent in response to what questions.*

Where can I store the data I collect?

Typically, collected data is stored in a database for easy retrieval and manipulation, but you can also store your data in a text file. Alternatively, you can have the data e-mailed to an e-mail account, in which case it will be formatted like the data in the "post" example above. If you e-mail the data, you don't really have to store it anywhere on the server.

FrontPage makes it very easy to save data either to an Access database or to a text file. Sending the data via e-mail is always easy, but sometimes processing it out of an e-mail message is messy. If you don't have an idea of what you want to do with the data, don't request it. Usually, when people create forms that send e-mail, nothing ever happens with the data because there's no good way to process field-value pairs out of e-mail. When that's the case, then you're wasting your visitors' time by requesting the data in the first place.

Will people give me their data?

Some will and some won't. If you can give people some assurance that their data is safe in your hands and if there's something in it for them, then chances are they'll give it to you. Some people are very paranoid about privacy and they won't give you their data no matter what. Most people are willing to trade personal data in exchange for a chance to win a trip, a computer, or money.

CREATING A FORM

How do I create a form using the Form Page Wizard?

The Form Page Wizard is the easiest way to create a form. If you already know exactly what type of data you want to collect, then you might be able to create your form using the

Privacy

Privacy is a big, big topic, both with consumers and with the government. The Federal Trade Commission has threatened to impose regulations on U.S.-based Web sites about privacy if private organizations don't help to make the Web safer. While most people aren't paranoid about privacy, everyone will feel a little bit safer giving you their data if you provide a clear, prominently placed privacy policy. Another way to raise people's comfort level with your site, and help them believe that you really won't do anything fishy with their data is to join a privacy group, like TrustE (www.truste.org) or BBBOnline (www.bbbonline.org). With both of these groups, you join by paying a hefty fee and signing a contract agreeing to their principles and to random data audits by them. They can show up any time and look through your data and your processes to confirm that you're only using the data as you say you are. They also act as an arbitrator with consumers who believe you've mishandled their data.

Form Page Wizard exclusively. Once you know what you'd like to see, follow these steps:

1. From FrontPage's select File | New | Page. You'll see the New dialog box.

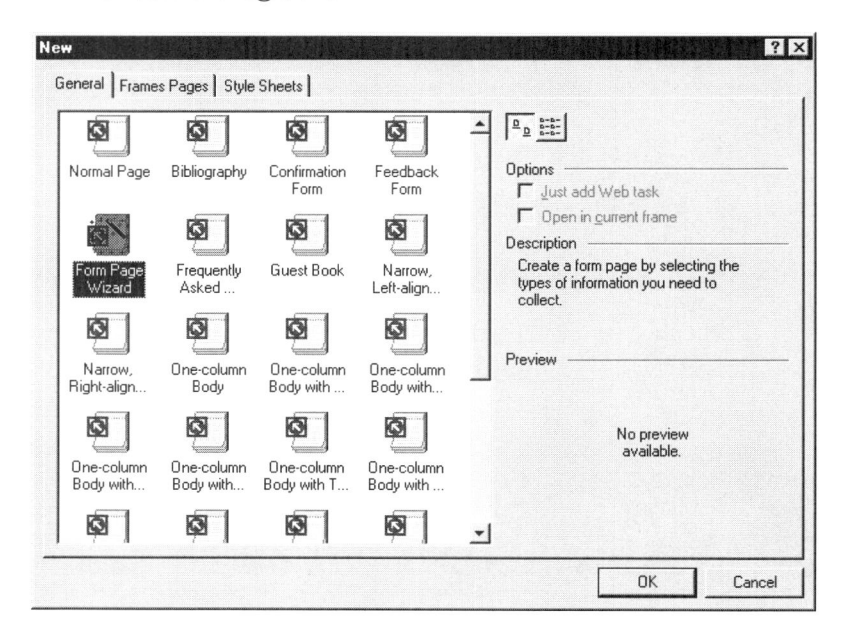

2. Click the Form Page Wizard icon in the window on the New dialog box.

3. The Form Page Wizard will display its first page, which is an introduction to the wizard. Click the Next option to begin entering data. FrontPage displays the second page of the Forms Page Wizard, shown in Figure 10-2.

4. When you see the dialog box in Figure 10-2, you can add sets of fields. Click the Add button to begin adding fields (questions) to your form. When you click the Add button, FrontPage displays the third screen of the Forms Page Wizard.

5. Select Personal Information to start adding form fields that request personal information. You can also change the prompt for this set of questions. Figure 10-3 shows

Creating a Form

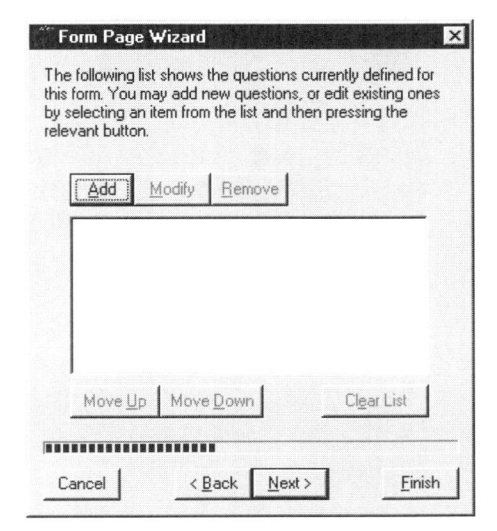

Figure 10-2 The list of questions (fields) to be included on your form; notice that it's empty right now

the default prompt that appears when you click Personal Information. When you select the Personal Information option, FrontPage displays the fourth screen of the Forms Page Wizard. From this screen, as shown in

Figure 10-3 Indicating the type of question you want to ask

Chapter 10 Creating Forms to Collect Data

Figure 10-4, you can select the type of data you want to collect as personal information.

6. By default, FrontPage will ask three questions as part of personal information, as shown in Figure 10-4: name, age, and sex. You can ask five more questions, if you wish: ID number, height, weight, hair color, and eye color. With respect to name, you can tell it to ask for either the full name (one single field), first and last names (two fields), or first, last, and middle names (three fields); with respect to age, you can tell it to ask for either age or date of birth. Finally, you can tell it what you want this set of questions to be called; it defaults to Personal.

7. When you're satisfied with the selections you've made, click Next either to add another set of questions or to move onto the next step of the wizard.

8. If you're clicking along with me, your list of questions now includes the set of questions about personal information. Click Add to add another set of questions.

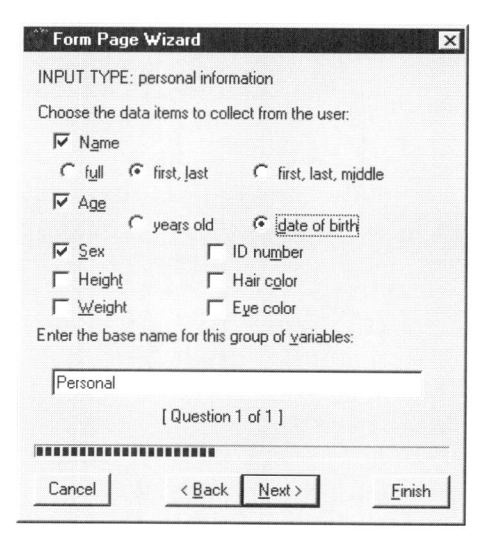

Figure 10-4 Choosing the data to include in personal information

Creating a Form   245

9. You'll see the list of questions you can add again. This time, select One of Several Options. You'll also want to change the prompt for this question.

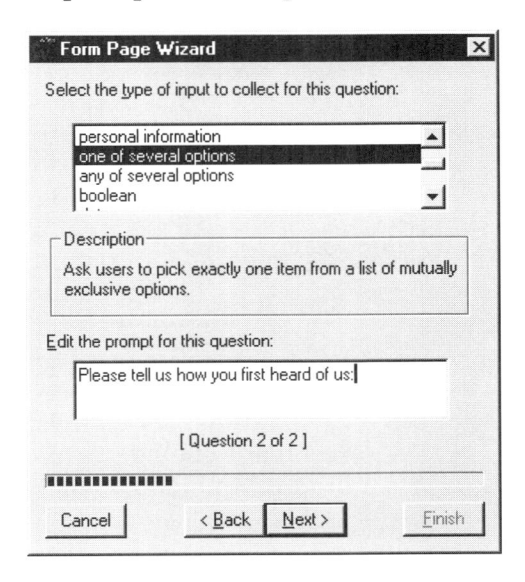

10. Click Next to specify the values that you want in the list, and the type of field you want FrontPage to use to collect this information, as shown in Figure 10-5.

Tip: *Select One of Several Options if you want the visitor to be able to select one option from a drop-down list. Select Any of Several Options if you want the visitor to be able to select multiple options from a series of check boxes.*

11. Suppose you want visitors to choose one option from a list. The three most common ways to indicate this is to provide a drop-down list, a list of radio buttons, or a list, which is just a drop-down list with more than one option visible. Choose a drop-down list, since it takes up the least room on the page. Now you need to tell it what values to use as the options. Figure 10-5 shows some of the values we've provided. Click Next when you're done entering options.

Chapter 10 Creating Forms to Collect Data

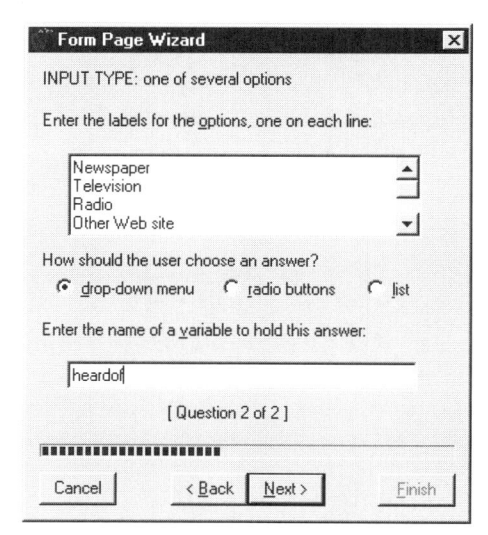

Figure 10-5 Giving values for your list and indicating the form field that FrontPage should use to collect information such as drop-down menu, radio buttons, or list.

> **Caution:** Don't use radio buttons if you have more than three or four options.

> **Tip:** Even though FrontPage doesn't give you an easy way to create a drop-down list for the visitor to check more than one option (by holding down the CTRL key on a PC or the OPTION key on a Mac, while clicking an option), you can do it yourself. Choose to create a One of Several Options question, then select List as the display type. After the form has been generated, go into the HTML and add the keyword "multiple" within the <SELECT> tag.

12. Again, if you're clicking along, you're looking at a screen similar to Figure 10-2, but now it's got two questions on it. Click Add to add another question, this time as a paragraph field.

Creating a Form 247

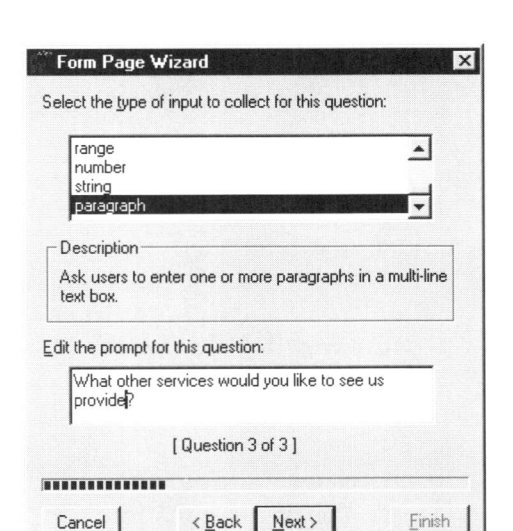

13. Here you can see that we've chosen to add a paragraph field, meaning that the visitor can answer at length, and we've changed what the prompt reads to "What other services would you like to see us provide?" Change the prompt to your satisfaction and click Next.

14. Now, you can give the field a name. As discussed in Chapter 9, the field name needs to match the field name in the database if your data is being written to a database. Click Next.

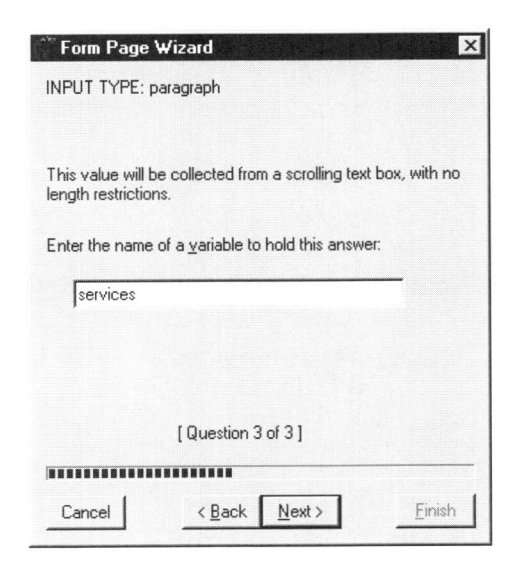

15. When you return to the list you saw in Figure 10-2, there will be three questions on the list. Click Add to include another question.

Note: A Boolean field is a field that is stored as either True or False, On or Off. You can define True to be Yes, or Up, or Male, or anything else that you want, as long as there are only two possible values for the field on your form, and as long as you understand what the value of True and False are when you do processing on the form data. Boolean fields are used most often for Yes/No questions.

16. Select Boolean from the list of question types. Now ask a Yes or No question. Change the prompt to read, "Would you like to receive information about updates to our site by e-mail?"

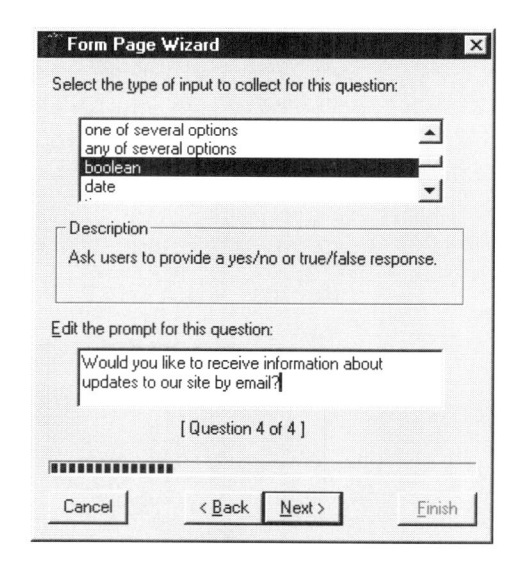

17. Since you want this field to appear as a checked check box (which means that you assume the answer is going to be Yes), you'll check the check box field, and provide a field name of e-mail.

Creating a Form

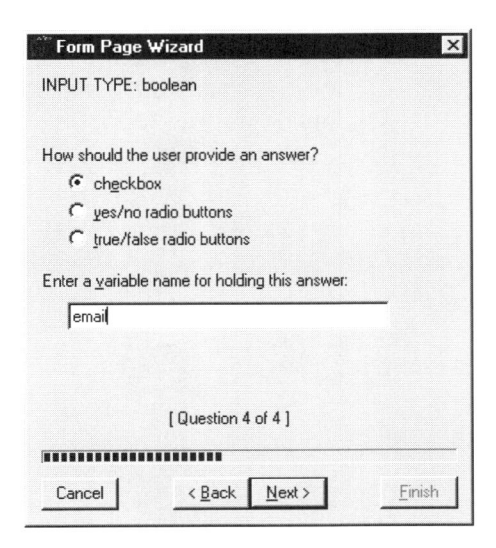

Form Page Wizard

INPUT TYPE: boolean

How should the user provide an answer?
- ⦿ checkbox
- ◯ yes/no radio buttons
- ◯ true/false radio buttons

Enter a variable name for holding this answer:

`email`

[Question 4 of 4]

Cancel | < Back | Next > | Finish

18. Again, the wizard returns to the list of questions shown in Figure 10-2. You have just one more question to ask. If the visitor would like to get updates by e-mail, then you'll need his or her e-mail address, so click Add to add the last field.

19. Select string and give the question a prompt. (A string field is also known as a *text input field*.) Here is the prompt you've chosen.

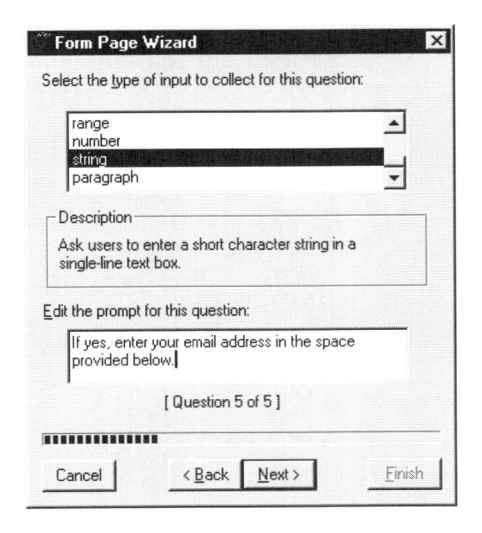

Form Page Wizard

Select the type of input to collect for this question:

- range
- number
- **string**
- paragraph

Description:
Ask users to enter a short character string in a single-line text box.

Edit the prompt for this question:

If yes, enter your email address in the space provided below.

[Question 5 of 5]

Cancel | < Back | Next > | Finish

Chapter 10 Creating Forms to Collect Data

20. If you want to limit the length of the data you'll accept, indicate that here. Also, you need to give the field a name.

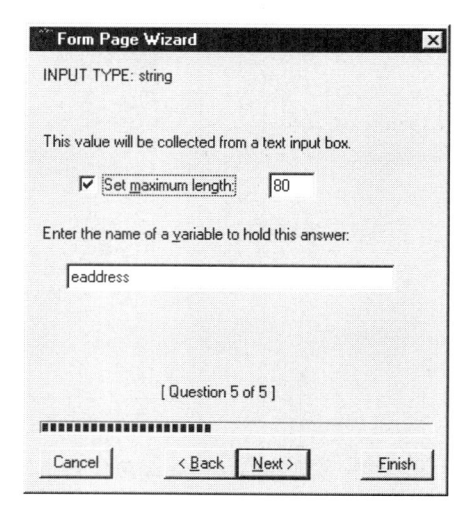

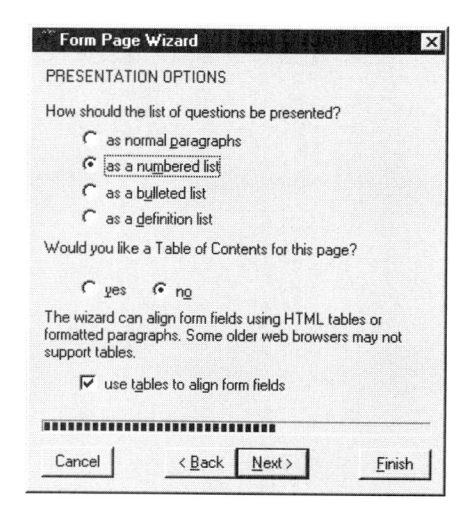

21. Finally, the list of questions is complete, as shown in Figure 10-6. If you need to modify any of the questions, click on the question you'd like to modify, and click Modify. Since you planned carefully, you don't need to modify anything. All the questions are just as you want them. Now click Next to wrap up the wizard.

22. It's time to address the presentation of the form. Tell FrontPage to display your questions as a numbered list, without a table of contents, and to use tables to align form fields (otherwise it'll look a mess).

Creating a Form

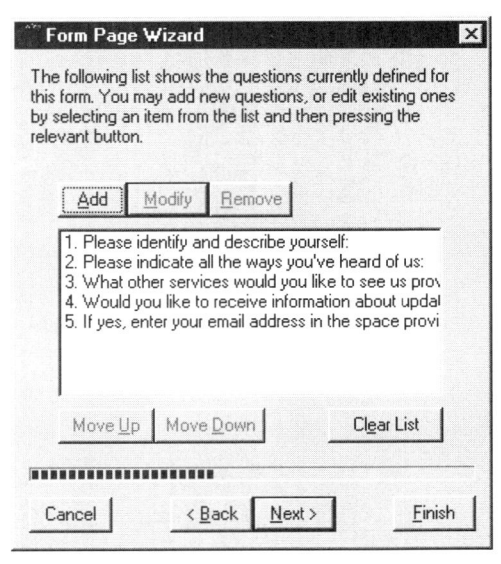

Figure 10-6 The complete list of questions

23. Now it's time to tell FrontPage how you want the server to process the data. Choose to use a CGI (common gateway interface) script.

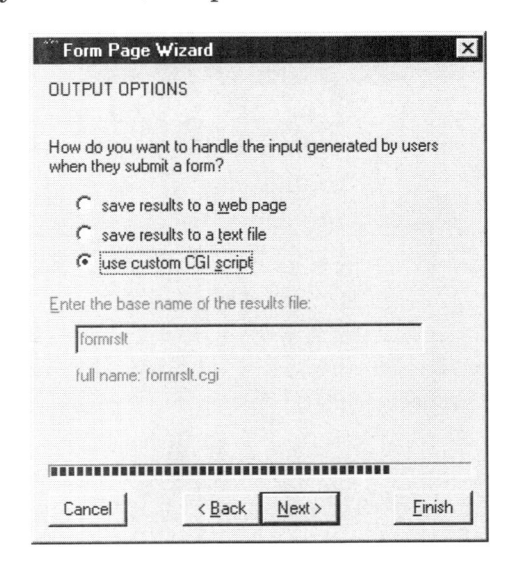

24. Figure 10-7 shows you your last chance to make any changes to your form from within the wizard. Once you click Finish, your form is generated. At that point, all

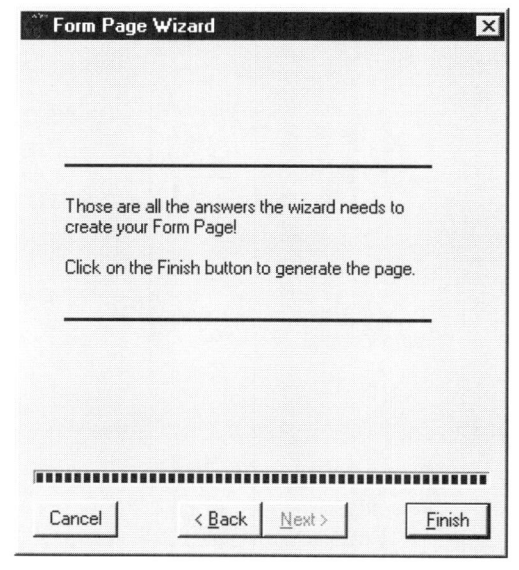

Figure 10-7 Finally, when you're absolutely sure that you're done, click Finish

changes will have to be made to fields on the form individually. Figure 10-8 shows the form that you've created, with a few formatting changes to the page.

User Interface Success

Computer users have very concrete expectations from buttons and fields on screens. Take advantage of the fact that most Windows software has a certain look and feel and behavior. Don't be creative about using fields in new ways.

Visitors to your site will have a more satisfying experience if you make your site more like other sites and more like existing Windows software, rather than trying to pave new ground for how the user interface should work. For example: a Yes/No question should be either a check box or radio buttons. A Boolean field, where there are only two possible values, should not be a drop-down list. People don't expect to see a drop-down list with two values in it. Save drop-down lists for questions where there are at least three possible values. Radio buttons are great for two or three options, but unless you're just trying to fill space, put options for questions that have more than three possible answers into a drop-down list.

Creating a Form 253

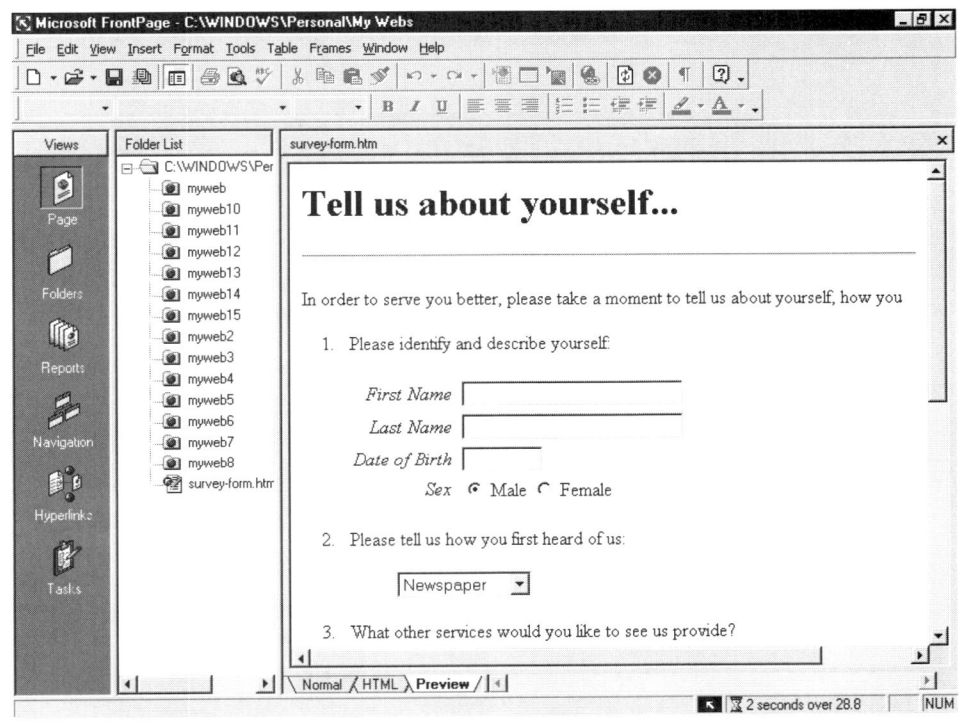

Figure 10-8 The finished form with a few formatting changes to the page

How do I ask for text data (such as a name)?

If you want to add a field to a form either outside of the Form Page Wizard, or after you've used the Form Page Wizard, you can do so from the Insert Menu. Follow these steps:

1. Select Insert | Form | One-line Text Box.
2. If you didn't already have a form on your page—indicated by a box on the screen drawn with long dashes—you have one now. You also have a Submit button, a Reset button, and a text field without a label. As you can see, it doesn't look too good at first.

3. You need to provide a caption for your field. In this example, the caption is "Please enter your ID." We've

also moved the buttons down a line, to make it look more the way a form is expected to look.

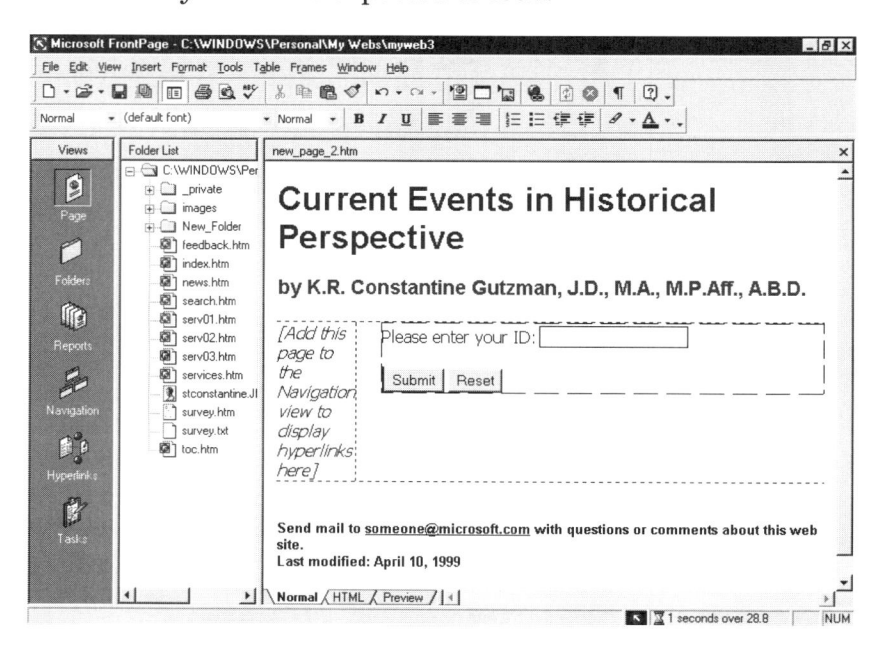

4. Now you need to give the field a field name that matches the name in your database, or at least a useful name that you'll recognize when it gets mailed to you. To edit the field name, double-click on the field to bring up the Text Box Properties dialog box.

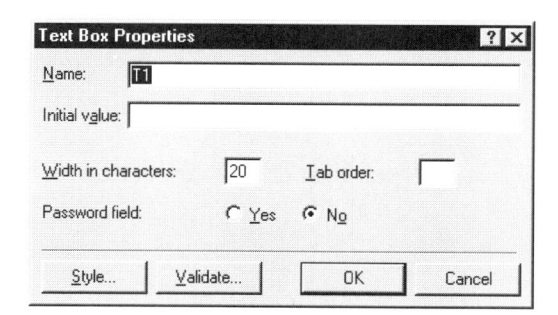

5. You'll notice that FrontPage will, in the absence of other data, give a text field the name T1. That's not going to be very helpful when that data tries to insert itself into

your database, when you look at a text file, or when it arrives in your mailbox. Give the field a useful name.

6. If you want the field to be populated when the page loads, then supply an initial value.

Caution: When you provide an initial value for a field, and the visitor doesn't overlay it with his own data, the initial data will be sent as if it was entered by the visitor.

7. Adjust the width of the field, as it appears on the screen. You can also modify how many characters a field will accept, but not in this dialog box.

8. If the field is for a password, check the box indicating that it is; when a visitor enters their password, it will appear as asterisks (or bullets on a Mac).

Tip: To modify the number of characters a field will accept, you must use field validation, which you can access from the Validate button. Assigning a maximum length to a field is the only kind of field validation that doesn't require FrontPage server extensions. Making the field required, however, does require server extensions, so the message you get from the Validate dialog box can be very confusing.

Can I keep visitors from entering garbage?

To some degree, you can keep garbage out of your database. For example, you can keep someone from entering "ABCDE" for the zip code or "aaa-aaaa" for the phone number, but you can't keep someone from typing "Mickey Mouse" as a name. Monitoring data that is entered before it's written into the database (or to a text file or mailed) is called *validating* the data.

You can perform data validation only on one-line text boxes, scrolling text boxes, radio buttons, and drop-down lists. Depending on the field, you can validate the following:

- Whether data is required
- A minimum and maximum field length

- What type of data must be provided, choosing from text, an integer, or a number; and if an integer or number, whether there must be a comma (U.S. style) or a period (European style) to group digits (for example, 1,234 or 1.234)
- If text, whether spaces, letters, and/or digits are permitted
- Whether the value of the field must be equal to, not equal to, greater than, greater than or equal to, less than, or less than or equal to a value you provide

How do I validate data for a text input field?

To validate a text input field, double-click on the field to bring up the Text Box Properties dialog box. Click the Validate button in the Text Box Properties dialog box. Select the type of validation you'd like, and click OK. As simple as this sounds, the tricky part is deciding how to set validation for the field. Here are a few ideas for how you might want to format common input fields.

Phone Number

In the case of a phone number, it's safe to say that a phone number is composed of digits (0-9), but it also includes, in most cases, a hyphen, and some people even enter parentheses when they provide their phone numbers and area codes. Use the interface that FrontPage provides for validating data, which you can access by clicking the Validate button in the Text Box Properties dialog box for a field (all fields but check boxes, for which there's nothing to validate). (See Figure 10-9.)

Figure 10-9 shows how we've chosen to validate data for a phone number. We could have told it that the field had no constraints, in which case anything entered by a visitor would pass muster. We could have told it that a phone number had to be numeric, either a number or an integer, but then if visitors had entered dashes, parentheses, or even spaces, the data would have been rejected. Instead, we told it that the data had to be text, and that digits, hyphens,

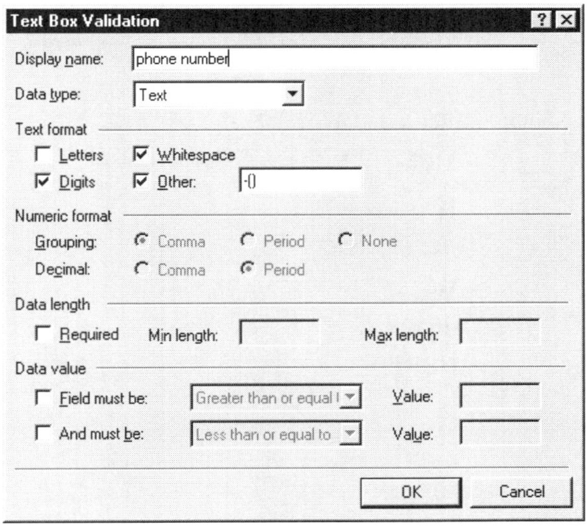

Creating a Form

Figure 10-9 Instructing FrontPage which characters a phone number is allowed to have

parentheses, or whitespace would be acceptable. Visitors can still input garbage, but we're less likely to get complete garbage in the database.

Name

To validate a name field, you probably want to limit the text field to letters and whitespace (in case someone has a last name with a space in it). Figure 10-10 shows how you might set the Text Box Validation dialog box to validate names. Notice that the Display Name field has Name in it. Whatever you enter for Display Name is what the server will return to the visitor along with a helpful message, if he or she tries to enter digits or other symbols. This field is set to allow a maximum length of 70.

Zip Code

In the U.S., the zip code can be either 5 digits, or 9 digits with a dash between the fifth and the sixth digits. If you want to accept postal codes from other countries, these guidelines wouldn't work, since most other countries have letters as well

Chapter 10 Creating Forms to Collect Data

Figure 10-10 Validating for name

as digits in their postal codes. For U.S. zip codes, you probably want to set the Data Type to Text, then agree to accept digits and hyphens.

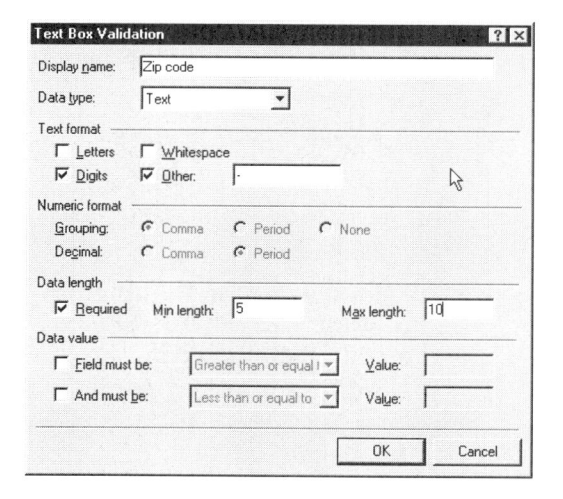

How do I ask a multiple-choice question?

There are four ways to ask a multiple choice question. Use Table 10-1 to help you decide which method is most appropriate to your needs.

Creating a Form

Field	Number of Responses Desired	Screen Space Used	Notes
Radio buttons	One	One line for each response	Sends back one response; ideal for up to three or four choices
Drop-down menu	One or more, but awkward for more	One line	Ideal for more than three or four choices
List	One or more, intuitive for more	Determined by you, but must be at least two, or it's just a drop-down list	Works well when you want more than one response sent back. You need to give clear instructions as to how to indicate multiple responses, since most people won't know how to do it.
Set of check boxes	More than one	One for each line	This actually sends Boolean results (True or False) for each question, so while it appears that these are answers to one question, they are really each Yes/No questions.

Table 10-1 Ways to Ask a Multiple-Choice Question

Radio Buttons

To create radio buttons, click in your form where you want your radio buttons to appear. If you don't already have a form, adding radio buttons to the page will create a form. A form is indicated on your page by a box with long dashed lines with a Submit button and a Reset button at the bottom of it.

1. Select Insert | Form | Radio Button.
2. If you didn't already have a form on your page, indicated by a box on the screen drawn with long dashes, you have one now. You also have a Submit button, a Reset button, and a single radio button without a label.
3. Radio buttons usually appear in groups, where each button represents a different value for the same field (variable). Radio buttons are essentially useless by

themselves, because you can only turn radio buttons *on*, not *off*. If you were thinking of putting only one radio button, then what you really want to use is a *check box*, which can be turned on and off. Go ahead and add at least one more radio button.

4. Here are three radio buttons. I've also moved the buttons down a line, to make it look more the way a form is expected to look.

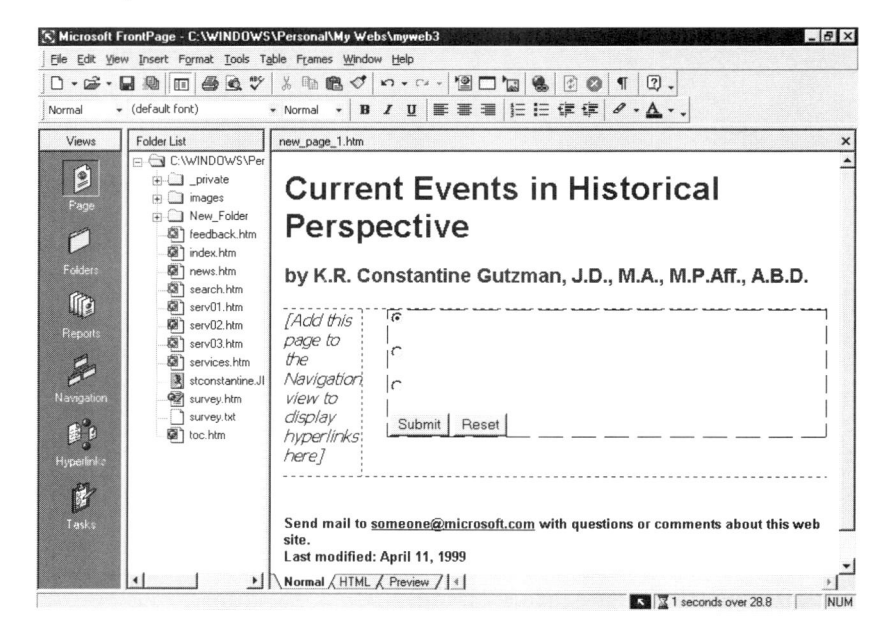

5. Go ahead and type in a question and give each of the radio buttons captions, so that the visitor will know what the options are. In this case, make it a question with three possible answers.

6. Now you need to modify the properties of the radio buttons so that the data sent to the server based on the answers provided by the visitor will be meaningful to you. Right now, if the visitor clicks on the first radio button, the following information will be sent to the server:

   R1=V1

7. You'll need to change the values for each radio button individually. Even though they're part of a group, each one has its own properties. Double-click the first radio button to edit the properties.

8. The Group Name should be the field name in your database, or at least a useful name that you'll recognize when it gets mailed to you. The Value is the value you want associated with the field in your database. The value for each radio button must be unique, so you know which radio button was selected. Here are the properties for the first radio button with the appropriate changes made.

Note: *If, in your group of radio buttons, none is selected by default, then you will have the option of performing validation just to require that one of the buttons is selected. If you load the page with one button selected, then the Validate button will be grayed out in the Properties box for each button in the group.*

9. In the Properties box, you can also indicate which of the buttons will be selected when the page loads. By default, the first in a group is the one that's selected.

10. Modify the properties of each of the other radio buttons in the group. Make sure that the Group Name for each button is the same or they won't really be part of the same group, and it will be possible for a visitor to check more than one button, and data will be sent back separately for each button.

Chapter 10 Creating Forms to Collect Data

Drop-Down Menu and List

The drop-down menu and the list are two forms of the same element. In both cases, the visitor is presented with a scrolling list of choices (unless the list window is the same size as the total number of options in the list). The following instructions are for creating a drop-down menu. The only difference between a drop-down menu and a list is the value of the height parameter. For a drop-down menu, only one choice is visible at a time (height is set to 1); for a list, more than one choice is visible at once (height is greater than 1).

1. From FrontPage's main menu, select Insert | Form | Drop-Down Menu.

2. If you didn't already have a form on your page, indicated by a box drawn with long dashes, you have one now. You also have a Submit button, a Reset button, and a very narrow, empty drop-down menu without a label.

3. Double-click on the drop-down menu to open the Drop-Down Menu Properties dialog box.

4. Begin by giving the field a useful name. The name either should match the name in the database, or should be something that will be meaningful when it arrives in your mailbox.

5. Now you need to add some values to the list. Click Add. You'll see this box.

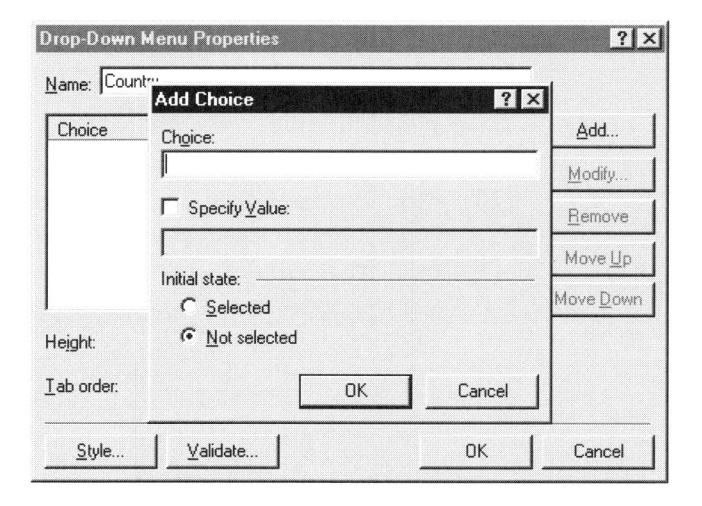

6. Give the option a name. This is the name that will appear on the list. Spaces are permitted. If you want something other than the exact same thing to be sent back to the database, click the Specify Value box and provide a value for this option. For example, if the list option were "People's Republic of China," you might want the value sent back to be only "China." You can determine which option will be in the window of the list when the page loads by clicking the Selected radio button. If you indicate that more than one option should be selected, the first one you indicate will be the only one selected.

7. Continue to add options to your list until you're satisfied with it. You can rearrange the options on the list by selecting an option, then moving it up or down with the buttons on the right. When you're happy with the list and the order of it, click OK. Figure 10-11 shows a complete list of choices with the first choice selected by default.

8. Test your drop-down menu in Preview mode. If you don't already have a question on your form for this drop-down list, provide one.

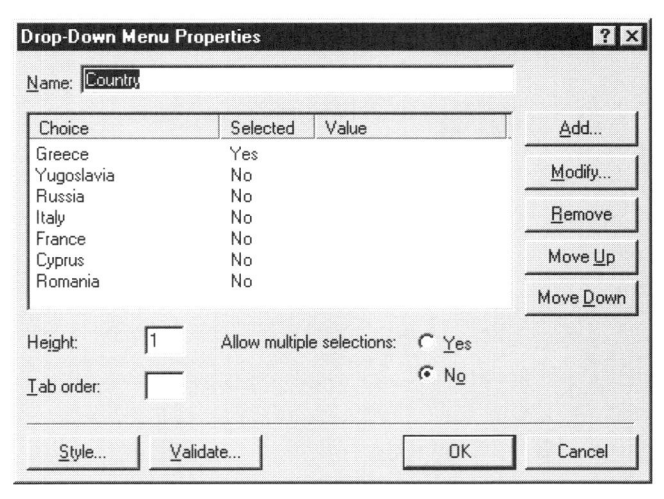

Figure 10-11 The completed list

Chapter 10 Creating Forms to Collect Data

If you want to make a list instead of a drop-down menu, follow these steps:

1. Double-click the drop-down menu to open the Properties dialog box.
2. Change the height from 1 to any number up to the number of items on the list. If you put a higher number, there'll be blank lines in your list. If you choose a number smaller than the number of items on your list, your visitor will be able to scroll through the list.
3. Click OK. Figure 10-12 shows the drop-down menu from above, converted into a list with four choices visible. The list doesn't look quite right in Normal view, but in Preview view it looks just fine.

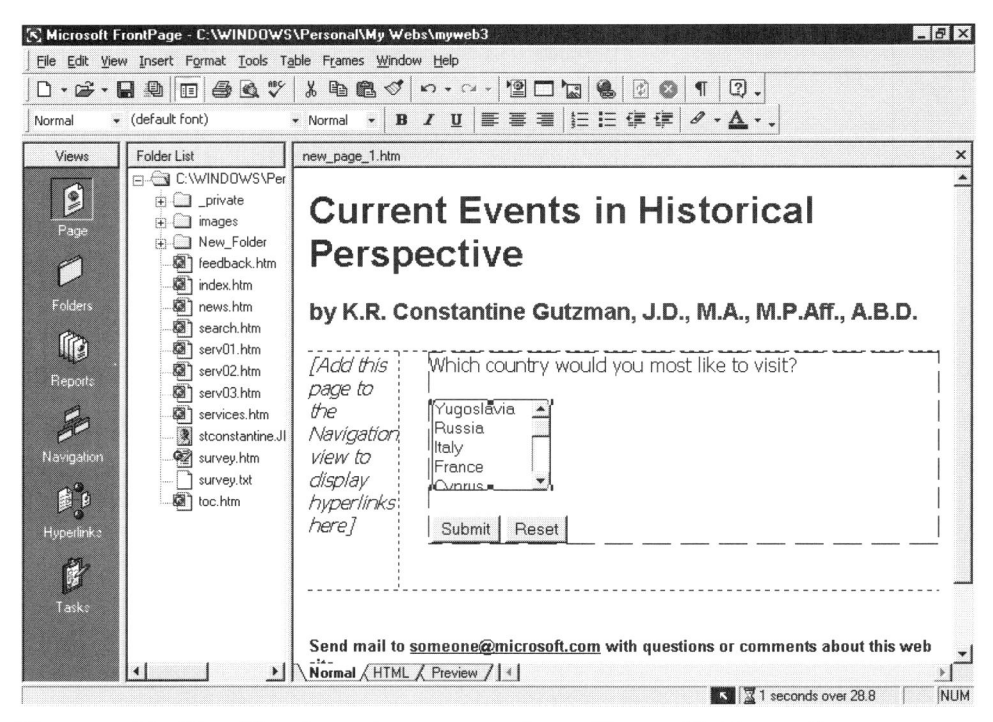

Figure 10-12 The drop-down menu from Figure 10-11 as a list

If you want to permit a visitor to select more than one option, follow these steps:

1. Double-click on the list (it should be a list for this, rather than a drop-down menu) to open the Properties dialog box.
2. Change Allow Multiple Selections from No to Yes.
3. Click OK.

Set of Check Boxes

Creating a set of check boxes isn't any different than creating one check box multiple times. To create a check box, follow these steps:

1. From FrontPage's main menu, select Insert | Form | Checkbox.
2. If you didn't already have a form on your page, indicated by a box drawn with long dashes, you have one now. You also have a Submit button, a Reset button, and a check box without a caption.
3. Double-click the check box to open the Check Box Properties dialog box.
4. Begin by giving the field a useful name; all check boxes default to being called C*n* where *n* is the number of the check box on that page. The name either should match the name in the database, or should be something that will be meaningful when it arrives in your mailbox. Value should be the value you want sent to your database as part of the field-value pair. If the field for the check box is defined as Boolean, then just leave the Value set to On. This is also where you can indicate whether you want the check box to be checked when the page loads; the default is not to have the check box checked when the page loads. Here are the properties after editing them.

Chapter 10 Creating Forms to Collect Data

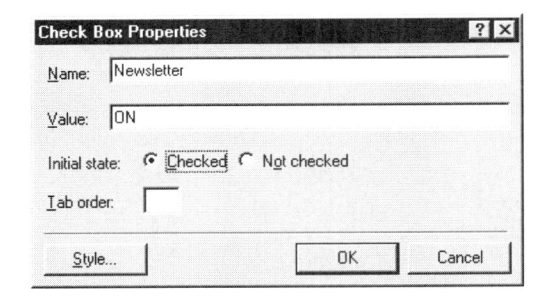

5. Make sure you give your check box a caption on the form, so visitors know whether they want to check the box.

How do I ask for more than one of many choices?

Table 10-1 shows your choices for asking for more than one of several choices. If you want the multiple values to be returned for a single field, then use a list. If you wanted to ask visitors to indicate all the ways they have heard about your site, you might provide the following options: television, radio, newspaper, magazine, other Web site, search engine, colleague, or other. The values that would be sent to the server for a list might be:

```
Heardof="other Web site", "search engine", "television"
```

If you want each value to be returned as a response to its own field, then use a set of check boxes. If you were to ask the same question with the same possible responses with a set of check boxes, the results sent to the server would be:

```
Other_web_site=yes
Search_engine=yes
Television=yes
```

How do I ask a Yes/No question?

The best way to ask a true Yes/No question is with a check box. Checked is Yes, unchecked is No. You sometimes also see radio buttons used in pairs for Yes/No questions. If the answers aren't simply Yes or No, but two other choices, such as Male or Female, then radio buttons are probably preferable to check boxes.

Creating a Form 267

? How do I collect answers to open-ended questions?

Open-ended questions require a *scrolling text box*, also known as a *paragraph* field (in the wizard) or a *text area* (in HTML). To create a scrolling text box, follow these steps:

1. From FrontPage's main menu, select Insert | Form | Scrolling Text Box.

2. If you didn't already have a form on your page, indicated by a box drawn with long dashes, you have one now. You also have a Submit button, a Reset button, and a small, empty scrolling text box without a caption.

3. Unless you want very short answers, you probably want to increase the size of the text box. In Normal view, double-click on the scrolling text box to open up the Properties dialog box.

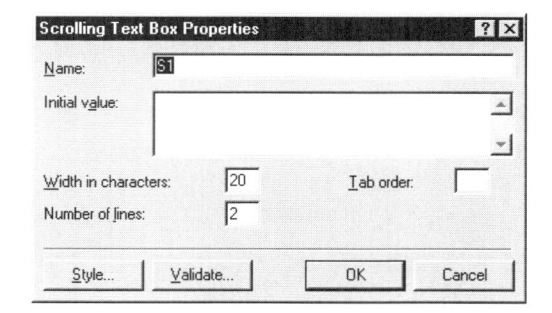

4. Begin by giving the field a useful name; all scrolling text boxes default to being called S*n* where *n* is the number of the scrolling text box on that page. The name either should match the name in the database, or should be something that will be meaningful when it arrives in your mailbox. Initial Value should be the text that you want to be sitting in the box when the page loads. This is also where you can set the width in characters and the number of lines; 60 and 4 provides a reasonably sized box. Click OK.

5. Make sure you give your scrolling text box a caption on the form, so visitors know what to enter in that space. Figure 10-13 shows the final scrolling text box, in Preview mode.

Chapter 10 Creating Forms to Collect Data

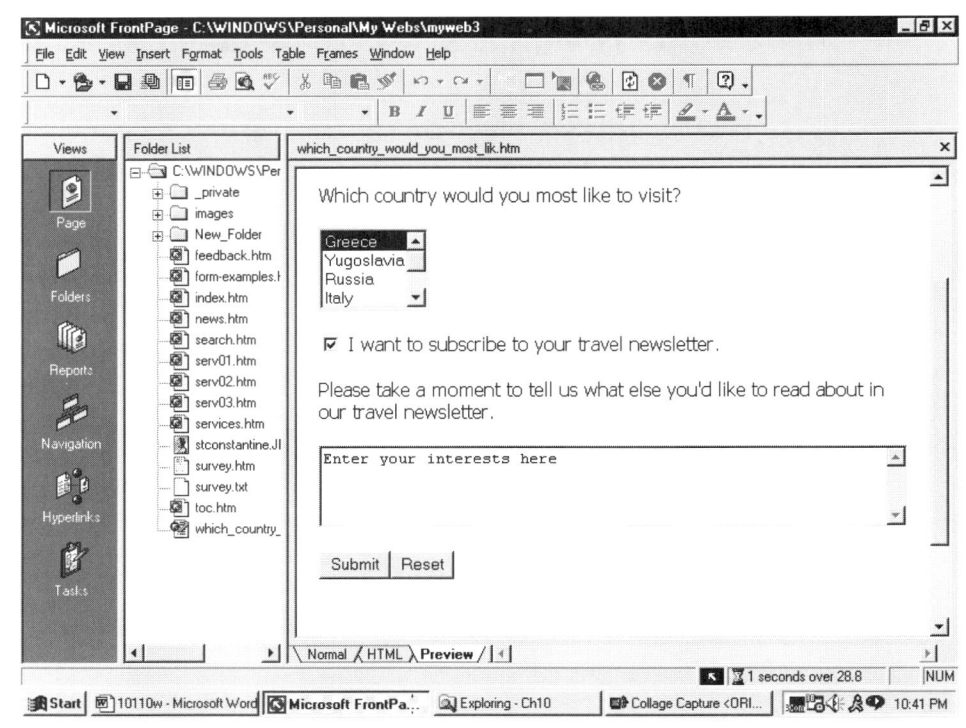

Figure 10-13 The final scrolling text box in Preview view

❓ I just thought of another form field I'd like to include in my form, but I've already finished the wizard. How can I add a field at this point?

Once you've clicked Finish on the wizard, the form is generated. At that point, if you want to add or modify fields you've created, you need to do it by following the detailed instructions earlier in this chapter. You can actually make far more detailed changes to the individual form elements through the individual properties boxes than you can through the wizard. Think of the wizard as a good first pass through the form, then modify the properties of the individual fields—especially the field names—after you've completed the wizard.

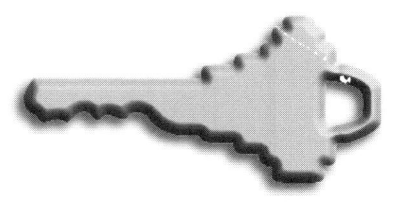

Chapter 11

Commerce and Security Issues

Answer Topics!

MAKING SENSE OF COMMERCE AND SECURITY ISSUES 271

? Buzzwords you should know

COMMERCE VIA "COMMERCIALS" 275

? Making your site income-generating or self-supporting
? Understanding affiliate programs
? Researching affiliate programs
? Signing up for an affiliate program

? Distributing your own targeted affiliate sales banner advertising
? Third-party add-ons to help you maintain your business Web site
? Setting up your site to accept credit card and other payment methods
? Online resources for information on Internet security
? Encouraging visitors to return to your site

Commerce and Security Issues @ a Glance

E-Commerce is hot, hot, hot! But how safe is it to count on the Web for a source of income? This chapter discusses how you can hacker-proof your site reasonably well and how you can use your site to generate income.

- **Making Sense of Commerce and Security** This section gives you an overview of the buzzwords associated with commerce and security online.
- **Commerce via "Commercials"** This section gives you lots of innovative ways and resources for turning your site into a cash cow.

MAKING SENSE OF COMMERCE AND SECURITY ISSUES

What are some of the buzzwords I should know?

It is wise to arm yourself with some tools of the trade that will enable you to deal with the subject of security measures for your commercial Web site. Here are a few of the principal buzzwords that will help you feel like an insider.

- **Asymmetric Encryption** Also called *public-key encryption*. An encryption method that uses two keys (a public one used by the sender and a private one known only to the recipient) instead of one. Invented in 1976 by Whitfield Diffie and Martin Hellman, this method is sometimes referred to as Diffie-Hellman encryption.
- **Certificates** A form of digital verification, most often used to confirm that the sender is who he claims to be.
- **Click-Through Rate** The means to measure a banner ad's effectiveness by keeping track of the number of people who view an ad versus the number who click on

it. Some such ads pay a set fee per click-through to the displaying Web site.

- **Cryptography** The process of transforming (via encryption) information into an unreadable format (sometimes called *cyphertext*) without the necessary secret key to translate it back into standard text.

- **Electronic Commerce (e-commerce)** Commerce or business transactions that take place over the Internet.

- **Encryption** The translation of data into a key-secured code.

- **Firewall** A hardware or software measure used to prevent unauthorized access to a private network or system.

- **Multi-Purpose Internet Mail Extensions (MIME)** An Internet standard for formatting non-ASCII messages so that they are readable within a text view (such as the message reader of an e-mail client).

- **Packets** Varying byte-sized (such as 4,096 bytes) units of electronically transmitted information.

- **Pretty Good Privacy (PGP)** A public-key encryption method created by Philip Zimmerman.

- **Proxy Server** A server that resides between a client browser and the real server to help improve performance and filter requests to the server.

- **Public-Key Encryption** *See* Asymmetric Encryption.

- **Security** Refers to the measures taken to ensure that data residing on a computer or online cannot be read, altered, or compromised by unauthorized personnel.

- **Secure Sockets Layer (SSL)** A protection protocol between two communicating devices, such as a server and a browser, that allows the server and client to authenticate one another via an "electronic handshake" before an action is completed.

- **Transport Layer Security (TLS)** Another electronic security means of providing a secure and authenticated channel between hosts on the Internet.

Is there such a thing as a hacker-proof site?

There's an old saying that goes: "It's impossible to make something foolproof, because fools are so ingenious." Sadly, that saying is especially true when it come to the fools who like to sabotage computer systems and networks. Whether the subversion is done by a disgruntled employee (the most common perpetrator of such crimes) or a hacker who needs to find a better hobby, such actions can create havoc for your business.

Therefore, the logical question is: How do I go about protecting myself so that a network or server hack doesn't happen? The answer is: You can't—completely. But there are some things you can do, if not to make such destructive action impossible, at least to lessen your risk that it will occur or decrease the devastation if it does.

Some say the only safe computer is one that's never plugged in and still in the box. That also isn't true. It just makes things easier for another class of criminal—a computer in the box is a burglar's best friend. To protect your valuable information, use the same logic that has you installing security measures in the hopes that a burglar will find it more attractive (easier) to simply go next door to lift somebody else's valuables.

Like street criminals, hackers are often opportunists. To understand this logic, first imagine you're in the market for a new car and as you walk down the street, you notice three cars of equal value parked in a row. One is locked. One is unlocked. One is unlocked and has the keys in the ignition. Are you going to bother to stop and compare mileage before you help yourself? Chances are, if you were the criminal, in less time than it took to ask that question, you'd already be turning the key and driving away.

- You want to "remove the keys" and "lock" your site for the same reasons. Why make things any easier for a hacker than they already are? We'll cover online sources of additional security information later in this chapter. In the meantime, you can decrease your vulnerability by following a few simple precautions. Check with your domain host to verify that similar password protection is in place for protection is in place for your online site. Limiting who can and cannot alter files on a site is akin to locking the door.

- Keep in mind that the more bells and whistles you add to your site, the greater your vulnerability. Some CGI and other scripts can be open invitations to "invade here!" But you can't let that worry detract from your goal to make your Web site one that attracts and impresses visitors. A well-written script will be heavily documented, so carefully read the stuff written between the <!-- and the -->'s for your own knowledge and protection. If you're still uncertain as to what a script provided by your site administrator or domain host does, check and find out. See if there is any additional documentation available. The more you know about how a script is to perform, the better informed you'll be about how to track site activity that can warn you if a sabotage attempt is taking place or has already occurred.

- Back up frequently. Rewriteable media such as Zip drives or CD "burners" (slang for writeable CDs) make creating backups a snap and make it easy to store such backups offsite as well. (Even the fastest LAN would take around four hours to transfer 600MB between machines; you can burn 600MB onto a CD in about 20 minutes.)

- Install virus scanning software on your computer or network and update the virus patterns frequently. It isn't a foolproof method. (See the first paragraph of this section.) The recent Melissa virus showed just how quickly devastation can occur. But it can limit your exposure to known viruses. If you question a file and it's been more than a few days since you updated your virus patterns, you can check it (or any others on your hard drive) online at http://housecall.antivirus.com/explorer.html.

You wouldn't feel safe going for a walk alone in a seedy neighborhood after dark. If you had to go, you'd at least appear less vulnerable if you hired a bodyguard to accompany you. Don't let your information travel to dark corners via your intranet and the Internet without similar protective measures.

COMMERCE VIA "COMMERCIALS"

I don't have a tangible product to sell, but I'd still like my site to generate income or at least support itself. What are my options?

Anyone who has earned a living from commissioned sales can tell you that there's a world of difference between knocking on doors (cold calling) and operating a sales office where the customers come to you. In the latter case, the clients (potential customers) are partially pre-screened or qualified. Granted, they may have the desire or the need for your product but be without the immediate ability to purchase. It's still a numbers game. But, the odds of making a sale do improve dramatically once the salesman finds that qualified prospect.

The big guys practice target marketing. (It's not a coincidence that corporations premiere their soft drink and beer commercials during the Super Bowl!) Webmasters who do the same find that their content-driven Web sites can become self-supporting, and in many cases, even profitable.

You don't have to be an entrepreneur to generate income from your site. But even if you are and do have products for sale (which we'll cover later in this chapter), your site still might benefit from the diversification of alternative profit centers, such as enhancing your Web site with ads via affiliate programs and the other e-commerce options we'll discuss in this chapter.

As you ponder such options, keep in mind the factors that will aid in your decision as to which choices are best for you and your site:

- **Common Sense**   If you mention a book on your Web site, supply a link via an associates program with barnesandnoble.com or amazon.com (or both) so that the visitor to your page can go directly to a site to purchase that book. If you put a link for your new book to amazon.com and barnesandnoble.com, you can increase sales greatly

Chapter 11 Commerce and Security Issues

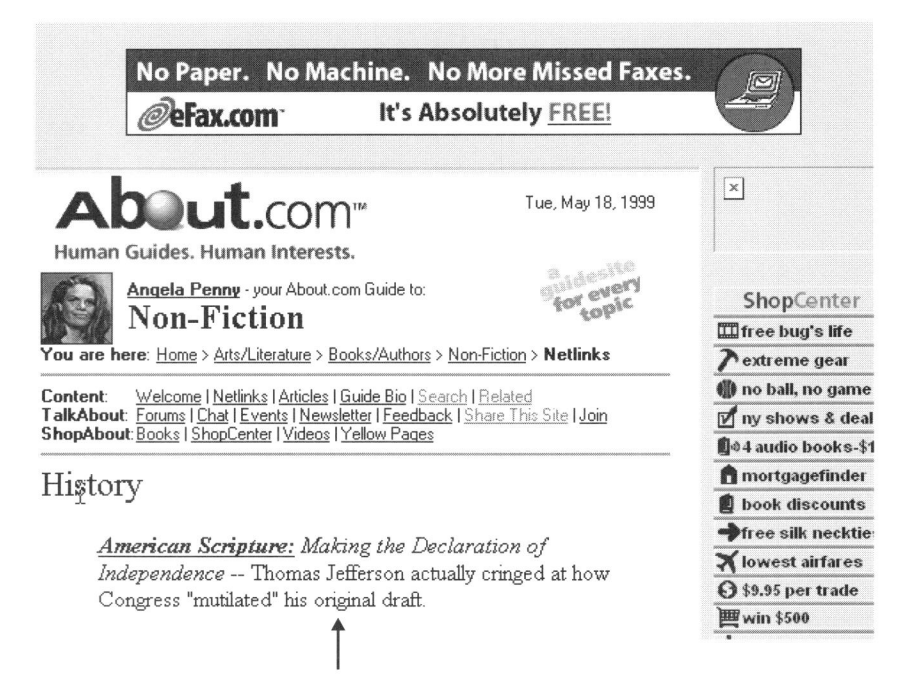

Links to associate sites can enhance your site

- **Knowing Your Audience and Anticipating Their Needs** Increase the odds that people who see the ad will be interested in what you're advertising by targeting ads to the likely site visitors. For example, your odds will be good that the visitors will be interested if you run a Viagra ad on a Men's Health site with an article about Coping With The Side Effects of Diabetes.

- **Reciprocal Links** Use the "you scratch my back and I'll scratch yours" concept. Even corporate Web sites can benefit from this arrangement. A contractor can link to a siding manufacturer's pages and vice versa. (Sometimes it pays to provide such links because they'll generate more traffic to your site, which in turn will mean more page views that ultimately result in more ad click-throughs and income for you.)

What are affiliate programs?

Affiliate program partnerships are those from which you earn a finder's fee, bonus, or commission each time someone from your Web site clicks through on an ad and then purchases the advertised service or product.

Several sites now operate that can help you pinpoint which associations will be most profitable for you, as described below.

AssociatePrograms.com
(http://www.associateprograms .com/)
This site is run by Allan Gardyne from Queensland, Australia and evolved out of the research and trial and error he did to market his own books online. He established the AssociatePrograms.com site because he wanted to create a site that was "useful for people who want to make money on the Internet without spending a lot of time learning how." In most cases, pay results when somebody buys something, but there are exceptions. Details are explained in the Associates Program Guide at http://www.associateprograms.com/guide.html, which is for people who want to make money with the Internet but who don't have a lot of time to spend learning about e-commerce. You can also sign up for a free newsletter in which Mr. Gardyne gives hints and suggestions on improving your site's income potential. Past issues of the newsletter are archived on the site.

Home | My Top 10 | Top Rated | Message Board | FREE newsletter
| New | Add your program | Change your program | Help!

AssociatePrograms.com
find a richer income stream . . .

Associate Programs Guide

32 useful hints about associate/affiliate/referral programs

How associate programs work

Associate programs (also called reseller or partnership programs) are revenue sharing arrangements set up by companies selling products and services. Webmasters are rewarded for sending customers to the business.

LinkShare   (http://www.linkshare.com/)
Claiming to be the largest affiliate program on the Web, LinkShare uses relationship-based selling models to help team your site with those affiliates mostly likely to benefit from exposure on your pages. (See Figure 11-1.) That, in turn, should result in more revenue for you. LinkShare is owned by the Boston AberdeenGroup, Inc. This site has a bit more sophistication (and uses bigger words) than the others. To learn more about how their ad impressions, click-through, and commissioned programs work, you'll need to complete the survey shown at http://merchant.linksynergy.com/fs/sregister.html.

linkShare affiliates program come join the largest on the web

Getting started is easy. Just follow these five simple steps to register your site. You will receive an immediate reply with detailed information on how to begin participating in our program.

Bold indicates required field.

Step 1: Site Information   Required

Please tell us the name of your site and your URL. If you don't know your URL, please copy and paste it from the location field at the top of your browser.

Site Name: [   ]
Site URL: [   ]

- Your site must be live.

Bold indicates required field.

Step 2: Contact Information   Required

ClickQuick   (http://www.clickquick.com/)
ClickQuick (see Figure 11-2) offers both "pay per click" and affiliate programs. The information on their affiliate programs at http://www.clickquick.com/affiliate/ includes an income-potential rating system. They currently list programs in 20 categories, including Art, Autos, Catalogs, Food & Drink, and Pay-per-Lead as shown in Figure 11-3.

Commerce via "Commercials"

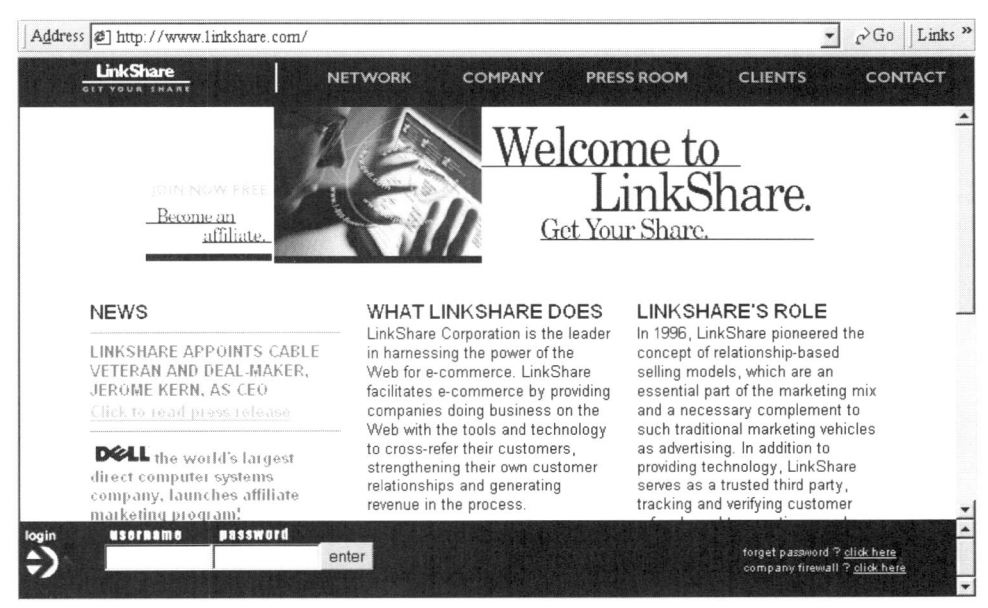

Figure 11-1 The LinkShare Web site

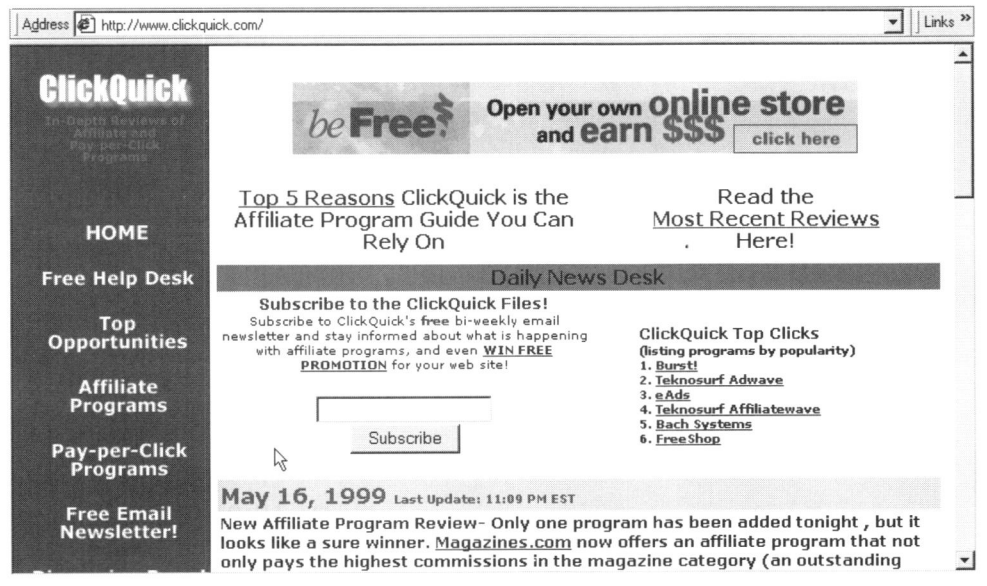

Figure 11-2 The ClickQuick Web site

Chapter 11 Commerce and Security Issues

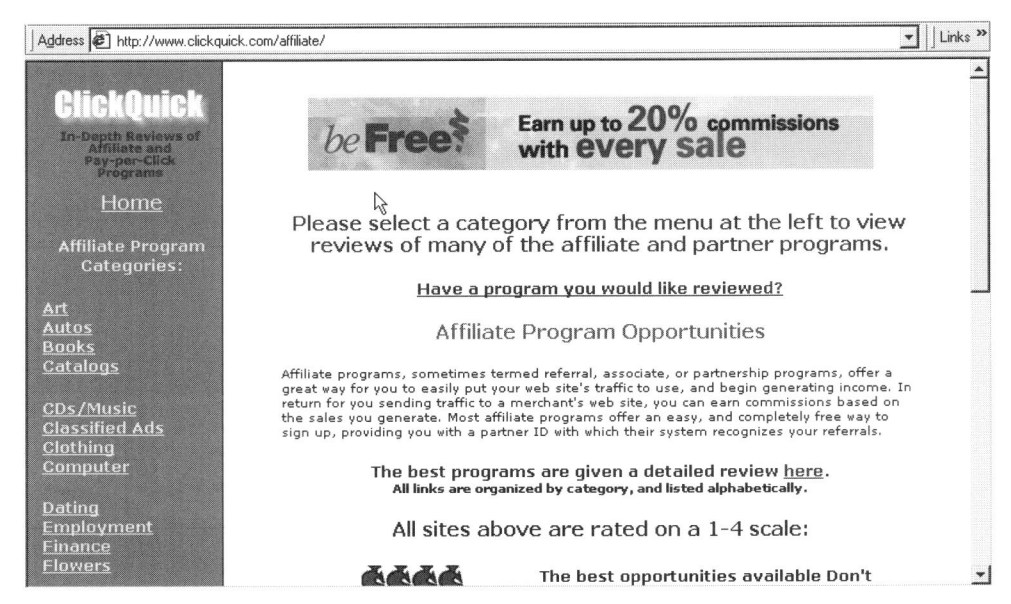

Figure 11-3 Information on ClickQuick's affiliate program opportunities

Refer-it.com (http://www.refer-it.com/)
Refer-It bills itself as "the search engine that pays." It offers more than 500 program listings in categories ranging from Accessories to Web Tools. To help you pinpoint your needs, Refer-It offers a page on the "Steps to Building a Successful Affiliate Program." Click on "Browse Affiliate Programs" for information on how to sign up.

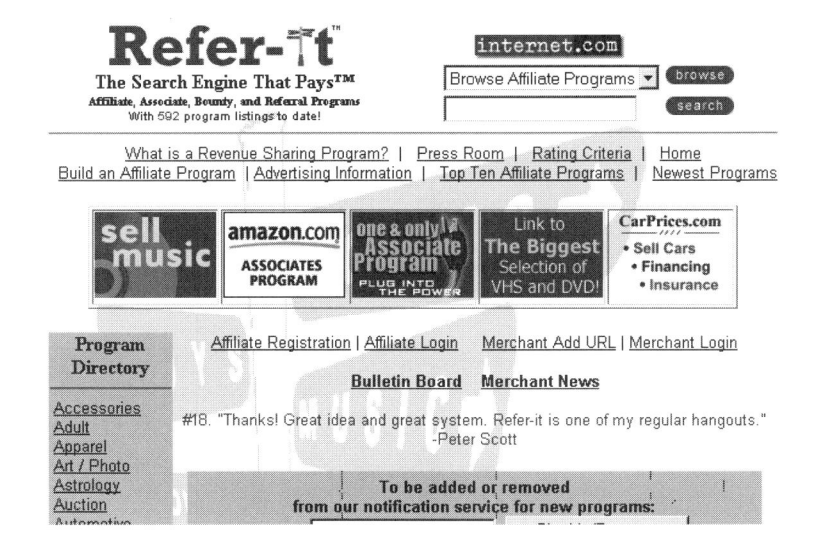

Sitecash   (http://www.sitecash.com/)
This is another site run by one person—in this case, Edwin Hayward. He takes a different approach by offering reviews of affiliate program offerings. His useful "The Affiliate's Guide" is at http://www.sitecash.com/guide.htm.

Is there a fast way to get started making money??

Absolutely. You can benefit by having ads on your site by signing up with one of the Ad networks online. Here is an overview of several.

SAFE-AUDIT   (http://www.safe-audit.com/)
Once you register your site with SAFE-AUDIT, you log onto their pages and select the banner ads you wish to host yourself. They provide the code for your pages and the necessary images. The company issues checks monthly, provided your site has earned at least $20; if your site earns less than that in a month, the amount is carried forward. They offer a download of a free Banner Wizard spreadsheet- style program that helps you to calculate your costs in site space to host banner advertising.

SAFE-AUDIT pays all sites before the 30th of the month for all monies earned during the previous month, if that amount exceeds $10; if it doesn't, the amount earned is carried over and kept on account. (They deduct a fee of 20 percent of revenue, which is their charge for providing the service.) Once you register with them, you can log onto their site to view statistics from your pages bearing the ads to determine whether or not you're getting the results you want.

ValueClick (http://www.valueclick.com/)
ValueClick uses what it calls a Cost-per-Click (CPC) model. In other words, they match ads to your site and each time a visitor clicks-through to the ad, your account is credited up to 17¢. They even offer custom contracts for high-traffic sites. There's no exclusivity required. You simply copy and paste the HTML code they provide in those spots where you wish the ads to appear. ValueClick ads reside on their server, so ValueClick pays for the bandwidth.

There is one catch. ValueClick must accept your site before you can participate in the program. According to ValueClick, "Only Web sites that are professionally designed and include useful content will be accepted as Hosts." (Not a problem since your site is designed using FrontPage 2000 and help from this book!) Figure 11-4 shows a Web site featuring an ad from this service. You can read their terms and conditions at http://valueclick.com/terms.html.

Is there an easier way to sign up for an affiliate program?

There sure is! Go to beFree's affiliate application site at http://www.reporting.net/networks/affiliates/bf_fast_app, complete the application, and choose between companies that

Figure 11-4 A Web site displaying a ValueClick ad

use the beFast FrontPage add-on software (described in the answer to the following question), such as GoTo.com, American Greetings, XOOM, barnesandnoble.com, and Fogdog Sports.

I use my site to sell my products. Is there an easy way I can distribute my own targeted affiliate sales banner advertising that focuses on merchandise from my business?

Of course! beFree: An Affiliate Network (http://www.befree.com/ 99frontpage.htm), as shown in Figure 11-5, has a FrontPage 2000 add-on software solution. The company will custom design software that meets your company's specific needs. Options can include the ability to enroll and approve affiliates; track impressions,

284 Chapter 11 Commerce and Security Issues

click-throughs and transactions; automatically manage your storefront displays; and more.

reporting.*net*
The **Affiliate** *Information Center*

sell online and **make $$$**

Welcome to the *FastApp* - the SIMPLE and EASY application form that you can use to apply to affiliate programs for merchants using Be Free! With *FastApp* we've made it possible to join multiple programs with a single click of a button.

Because you have accessed this page without logging on first, the fields have not been pre-filled with any information. Please complete and review your application information! This information will be sent to all the merchants whose networks you apply for and will be used for processing your commissions.

NOTE: Clicking on the APPLY button means you are agreeing to be bound by the Affiliate Agreement terms outlined by the merchant.

Site Information

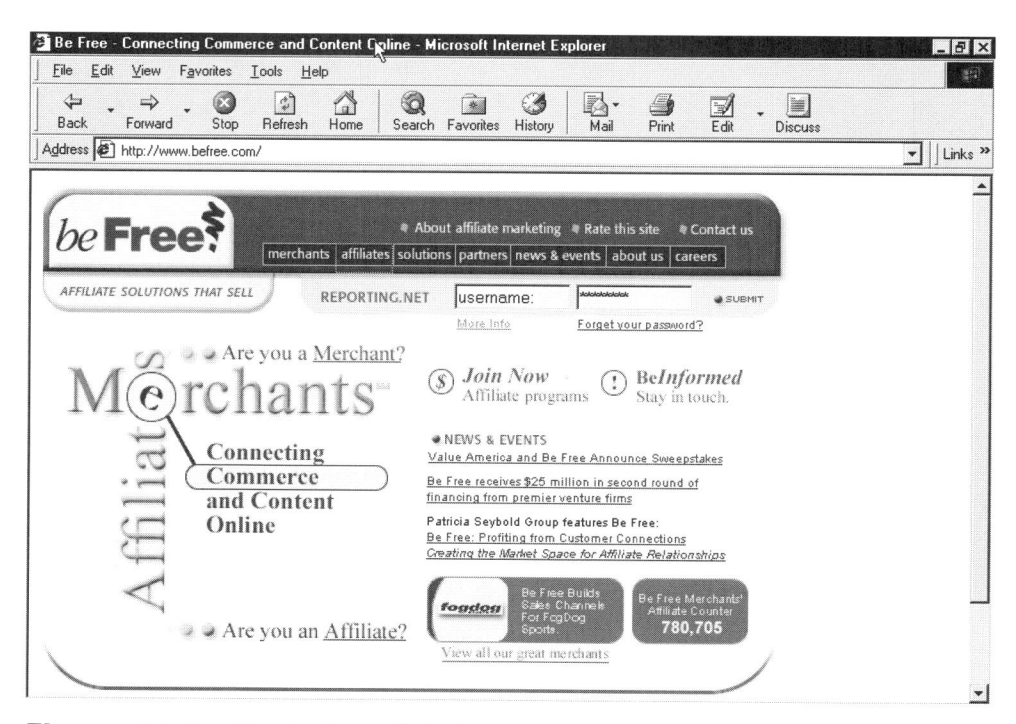

Figure 11-5 The beFree Web site

Are there any other FrontPage third-party add-ons that can help me maintain my business Web site?

Absolutely! There are businesses out there that appreciate that you use FrontPage 2000 to design and maintain your Web site because your time is valuable. Therefore you want the business maintenance aspects of your site to be easy, too. Following are descriptions of such products.

JustAddCommerce™ from Rich Media Technologies, Inc. (http://www.richmediatech.com/) JustAddCommerce™ is a complete integrated shopping cart—no programming skills required. It runs on all SSL browsers, including AOL and WebTV. Because it doesn't require FrontPage Server Extensions, it can run on Linux, Unix, NT, and other servers. You can customize up to two drop-down menu options (such as color and size) per item. The program allows for flexible shipping options (base rate or according to the order total, for example). If you wish, you can receive e-mail notification and verification of orders. New features include currency options and automatic credit card verification.

Pricing information and program instructions are available on the Web site.

Mercantec StoreBuilder™ for Microsoft® FrontPage® (http://www.mercantec.com/frontpage/) Mercantec StoreBuilder for Microsoft FrontPage has three major components:

- Web Templates
- Page Templates
- Commerce Bots

With Mercantec's StoreBuilder you can create an electronic shopping cart without doing any programming. The entire application is managed through FrontPage. The product costs $149, and more information is available at the Mercantec site.

PDG Shopping Cart Componenet for Microsoft FrontPage (http://www.pdgsoft.com/frontpage/) Another shopping cart add-on, but in this case the free 30-day trial version is a fully-functioning one with no obligation to buy. The company offers free tech-support and upgrades during this time, too. It includes a WebBot to help you add new items to the PDG Shopping Cart "administrator." It includes an integrated index and search function, internationalization of currency that displays in the new Euro currency as well as U.S. dollars, the ability to change price based on options, the ability to import information from any database, and multiple shipping options. Figure 11-6 shows a Web site featuring a PDG shopping cart.

Figure 11-6 A site that uses PDG's shopping cart

SalesCart™ Virtual Shopping Cart
(http://www.salsescart.com/3rdparty.htm/)
This company boasts that their shopping cart is 100 percent configurable. Because it fully integrates with FrontPage, there are no tools to learn.

Download a Free 30 day Trial Demo

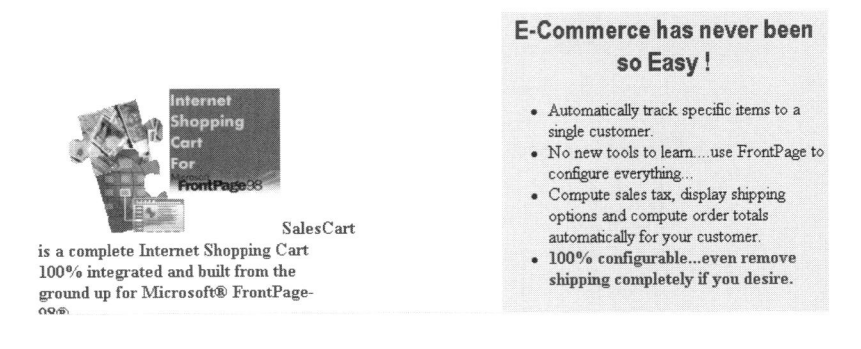

SalesCart is a complete Internet Shopping Cart 100% integrated and built from the ground up for Microsoft® FrontPage-98®.

E-Commerce has never been so Easy!

- Automatically track specific items to a single customer.
- No new tools to learn....use FrontPage to configure everything...
- Compute sales tax, display shipping options and compute order totals automatically for your customer.
- 100% configurable...even remove shipping completely if you desire.

ShopSite Express   (http://www.frontpage.shopsite.com/)
This company bills their program as the FrontPage
Companion. ShopSite Express (SSE) lets you create a new
Web site or even convert your existing one into a customized
full-featured commerce site. Much of the updating is done by
dragging and dropping elements (such as order buttons) from
SSE into FrontPage. The program lets you easily add
shopping carts, incorporate e-mail receipts, include credit
card transaction handling, and more. They have a "live demo"
on their site at http://frontpage.shopsite.com/demo.html that
lets you try out the program with FrontPage while you're
online.

StoreFront E-Commerce for Microsoft FrontPage
(http://www.storefront.net/frontpage/)
StoreFront is a complete e-commerce package, specifically
designed for FrontPage. (See Figure 11-7.) The company
offers a free downloadable demo of the $195 software package
so you can try before you buy. According to information on
their site, "StoreFront gives you the tools to create
graphically compelling catalog pages as well as the back end
functionality to dynamically build product pages based on

shoppers' individual needs." Companies using this software includes The Microsoft Store, The Pepsi Store, Gift of the Month.com, and Prim and Proper, a one-of-a-kind Victorian gifts and collectibles site at http://www.primproper.com/.

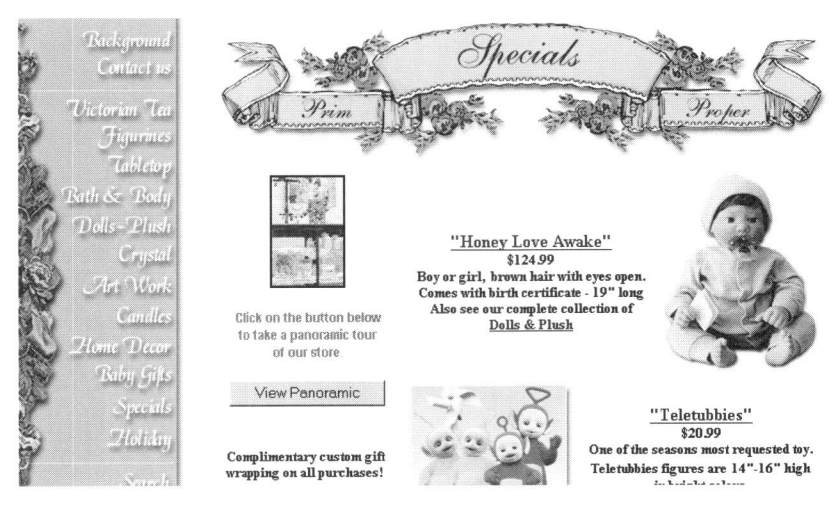

SecuredForm from Internet Technologies, Inc.
(http://www.securedform.com/frontpage.htm/)
For those sites that don't require a complicated shopping cart storefront set up, SecuredForm might be the answer. They, too, offer a 30-day free trial; after that it's $12.95 a month. (They also offer discounts if you pay quarterly or annually.)

Chapter 11 Commerce and Security Issues

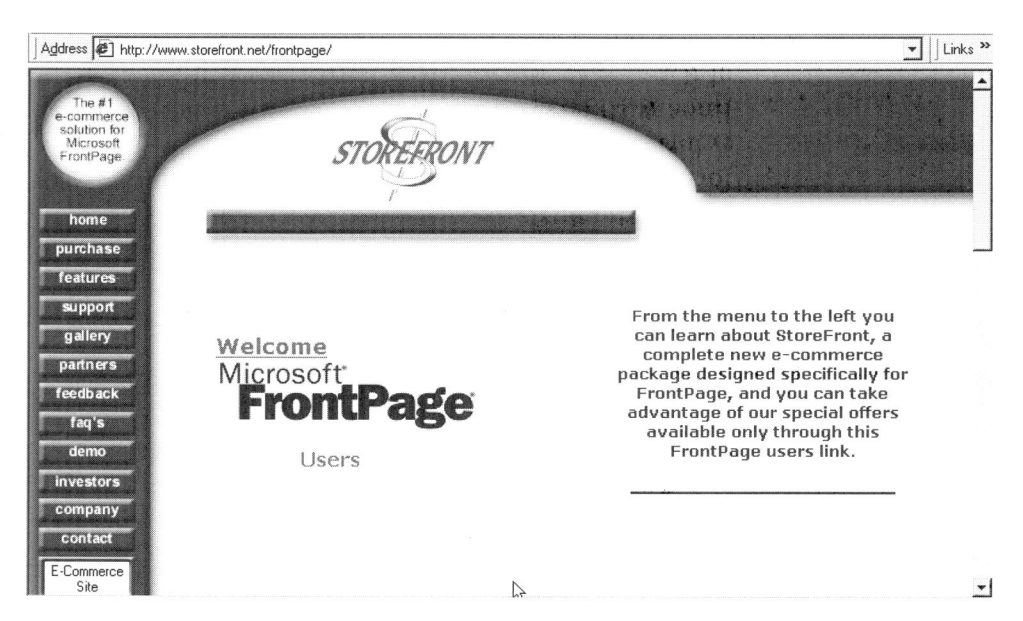

Figure 11-7 The StoreFront e-commerce add-on for FrontPage

How do I set up my site to accept credit card and other payment methods?

As your e-commerce Web site matures and your business grows, you may want to explore some of the add-on enhancements we've discussed in this chapter. If you're expanding an existing storefront enterprise and taking it online, that's another story. (We'll address that in a minute.) However, if you're starting from scratch, any expense in addition to your monthly domain and ISP fees may be beyond your budget. Sites that offers credit card and other payment options you may want to consider include:

- **Cardhost.co** (http://www.cardhost.com/) This company offers a $19.95 program that allows you to accept payment by check via e-mail.

- **iBill.com** (http://www.ibill.com/) If you only anticipate handling the occasional online transaction, check out iBill's Reseller Subscription Sales (iBill retains 15 percent of sales up to $9,999 a month in exchange for handling the credit card transaction) or their Web 900 (customer pays via a 900 number) services.

Payment Processors

If you know you'll be handling enough credit card transactions online to warrant the initial set-up fees (fees vary greatly, usually ranging from $300-$600), monthly service charges (in the $50 range), and per-transaction costs, then it's time to consult a company whose primary business is furnishing credit card solutions for merchants. Several such companies you can check out online are:

- Bank America Merchant (http://www.bankamerica.com/)
- Credit Card Network   (http://www.creditnet.com/)
- Charge Solutions   (http://www.chargesolutions .com/)
- Epoch Transaction Services (http://www.epochsystems.com/)
- First Data   (http://www.firstdata.com/)
- iBill   (http://www.ibill.com/)
- Paymentech   (http://www.paymentech.com/)

I'd like to know about security issues on the Internet. Are there any online resources you can recommend?

Ignorance isn't always bliss. So, while you may prefer that FrontPage 2000 handle all of the "HTML knowledge" and do your coding for you, when it comes to ensuring that you're running a safe and truly secure e-commerce site, you'd feel better knowing a bit more about security. With a world of knowledge at one's fingertips via the Internet, it's easy to achieve the Henry Ford–level of intellectual competence, which, paraphrased states: "I don't have to know everything if I surround myself with people who do." Here are three suggestions on where you can go when you need more answers:

- **Authentication and Encryption Software** (http://www.alw.nih.gov/Security/prog-auth.html)   In addition to information on public domain authentication and encryption software, this site is a source of additional information and FAQs (Frequently Asked Questions

Chapter 11 Commerce and Security Issues

documents) on such topics as firewalls, MIME, and many online security issues.

- **The Electronic Commerce guide**
  (http://e-comm.internet.com/) This site offers a free newsletter and discussion forum covering online security issues as well as reviews of e-commerce and storefront software.

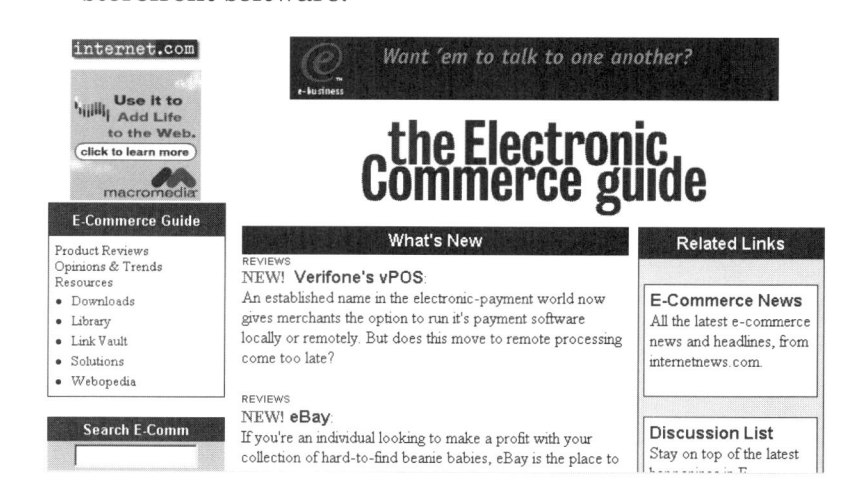

- **World-Wide Web Consortium Security Resources**
  (http://www.w3.org/Security/) The World-Wide Web Consortium (W3C) is the governing body that determines HTML standards. In addition, they now sponsor The Electronic Commerce Interest Group (http://www.w3.org/ECommerce/). You can find the

Commerce via "Commercials"

W3C's WWW Security FAQ at http://www.w3.org/Security/faq/www-security-faq.html.

W3C Security Resources

Introduction

Web security is a complex topic, encompassing computer system security, network security, authentication services, message validation, personal privacy issues, and cryptography. This page contains links to various aspects of Web and Internet security.

Overview: The World Wide Web Security FAQ

The World Wide Web Security FAQ (Frequently Asked Questions with answers) provides an overview of Web security issues, security hole alerts, and practical advice for avoiding unpleasant surprises. It is recommended as a starting point for exploration.

Security Initiatives at the W3C

The W3C is involved in the development of several protocols that relate to Web security. Presently, the main areas of work is on the signed-XML proposed activity. Other related activities include the HTTP/1.1 protocol and eCommerce. The W3C also produces software

Other Security Links

Protocols and Standards

- The HTTP/1.0 Basic authentication scheme.
- HTTP/1.1 Digest Authentication.
- Secure Sockets Layer (SSL) pages.
- TLS specification (IETF protocol based on SSL)
- A Distributed Authorization Model for WWW by Jose Kahan

❓ Now that I have a security-conscious, well-maintained e-commerce site, can you offer any suggestions on how I can encourage visitors to return to my site once they've found it?

One of the best ways to get visitors to return to your site is to request some information from them on the first visit, then send them friendly reminders and updates from time to time. That's called opt-in e-mail. It can be effective in generating return visits. Even more effective, however, is targeted e-mail. If you can get your visitors to profile themselves, then you can send mail to them only about things about which they care. Over The Web provides just this service. By subscribing to their $49 per month service, you can send targeted direct mail to visitors to your site who are inclined to join your list. Sign up at http://www.overtheweb.com.

Over the Web

Putting the Web to Work for You.

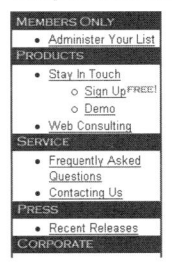

MEMBERS ONLY	
• Administer Your List	Try our *Stay In Touch* instant newsletter service for FREE.
PRODUCTS	◆
• Stay In Touch	
○ Sign Up FREE!	The Web allows you to instantly communicate with your customers, members, and clients. Are you taking advantage of that? With Over the Web's *Stay In Touch* instant newsletter service, you can. We're so sure you'll be hooked, we'll let you try it for 3 months for free.
○ Demo	
• Web Consulting	
SERVICE	
• Frequently Asked Questions	◆
• Contacting Us	
PRESS	You need to inform your members, inform your customers, update your clients with breaking news about your services. How can you do that without a programming staff? Over the Web's *Stay In Touch* is the
• Recent Releases	
CORPORATE	

Chapter 12

Publishing Your Site

Answer Topics!

ISP VS. PRIVATE SERVER 297

- ? Determining whether to host a site on a Web Presence Provider's (WPP's) server
- ? The difference between an ISP and a Web Presence Provider (WPP)
- ? Knowing what to look for in a good WPP

SERVER SOFTWARE 302

- ? Determining the need for special server software to use FrontPage's publishing functions
- ? Publishing to a Web server with FrontPage extensions installed
- ? Publishing to a Web server without FrontPage extensions installed
- ? Why Publish Web is grayed out on my File menu

UNIX SERVERS 305

- ? Using a WPP with a Unix Web server
- ? Losing functionality when FrontPage extensions aren't installed on the Web server

WINDOWS NT SERVERS 307

- ? Publishing a web to an NT server
- ? Publishing each page as you go vs. waiting and publishing the entire web at once

FILE SAVES AND FTP 308

- ? Publishing to a local hard drive
- ? Using a local hard drive on a network
- ? Using an NT server that is not local

Publishing Your Site @ a Glance

Publishing your Web site, in FrontPage lingo, is publishing your *web*. In order for your site to be accessible to the world on the World Wide Web, you'll need to publish your web to a Web server. This chapter tells you everything you need to know to use FrontPage's publishing capabilities, plus a few things that you need to know that are independent of the software you are using.

- **ISP vs. Private Server** Do you have your own Web server? Should you have your own server? This section discusses the advantages and disadvantages of publishing your web to your own server and the advantages and disadvantages of using an ISP or WPP.

- **Server Software** There are many flavors of Web server software. If you don't have your own server, there's some information you'll need to collect from your WPP.

- **Unix Servers** The first Web servers were Unix servers. Many ISPs and WPPs still use Unix Web servers because they're fast and reliable. If you do want to include server-side processing on your site, check with your WPP to see what's installed. You may be limited to CGI (common gateway interface) processing with Perl or C++. Unless you're a decent programmer, that's going to be a real problem. For most basic functions, you can find "off the shelf" CGI scripts on the Web, or you can get these scripts from your WPP (usually for a fee).

- **Windows NT Servers** Windows NT is rapidly taking over the server market. Because of the relative ease of installation and maintenance of Windows NT servers, many WPPs are moving away from Unix servers to NT servers. Because IIS is free and automatically installs with NT, unless you tell it not to, many NT servers run IIS as the Web server software.

- **File Saves and FTP** There's more than one way to save your files. To begin with, you definitely want to publish your site locally, so you have a mirror of your production site, in case anything happens to your Web server (referred to as an "act of God" in your WPP contract). But did you know that you can also publish to a local hard drive that isn't on your local computer?

THE LANGUAGE OF WEB COMMUNICATION

One of the things you need to know, independent of FrontPage, is how the publishing process works. Consider the following illustration:

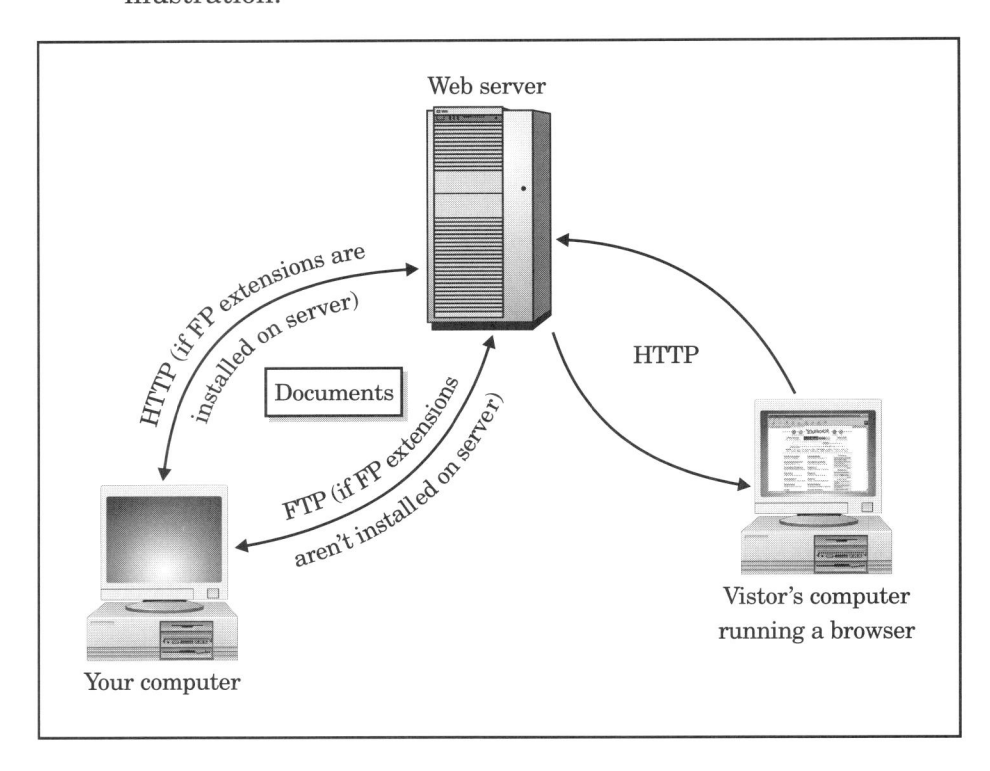

Diagram: Your computer connects to a Web server via HTTP (if FP extensions are installed on server) or FTP (if FP extensions aren't installed on server), transferring Documents. The Web server communicates with the Visitor's computer running a browser via HTTP.

You'll see several acronyms in this chapter. Some of them may already be familiar to you, but to help dissolve that line between those who know and those who want to know, I'll define them here for you:

- **ISP (Internet Service Provider)** A company that sells you access to the Internet, which usually includes a dial-up connection via your modem, an electronic mailbox (commonly known as *e-mail*), and a small amount of space on one of their servers to publish your Web site. Unless you make other arrangements (and pay additional fees), your Web site won't have your own domain. My own is: http://www.alexisgutzman.com (alexisgutzman.com is the *domain name*). For a more thorough explanation of acquiring domain names, take a look at *Internet: The Complete Reference, Millenium Edition* by Margaret Levine Young (an Osborne/McGraw-Hill book, ISBN: 0-07-211942-X).

- **FTP (File Transfer Protocol)**   The way your files are normally transferred across the Internet, up to your Web server, or down to your local computer.

- **HTTP (Hypertext Transfer Protocol)**   The protocol that paved the way for graphics to be displayed on Web pages. You probably recognize "http" from "http://". This is the way your files are normally *served* to the browser of your visitors via the Internet. With FrontPage, you can upload your files, whether they be pages, graphics, sound, video, or animation, to your Web server, as well.

- **SSL (Secure-Sockets Layer)**   The security technology that your browser and your server use to ensure that data that must be kept secure when traveling across the Internet will remain encrypted while in transit.

Note: *Chapter 11 discusses security in depth.*

- **URL (Uniform Resource Locator)**   The address by which a Web site is identified (for example, www.alexisgutzman.com).

- **WPP (Web Presence Provider)**   A company that will host your Web site and provide a full-featured Web server, but it won't necessarily offer any way for you to connect to the Internet. When you use a WPP, you'll probably want to go to the trouble of purchasing your own domain name.

ISP VS. PRIVATE SERVER

Should I host my site on a Web Presence Provider's (WPP's) server or should I get my own server?

Setting up your own server is a relatively simple task. Nowadays, many server-grade computers come with Windows NT Server pre-installed, and since Internet Information Server (IIS) is a standard part of Windows NT Server, with relatively little up-front effort, you can have a Web server for little more energy than you need to invest to set up a workstation. But the cost of ownership of a Web server is far more than the initial cost of a more expensive operating system. Hosting a Web server on your own workstation might sound convenient, but there are trade-offs. There are many legitimate reasons for maintaining your own Web server, but before you install your own, consider the pros and cons in the following table.

PROS	Maintaining Your Own Web Server
You can have all the disk space you want.	If you need to use a lot of disk space, you just add a hard drive. You don't have to pay the WPP for the hard drive space month after month. Most WPPs charge you for hard drive space after you use the small amount that's included with your contract.
You can create as many virtual directories as you like.	A *virtual directory* is a pointer to files. It may or may not map to an actual directory. Using virtual directories helps your visitors navigate around your site. Consider the URL http://www.alexisgutzman.com/books. You know that there is a server called "www.alexisgutzman.com," but is there really a directory called "books?" It doesn't matter. Your Web server can create virtual directories, called *mappings,* that point visitors to some remote location on the Web server with one easy-to-remember virtual directory name. Some WPPs charge for creating mappings. Because they create links between documents, they are very convenient for you as a developer, as well as for visitors, too.
You can use whatever server-side processing you want.	Rather than limit yourself to the server-side processing that your WPP supports, install whichever ones you want. Test new or experimental technologies on your own space. Most WPPs don't support every type of CGI (Common Gateway Interface), and will charge you for anything more than a basic account. CGI is the way that your Web pages perform actions on the server. When you choose a WPP or an ISP, you need to make sure that they support whatever type of CGI you're planning to use. They'll usually charge you for creating ODBC entries (see Chapter 9) and for using an enterprise database. If you administer your own server, you'll buy the software yourself, and won't have to pay someone else every time you make a change.

ISP vs. Private Server

PROS	Maintaining Your Own Web Server
You can publish a page by saving to your local hard drive.	What could be more convenient than publishing a page with your own computer? You don't need to worry about a network being down, or about file permissions.

CONS	Maintaining Your Own Web Server
You'll need to start supporting your server in the wee morning hours, the way *real* Web server administrators do.	Forget about just rebooting your server or installing software at your convenience. You'll need to schedule your maintenance outside of the hours that people are likely to want to see your site. It doesn't look very professional to have a Web site going up and down all the time.
You'll need to become an expert in Web server administration.	Are you ready to start worrying about registry entries in Windows 95 or NT? Not being responsible for all the minutia of server administration leaves you free to develop a professional site. Will you have the time to do both? Don't think of this as some big loss of autonomy. You don't learn how to dry clean just so you can dry clean a few suits and sweaters, do you? No.
You have to have a direct connection to the Internet with a permanent IP address.	A dial-in connection to the Internet is inadequate. You'll need to purchase an ISDN (Integrated Services Digital Network) line, DSL (Digital Subscriber Line), or a T1 line or better that will be connected directly to your own server. What you settle on will be determined in large part by what's available from your local phone companies and Internet Service Providers. There's usually a cost associated with having these lines installed. All three of these types of lines are dedicated to your use (so they won't slow down at peak times). Therefore, they guarantee you the bandwidth. With cable modems, you might get great bandwidth at off-peak times, but you're sharing the pipe with other users and things can really slow to a crawl during peak times. You can't rely on a dial-up line for serving a site.

❓ What's the difference between an ISP and a Web Presence Provider (WPP)?

Usually an ISP has dial-in lines and a WPP expects you to have your own connection to the Internet. With a WPP, you pay for space on a server; with an ISP, you pay for access to the Internet. If you're serious about publishing Web sites, you'll want to make sure you've selected either an ISP that also hosts many sites, or a good WPP. If you want to make a business of developing Web sites, take the time to find the right WPP for you and forge a good relationship with the folks there.

What should I look for in a good WPP?

A WPP should provide you with basic Web services at a reasonable price. If you need special server-side processing, like ASP, Cold Fusion, or CGI/Perl scripts, or other less-common Web development tools, make sure your WPP can provide it. Additionally, your WPP should have some way of keeping you informed of changes to the system, and of system downtime. Ideally, a WPP will have redundant network access, so that if one of its own sources of connectivity is down, your site stays up. You can use the checklist in Table 12-1 to help compare WPPs.

Start by asking your friends and colleagues who they use. Make a list of what you need and compare your list to the recommended list you get from associates. If you use arcane CGI, see if there's a newsgroup for that software and ask there which WPPs support that CGI. With a WPP, there's no obvious reason to limit yourself to one in your area. You'll be connecting to it via the Internet, anyway.

Figure 12-1 shows you a WPP that meets all of the requirements in the following checklist. With the help of the checklist, you will be able to identify quality providers when you see them. They're out there.

ISP vs. Private Server

What to Expect From Your WPP

✓ **Consistent Up-Time** Expect your WPP to be up the vast majority of the time. The contract you sign with your WPP will say something about not being responsible for network downtime—because they can't control where their own network connectivity comes from—but you should still demand that they have redundant connections to the Internet, so that if one of their own services goes down, there's a backup.

✓ **Good Bandwidth** *Bandwidth* is the volume of data you can transmit to visitors in a second. It's usually measured in thousands of bits per second (Kbps) or millions of bits per second (Mbps). A 28.8 modem allows 28.8Kbps bandwidth as the ceiling. That's pretty small bandwidth. The bigger the bandwidth, the faster your page will be delivered to your visitors and the more visitors you can serve at once.

Half the visitors to your site will leave if it takes longer than 20 seconds for your page to load. Can you afford that? If your target visitor is likely to be connecting from a home computer, load your own page (or another page of a client of your prospective WPP) from a 28.8 modem and time how long it takes. You can adjust the content of your page by reducing the size and bit-depth of graphics, but you should be able to load a reasonably well-designed page in well under 20 seconds.

✓ **A Turn-Key Environment** Don't be your WPP's first client. Look for a WPP that has processes and policies in place. It should be just a couple hours of work to publish your site the first time. You'll need the basic security information to publish to your account. You'll also want to allow a day or so for your WPP to set up your domain on its servers.

✓ **A Good Backup Schedule** Don't accept any lines about the WPP not being responsible for whatever. They should perform nightly backups so that you never lose more than a day of work (and you should have backups on your local drive so you never even lose that much).

✓ **Fast, Responsive Customer Service** If they don't answer your inquiries promptly, find someone else. Ideally, they will have a Web site that you can go to for frequently asked questions and assistance with system downtime. The most professional WPPs also have newsletters that they distribute by e-mail to inform their clients about server changes and software upgrades.

✓ **Reasonable Rates** Check to see what's included with basic service. Determine the minimum level of service you need. Don't ever accept a contract in which you're charged for bandwidth. That will punish you for having a successful site.

✓ **Traffic Reporting Tools** Most good WPPs will give you a weekly or monthly report (usually in the form of a Web page) of traffic to your site. You shouldn't have to pay extra for it. Without good data, how will you know whether your advertising or strategic partnerships are paying off?

Table 12-1 Checklist for Comparing Web Presence Providers

Chapter 12 Publishing Your Site

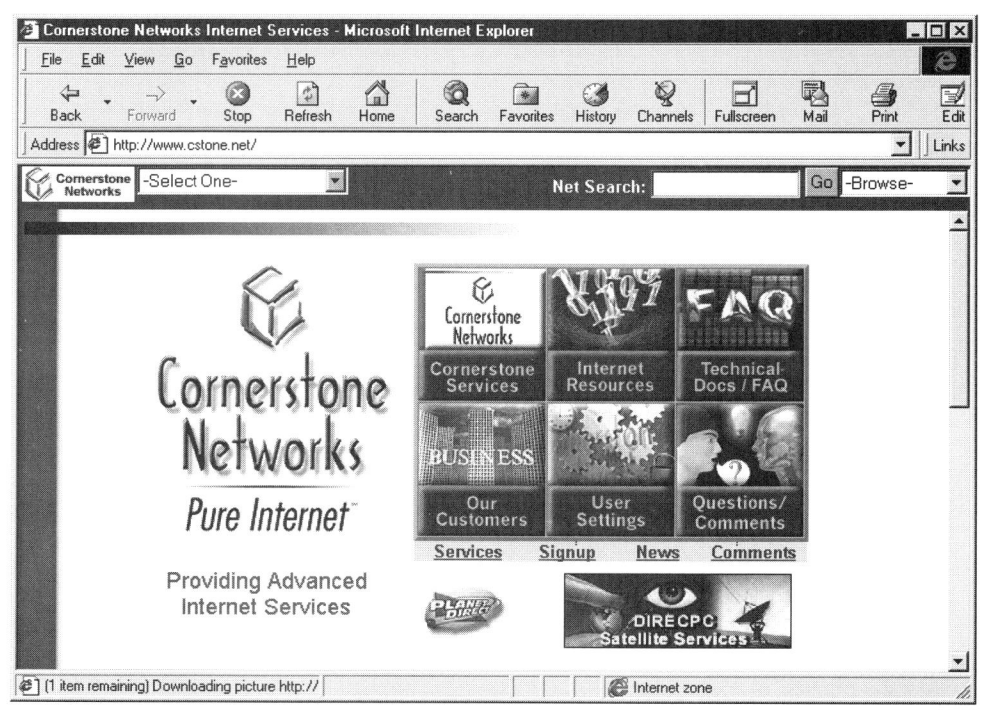

Figure 12-1 An example of a Web Presence Provider that meets these requirements

SERVER SOFTWARE

Do I need any special software installed on the server to be able to use FrontPage's publishing functions?

FrontPage gives you two ways to publish your Web. The better way to publish your web is to have the FrontPage extensions installed on the server. If you don't have the FrontPage extensions installed on your Web server, you can still publish your web via FTP, which basically just lets you copy your files across a network, as if the server were a local hard drive.

Server Software 303

Tip: It's important to find out from your WPP whether the FrontPage extensions are installed on the Web server. Also, be sure to ask whether the FrontPage 2000 extensions are installed. The older ones will provide only a subset of the FrontPage 2000 functionality.

How do I publish to a Web server that has FrontPage extensions installed?

The easier way to publish your web is to publish to a Web server with the FrontPage server extensions installed. In this case, you'll publish using HTTP.

To publish your web to a Web server with FrontPage server extensions installed:

1. Select File | Publish Web.
2. Click Options to expand the dialog box, as shown here.

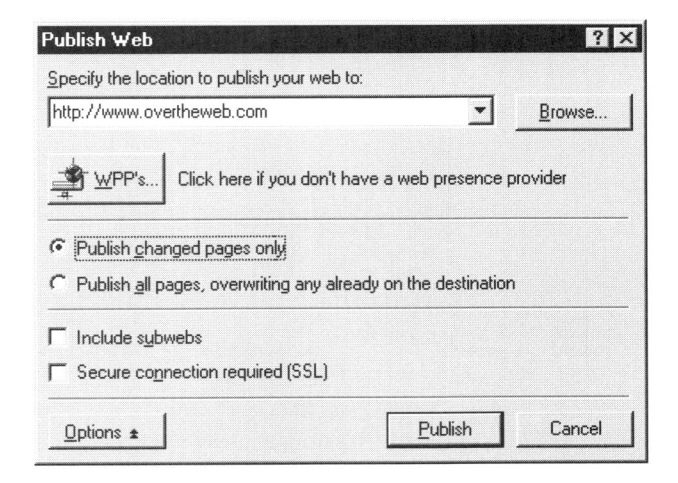

3. Indicate whether you want to publish only pages that have changed, or all pages.
4. To publish subwebs, if you have any, click the check box next to Include Subwebs. A *subweb* is a web nested inside another web. The web that contains a subweb is called the *parent web*.

5. If a secure connection (SSL) is required, check that check box. This requirement would be imposed on you by the server.
6. Type the location of the Web server (the URL) in the Specify the Location to Publish Your Web To box. If you've published before, click the down arrow to select from the list of Web servers to which you've already published. If you are publishing to a local harddrive, click Browse to find the publishing location.
7. Click Publish.

Can I publish to a Web server without FrontPage extensions installed?

Yes you can. You will be publishing to the Web server using FTP, rather than HTTP. To publish your web to a Web server without FrontPage extensions installed:

1. Select File | Publish Web.
2. Click Options to expand the dialog box.
3. Indicate whether you want to publish only pages that have changed, or all pages.
4. To publish subwebs, if you have any, click the check box next to Include Subwebs.
5. Type the location of the FTP server (which may also be the Web server) in the Specify the Location to Publish Your Web To box. If you've published before, click the down arrow to select from the list of Web servers to which you've already published. You'll probably have to precede the FTP server's name with **ftp://**.
6. Click Publish.

Why are the words "Publish Web" grayed out on my File menu?

Chances are that either you haven't yet created a web to publish or that you're not in the web you want to publish. Try opening up one of the pages for editing, then check again to see whether you can access Publish Web on the File menu.

UNIX SERVERS

What if my WPP has a Unix Web server?

No problem. You can still publish your web, but you'll use FTP, rather than HTTP to send the files across the Internet. The other limitations are the same whether your WPP is running Microsoft's Internet Information Server without the FrontPage server extensions running, or your WPP is running Apache (the most popular Unix server) or any other Unix- or NT-based server. In any case, you won't have access to a few of the types of server-side processing that FrontPage provides.

In order to avoid using functionality that isn't supported by your server through FrontPage extensions, modify the Compatibility tab of the Page Options dialog box.

1. Select Tools | Page Options.

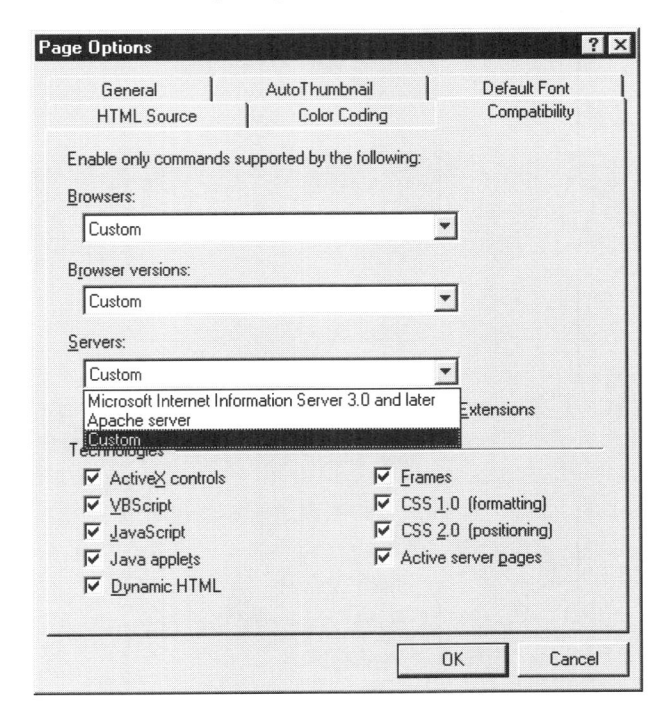

2. Click on the Compatibility tab.
3. Click on the down arrow next to the Servers list.

4. Select your server. If you know that your Web server has Microsoft's Internet Information Server installed, select that. If you know that your Web server has Apache server installed, select that. Otherwise, leave the option set to Custom. Notice that there's also a check box to indicate whether FrontPage extensions are installed. Uncheck it if your server is Unix, or if you don't know for a fact that the extensions are installed.

What functions will I lose if I don't have FrontPage extensions installed on my Web server?

You'll lose bells and whistles, such as a hit counter, a search form, and a confirmation field. A hit counter counts the number of times the page featuring the hit counter is loaded (see the following sidebar, What's This About Hit Counters?). Both of the other two functions are more complicated to create, but can be created manually using other FrontPage functionality. You will also lose the ability to save *form* data to a database without programming.

What's This About Hit Counters?

You often see *hit counters* on Web sites. Do they mean anything? Do they really count *hits*?

That depends on what you mean by a "hit." If what you mean is that the page was requested from the server, then you'll get what you expect from the hit counter. If you really want to know the number of times your page was visited by a *person*, then a hit counter will be misleading. To your server, a page request is a page request, whether that page is requested by a person sitting at a computer, by a search engine indexing a site, or by an agent (also called a *spider*) searching for e-mail addresses or other information.

It's been estimated that 40-50 percent of hits on Web pages are not by people, but by automated processes. If you really want to know what kind of traffic your site is seeing, check with your WPP and see what kinds of tools they have for parsing traffic data. They should be able to tell you the domains from which the page requests originated. Some of the fancier traffic-tracking packages can even identify the patterns of agents and other tools used to index sites (such as different pages being requested in rapid succession with fixed intervals between page requests). Ask your WPP what kinds of tools they provide for analyzing site traffic. You shouldn't have to pay an additional fee for these services and they're far better than hit counters.

WINDOWS NT SERVERS

What's involved in publishing a web to an NT server?

That depends on what the Web server software is running on the NT server to which you're publishing. If the Web server is Internet Information Server with FrontPage extensions installed, then you can publish your web using HTTP (see the sidebar at the beginning of the chapter). Otherwise, you'll publish your web by using FTP. Both options are readily supported in FrontPage.

To publish your web to a Web server without FrontPage extensions installed using FTP, see the answer to the question "Can I publish to a Web server without FrontPage extensions installed?" earlier in this chapter.

To publish your web to a Web server with FrontPage extensions installed using HTTP, see the answer to question "How do I publish to a Web server with FrontPage extensions installed?" earlier in this chapter.

Secure Sockets Layer (SSL)

SSL is the standard for Web security. When you use SSL, your client (either a browser or FrontPage) initiates the connection with the Web server. The Web server and the client exchange keys. All subsequent communication is then encrypted with the keys. Only the opposing party (the client for the server, and the server for the client) has the correct key to unlock the encrypted message. When you communicate with a *secure server,* you preface the URL with https:// to tell the server to direct you to the secure directories.

The name "secure server" is really a misnomer. What is really secure on a secure server is the connection. Usually, on a Web server there will be some directories that don't require a secure connection, and some directories that do. Ask your WPP to tell you where to put your files that require a secure connection.

Is it better to publish each page as I go, or to wait and publish and the entire web at once?

Fortunately, if you're publishing to a Web server with IIS installed, you can actually edit your files right on the Web server. That way, you don't need to make a choice about how you're going to work.

If your server doesn't have IIS installed, it's your choice whether to move each page individually onto the Web server, or to wait and publish the web all at once. Whichever route you take, test your work thoroughly so you don't publish work that's only half done.

FILE SAVES AND FTP

Can I publish to a local hard drive?

Yes, you can. In fact, I'd recommend that you publish all your work to a local hard drive first, then open up the pages from the browser by pointing the browser at the local hard drive. Figure 12-2 shows how you can open a local site in a browser.

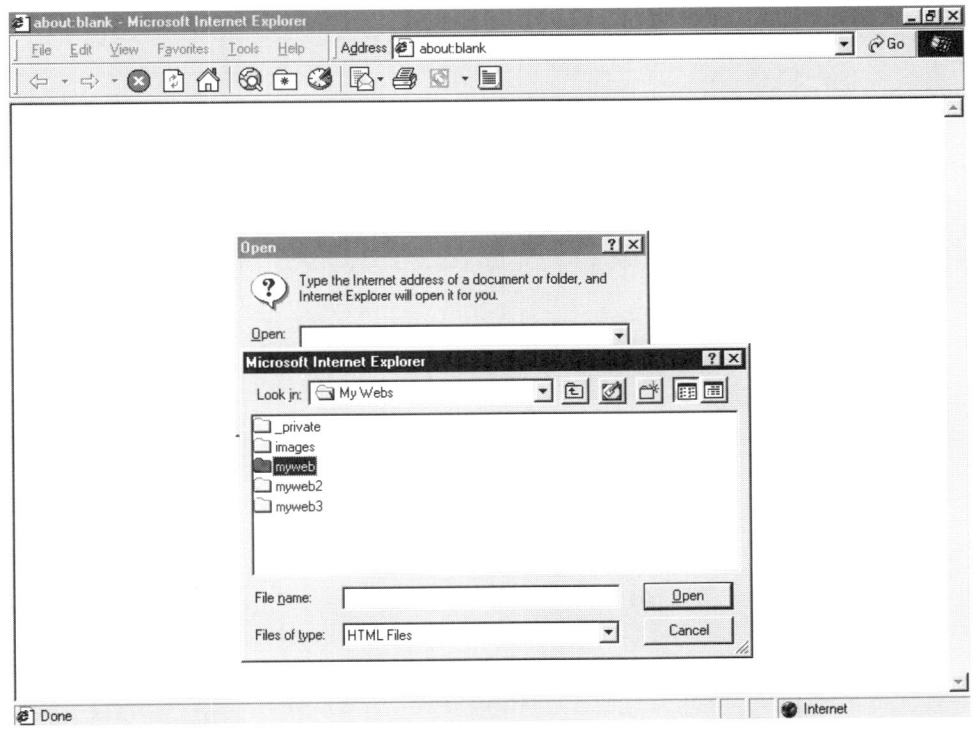

Figure 12-2 Opening a local site in a browser

What if my local hard drive is on a network?

If you have a network file server mapped to behave like a local hard drive (assuming that your desktop computer is some type of Windows machine), then you can publish to your local drive even if your local drive is on the server. If you're fortunate enough to have a server that you can map to, then by all means, publish there.

What if my server is NT, and is not local?

This is one of the really nice but undiscovered virtues of publishing to an NT server (even if it's not running IIS). If your Web server is running Windows NT, and you're working on Windows 95, Windows 98, or Windows NT, and your server administrator gives you permission (which means that you have to buy an NT user license through the administrator), you can map a local drive to the remote server across the network.

Chapter 12 Publishing Your Site

In order for this to work, you'll need to log into your Windows 95 session with the ID and password you are supposed to use on the server. If you're using Windows NT, after step 4 in the steps that follow this paragraph, you can enter your login and password for the remote server separately.

From Windows 95, Windows 98, or Windows NT

1. Make sure you have Client for Microsoft Networks and NetBEUI running. You can do that by following the lettered steps below. If you've already got NetBEUI running, then jump to Step 2.

   a. From the Start Menu, select Settings | Control Panel.

   b. Select the Network Control Panel.

   c. On the Configuration tab, make sure you have both Client for Microsoft Networks and NetBEUI listed.

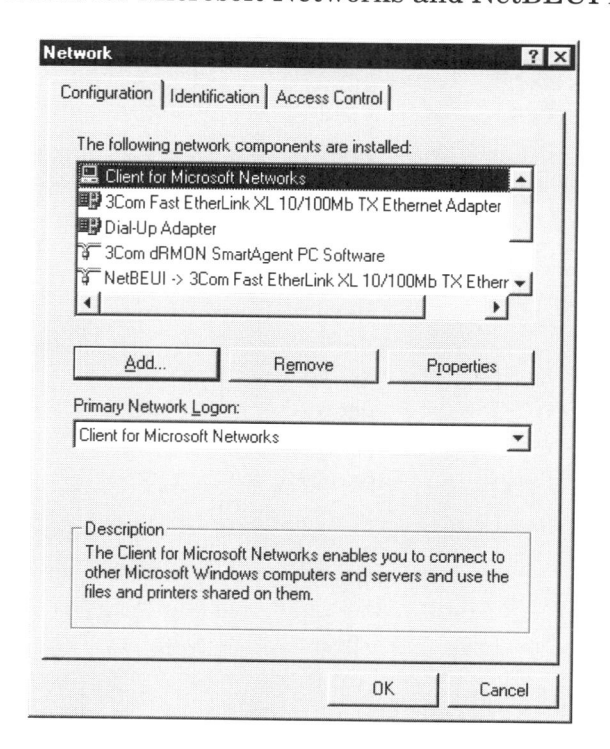

    d. If you don't, you'll have to add them, then restart your computer. On the computer used in this example, there are actually two NetBEUI protocols running; one is for an Ethernet connection, and one is for a dial-up connection. Be sure you install the right one for your computer.

2. Right-click on the Network Neighborhood icon on your desktop.

3. Select Map Network Drive.

4. Select the drive letter you want to associate with the NT server. If you're using Windows NT, this is where you can enter your ID; it will prompt you for your password.

5. Indicate the address of the server, for example:

    \\nautilus\overtheweb\

Be sure to include the *share* name that your server administrator gives you or it won't work.

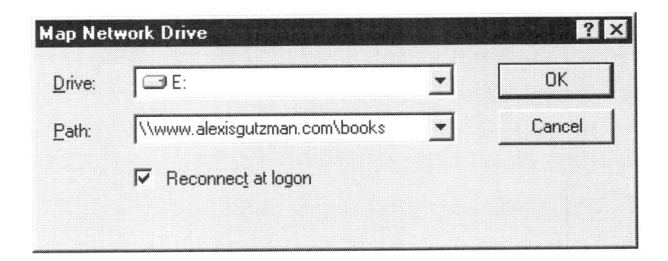

6. Check the Reconnect at Login box if you want to map to this drive every time you log in. If you don't check this box, you'll have to repeat steps 2-6 every time you want to copy or save files to your NT server. If you check this box and you have a dial-up connection, you'll have to keep telling your computer to go ahead and maintain the share even though you won't have a connection when you log in.

Chapter 13

Giving Your Site a Facelift

Answer Topics!

TEMPLATE OVERVIEW 314
- ? Types of templates

SHARED BORDERS 315
- ? Understanding shared borders
- ? Why you should use shared borders
- ? Ways to use shared borders
- ? Applying shared borders to all pages in your Web site
- ? Using shared borders on only a few pages
- ? Adding content to shared borders
- ? Viewing shared border page files stored on a Web site
- ? Creating shared borders in the middle of pages
- ? Using shared borders on a server that doesn't support FrontPage extensions

INCLUDE PAGE COMPONENT AND SERVER-SIDE INCLUDES 320
- ? The Include Page Component
- ? Including a page on another page
- ? How the Include Page Component differs from shared borders
- ? Including pages in other pages if your web server doesn't use FrontPage extensions
- ? Inserting a Server-Side Include in your pages
- ? Formatting the document you want to include
- ? Using the Include Page Component or Server-Side Includes versus shared borders

PAGE TEMPLATES 324
- ? What a template is
- ? The difference between global and web-specific templates
- ? Creating a page template
- ? Associating more than one page template with your web

REPLACING TEXT AND GRAPHICS GLOBALLY 329
- ? Replacing items in HTML code across a Web page

- ? When to replace items in HTML code
- ? Sizing a replaced graphic
- ? Other ways to change the look of all pages at once

UNDERSTANDING ELEMENTS 338

- ? Understanding elements
- ? How changing just a few elements affects the look of a site
- ? Knowing which fonts are safe to use

FONTS AS ELEMENTS 341

- ? Which fonts you should use
- ? Using specialty fonts or fonts that your visitors may not have
- ? Embedding fonts on pages
- ? The best point size for body text

GRAPHIC ELEMENTS 343

- ? Using art provided in themes without applying an entire theme
- ? Creating thumbnail images
- ? Sizing thumbnail images
- ? Creating instant buttons
- ? Screening back an image for a background or button
- ? Resources for graphics for your Web site

LAYOUT AS AN ELEMENT 349

- ? Understanding layouts
- ? Maintaining consistency in layouts
- ? Using the grid system in FrontPage
- ? Ensuring that all browsers and computers will display pages the way you intend them to look

Giving Your Site a Facelift @ a Glance

Styles change. Technology changes. What looked like a cutting-edge site a few years ago now looks stale and tired. Web designers stay busy by doing site makeovers, and you'll learn some tricks of the trade in this chapter that you can apply to your own site. You'll learn techniques for changing many pages or elements at once, and for setting up your web so that when you want to change it again, it'll be a breeze rather than a nightmare.

- **Template Overview** discusses what templates are, why to use them, and what FrontPage offers.
- **Shared Borders** provides an in-depth discussion of Shared Borders, how they're used and what their limitations are.
- **Include Page Component and Server-Side Includes** discusses the Include Page Component and server-side includes. These are two ways to include a page of HTML within another page. Limitations of each method are elaborated.

- **Page Templates** covers designing pages that have a consistent look and feel, and describes how to think of your content in levels and design pages accordingly.
- **Replacing Text and Graphics Globally** shows you techniques for changing separate elements across your web and looking at the HTML code.
- **Understanding Elements** helps you identify what the elements on your site are, and how you can change only a few elements to give your site an entirely fresh look.
- **Fonts as Elements** discusses how you can use fonts effectively on your site, limitations of embedding fonts, and guidelines for using fonts.
- **Graphic Elements** discusses how to use graphics effectively, create thumbnails, size thumbnails, create buttons quickly, screen back images to make them effective background images, and provides a list of resources for getting clip art and other materials.
- **Layout as an Element** discusses layout, what it is, how you can find a layout you like and stick with it, and browser compatibility issues.

TEMPLATE OVERVIEW

What does FrontPage provide in the way of templates?

There are six ways to use templates in FrontPage:

- **Themes** Themes are the easiest way to give your site a uniform look and revamp it in a jiffy. Chapter 2 discusses Themes at length.
- **Shared borders** Shared borders give you a quick way to have navigational elements in the same places on every page. Consistency is the hallmark of a good site; and shared borders give you consistency for very little overhead.
- **Include Page Component** The Include Page Component gives you an easy way to include a page within another page. This is FrontPage's own version of server-side includes.

- **Page templates** You can create your own page templates so that once you've developed a page you like, you can use it as the starting point for all subsequent pages.
- **Cascading style sheets (CSS)** Style sheets permit you to define rules, in a separate file, governing how elements will appear, with links to that file from every page so that styles are reflected on the pages. Chapter 7 discusses CSS at length.
- **Applying the background and colors of one page to another** This little trick permits you to develop one beautiful page, then transfer the background and colors to other pages in a snap.

SHARED BORDERS

What are shared borders?

A shared border is a portion of a page that is common to one or more pages in a Web site. A shared border may be a place at the top of the page (like a page header), at the bottom (like a page footer), at the left, or at the right. Use shared borders to place the same content on multiple pages once, rather than editing each page.

Why use shared borders?

The advantage to using shared borders is that you only have to edit content in one place to update all your pages. For example, to change the logo on a site of 40 pages, you only need to change it on one page if the logo is contained inside a shared border.

What are some ways to use shared borders?

Shared borders are a quick and easy way to give your pages a consistent look. Here are some examples of ways to use shared borders:

- Add a banner or logo to a shared top border to make sure each page has a title.
- Add a navigation bar containing main sections of your web on each page.

Chapter 13 Giving Your Site a Facelift

- Add copyright information in a shared bottom border.
- Add the date and time the web was last updated.
- Add an e-mail address for comments from your visitors.

How do I apply shared borders to all the pages in my web?

1. Select Format | Shared Borders. FrontPage displays the Shared Borders dialog box, shown here:

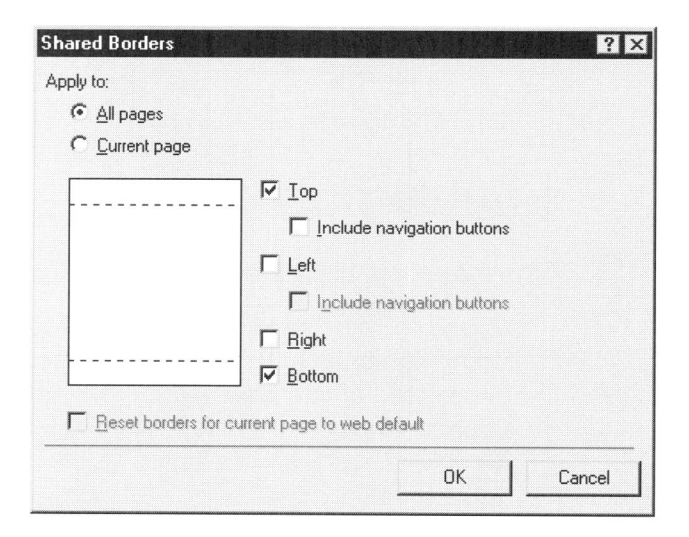

2. Choose All Pages.
3. Select the borders that you want to appear on every page in the current Web site. If you select Top or Left, you can also opt to include navigation bars.
4. Dashed lines are displayed to show where the shared borders will appear. If you included a navigation bar, it is displayed in the shared border.

What if I don't want content in shared borders to appear on every page?

You can set shared borders on individual pages. For example, the default setting for a web might be to share top and bottom borders; each new page would then have these shared borders. However, you can turn off a shared border on certain pages if you don't want it. You can also set up a web that has no shared borders by default. You could then set shared borders on specific pages as needed.

How can I add my own content to my shared borders?

After you set a shared border, you can add content to it. At any point, you can change or delete what's in a shared border. For example, you can add a company logo to a shared top border, change the navigation, or add or delete text. Figure 13-1 shows an example of the Virginia Wine Company's Web site, which features a shared border at the top of the page.

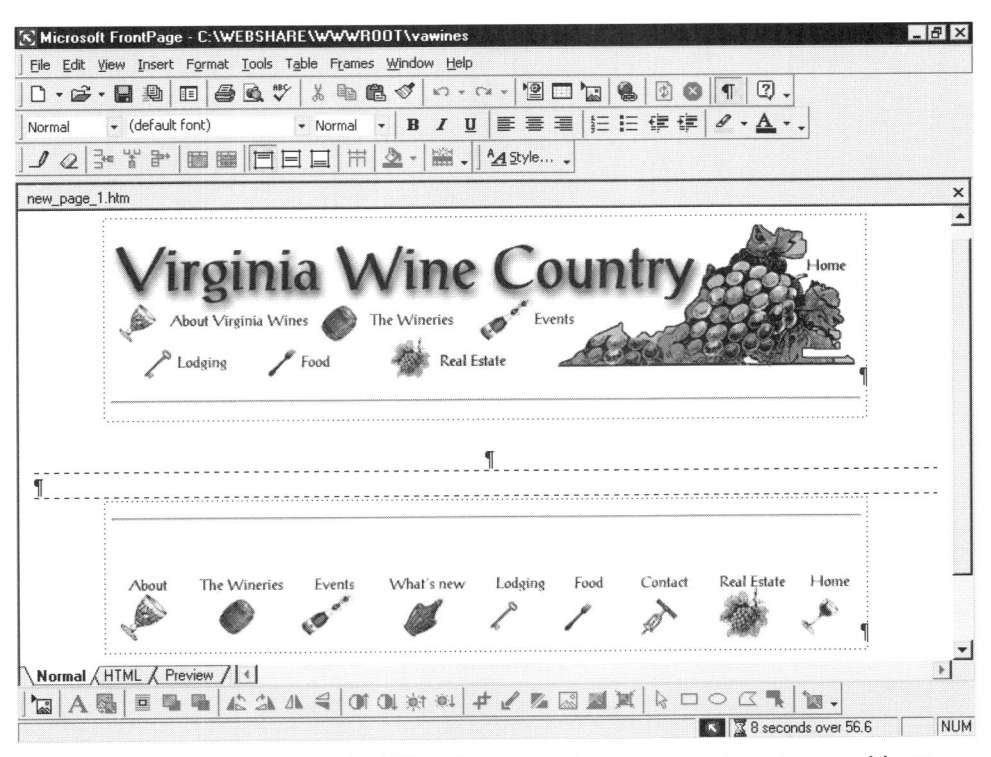

Figure 13-1 The Virginia Wine Country site uses custom top and bottom shared borders as navigational elements

To set up shared borders with your own content, follow these steps:

1. Open a page that uses the shared border you want to change.
2. In Page view, click inside the shared border region, which is outlined with a dashed line. When you click the area, the outline changes to a solid line.
3. Make your changes to the content inside the shared border region. For example, add text or include an image.
4. Click Save. Your changes will appear on all pages that share the border.

Why can't I see where the shared border pages are stored on my web?

Shared borders are HTML pages like the others on your web. They live in a folder called _borders, which is hidden. FrontPage hides these pages from you, but here's how you can see them:

1. Select Tools | Web Settings.
2. Choose the Advanced tab.
3. Choose the Show Documents In Hidden Directories box to show files in hidden folders, as shown in the following illustration.

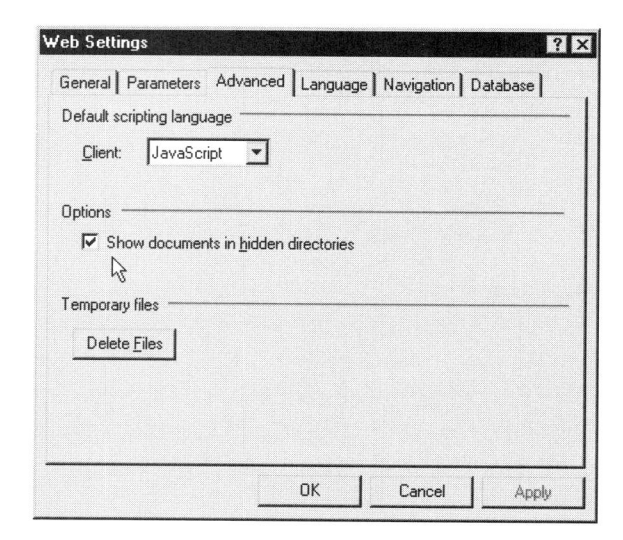

Figure 13-2 shows the Folder view after you have unhidden the shared border files. Shared Borders have only four names: top.htm, bottom.htm, left.htm, and right.htm.

Tip: *Hidden folder names begin with an underscore character (for example, _borders).*

Can I create my own shared borders? Like an invisible frame in the middle of every one of my pages?

No. Top, bottom, left, and right are your only options. FrontPage doesn't give you the option of putting shared borders in the middle of pages. If you want to put something in the middle a page, consider using the Include Page Component or server-side includes.

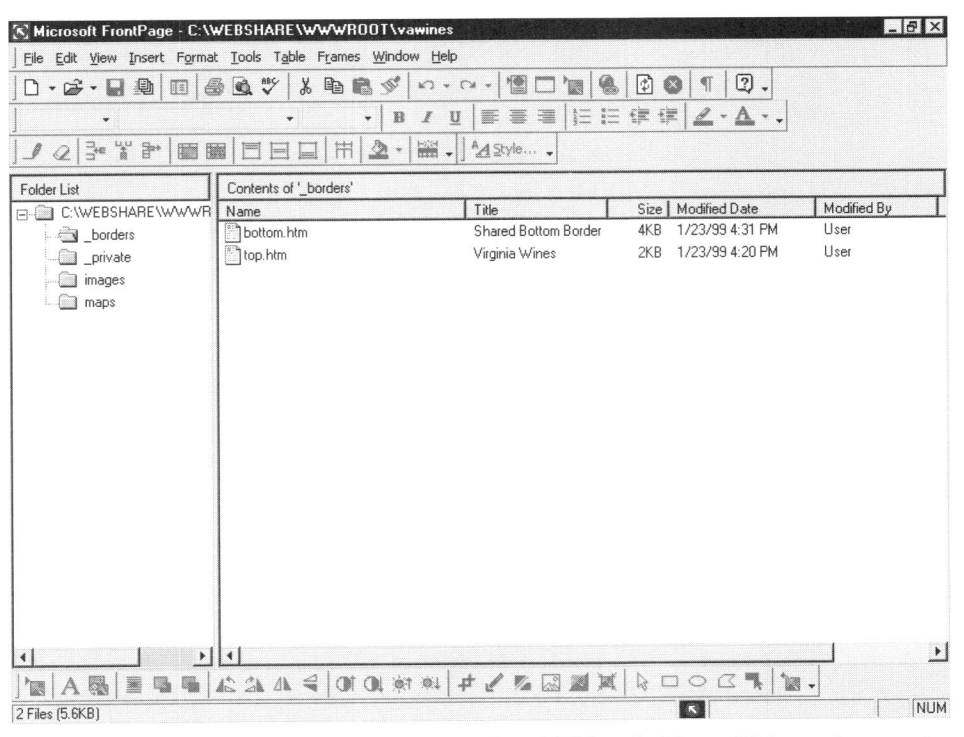

Figure 13-2 Folder view after showing hidden folders. This web uses top and bottom shared borders, always named top.htm and bottom.htm

Chapter 13 Giving Your Site a Facelift

? Can I use shared borders if the server I'm using doesn't support the FrontPage extensions?

Yes, you can. Shared borders are not dependent on the FrontPage extensions. They take up a lot less room than themes, which is a great reason to use them!

INCLUDE PAGE COMPONENT AND SERVER-SIDE INCLUDES

? What does the Include Page Component do?

You can display an HTML page on another page in the web, allowing you to maintain separate pages. For example, to show a disclaimer on several pages in a web, make one page that contains disclaimer text and include that page on other pages in the web. When you change the disclaimer, you change that one page—and all the other pages that include the disclaimer will be automatically changed.

? How do I include a page on another page?

1. In Page view, put the cursor where you want to include a page.
2. Select Insert | Component | Include Page. FrontPage will display the Page to Include box.
3. In the Page to Include dialog box, type the filename of the page to include, or choose Browse to locate the file. You must already have created the include page before you can use this function.

? How does the Include Page Component differ from shared borders?

It differs in two ways. First, the Include Page feature is a FrontPage Component, meaning that the FrontPage extensions must be installed on the Web server in order for this feature to work. Secondly, shared borders contain content that resides only on the top, bottom, left, or right sides of your pages. The Include Page Component can be placed anywhere on your page.

How can I include pages in other pages if my Web server doesn't use the FrontPage extensions?

You can use what's called a Server-Side Include. A Server-Side Include (SSI) does what the Include Page Component does, but doesn't require the FrontPage extensions. It does, however, require that the server be configured to handle includes. Check with your Internet Service Provider or Web Presence Provider to find out more.

How do I insert a Server-Side Include in my pages?

First, you must put the content you want included into an include file. Then, you'll use a special tag (Figure 13-3) that automatically inserts whatever text is included in the Server-Side Include file into your page at run time and presents the finished document to your viewer. In other

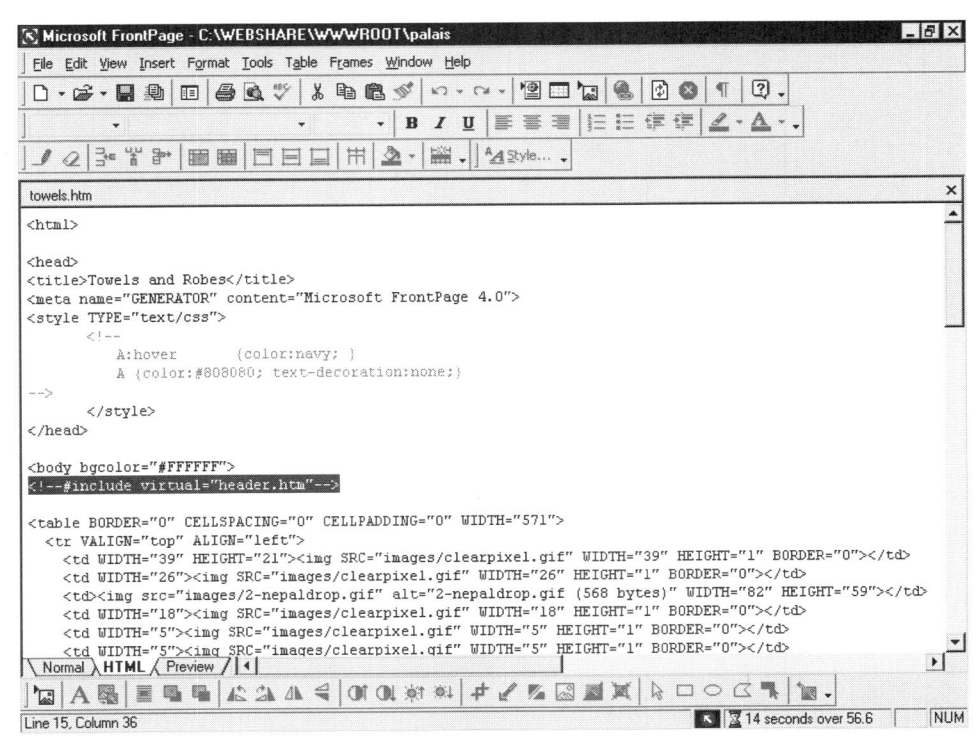

Figure 13-3 How the Server-Side Include tag looks in the HTML code

words, when visitors view your source code, they don't see the include tag, they see the results. Here's the format of the tag:

`<!--#include virtual="somefile.htm"-->`

Wherever this tag appears in your HTML document, the file you specify will be inserted. Figure 13-3 shows how the SSI tag looks in the HTML code.

In this case, the SSI is inserting the navigation that runs across the top. Figure 13-4 shows the file that's being inserted.

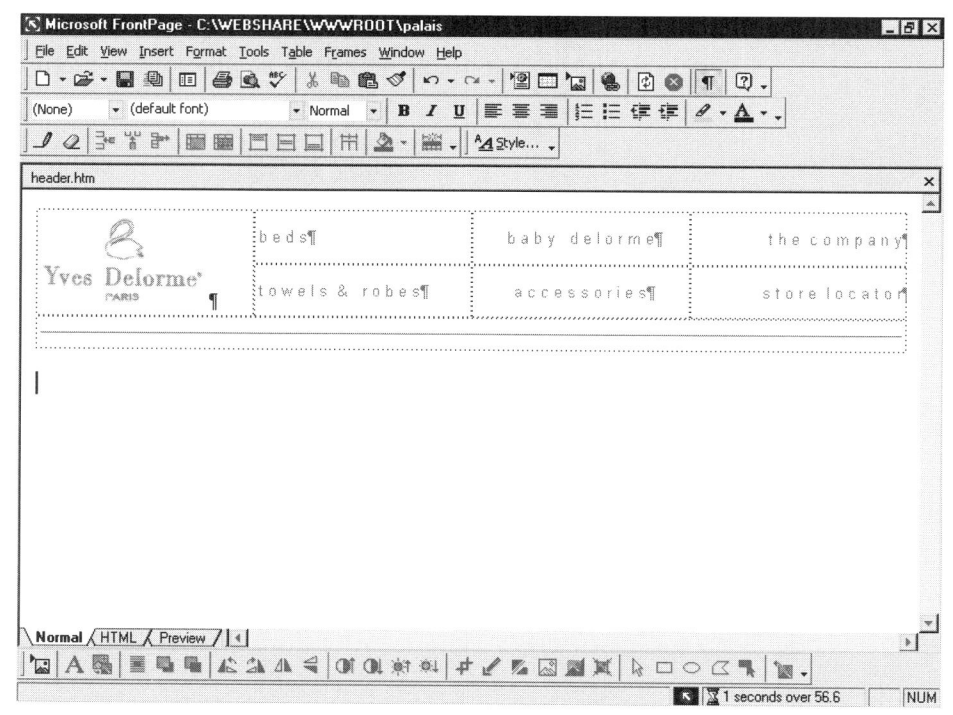

Figure 13-4 The navigational element the SSI inserts on the page

Include Page Component and Server-Side Includes

? Do I have to format the document I want to include in a special way?

Yes. Remember, the Server-Side Include inserts the entire file into your page. If you are inserting content in the middle of a page, you will need to access the file you want to include in HTML view, and strip out all HEAD, HTML, and BODY tags so they aren't inserted into your document twice. Figure 13-5 shows the page with the tags stripped out, and Figure 13-6 shows the final results running on the server.

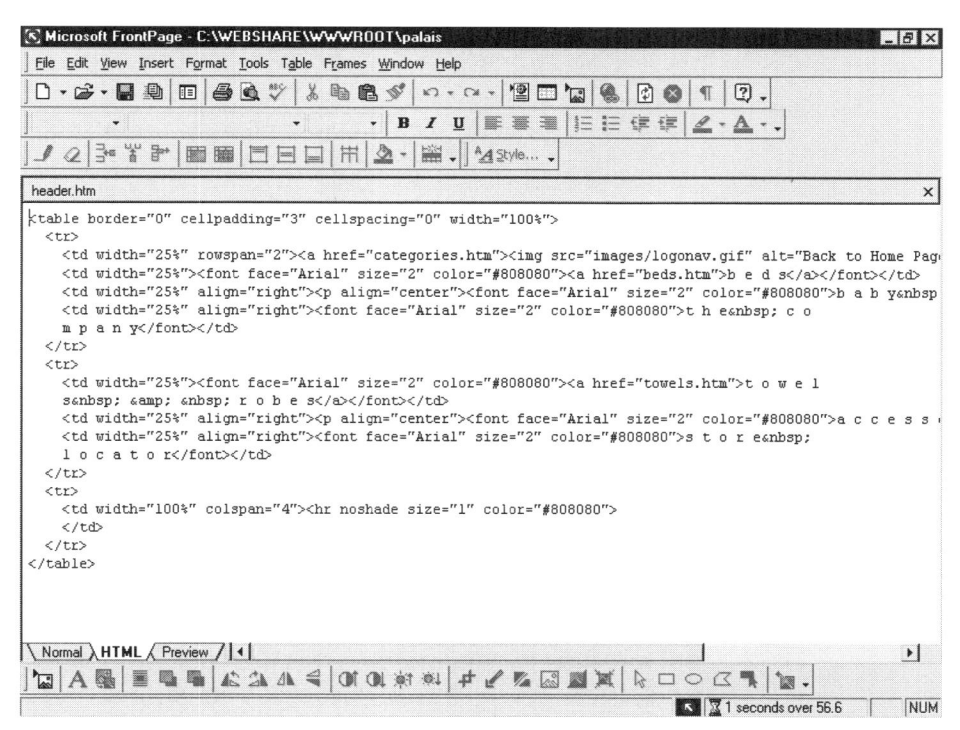

Figure 13-5 The HTML for the Server-Side Include with extraneous tags stripped out

Figure 13-6 The results of an SSI in a page

Why would I want to use the Include Page Component or Server-Side Includes rather than shared borders?

Shared borders allow you to include content on only the top, bottom, left, or right sides of your pages. If you want content to appear in other areas, like in the middle of a page, you'll need includes. Think of includes as "boilerplate" text in word processing. It's something that you might want to include on specific pages or all pages, such as a table or several paragraphs. You can also use Server-Side Includes or the Include Page Component to handle your navigation if you don't want to use shared borders. You can use Server-Side Includes or the Include Page Component to handle subnavigational elements as well.

PAGE TEMPLATES

What's a template?

A template is a page that contains formatting for page elements. You can design your own page templates so that you can create pages for your web quickly and consistently. Templates are very useful in a multiple-author environment because they help authors create pages in the same way.

For example, if all your pages always have a graphic and tagline at the top of the page, create a template with those elements. Then, use your template when you want to create a new page, and the graphic and tagline will automatically be placed on the page.

FrontPage comes with lots of predesigned templates that cover most of the standard types of page layouts. When you click on File | New, you'll see the list. You can create templates that are global or specific to a particular web.

What's the difference between global and web-specific templates?

A global page template is available during all sessions of FrontPage. It's like the Normal template in Word.

A web-specific template is available only in one web, and isn't available when you are working on a different web. Web-specific templates are handy for keeping templates together within a particular web.

When you create a page template, you make a page with the settings you want, and then save the page as a template. The template will show up with the other templates provided in FrontPage. When you want to create a new page using your template, pick your template from the list. If the template is web-specific, you will only see the template listed if that web is open.

How can I create a page template?

When you create a page template, you're basically just creating a page and saving it as a template file so that you can use it more easily the next time you create pages.

1. In Page view, make a page with the graphics, rules, and layout you want. Don't include content—just the elements that make up the page.

2. Select File | Save As. FrontPage displays the Save As dialog box.

3. From the Save As dialog box, find the Save As Type box, and click the FrontPage Template (*.tem) option from the drop-down list.

4. Click Save. FrontPage displays the Save As Template dialog box.

5. In the Title box type a title for the template, which will appear with the along with the other templates on the General tab in the New dialog box.

6. In the Name box give the new template a filename. FrontPage will automatically add the correct extension.

7. In the Description area, enter a description of the template. For example, type something like "Acme Web-Level 1 page." When you create a new page, this description will appear in the New dialog box when you select the template.

8. If you want the template to be available only to this web, check the Save Template In Current Web check box. If you want the template to be available during all sessions of FrontPage, clear the box. Click OK.

Can I have more than one page template associated with my web?

Yes, you can have as many as you want, and it's a good idea to create them. One really handy way to think about layout is to think of your pages in *levels*. You probably already have your web structured navigationally in levels—Parent level, Child level, and so on, and your page design should reflect that as well. For example, the home page or "splash" page should have a certain look. Your "level 1" pages, which the visitor comes to following the home page, should also have a unified look. When a visitor drills down to the next level, he or she should also find a consistent look for "level 2" pages. If you make templates for each level, your web will have certain consistency of form and style that your visitors will appreciate.

Figures 13-7, 13-8, and 13-9 show Home, Level 1, and Level 2 pages in the Virginia 2020 web.

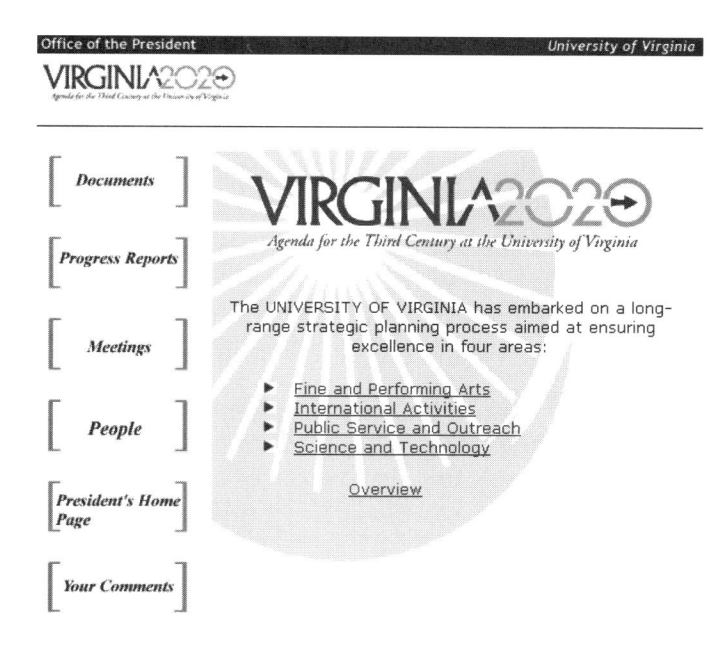

Figure 13-7 The Virginia 2020 Home page (www.virginia.edu/virginia2020)

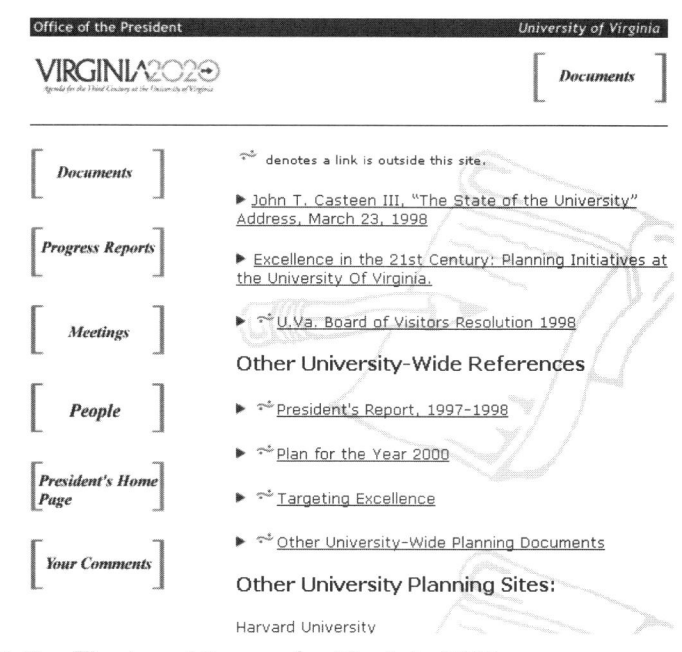

Figure 13-8 The Level 1 page for Virginia 2020

Chapter 13   Giving Your Site a Facelift

Figure 13-9   The Level 2 page for Virginia 2020

The home page introduces the navigation, which runs down the left side of the page. It contains the splashy graphic and gives the visitor the options of clicking on the four links that contain the main sections of the site. The Level 1 page is what the visitor sees when he or she is on the first level of the navigation—anything off the main page. The Level 2 page is designed to display text-rich documents, which contain the "meat" of the content. The navigation is modified to flow across the top, rather than down the left, leaving more room for the text.

REPLACING TEXT AND GRAPHICS GLOBALLY

How can I replace all occurrences of text in my web?

You can search for and replace text in one or more pages in the current web. You can either search the entire web or select the pages you want. Follow these steps:

1. Change to Folder view.
2. If you do not want to search each page in the web, specify the pages you want to search. You can do this by clicking on each of the pages while holding down the CTRL key.
3. Select Edit | Replace. FrontPage displays the Replace dialog box.
4. In the Find What box enter the text you want to search for.
5. In the Replace With box enter the replacement text.
6. To find text in the HTML code, select the Find In HTML check box. For example, you can search for text that is not visible or editable on the page, like an image.
7. Click Find In Web. When FrontPage lists the pages on which the text was found, you have some additional choices:
   - To add a task for a page, click the page in the list, and then choose Add Task.
   - To open a page in Page view, double-click the page in the list. The text that FrontPage found is highlighted. Click Replace to replace this occurrence, or click Find

Next to find the next occurrence. Choose Replace All to replace all occurrences on the current page.

When you have been presented with all occurrences of the text on the page, you'll be prompted to save and close the page and go on to the next page where the text was found.

How do I replace items in my HTML code across my web?

You can find or replace text in tags, attributes, values, comments, and script in HTML. Save any open pages first so the most current version of your page or web is checked.

If you want to find or replace text in HTML only in selected pages in your web, switch to Folders view, and then select those pages in the file list before continuing.

1. On the Edit menu, choose either Find or Replace.

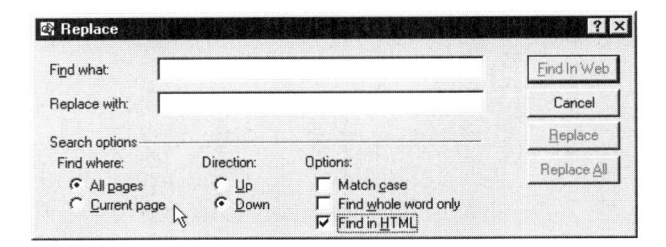

2. In the Find What box, type the text that you want to find or replace in HTML. If you're replacing text, type the replacement text in the Replace With box.

3. Choose All Pages to find or replace the text on every page in your web. Choose Selected Pages to find or replace the text on the pages you selected in Folders view.

4. Click Up or Down to tell FrontPage the direction to search.

Replacing Text and Graphics Globally

5. If you wish, you can choose the Find Whole Word Only or Match Case check boxes to refine the search.

6. Select the Find In HTML check box, and then click Find Next (for selected pages) or Find In Web (for an entire web) to find the first occurrence.

At the bottom of the dialog box, you'll see each page that contains the search text, including the number of times of the search text is located on each page. To edit a page containing the search text, double-click that page in the list. Click Find Next to skip this and find the next instance, Back to Web to cancel editing and restore the list of occurrences in the Find or Replace dialog box, Replace to replace this occurrence on the page and find the next, or Replace All to replace every occurrence in the web.

Why would I ever want to mess around with replacing my HTML code? How do I know what to choose if I don't know HTML?

HTML is the language of the web. In Preview view, you see the results of the HTML that FrontPage is generating behind the scenes. If a page doesn't look quite how you intend, or you make changes to your page and things look odd, you should take a look at the code. Here's an example. Your company replaces its old logo, shown in Figure 13-10, with a newly designed logo, and it's been used throughout your site. You haven't used shared borders, so you can't replace it on just one page and have the change replicated throughout your site. You can't find an image using the Find and Replace menu item for either a page or web, because your image isn't text. You have to do it in the code. Follow these steps to see how it's done.

Chapter 13 Giving Your Site a Facelift

1. Click on the image in Normal view, so that it's selected. Figure 13-10 shows the logo we'd like to replace.
2. Go into HTML view by clicking on the HTML tab. The code for the image you've selected will be highlighted. Fix the highlighted area so that only the src attribute and value (the file name of the image) are highlighted, as in Figure 13-11. Copy it onto your clipboard by clicking CTRL-C or Edit | Copy.
3. Select Edit | Replace, or CTRL-H to bring up the Replace dialog box, as shown in Figure 13-12. Paste the current src attribute and value into the Find What box by clicking CTRL-V or selecting Edit | Paste. Type the new src attribute and value into the Replace With box. Make sure the Find In HTML box is checked. If you want to replace it across your web, make sure the All Pages radio button is checked. Click Replace to execute.

Figure 13-10 The old logo

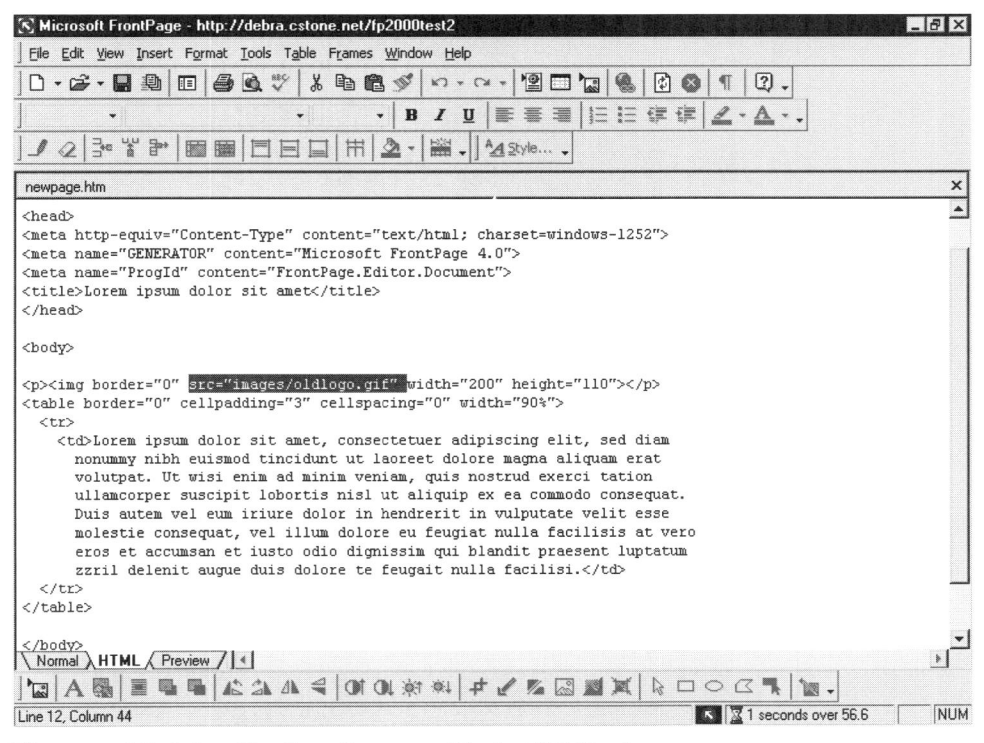

Figure 13-11 Finding the logo file in HTML view

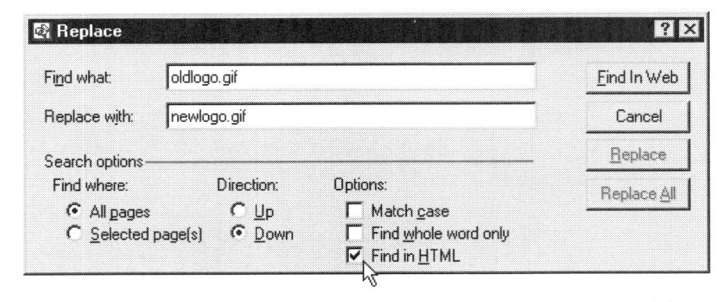

Figure 13-12 Using the Replace feature to replace the old logo in the HTML code

? I replaced my graphic in HTML code, but it's all stretched and weird looking. Where did I go wrong?

If the old graphic and new graphic are different sizes, you have to replace the dimensions, too. Figure 13-13 shows how a new graphic might look after it's replaced if the two images

Chapter 13 Giving Your Site a Facelift

Figure 13-13 A misshapen new graphic when the image sizes are different and you have changed only the image name in the HTML

are different sizes and you haven't changed the whole line. Figure 13-14 shows where the size properties for an image are in the code. Figure 13-15 shows how to do the Replace operation correctly.

1. Click on the image in Normal view, so that it's selected. Figure 13-13 shows the mangled logo.

2. Go into HTML view by clicking on the HTML tab. The code for the image you've selected will be highlighted. Fix the highlighted area so that only the src, height, and width attributes and values (the file name and dimensions of the image) are highlighted, as in Figure 13-14. Copy that onto your clipboard by clicking CTRL-C or Edit | Copy.

Replacing Text and Graphics Globally

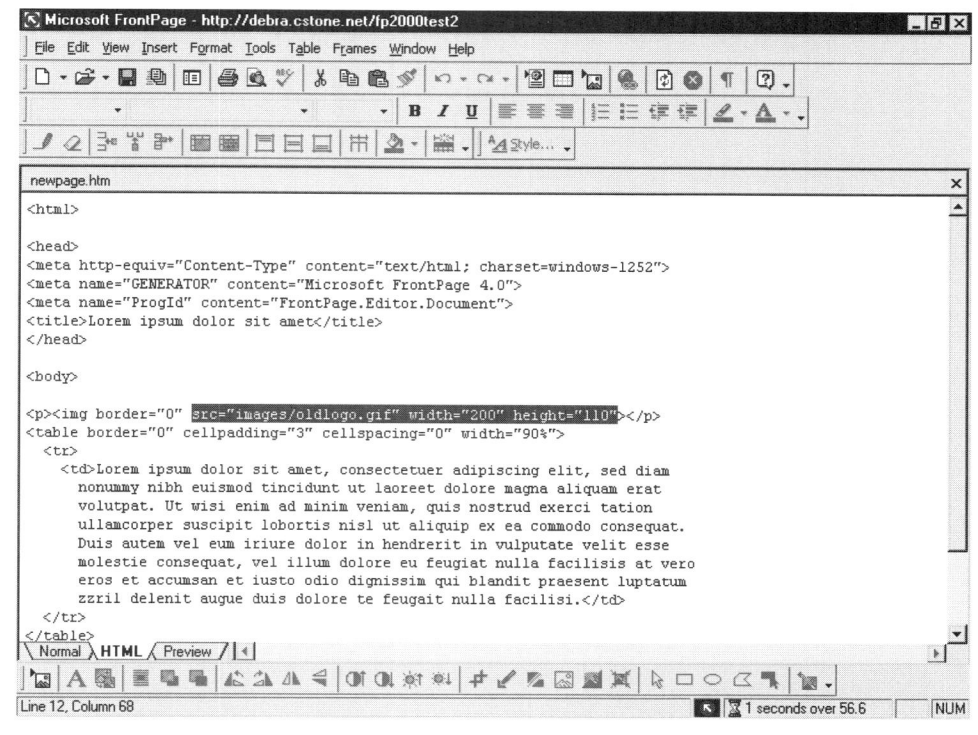

[screenshot of Microsoft FrontPage showing HTML source of newpage.htm with the src="images/oldlogo.gif" width="200" height="110" portion highlighted]

Figure 13-14 Finding the size properties in the HTML

3. Select Edit | Replace, or CTRL-H to bring up the Replace dialog box, as shown in Figure 13-15. Paste the current src, height, and width attributes and values into the Find What box by selecting Edit | Paste or CTRL-V. Type the correct src, height, and width attributes into the

[screenshot of the Replace dialog box with Find what: "images/oldlogo.gif" width="200" height="110" and Replace with: "images/newlogo.gif" width="110" height="200", with Find in HTML checked]

Figure 13-15 Using the Replace operation correctly

Replace With box. Make sure the Find in HTML box is checked. If you want to replace it across your web, make sure the All Pages radio button is also checked. Click Replace to execute.

Are there any other ways to change the look of all my pages at once?

Yes. If you have set the background picture, background color, hyperlink colors, and text colors for one page, you can apply these settings to another page in the current web.

Caution: *If the current page uses a theme, this feature is unavailable!*

Follow these steps to assign a page's attributes to those of another page in the web:

1. In Page view, open the page to which you want to apply a background and color.
2. Right-click the page, and then choose Page Properties from the menu. The Page Properties dialog box will open, as shown in the following illustration.

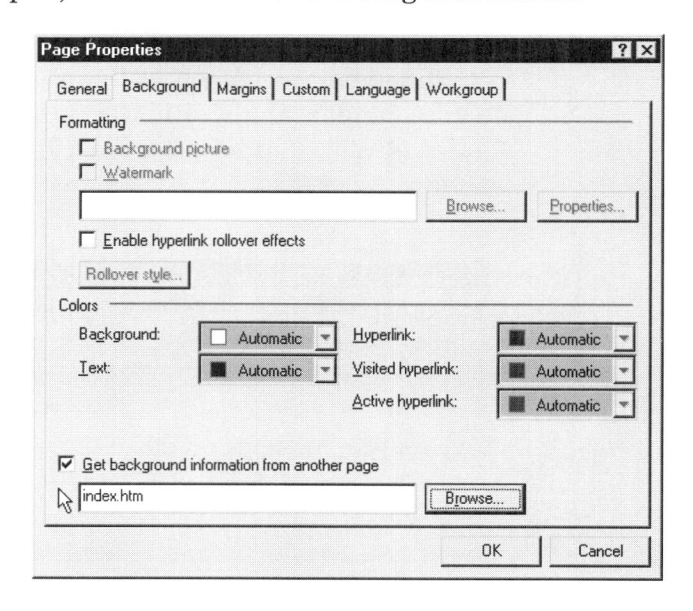

3. Select the Background tab.
4. Click to select the Get Background Information From Another Page box.
5. Click Browse.
6. Select the page that contains the background and colors you want to use. Click OK.

Figure 13-16 shows an example of a web page to which new background information from another page will be applied. Once I've applied the new background information to the example page, it transforms itself into the new look, which is shown in Figure 13-17.

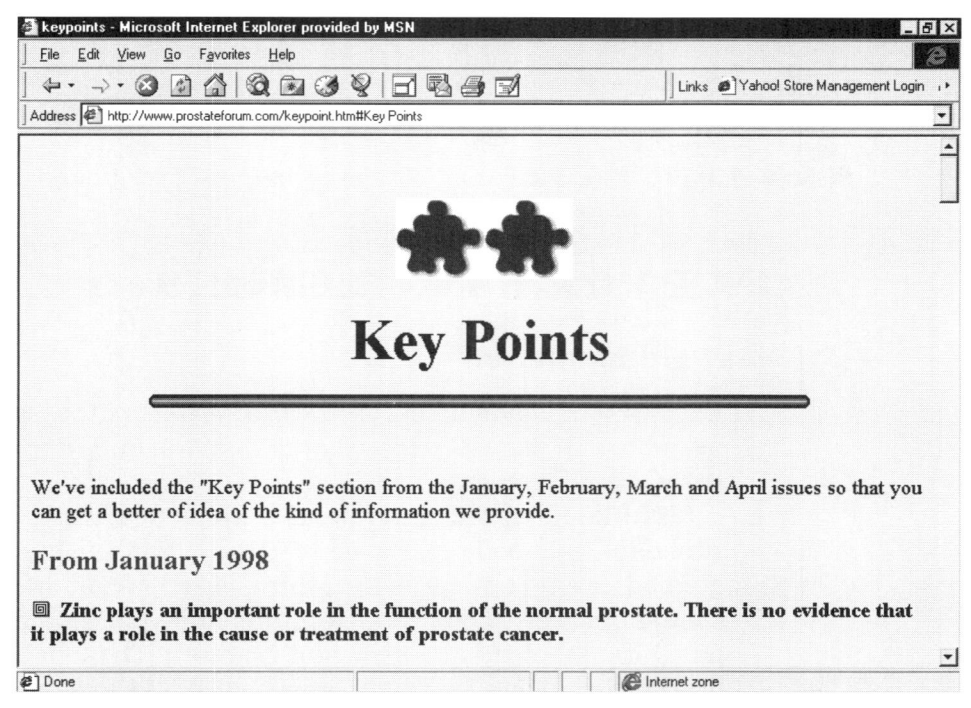

Figure 13-16 Prostate Forum before applying new background information

Chapter 13 Giving Your Site a Facelift

Key Points

We've included the "Key Points" section from the January, February, March and April issues so that you can get a better of idea of the kind of information we provide.

From January 1998

- Zinc plays an important role in the function of the normal prostate. There is no evidence that it plays a role in the cause or treatment of prostate cancer.

- Severe oxidative damage kills cells, low levels of oxidative damage can cause cancer.

- In the prostate, oxidative damage appears to be chronic and at low levels. Antioxidants do not cause cancer, but they may prever or delay the development of cancer.

- When hormonal therapy lowers your testosterone level, you will develop osteoporosis just like women do after menopause. This can lead to bone fractures if you are on hormonal therapy for more than several years.

- Calcitriol, the active form of vitamin D, can prevent osteoporosis while you are on hormonal therapy.

- At high doses, calcitriol can kill prostate cancer cells. However, the high dose required to do this will also cause your blood calcium to increase, causing heart and kidney problems.

- Chemical modification of calcitriol may create promising new drugs for prostate cancer. .We revisit the issue of green tea to give you newly published information. In addition, we list sourcesfor green tea and green tea extract.

- We do not recommend that you use either margarine or butter.

Figure 13-17 Prostate Forum after applying new background information

UNDERSTANDING ELEMENTS

What are elements?

Every site is made up of items called *elements* that repeat from page to page. Buttons, banners, bars, and horizontal rules are all elements.

Additionally, text treatments such as headlines, subheads, and body text used from page to page are also defined as elements. Further, think of the layout as an element as well. The layout would include placement of the navigational elements, text, and graphics. The following illustration shows an example web with all the elements highlighted.

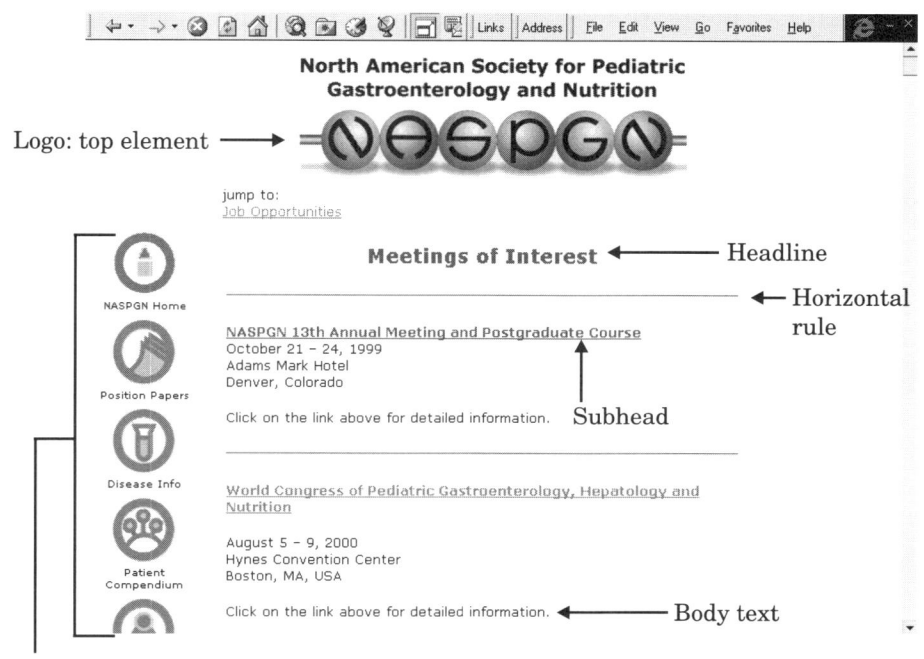

Understanding Elements 339

[Figure showing a web page screenshot with labels: "Logo: top element" pointing to the NASPGN logo, "Headline" pointing to "Meetings of Interest", "Horizontal rule" pointing to the line below the headline, "Subhead" pointing to the meeting title, "Body text" pointing to the description text, and "Navigational elements" pointing to the icons on the left side.]

How does changing just a few elements affect the look of my site?

Changing just a few elements can be fairly dramatic. If you look back at Figure 13-16, you'll see the example home page of The Prostrate Forum, a site badly in need of a makeover. First, let's identify the existing elements. The puzzle piece graphic is blue, and it's used as the current logo treatment. There's the thick horizontal rule and the little square spiral bullet. The text is 14-point Times New Roman. The background color is a light blue. Let's not change the layout yet. We'll just change the elements.

Figure 13-17 shows the results after the elements are changed. Content-wise, everything's the same. The headline font is a different font and size. The body text is now Arial 10.

The horizontal rule has been removed, replaced with a simple underline. The bullet is a different graphic, and the background contains the puzzle piece, screened way back. It's looking cleaner already.

When choosing fonts, how do I know which fonts are safe to use?

When you choose fonts, you see a list of all the fonts you have on your computer. Keep in mind that in order for your visitors to see the fonts that you've chosen, they have to have the same fonts installed. The following is a list of what are considered "safe fonts:"

Fonts Installed with Microsoft Internet Explorer	**Fonts Supplied with Apple Macintosh System 7**
Arial	Chicago
Arial Bold	Courier Regular
Arial Italic	Geneva
Arial Bold Italic	Helvetica
Arial Black	Monaco Palatino
Comic Sans MS	New York
Comic Sans MS Bold	Symbol
Courier New	Times
Courier New Bold	
Courier New Bold Italic	
Courier New Italic	
Georgia	
Georgia Bold	
Georgia Italic	
Georgia Bold Italic	
Impact	
Times New Roman	
Times New Roman Bold	
Times New Roman Bold Italic	

Fonts Installed with Microsoft Internet Explorer
Times New Roman Italic
Trebuchet MS
Trebuchet MS Bold
Trebuchet MS Italic
Trebuchet MS Bold Italic
Verdana
Verdana Bold
Verdana Italic
Verdana Bold Italic
Webdings

Source: http://www.microsoft.com/typography/web/fonts/fonts03.htm

FONTS AS ELEMENTS

Which fonts should I use?

In general, fonts should be chosen for readability. A good rule of thumb to use is to choose one font family for your body copy, and another font for your headlines and subheads. You'll notice that most newspapers and magazines choose a serif font, like Times New Roman for the articles, and a sans-serif font like Arial. On the web that's true as well, although often it's reversed, because sans-serif fonts like Arial, Helvetica, and Verdana tend to be very readable on the computer monitor. Try not to use more than two font families. It really helps things stay consistent.

What if I really want to use specialty fonts, or fonts that I'm not sure most of my visitors will have?

You can set your headlines, subheads, text on your buttons, and so on, as graphic images, rather than text. This technique ensures your visitors will see your fonts as you intend. Avoid setting large blocks of body copy as images. Those take too long to download to the browser.

Another alternative is to embed copies of the fonts you want to use within your web. Internet Explorer 4.0 (and later versions) will use those embedded font copies to display your text. Other browsers will simply ignore the embedded-font instructions and continue to use a default font.

How can I embed fonts on my pages?

Microsoft's TrueType font embedding technology is based on Cascading Style Sheets (CSS). In addition to requiring a CSS-compliant browser, the technology requires you to use fonts that have embedding permission encoded into them. The core Windows fonts will work as will some newer fonts from other companies.

Finally, you'll need a copy of Microsoft WEFT, the Web Embedding Font Tool. You can download this free utility from http://www.microsoft.com/typography/Web/embedding/weft/

WEFT analyzes the fonts you've used in your site and then creates font objects. A *font object* is a compressed file containing just the font characters you've used in your HTML document. WEFT also adds a CSS font definition to your Web pages to refer to the font object. WEFT works in FrontPage and if you want to use it, there's a great step-by-step tutorial on Microsoft's Sitebuilder Network at http://www.microsoft.com/workshop/languages/fp/design/mfp9935.asp. Note, though, that this technique won't work in all browsers, so before you use it, know your audience.

Caution: *IE 5 is nearly fully CSS-compliant. Netscape Navigator 4.5 is quite CSS-compliant, comparable to IE 4. IE 4 is much more CSS-compliant than Navigator 4. IE 3 is somewhat CSS-compliant, and Navigator 3 is not at all CSS-compliant. However, don't assume your visitors have the latest browsers. There are still a lot of version 3 browsers in use.*

What's the best point size for body text on my site?

The best point size for body text on your site is no smaller than 10 points, and no larger than 12 points. Anything smaller is going to be too hard to read, and anything larger is going to look like you are screaming at your visitor.

GRAPHIC ELEMENTS

Can I use art provided in themes without applying an entire theme to my site?

Like the bullet in one theme and a horizontal rule in another? There is a way to save specific graphics from themes to your current web, and it's a pretty good trick! Here's how:

1. Open up a second window with FrontPage concurrently running by clicking the Windows Start button, and selecting the FrontPage icon.
2. Don't create a new web. You'll be using a blank page.
3. Choose Format Theme. FrontPage will display the Themes dialog box.
4. Choose the theme you want and click Apply. Since you don't have a web open, the theme is applied to just that page. Go ahead and insert the elements you'd like to use for the theme.
5. Click the Preview tab.
6. In Preview view, right-click on any element you want and choose Save As.
7. In the Location box, choose the Images folder from web where you're going to use the image. Click OK.

Repeat this procedure by applying other themes to your blank page, and saving the graphics you want. You can use

Chapter 13 Giving Your Site a Facelift

the elements to create your own theme, or insert them whenever you want.

Figure 13-18 shows two windows running FrontPage concurrently. The second window has no web open, just a blank page. The Canvas theme was applied. A bullet and horizontal rule were inserted onto the page. The page is shown in Preview view. The horizontal rule is right-clicked with the mouse, prompting a shortcut menu with the Save Picture As command. The location for the save will be the other web's Images folder.

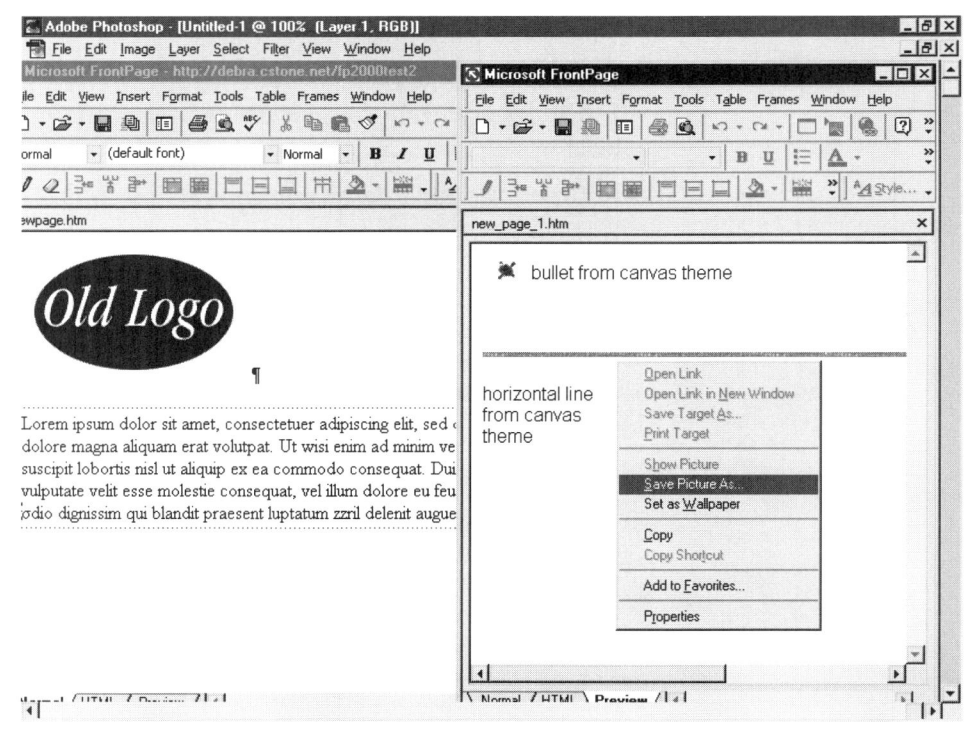

Figure 13-18 Saving specific graphics from themes in FrontPage.

Graphic Elements 345

? I want to show a bunch of products on my page. I have fairly large images, and would like to present a page of smaller images that viewers can click on to get the larger view. How can I do that without creating two sets of each image myself?

You can use FrontPage to create a *thumbnail*, which is a small version of a picture that a visitor clicks in order to follow a hyperlink to the full-size picture.

A thumbnail is handy when you have a large picture that might take a long time to load. Rather than forcing the visitor to wait around, you can provide a thumbnail, enabling the visitor to choose whether or not to view the bigger version.

To create a thumbnail, follow these steps:

1. In Page view, click the picture.
2. On the Pictures toolbar, click Auto Thumbnail.
3. FrontPage creates the thumbnail picture and a hyperlink to the original.

Note: *Auto Thumbnail will not work if the picture you selected is smaller than a thumbnail, if the picture has a hyperlink or hotspots set for it, or if the picture is animated.*

Chapter 13 Giving Your Site a Facelift

> **Tip:** *Auto Thumbnail is a very quick way to create custom buttons for your site.*

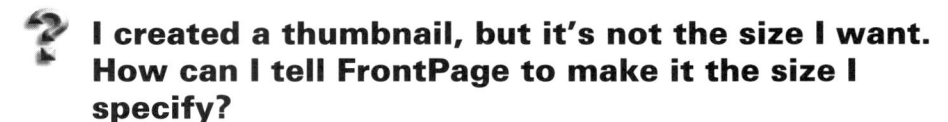

I created a thumbnail, but it's not the size I want. How can I tell FrontPage to make it the size I specify?

You can set properties for the thumbnail size and borders. Any changes you make to thumbnail properties do not affect thumbnails you have previously created, so keep this in mind before you start creating your thumbnails in the first place.

1. Select Tools | Page Options. FrontPage will display the Page Options dialog box. Click the AutoThumbnail tab, as shown in Figure 13-19.

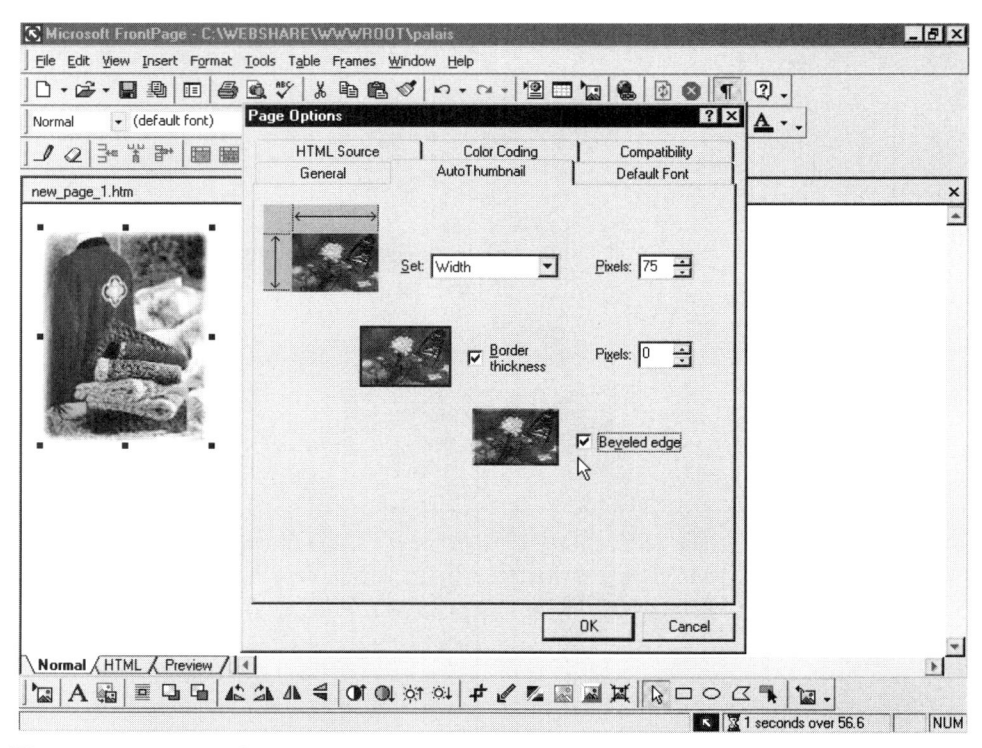

Figure 13-19 Setting the properties for Auto Thumbnails

Graphic Elements

2. In the Set box, click the option you want to use for specifying a size, then in the Pixels box, enter the value in pixels.

   For example, if you want thumbnail pictures to be 32 pixels wide, click Width and then enter 32. The height of the thumbnail will be sized to maintain the proportions of the original picture. Or, if you select Shortest side and then enter 32, the shortest side of any thumbnail picture, will measure 32 pixels, whether it's the height or the width.

3. To specify a border, select Border Thickness, and then in the Pixels box, enter a number for the thickness of the border in pixels.

4. If you want the graphic to be beveled, choose Beveled Edge. Beveled edges give your thumbnail a more button-like look. If you have also specified a border thickness, the thumbnail will have a beveled edge inside of a border, which can sometimes look quite odd, so experiment with this.

5. Click OK.

Can I draw a shape, fill it with color, and bevel the edge to create an instant button?

Unfortunately, no. FrontPage doesn't support drawing features. However, you can create the shape in Image Composer or another program and import it into your web for beveling and other effects. You can create an auto thumbnail out of an existing image, bevel it, and use that for your button.

I have an image I'd like to use for a background or button, but the text on top of it is too hard to read. How can I reduce the contrast so it makes a better background?

You can reduce the contrast and increase the brightness of an image, which is useful for creating a watermark or background picture.

Chapter 13 Giving Your Site a Facelift

1. In Page view, click to select the image you want to change. (If you want to wash out the background picture, you don't need to choose anything.)

2. On the Pictures toolbar, which appears at the bottom of the FrontPage screen, click Wash Out. Figure 13-20 shows two images, one without any effects and one with the washout effect.

Where are some good places to get art and other stuff for my web?

There are innumerable clip art sites on the web, but highly recommended is Art Today at http://www.arttoday.com. There is a free section of 40,000 web images—icons, rules, buttons, animated gifs, and more, and for about $30 per year, you get all 750,000 images, fonts, and so on. The searches are fast and the images are quite nice.

Figure 13-20   Two images: one washed out, the other normal

LAYOUT AS AN ELEMENT

What's a layout?

The positions of recurring elements on a page such as the navigation elements, images, text, and horizontal and vertical rules make up the *layout* of a page. Changing the page position of elements without changing the existing content or images can make a noticeable difference.

Let's revisit this chapter's earlier example of the Prostate Forum, which was shown in Figures 13-16 and 13-17. Figure 13-21 shows the same elements contained in the two previous

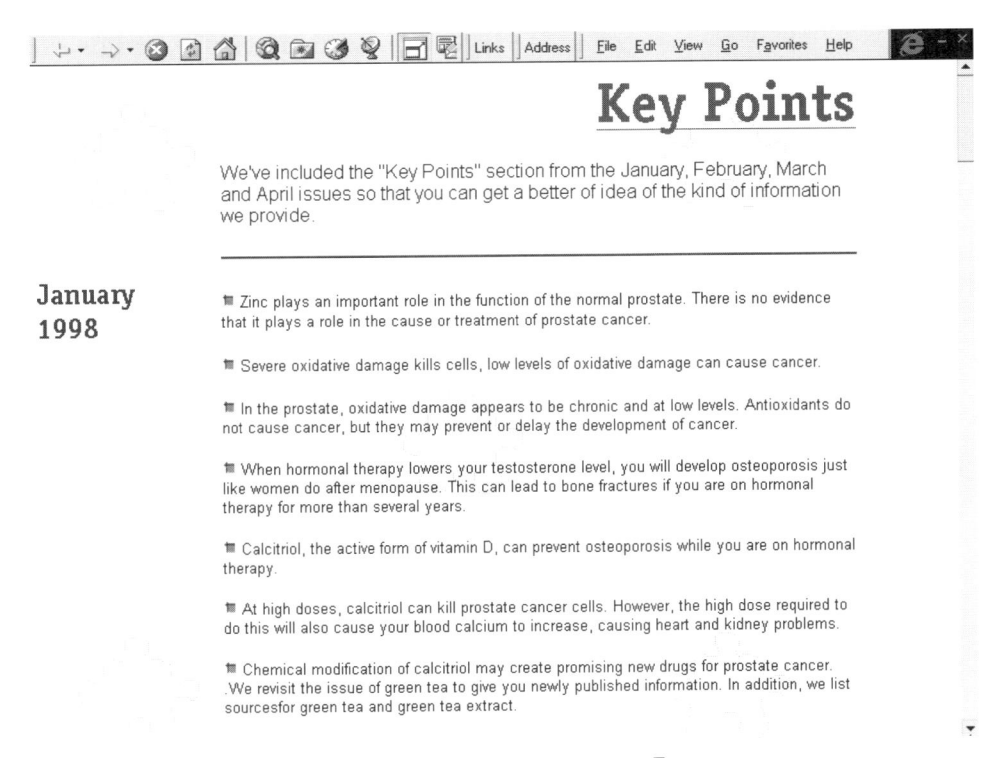

Figure 13-21 The new layout for the Prostate Forum

example screens of this web, but we've changed the elements into yet another new layout. The headline has been moved to the right, the months are running down in a timeline style on the right, and the text is pretty much centered on the page. The explanatory text is a little larger, and a horizontal rule separates the explanatory text from the main body of the page.

How can I maintain consistency in my layouts?

One way is to use the grid system, which has been in use forever in graphic design. The grid system uses an underlying grid as the basis for your page. Your grid might consist of 2, 3, 4, or even 6 columns that you use in combination to place your elements in a consistent way. Look at newspapers and magazines and you'll start to see this technique used everywhere. If you've done much desktop publishing, you'll remember that most documents use a series of frames as underlying elements for placement of graphics and text. You can do the same thing when you design web pages.

How can I use the grid system in FrontPage?

You can create a grid image in Photoshop or Image Composer and use it as a temporary background for placement of elements on your page. Figure 13-22 shows a grid created in Photoshop. It's handy to turn the rulers on. The lines are Photoshop's guidelines. The sections have been filled with a light gray.

Hide all the tools, palettes, and so on, and take a screenshot of the grid by pressing the PRINT SCREEN key. The result will be an image with the guidelines showing. Crop everything out of the image except the rulers and the grid, and save it as a .gif or .jpg file. Use this image as a temporary background for pages in your web. You can draw tables on the background to use as guidelines for image and text placement. Figure 13-23 shows how this looks in Page view.

Layout as an Element 351

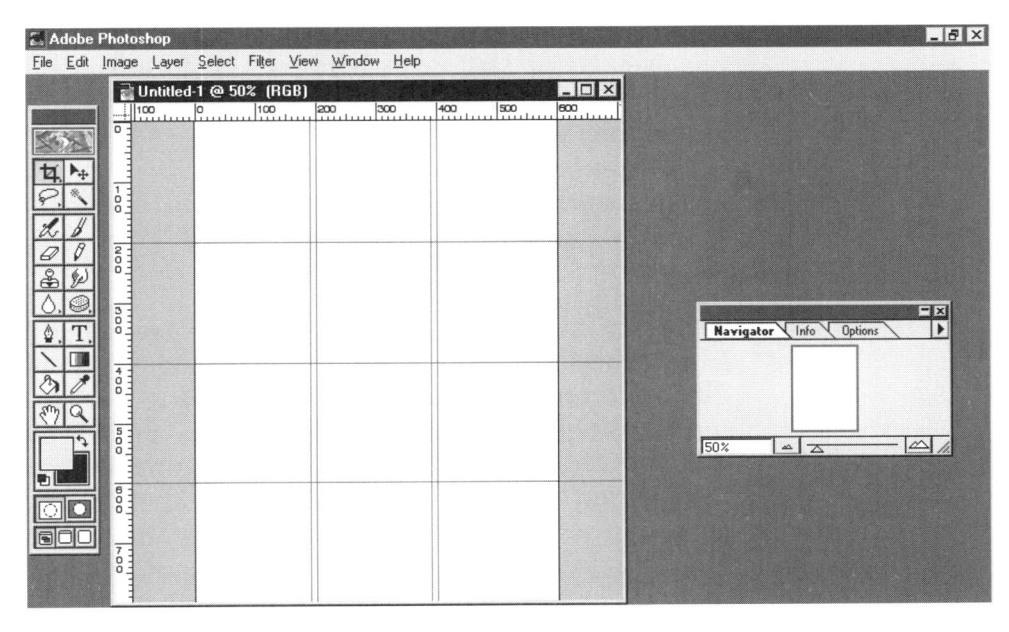

Figure 13-22 A Photoshop grid

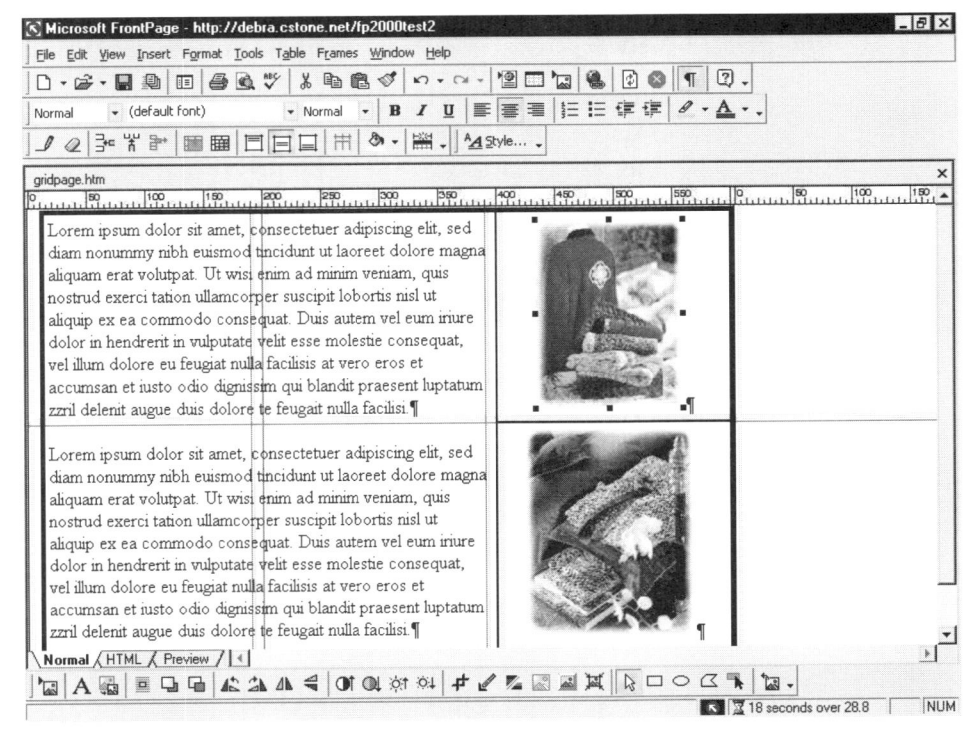

Figure 13-23 The grid as the background image for your pages in FrontPage

Chapter 13 Giving Your Site a Facelift

(For illustration purposes, the table drawn on top of the grid has been given dark black borders so you can see it.)

When you're all done, remove the grid background and put in your real background, if you have one.

How can I ensure that all browsers and computers are going to see my pages the way I intend them to look?

That's the question that plagues all web designers. Fonts look smaller on Macs than on the PC. People view web pages at different screen resolutions. What looks great on your 21-inch monitor at 1,024 × 768 resolution is going to look vastly different on a 13-inch monitor running at 640 × 480. Systems that display only 256 colors are going to show pages that are designed with millions of colors. However, if you stick with safe fonts, web-safe colors, and tables set at fixed pixel widths, you can be fairly certain that your pages will look similar on different systems. The best thing to do is test your pages on a variety of different computers and browser versions.

Chapter 14

Managing Your Web Site

Answer Topics!

IMPORTING A WEB 357
- ? Getting your existing Web site into FrontPage
- ? Importing your site if you use ASP or other server-side processing

DIAGNOSING PROBLEMS 361
- ? Tools FrontPage provides to help catch and fix errors
- ? If the reports don't show all the files in your web

WORKING WITH TEAMS 363
- ? Organizing all the people who are working on your web

- ? Organizing files to keep track of who's doing what
- ? Seeing a list of all your assignments
- ? What "review status" means
- ? How people on your team do the tasks assigned to them
- ? How one indicates a task is complete
- ? How to prevent two people from working on the same file at the same time
- ? How to enable the source control feature
- ? How to monitor which files are checked in and out

FINAL CONSIDERATIONS BEFORE YOU PUBLISH 372
- ? Final considerations

Managing Your Web Site @ a Glance

Maintaining your growing Web site doesn't have to be a daunting task. FrontPage 2000 makes it so easy that it's even making converts of the HTML purists who used to believe the only true way to code a Web site was by using TextPad to write the HTML and a browser to view the results.

So, regardless of which stage you're at in your Web site development—whether you're ready to publish a Web page or two for the first time, perform maintenance on a growing Web site, or manage a team of Web page designers, graphic artists, and scripting technicians—this chapter provides an overview of some of the ways FrontPage 2000 can help simplify your work.

As you'll soon discover, Web site housekeeping doesn't have to be a chore.

- **Importing a Web** shows how to import your existing Web site into FrontPage in a way that FrontPage can use it.
- **Diagnosing Problems** considers how FrontPage tools can help you find and fix problems.
- **Working with Teams** discusses how to use the features of FrontPage to manage site development by a team. This includes assigning tasks to individuals, categorizing files, and monitoring the status of development.
- **Final Considerations Before You Publish** reviews a few dos and don'ts of Web site development with relevant examples.

COMMON FILE EXTENSIONS

Before we dig into the questions you may have about managing your Web site, here is some preliminary information about the most commonly used file extensions:

- **Active Server Pages (.asp)**   An Active Server Page (ASP) is a type of Web page generated via a script on the server in response to a user query.

- **Audio Files (.au, .wav, .aiff, .midi, .mp3)**   You'll work with these file extensions if you put sound on your pages; only .au files work if you want sound on a rollover.

- **Cascading Style Sheets (.css)**   As described in Chapter 7, style sheet documents contain formatting instructions for text and other page elements on a Web site. These pages are never executed; they're just referenced by other pages.

- **Executable Files (.exe)**   An executable file associated with programs and ActiveX controls.

- **Hypertext Markup Language (.htm or .html)**   The set of codes you see when you click on the HTML tab; they are used to format your Web pages.

- **Image Files (.gif, .jpeg, .png)**   The Web-friendly image formats that browsers can open. FrontPage normally stores these formats in an Images folder in your web.

- **Java Applets (.class)**   Small files that contain programming controls written in Java.

- **JavaScript Scripts (.js)**   Scripts created automatically by FrontPage when you create animated special effects for your pages, such as hover buttons and other special components.

- **Microsoft Office Files (.doc, .xls, .ppt, .pub, and .mdb)**   The file extensions for Word documents (.doc), Excel workbooks (.xls), PowerPoint presentations (.ppt), Publisher publications (.pub), or Access databases (.mdb); FrontPage lets you import such documents into your Web page.

Importing a Web

- **Server Scripts (.cgi and .pl)**   Common Gateway Interface (.cgi) scripts that run on a server; Perl (.pl) is a popular language for writing CGI scripts. If you have your own domain or if your Web site existed before you or your company installed FrontPage, you may find such scripts normally stored on the server in a folder called CGI_Bin or CGI_Win.
- **Text Files (.txt)**   Information generated from response to a Web form can be saved to a plain text file which FrontPage usually stores in the _private folder.
- **Video Files (.avi, .vfw, .mov, .mpeg)**   You'll encounter these file extensions if you decide to put movies on your Web site.

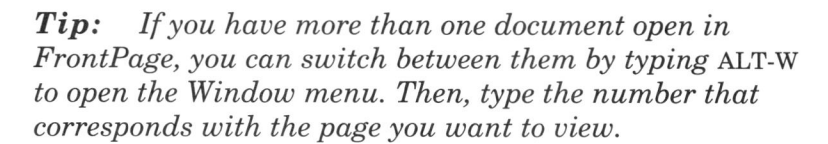

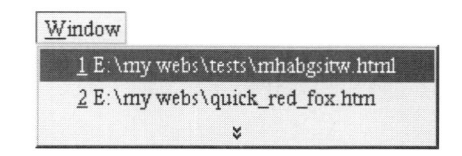

Tip: *If you have more than one document open in FrontPage, you can switch between them by typing* ALT-W *to open the Window menu. Then, type the number that corresponds with the page you want to view.*

IMPORTING A WEB

How do I get my existing Web site into FrontPage?

You basically have two choices. If your site does not have any server-side processing, then you can let FrontPage import the site directly from the Web. If your site does have server-side processing, then you're better off moving your entire site into a folder on your hard drive, then letting FrontPage convert the folder into a web.

Importing from the Web

To import from the Web, begin by creating an empty web in FrontPage:

1. Select File | Import | Empty Web. This will give you an empty web with two empty folders: _private and images. Now, you're ready to import from the Web.

2. Select Import, which will open the Import dialog box.
3. Click From Web to begin the Import Web Wizard.

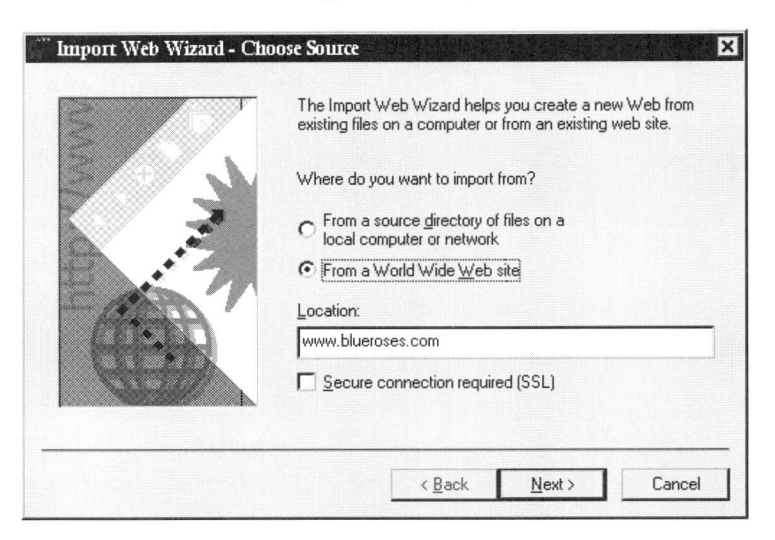

Tip: *If you don't have an accurate backup of your site, letting FrontPage import it from the Web is a great way to create one.*

Caution: *Don't import from the Web a site that you don't own. You can use the wizard to download pages from someone else's site, but if you do, it should be because you either want to study how the site is constructed or to read it while you're offline. To use any of the code, text, or images from the site without permission constitutes a copyright violation.*

4. Check the appropriate radio button to indicate that you want to import files either from a source directory of files on a local computer or network, or from a World Wide Web site.
5. Fill in the Location information. (For a WWW location, you type in the URL.) Click Next.

Importing a Web | 359

Note: *If you only want to download a single file, such as a Web page, you'll need to type in the exact URL, such as http://www.overtheweb.com/index.html.*

6. If you want to limit the depth of a site that you import, check the first box, Limit To This Page Plus, and indicate the number of levels below the home page you want included. If you want to limit the total amount of data you download by size, indicate the number of kilobytes (that's 1/1000 of a megabyte; 1,440KB fills up a floppy disk) you want to download. If you're including images in the download, then you need to make sure you allow enough space because images will take up significantly more space than text files. Finally, if you only want to download images and text, rather than other types of media files, check the appropriate box. Click Next, then click Finish on the final screen.

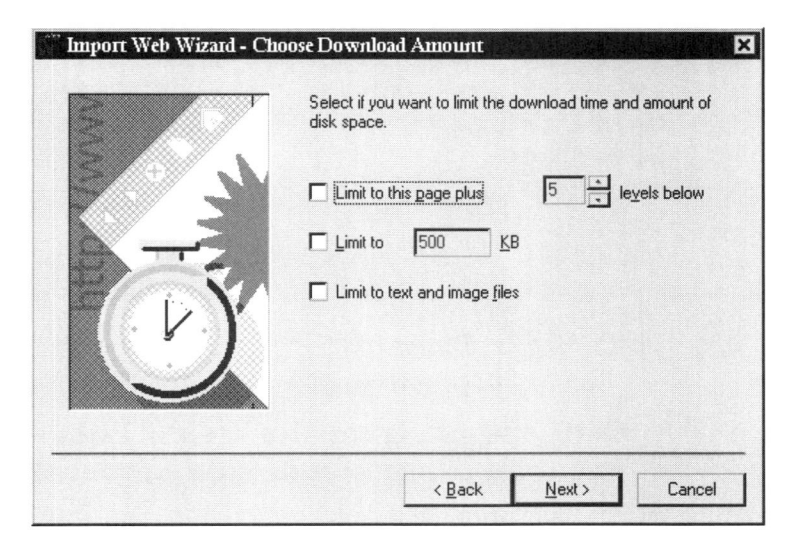

Tip: *For those times when it isn't convenient to lift your fingers from the keys and grab your mouse to click on a Normal, HTML, or Preview tab in FrontPage, you can cycle through them by pressing CTRL-UP ARROW (to go counterclockwise) or CTRL-DOWN ARROW (to go clockwise).*

Automatically Redirecting Users to a New URL

If your Web site changes locations, your old URL may appear in the search engines and directories for quite a while (and within visitors' Favorites lists for even longer). To prevent visitors from getting an error message that the page isn't found whenever they try to visit your old site, it's much wiser to set up an easy way to direct them from the old URL to the new one. In FrontPage, open the file for your home page at the old URL, then click the HTML tab to switch to HTML view. Just above the </HEAD> tag, add the following line:

```
<meta http-equiv="refresh" content="10;
   url=http://www.yournewurl.com">
```

where *ten* is the number of seconds and http://www.yournewurl.com is the page to jump to (with, of course, *your* new, real address placed after www).

You can delete all remaining content on the page in Normal view if you wish, although it's a good idea to leave your logo or other identifying features and type in a message that tells the visitor what's about to occur, such as: "We've moved to *www.thenewURL.com*. This page will automatically refresh to our new location in *ten* seconds." It's a good idea to also include a regular hyperlink on the same page for those users who don't want to wait ten seconds.

? Can I import from the Web if I have Active Server Pages or other server-side processing in my web?

No. If you have any kind of server-side processing on your site, then you must copy the files to a folder and let FrontPage convert the folder into a Web, rather than let FrontPage import it from the Web. You can still use the Import Web Wizard—just follow these steps:

1. Select File | Import to open the New Web dialog box. The Import Web Wizard icon is highlighted. In the text

entry field on the right side of the box, enter the exact filename, including the directory information for where you want FrontPage to put the web. If you already have created the directory, you'll see a dialog box warning you that FrontPage needs to convert the folder into a web. Don't use the same folder as the place that your current web site resides. Click Yes. All that this will do is add some extra folders to your folder. It's a shortcoming of FrontPage that there's no Browse button; that would be a welcome enhancement. Click OK to let FrontPage create a folder for your web.

2. The Import Web Wizard will begin. Click on the From A Source Directory Of Files On A Local Computer Or Network radio button. The Browse button will appear. Click Browse to locate the folder that contains your Web site. Click Next.

3. Indicate whether you want to limit the amount of data imported either by levels deep, by file size, or by limiting the import to text and images. Click Next, then click Finish on the final screen.

DIAGNOSING PROBLEMS

What tools does FrontPage provide to help me catch and fix errors?

Errors are inevitable, especially if you're the only one who edits your Web page work. Try as you might, you're bound to overlook something. FrontPage can check your spelling, search and replace text throughout your Web site, verify that all of your links work, and, for those times you can't "do it now," help you create your own To Do List-style Task Report as a reminder of work you need to do later.

Tip: *One tried and true proofreading technique is to read the content of your pages out loud. If you have to do so at the office, read quietly. But, you must take the time to pronounce each word or you're apt to skim past something that's wrong. Your ear can help you detect errors. (The downside is that your co-workers may start to think you can't read without moving your lips.)*

Why don't the reports show all the files in my web?

FrontPage runs reports from temporary files. If the temporary files are out of synch with the web, then the reports will be inaccurate. These temporary files have information about the web files that let FrontPage open the files without returning to the server to download the additional information. The intent is to keep things running as quickly as possible.

However, over time, this can result in temporary files that are not current with the web information stored on the server. The most common indication that the temporary files are not current is that your reports don't show all the files in the web or you notice you have hyperlinks that won't work. You can solve this situation and synchronize your local temporary files with the latest information from the server by following these steps:

1. Click Refresh.
2. Select Tools | Recalculate Hyperlinks. If you have a large Web site, especially one with a lot of hyperlinks, it can take awhile to perform this task.
3. Select Tools | Web Settings, and then select the Advanced tab. Then click Delete Files.

Caution: *Once you delete the temporary files for a large web, you'll find that it takes much longer to open it the next time because FrontPage must recopy some information from the server to update your local temporary files.*

Maintaining a Mirror Site

It's often hard to keep track of where the most current version of your site resides. Because FrontPage lets you edit directly on your site using the HTTP protocol, it's even easier to get confused as to which copy of a file has the most recent material. To help avoid making changes to a file that is not the most recent copy of that file, be sure to keep a mirror site on a local hard drive.

Discipline yourself only to make changes to the mirror site. Then once you've tested the changes, publish them to your production site. It may seem like an inconvenience, but it will save you hours down the road when you find yourself unsure of what's where. It will also save you the trouble of having to reconstruct your site if anything happens to the Web server and the backup isn't up to date.

WORKING WITH TEAMS

How can FrontPage help me organize all the people who are working on my web?

FrontPage provides a very full-featured Task Manager. If you're upgrading from a previous version of FrontPage, you'll notice that there's been a lot of thought put into this version. The Task Manager enables you to:

- Assign files and tasks to people or workgroups
- Categorize pages
- Monitor and update the status of tasks
- Indicate the review status of files to be released for publishing

When you work with tasks, you'll work either from Tasks view or from Reports view. To enter Tasks view, select View | Tasks. To enter Reports view, select View | Reports.

? How do I organize my files to keep track of who's doing what?

If you're working with a web team, you probably have different groups working on different sections. You might have a Content or Editorial group working on copy. You might have an Art group creating images. You also might have a Legal group which makes sure all copyright and disclaimer information appears correctly.

The first step is to define users. Then create categories that are appropriate to your project by modifying the Master Category List. Next, organize your files into the categories you've created. Finally, assign tasks.

Defining Users

Begin in Reports view. Right-click any file, and select Properties from the shortcut menu; select the Workgroup tab. Click the Names button opposite the Assigned To list box, as shown here:

Modify the Master Category List

You want the Category list to reflect your environment, and you'll most likely want to customize it for your web.

1. Begin in Reports view. Right-click any file, and select Properties from the shortcut menu.

2. Click the Workgroup tab. Click the Categories button to display the Master Category List, shown here:

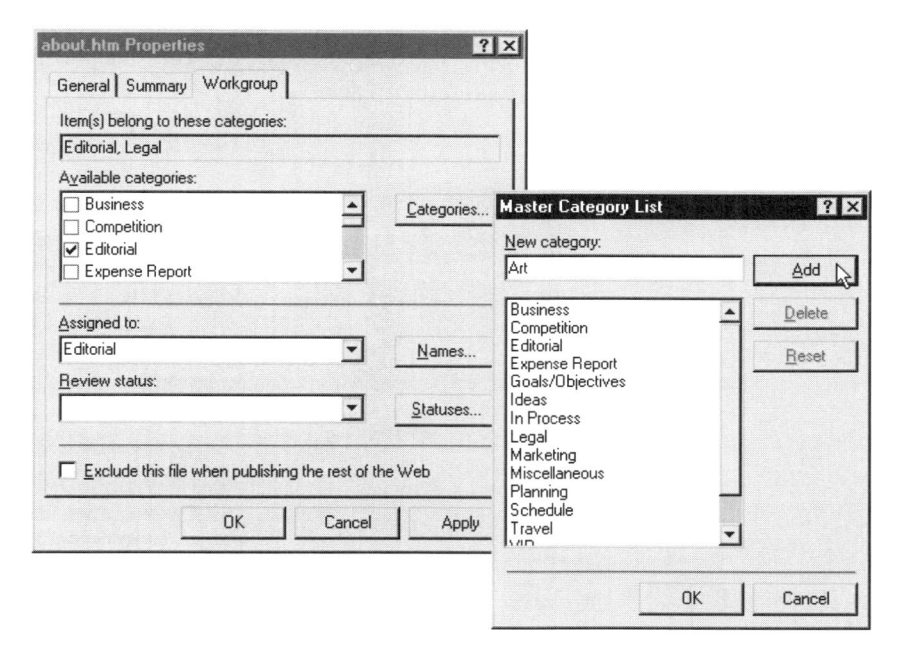

3. To add a new category, type its name in the New Category box, and then click Add.

4. Add the rest of your categories the same way.

Categorizing Files

You can group art, sounds, and other files into any available categories. In Reports view, sort by file type, and choose files or groups of files. You can choose several files by holding down the SHIFT key and clicking on a contiguous group, or by

Chapter 14 Managing Your Web Site

holding down the CTRL key and clicking on a non-contiguous group. Choosing the Categories report within Reports view displays your categories. (See Figure 14-1.)

1. Start in Reports view. Click the Type column head to sort by type. Click on the file to which you want to assign a category. FrontPage will display the Properties dialog box, which will bear the name of the file you selected.
2. Click on the Workgroup tab.
3. Check the box next to any categories to which you want to assign this file.

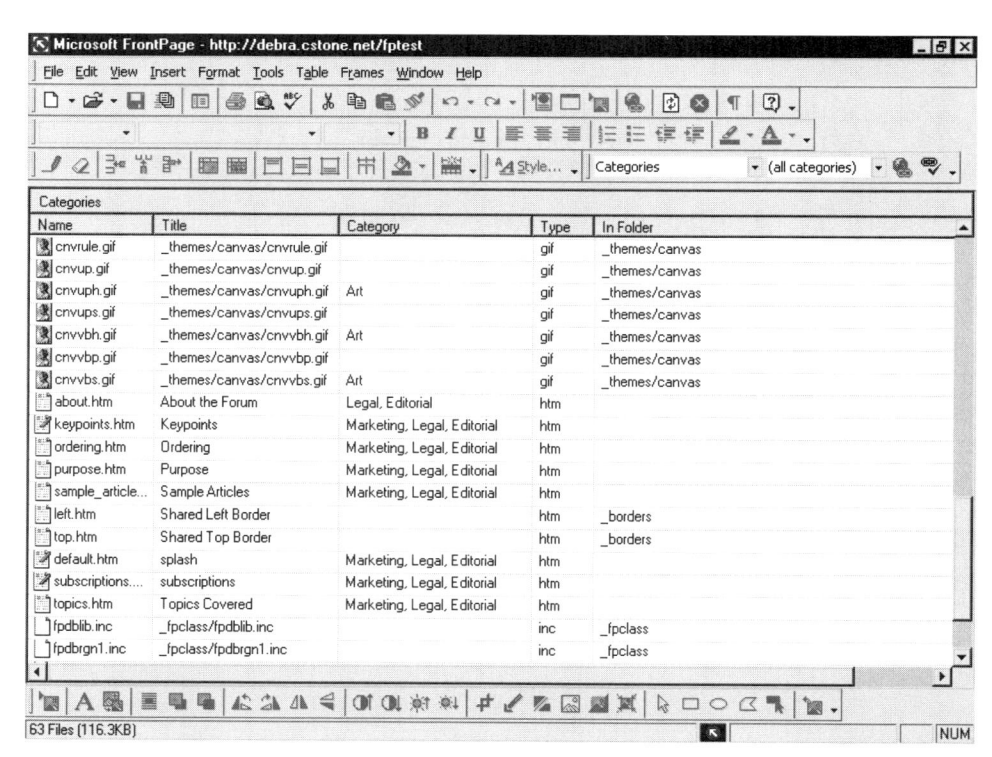

Figure 14-1 Reports view shows the category assigned to files in the web

Working with Teams

Tip: *To view files and categories in the same report, choose the Categories report.*

Creating and Assigning a Task

You can begin this process in two ways. If you are in Folder or Reports view, right-click on any file and choose Add Task. If you are in Page view, select Edit | Task | Select Task. FrontPage will display the New Task dialog box, as shown in the following illustration. Choose whom to assign the task to, add your comments, and click OK.

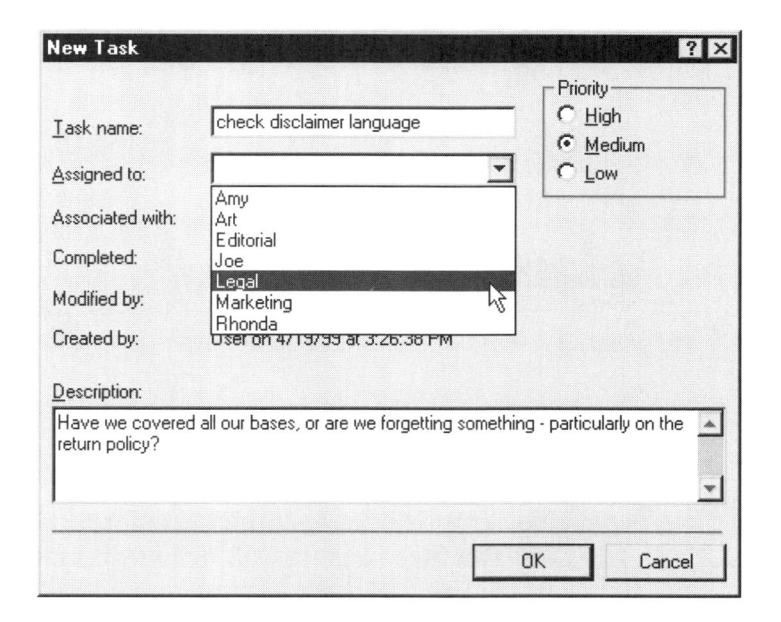

Monitoring the Status of Assigned Tasks

FrontPage provides Tasks view for just this purpose. Select View | Task and you'll see a list of all your assigned tasks, along with their status. (See Figure 14-2.)

Chapter 14   Managing Your Web Site

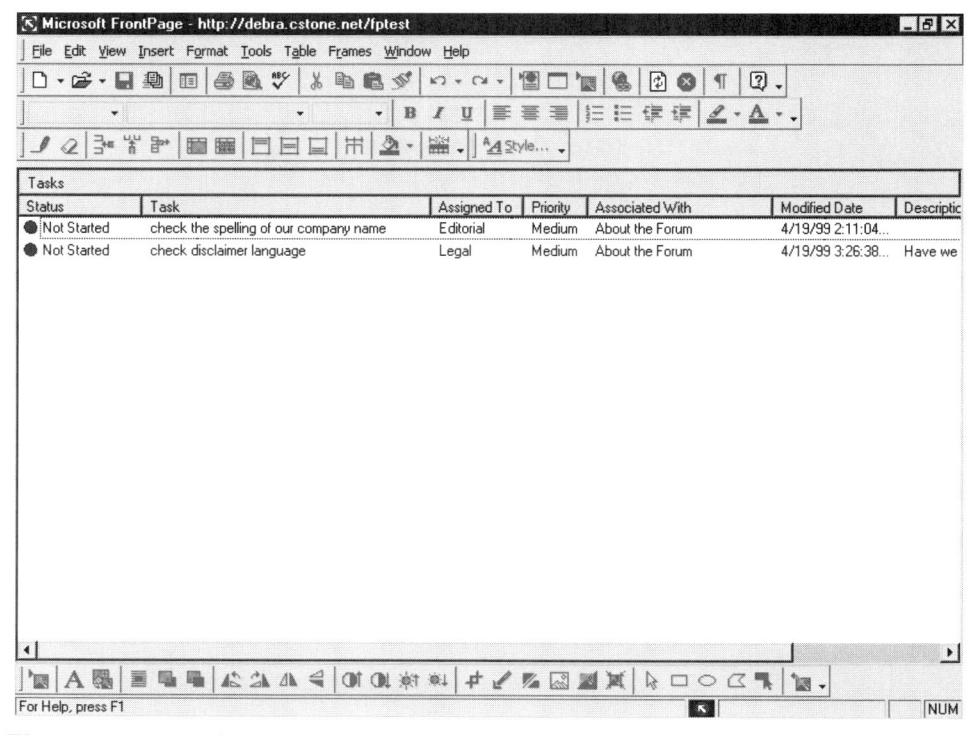

Figure 14-2   Seeing the status of tasks using Tasks view

How can I see a list of all my assignments?

You can use the Assigned To report, shown in Figure 14-3, to list the files in your web by assignment, as well as see the dates the files were assigned, who assigned them, and what comments have been added to the files.

1. Select View | Reports | Assigned To.
2. To sort the report by assignment dates or team member names, click the Assigned Date or Assigned To column heading.
3. You can assign multiple files at one time. In the Assigned To report, select the files you want to assign (or re-assign), then right-click to display the shortcut menu.

Working with Teams

[screenshot of Microsoft FrontPage showing the Assigned To report]

Figure 14-3 The Assigned To report

Choose Properties. In the Properties dialog box click the Workgroup tab. In the Assigned To box, choose the person or workgroup to whom you want to assign the files.

What does "review status" mean?

Review status is another way to keep track of pages, pictures, and other files as they are prepared for publishing to your live web. For example, "Code Review" might mean that a programmer should do some debugging on a page, "Legal Review" may mean that a page needs to be approved by your Legal department, and so on.

To assign a review status, follow these steps:

1. In any view except Tasks view, right-click the file. From the shortcut menu, choose Properties, and then click the Workgroup tab.

2. In the Review Status box, select a review status from the list or type a new one, as shown here:

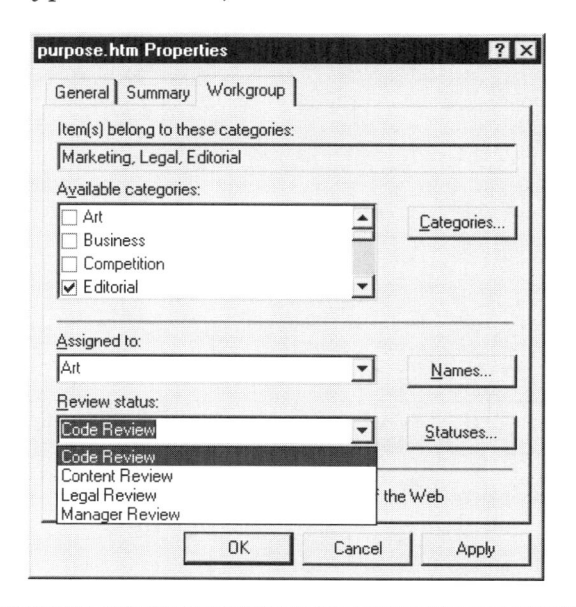

Tip: If you can't see the review status, it's probably because you're in Tasks view. Switch to another view and you should be able to find it easily.

How do people on my team do the tasks assigned to them?

To do an assigned task they should view the web in Tasks view, right-click the task they want to start, and then click Start Task on the shortcut menu. When they start a task associated with a page, FrontPage opens that page in Page view. When they start a task associated with another type of file, FrontPage opens the file in its associated editor (for example, Photoshop for .jpg files, Word for .doc files, Notepad for .txt files, and so on), which is a pretty slick feature!

How does one indicate that a task is complete?

You can mark a task as completed in two ways:

- In Tasks view, right-click the task that you want to mark as completed, and then click Mark as Completed on the shortcut menu.
- If you started a task associated with a web page, the first time you save the page in Page view, FrontPage will ask if you want to mark the task as complete. Choose Yes.

We have a bunch of people working on the same set of files, doing different things. How do I prevent two people from working on the same file at the same time?

That's called *source control*. Source control is a way for you to ensure that only one person at a time edits a file, which is necessary in a multi-authoring environment. FrontPage provides a built-in source control feature that lets web authors perform basic source control tasks:

- A web author can check out a file. When a file is checked out, other authors can open the file, but cannot modify it. A file that has been checked out is indicated by a check mark if the file is checked out to you, or a padlock if the file is checked out to a different author.
- A web author can check in a file after editing and saving it. The file is then available to other authors for checking out. A file that is checked in and available is indicated by a green diamond.
- A web author can undo a file checkout. The file is checked in without applying any of the changes that were made since the file was checked out.

The FrontPage extensions must be installed in order to use this feature.

Chapter 14 Managing Your Web Site

? How do I enable the source control feature?

Before you can use the built-in source control in FrontPage, you must enable it. You can enable source control only if you have administrator privileges.

1. Select Tools | Web Settings. FrontPage will display the Web Settings dialog box, shown here:

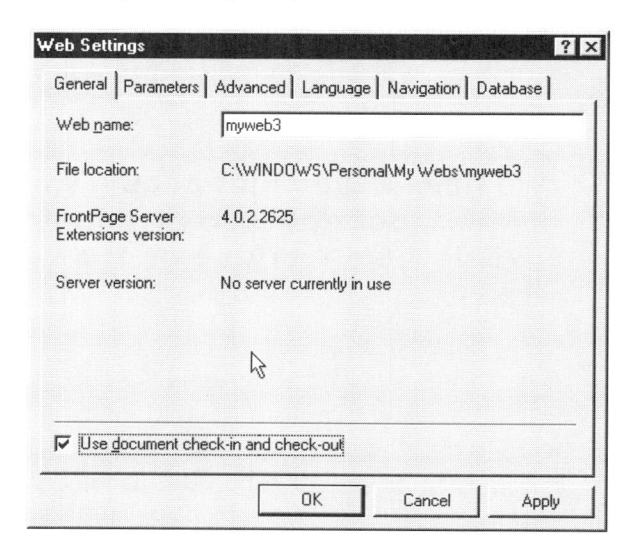

2. On the General tab, select the Use Document Check-In and Check-Out check box.
3. Click OK to close the dialog box.

? How do I monitor which files are checked in and out?

To see the checkout status of files, select View | Reports, and then choose Checkout Status.

FINAL CONSIDERATIONS BEFORE YOU PUBLISH

? What should be my final considerations before I publish?

Even with FrontPage making the process a lot easier, you'll still spend a lot of time (not to mention blood, sweat, and tears!) in designing and creating your Web site. Once you go "live" with your site, you want your visitors to see you at your bright, shiny best. Here are some additional suggestions on how you can insure that what gets published online is indeed your best work.

Browse Your Web Site

Even with the Preview tab option available to you in FrontPage, it's still a good idea to preview your pages within your browser (Internet Explorer). This activity gives you a chance to see your site in its actual environment, as well as follow the links and test any components to make sure your Web site looks and behaves as you expect it to. The easiest way to do this is to open your pages in FrontPage and click the Preview in Browser toolbar button. If you've already published your site online (but haven't announced publication yet), you can launch your browser, enter the URL for the home page of your Web site, and view the pages online.

Don't Announce Your Site as Being Under Construction

A Web site is an ever-evolving work. Putting an "under construction" sign on a page is akin to hanging a "my tailor hasn't gotten around to finishing these alterations" sign around your neck if your suit doesn't fit. It's just not something that's done in a normal business environment. (If, on the other hand, you work in an abnormal business environment, handle this issue as you see fit.) Instead, a note advising that content is updated frequently and an invitation for visitors to return often is a better solution. But even that isn't necessary. Today's savvy Web users know the only online constant is change. If they like your site, they'll return. Therefore, your job is to make sure that on each visit they like your site!

Eliminate Stuff That Just Doesn't Work

This is where testing all of your pages in your own Web browser (as mentioned above) comes in handy. You can verify that the FrontPage components, plug-ins, and animated special effects work correctly. It's a good idea to test all internal links (those that take you to and from pages on your own site), too.

Avoid a Page with a Carnival Atmosphere

You know the type: gazillions of animated GIFs, special effects, FrontPage components, text marquees, busy background images, background sounds (with no way to turn them off! Grrrrrr!), and streaming multimedia files. Posting a fun page to which you can direct your family and friends is a nice diversion. But remember, there are some things about you (and therefore your pages) that only your mother can love.

Note: There will always be exceptions. To see one, visit http://www.hamsterdance.com. This site, originally online with a single link to the design firm who posted it (a link hidden at the bottom of the page, after a lengthy scroll to reach it) now has a booming T-shirt and coffee mug business on the side.

Make Sure Visitors Can Actually Read What's on Your Page

Avoid using fonts that are too small or a font color with too little contrast against your background color or image choice. Have others check the layout. You want your site navigation to be as intuitive as possible. Make sure visitors can find the links, too.

Index

NOTE: Page numbers in *italics* refer to illustrations or charts.

A

<A> element, elements that take styles, *160*
<ABBR> element, elements that take styles, *160*
Access 2000 connections, ODBC-compliant databases, 217–219
Access 2000 databases, 207–210
    adding tables to, 207–208
    Documenter dialog box, 209–210
    See also databases
<ACRONYM> element, elements that take styles, *161*
active graphics, 22–23
    defined, 22
    disadvantage of, 23
    downloading and, 23
    extensions and, 23
    See also themes
Add Database Connection dialog box, Import dialog box, 224–225
<ADDRESS> element, elements that take styles, *161*
affiliate programs and commercial advertising, 276–284
    Associate Programs, 277
    beFree program, 282–284
    ClickQuick, 278, *279*, *280*
    LinkShare, 278, *279*
    overview, 276–277
    Refer-it.com, 280
    ValueClick, 282, *283*
aligning text in cells, 154
Alignment property, described, *143*

All Pages option, shared borders, 316
Allow Zero Length property, mapping columns to form fields, 222
ALT attributes, graphics and the handicapped, 61–62
ALT tags, navigation tips, 110
ALT text, associating with hotspots, 90–91
animated GIFs, reducing size of, 70–72
animation, DHTML (Dynamic HTML), 192
anti-aliasing
    color, 51, *52*
    display fonts, 49
<APPLET> element, elements that take styles, *161*
Archipelago Web site, navigation tips, *106*
<AREA> element, elements that take styles, *161*
artifacts, graphics, 75
Assigned To report, teams, 368–369
Associate Programs, affiliate programs and commercial advertising, 277
asymmetric encryption, defined, 271
attributes
    copying, 336–337, *338*
    style, 167–178
authentication software, commerce and security issues, 291–292
Auto Thumbnail command, 345–346
automatically redirecting URLs, 360

B

\<B\> element, elements that take styles, *161*
Background Color property, described, *143*
Background Image property, described, *143*
backgrounds, tiling graphics and, 67
backing-up data, commerce and security issues, 274
banners
    fonts and, 32–33
    themes and, 30–33
\<BASE\> element, elements that take styles, *161*
\<BASEFONT\> element, elements that take styles, *161*
beFree program, affiliate programs and commercial advertising, 282–284
\<BGSOUND\> element, elements that take styles, *161*
\<BIG\> element, elements that take styles, *161*
Black and White option, graphics, 65–66
\<BLINK\> element, elements that take styles, *161*
block-level elements, inheritance, 135
\<BLOCKQUOTE\> element, elements that take styles, *161*
\<BODY\> element, elements that take styles, *161*
Boolean fields, Form Page Wizard, 248
Border Color Dark property, described, *143*
Border Color Light property, described, *143*
Border Color property, described, *143*
Border Style property, described, *143*
Border Width property, described, *143*
borders, 142–148
    Cell Properties dialog box, 150–152
    DHTML (Dynamic HTML), 193–194
    partial, 148–152
    setting, 144–146
    shared. *See* shared borders
    Style dialog box, 173–174
    style sheets alternatives, 146–147
    table properties, 142, *143*
    Table Properties dialog box, 144–148
    See also tables
Borders and Shading dialog box, 173–174
    DHTML (Dynamic HTML), 193–194
    margins, 174
    Modify Style dialog box, 173–174
    padding, 174
    shading, 174
\<BR\> element, elements that take styles, *162*
brightness, graphics and, 347–348
broken hyperlinks, Site Summary reports, 120–121
browser/server interaction, forms, 238–239
browsers
    compatibility issues and shared borders, 7
    image maps and, 93–95
    style sheet limitations, 183
Bullets and Numbering dialog box, Modify Style dialog box, 175–176
\<BUTTON\> element, elements that take styles, *162*
buttons
    navigation. *See* navigation buttons
    radio. *See* radio buttons

C

caches, browsing and graphics, 73–74
\<CAPTION\> element, elements that take styles, *162*
Cardhost.com, credit cards and security issues, 290
categorizing files, teams, 365–367
Cell Padding property, described, *143*
Cell Properties dialog box, partial borders, 150–152

Cell Spacing property, described, *143*
cells
    aligning text in, 154
    padding, *143*, 152–153
    spacing, *143*, 148
<CENTER> element, elements that take styles, *162*
certificates, defined, 271
CGI scripts
    commerce and security issues, 274
    Form Page Wizard and, 251–252
Character Spacing tab, Font dialog box, 171
check boxes
    forms and, 265–266
    mapping columns to form fields, 220
Checkout Status option, teams, 372
circular hotspots, 89
<CITE> element, elements that take styles, *162*
classes, styles and, 180
click-through rates, defined, 271–272
ClickQuick, affiliate programs and commercial advertising, 278, *279*, *280*
<CODE> element, elements that take styles, *162*
<COL> element, elements that take styles, *162*
collapsible outlines, DHTML (Dynamic HTML), 200–201
collecting data. *See* forms
Colonnade Realty, navigation tips, *107*
color, 50–52
    anti-aliasing, 51, *52*
    dithering, 50–51
    headings and themes, 34
    reduction and image size, 64–65
    rows and columns in tables, 152
    text in tables, 153–154
    themes and, 28–30
    "Web-safe" palette, 52, 76–77
    See also graphics
Colormix Web site, colors outside of "Web-safe" palette, 76

ColorSafe Web site, colors outside of "Web-safe" palette, 76–77
columns
    colored, 152
    mapping to form fields, 219–222
commerce and security issues, 270–293
    authentication software, 291–292
    backing-up data, 274
    CGI scripts, 274
    commercial advertising, 275–284
    credit cards, 290
    Electronic Commerce guide, 292
    encryption software, 291–292
    "hacker-proofing" sites, 273–274
    JustAddCommerce, 285
    ListBot, 293
    Mercantec StoreBuilder, 286
    online resources, 291–293
    overview, 271
    payment processors, 290–291
    PDG Shopping Cart, 286, *287*
    SalesCart, 287
    SecuredForm, 289
    ShopSite, 288
    StoreFront E-Commerce, 288–289, *290*
    terminology, 271–272
    third-party add-ons, 285–291
    virus scanning software, 274
    World-Wide Web Consortium Security Resources, 292–293
Compatibility tab (Page Options dialog box), DHTML menu items, 189–190, *189*
configuration scenarios, ODBC-compliant databases, 212
connection scenarios, ODBC-compliant databases, 212–219
content
    adding to shared borders, 317–318
    Web sites and, 35
contrast, graphics and, 347–348
Convert Text to Table dialog box, 137–138

copying attributes, replacing graphics globally, 336–337, *338*
Create Hyperlink dialog box
    creating hotspots, 90
    image maps as single hotspots, 86–87
credit cards, commerce and security issues, 290
criteria, Database Results Wizard, 233
cropping graphics, 63–64
    versus resampling, 64
cryptography, defined, 272
CSS (Cascading Style Sheets), 180–181
    defined, 180
    overriding styles, 181
    templates and, 315
    See also style sheets; styles

D

data
    collecting. *See* forms
    validating. *See* validating data
databases, 202–235
    Access 2000, 207–210
    creating, 206–207
    criteria, 233
    Database Results Wizard, 230–235
    fastest way to create, 206–207
    Form Properties dialog box, 227–230
    forms and, 240–241
    mapping columns to form fields, 219–222
    ODBC-compliant, 211–219
    Options for Saving Results to Database dialog box, 227–230
    overview, 203–204
    Page Options dialog box, 223–225
    relational, 205–206
    terminology, 204
    text files and results, 210
    Web Settings dialog box, 225–226
<DD> element, elements that take styles, *162*
default hyperlinks, image maps and, 92

<DEL> element, elements that take styles, *162*
design tips
    graphics, 48–50
    layout, 349–352
    themes, 2–5
<DFN> element, elements that take styles, *162*
DHTML (Dynamic HTML), 184–201
    adding font effects to hyperlinks, 198–199
    animation, 192
    Borders and Shading dialog box, 193–194
    changing images when pointing at, 77–78, 80
    collapsible outlines, 200–201
    Compatibility tab (Page Options dialog box), 189–190, *189*
    creating effects for hyperlink images, 199–200
    defined, 186
    DOM (document object model), 186, 187
    effects, 191–201
    Effects toolbar, 188–189, 190
    enhancements, 187
    font effects, 192–193
    Format Painter to copy effects, 197
    JavaScript and, 191
    menu items related to, 189–190
    objects and effects (determining), 190
    overview, 185
    Page Properties dialog box, 198–199
    Page Transitions dialog box, 194–197
    previewing effects, 190–191
    Remove Effect button, 197
    shading text, 192–193
    swapping graphics, 77–78, 80, 191–192
    toolbar, 188–189, 190

Index 379

<DIR> element, elements that take styles, *162*
Display Properties dialog box, resolution options, 68–69, *70*
dithering, color, 50–51
<DIV> element, elements that take styles, *163*
<DL> element, elements that take styles, *163*
Documenter dialog box, Access 2000 databases, 209–210
DOM (document object model), DHTML (Dynamic HTML), 186, 187
download time
    optimizing graphics, 58–60, 70, *71*, *72*
    Reports view and graphics, 57–58
downloading
    active graphics and, 23
    image maps and, 93–95
Draw Table tool, 134–137
    formatting tables, 141–142
drop-down lists
    adding to forms, 262–265
    Form Page Wizard, 245, *246*
    mapping columns to form fields, 222
<DT> element, elements that take styles, *163*

E

e-commerce, defined, 272
e-mail, sending form results via, 9–10
Edit Hyperlink dialog box, 92–93
editing
    HTML manually, 8
    Preview view and, 8
    themes, *5*
effects, DHTML (Dynamic HTML), 191–201
Effects toolbar, DHTML (Dynamic HTML), 188–189, 190
Electronic Commerce guide, commerce and security issues, 292

elements, 338–352
    defined, 338
    definitions and themes, 20, *21*
    fonts and, 340–343
    graphic, 343–348
    impact of, 339–340
    layout as, 349–352
    overview, 338, *339*
elements that take styles, *160–167*
    <A> element, *160*
    <ABBR> element, *160*
    <ACRONYM> element, *161*
    <ADDRESS> element, *161*
    <APPLET> element, *161*
    <AREA> element, *161*
    <B> element, *161*
    <BASE> element, *161*
    <BASEFONT> element, *161*
    <BGSOUND> element, *161*
    <BIG> element, *161*
    <BLINK> element, *161*
    <BLOCKQUOTE> element, *161*
    <BODY> element, *161*

 element, *162*
    <BUTTON> element, *162*
    <CAPTION> element, *162*
    <CENTER> element, *162*
    <CITE> element, *162*
    <CODE> element, *162*
    <COL> element, *162*
    <DD> element, *162*
    <DEL> element, *162*
    <DFN> element, *162*
    <DIR> element, *162*
    <DIV> element, *163*
    <DL> element, *163*
    <DT> element, *163*
    <EM> element, *163*
    <EMBED> element, *163*
    <FIELDSET> element, *163*
    <FONT> element, *163*
    <FORM> element, *163*
    <FRAME> element, *163*
    <HEAD> element, *164*
    <Hn> elements, *163*

<HR> element, *164*
<HTML> element, *164*
<I> element, *164*
<IFRAME> element, *164*
<IMG> element, *164*
<INPUT> element, *164*
<INS> element, *164*
<ISINDEX> element, *164*
<KBD> element, *164*
<LABEL> element, *164*
<LAYER> element, *164*
<LEGEND> element, *164*
<LI> element, *165*
<LINK> element, *165*
<MAP> element, *165*
<MARQUEE> element, *165*
<MENU> element, *165*
<META> element, *165*
<NOBR> element, *165*
<NOEMBED> element, *165*
<NOFRAMES> element, *165*
<OBJECT> element, *165*
<OL> element, *165*
<OPTGROUP> element, *165*
<OPTION> element, *165*
<P> element, *165*
<S> element, *166*
<SAMP> element, *166*
<SCRIPT> element, *166*
<SELECT> element, *166*
<SMALL> element, *166*
<SPAN> element, *166*
<STRIKETHROUGH> element, *166*
<STRONG> element, *166*
<STYLE> element, *166*
<SUB> element, *166*
<SUP> element, *166*
<TABLE> element, *166*
<TD> element, *166*
<TEXTAREA> element, *167*
<TFOOT> element, *167*
<TH> element, *167*
<THEAD> element, *167*
<TITLE> element, *167*
<TR> element, *167*
<TT> element, *167*
<U> element, *167*
<UL> element, *167*
<VAR> element, *167*
<EM> element, elements that take styles, *163*
<EMBED> element, elements that take styles, *163*
embedded links, navigation and, 112
embedding fonts, 342
encryption
    asymmetric, 271
    defined, 272
    public-key, 272
encryption software, commerce and security issues, 291–292
exit signs, navigation and, 112–113
extensions
    common file, 356–357
    FrontPage. *See* FrontPage extensions
    server. *See* server extensions

F

FAQs (Frequently Asked Questions), xxii–14
    designing themes, 2–5
    editing HTML manually, 8
    FrontPage 2000 resources, 13–14
    navigation buttons (location of), 5–6
    navigation buttons (text), 10–11
    overview, 1
    Preview view, 8
    publishing pages without server extensions, 11–12
    sending form results via e-mail, 9–10
    shared borders, 7
    shared borders and include files, 13
<FIELDSET> element, elements that take styles, *163*
file extensions, common, 356–357

file organization, 116–120
    filenames, 117–120
    folders and, 116
    teams, 364–367
    See also navigation
filters, JPEG graphics, 75
firewalls, defined, 272
Fireworks Slice tool, cutting graphics and reassembling, 56, *57*
Float property, described, *143*
folders, file organization and, 116
Font dialog box, 170–172
    Character Spacing tab, 171
    Indents and Spacing tab, 172
font effects
    adding to hyperlinks, 198–199
    DHTML (Dynamic HTML), 192–193
<FONT> element, elements that take styles, *163*
fonts, 340–343
    anti-aliasing, 49
    banners and, 32–33
    choosing, 340–341
    elements and, 340–343
    embedding, 342
    graphic images versus text, 341–342
    point size, 343
    themes and, 26–30
    See also text
<FORM> element, elements that take styles, *163*
Form Page Wizard, 241–268
    Boolean fields, 248
    CGI scripts and, 251–252
    creating forms, 241–252
    drop-down lists, 245, *246*
    Insert menu, 253–255
    modifying forms after completing, 268
    naming fields, 247
    New dialog box, 242
    numbered lists, 250
    One of Several Options option, 245
    paragraph fields, 246–247
    Personal Information option, 242–244
    text input fields, 249–250
    validating data, 255–258
Form Properties dialog box
    databases, 227–230
    sending form results via e-mail, 9–10
Format Painter, copying DHTML effects with, 197
formats, graphics, 44–50
formatting
    Include Page Component and, 323–324
    removing from text, 36
formatting tables, 139–142
    Draw Table tool, 141–142
formatting text
    color in tables, 153–154
    tables and, 130–131, 138, 153–154
    themes and, 131
forms, 236–268
    browser/server interaction, 238–239
    check boxes, 265–266
    components of, 239
    creating, 241–268
    databases and, 240–241
    defined, 239
    drop-down menus, 262–265
    Form Page Wizard, 241–268
    mapping columns to fields, 219–222
    multiple-choice questions, 258, *259*, 266
    overview, 237–241
    processing of, 238–240
    radio buttons, 259–261
    scrolling text boxes, 267, *268*
    sending results via e-mail, 9–10
    server/browser interaction, 238–239
    Yes/No questions, 266

FrontPage 2000 Answers!

<FRAME> element, elements that take styles, *163*
frames, navigation and, 115
Frequently Asked Questions. *See* FAQs
FrontPage 2000
    commerce and security issues, 270–293
    databases, 202–235
    DHTML (Dynamic HTML), 184–201
    elements, 338–352
    FAQs (Frequently Asked Questions), xxii–14
    forms, 236–268
    graphics, 42–80
    image maps, 82–95
    importing Web sites into, 357–361
    Include Page Component, 320–324
    layout, 349–352
    managing Web sites, 354–374
    navigation, 96–125
    page templates, 324–328
    publishing Web sites, 294–311
    resources, 13–14
    shared borders, 315–320
    styles, 156–183
    tables, 126–154
    templates, 314–315
    themes, 16–40
FrontPage extensions
    Include Page Component and, 321
    shared borders and, 320
    See also server extensions
FTP (File Transfer Protocol), publishing Web sites, 297, 304

G

GIF graphics format, 44–47
    animation, 70–72
    interlaced versus non-interlaced, 47
    JPEG comparison, 46
    modifications, 75–76
    transparency, 47
    See also graphics

global page templates, web-specific page templates comparison, 325
graphics, 42–80
    active, 22–23
    ALT attributes and the handicapped, 61–62
    animated, 70–72
    anti-aliasing display fonts, 49
    artifacts, 75
    banners and themes, 30–33
    "bells and whistles," 50
    Black and White option, 65–66
    brightness, 347–348
    caches and browsing, 73–74
    changing images when pointing at, 77–80
    color, 50–52
    color reduction and image size, 64–65
    colors outside of "Web-safe" palette, 76–77
    consistency of, 48
    contrast, 347–348
    creating with tables, 139–141
    cropping, 63–64
    cutting into smaller sizes and reassembling, 54–57
    design tips, 48–50
    DHTML effects for hyperlink images, 199–200
    download time (optimizing), 58–60, 70, *71*, *72*
    download time (Reports view and), 57–58
    elements as, 343–348
    formats, 44–50
    Hover Button Properties dialog box, 78–79
    HTML and scaling images, 66
    image maps, 53–54, 82–95
    JPEG modifications, 74–75
    Macromedia's Fireworks Slice tool, 56, *57*
    optimizing, 74–80

optimizing download time, 58–60, 70, *71, 72*
overview, 43–44
Picture toolbar, 77
replacing globally, 329–338
Reports view, 57–58
resampling, 62–63
resampling versus resizing, 62
resolution options, 68–69, *70*
saving themes, 343–344
sizing when replacing, 333–336
slicing, 54–57
styles and, 49
swapping on Web pages, 191–192
in tables as alternative to image maps, 95
tables and, 54–57, 70, *71, 72*
of text in tables as alternative to image maps, 94
themes and, 36–38
thumbnails, 345–347
tiling, 67–68
typographical marks, 49
vertical rules, 67
ways to use images on Web sites, 53–74
Web sites, 348
"Web-safe" palette, 52
"Web-safe" palette (colors outside of), 76–77
white space and, 50
graphics formats, 44–50
GIF, 44–45, 46, 47
GIF modifications, 75–76
JPEG, 45
JPEG modifications, 74–75
JPEG versus GIF, 46
PNG, 45–46
grid system, layout, 350–352
groups. *See* teams

H

<HEAD> element, elements that take styles, *164*
heading colors, themes and, 34
heading styles, 159–160
Height property, described, *143*
Hidden Directories option, shared borders, 318–319
hierarchical displays, navigation, 111
Highlight Hotspots tool, 91
hit counters, publishing Web sites, 306–307
<Hn> elements
elements that take styles, *163*
heading styles, 159–160
home pages, navigation and, 103
hotspots, 53–54, 86–93
associating text with, 90–91
circular, 89
Create Hyperlink dialog box, 90
creating, 87–90
default hyperlinks, 92
Edit Hyperlink dialog box, 92–93
Highlight Hotspots tool, 91
image maps as single, 86–87
Image Properties dialog box, 92
modifying, 92–93
Picture toolbar, *88*
polygonal, 89
rectangular, 89
See also image maps
Hover Button Properties dialog box, changing images when pointing at, 78–80
<HR> element, elements that take styles, *164*
HTML (Hypertext Markup Language)
Dynamic. *See* DHTML
editing manually, 8
replacing text and graphics globally, 330–336
scaling images and, 66
<HTML> element, elements that take styles, *164*
HTTP (Hypertext Transfer Protocol), publishing Web sites, 297
hyperlinks
adding font effects to, 198–199
broken, 120–121

creating DHTML effects for images, 199–200
default for image maps, 92

I

<I> element, elements that take styles, *164*
iBill.com, credit cards and security issues, 290
iconographs, navigation, 109
ideagraphs, navigation, 109
<IFRAME> element, elements that take styles, *164*
image maps, 53–54, 82–95
    alternatives to, 93–95
    browser and download issues, 93–95
    Create Hyperlink dialog box, 86–87
    default hyperlinks, 92
    graphics in tables as alternative to, 95
    graphics of text in tables as alternative to, 94
    hotspots, 53–54, 86–93
    illusion of, 84
    limitations of, 93
    overview, 83
    selecting images, 84–87
    as single hotspots, 86–87
    text as alternative to, 94
    text and, 85
    text in tables as alternative to, 94
    text-only navigation bars and, 87
    "Web-worthy" checklist, 85
    See also graphics
Image Properties dialog box, default hyperlinks for hotspots, 92
images. *See* graphics
<IMG> element, elements that take styles, *164*
Import dialog box, Add Database Connection dialog box, 224–225

importing Web sites into FrontPage 2000, 357–361
    Limit To This Page Plus checkbox, 359
    server-side processing and, 360–361
    from the Web, 357–359
include files
    shared borders and, 13
    See also server extensions
Include Page Component, 320–324
    described, 320
    formatting and, 323–324
    FrontPage extensions and, 321
    Page to Include dialog box, 320
    Server-Side Includes and, 321–324
    shared borders comparison, 320, 324
    templates, 314
Indents and Spacing tab, Paragraph dialog box, 172
inheritance
    styles and, 168
    tables and, 135
inline elements, inheritance, 135
<INPUT> element, elements that take styles, *164*
<INS> element, elements that take styles, *164*
Insert menu, Form Page Wizard, 253–255
Insert Table dialog box, 133–134
Insert Table tool, 134
installing themes, 3–5
Internet Service Providers. *See* ISPs
<ISINDEX> element, elements that take styles, *164*
ISPs (Internet Service Providers)
    private servers comparison, 297–302
    publishing Web sites, 296–297

Index

J
JavaScript, DHTML (Dynamic HTML) and, 191
JPEG graphics format, 45
    artifacts, 75
    filters, 75
    GIF comparison, 46
    modifications, 74–75
    See also graphics
JustAddCommerce, commerce and security issues, 285

K
<KBD> element, elements that take styles, *164*

L
<LABEL> element, elements that take styles, *164*
<LAYER> element, elements that take styles, *164*
layout, 349–352
    defined, 349
    grid system, 350–352
    overview, 349–350
    testing, 352
<LEGEND> element, elements that take styles, *164*
levels, multiple page template, 326–328
<LI> element, elements that take styles, *165*
Limit To This Page Plus checkbox, importing Web sites into FrontPage 2000, 359
<LINK> element, elements that take styles, *165*
links. *See* hyperlinks
LinkShare, affiliate programs and commercial advertising, 278, *279*
List Properties dialog box, collapsible DHTML outlines, 200–201
ListBot, commerce and security issues, 293
lists
    Bullets and Numbering dialog box, 175–176
    drop-down. *See* drop-down lists
local hard drives
    mapping to remote servers, 309–311
    publishing Web sites via, 308–309
logo example, replacing text and graphics globally, 331–332

M
Macromedia's Fireworks Slice tool, cutting graphics and reassembling, 56, *57*
managing Web sites, 354–374
    automatically redirecting URLs, 360
    common file extensions, 356–357
    importing Web sites into FrontPage 2000, 357–361
    overview, 355
    teams, 363–372
    troubleshooting, 361–363
<MAP> element, elements that take styles, *165*
mapping columns to form fields, 219–222
    Allow Zero Length property, 222
    check box fields, 220
    drop-down lists, 222
    radio button fields, 221
    scrolling text box fields, 222
    text input boxes, 219–220
mapping local drives to remote servers, 309–311
mapping Web sites. *See* site maps
margins, Borders and Shading dialog box, 174
<MARQUEE> element, elements that take styles, *165*
Master Category List, teams, 365
<MENU> element, elements that take styles, *165*

menu items, DHTML (Dynamic HTML) and, 189–190
Mercantec StoreBuilder, commerce and security issues, 286
<META> element, elements that take styles, *165*
MIME, defined, 272
mirror sites, 363
mnemonic symbols, navigation, 109
Modify Style dialog box
    Borders and Shading dialog box, 173–174
    Bullets and Numbering dialog box, 175–176
    Position dialog box, 177
More Colors dialog box, themes and, 30
multiple page templates, 326–328
multiple themes, 24–26
multiple-choice questions, forms and, 258, *259*, 266

N

names, validating, 257
naming fields, Form Page Wizard, 247
naming files, navigation and, 117–120
navigation, 96–125
    ALT tags, 110
    Archipelago Web site, *106*
    Colonnade Realty, *107*
    ease-of-use, 110–111
    embedded links, 112
    exit signs, 112–113
    file organization, 116–120
    filenames and, 117–120
    frames and, 115
    hierarchical displays, 111
    home pages, 103
    iconographs, 109
    ideagraphs, 109
    mnemonic symbols, 109
    organizing principles, 100
    overview, 97
    planning, 98–99
    preventing pages from being published, 124–125
    Publish Status command, 124
    shared borders, 104–105
    site maps and, 99–103, 114–115
    site structure, 98–100
    Site Summary reports, 120–125
    Slow Pages report, 121–123
    splash pages, 103
    storyboarding and, 100
    strategies, 101–115
    subfolders and, 116, *117*
    supplemental, 112
    symbols, 109, *110*
    table of contents, 113–114
    text links, 107–108
    That Patchwork Place, 107–108
    tips, 106–113
Navigation Bar Properties dialog box
    including Web pages on, 38–39
    shared borders, 6
navigation bars
    outside of shared borders without graphics, 38
    shared borders without graphics, 37–38
    text-only and image maps, 87
navigation buttons
    changing text of, 10–11
    location of, 5–6
    themes and, 33–34
NetBEUI, mapping local drives to remote servers, 310–311
networked computers, ODBC-compliant databases, 219
New dialog box, Form Page Wizard, 242
New Style dialog box, 178
New Task dialog box, teams, *367*
<NOBR> element, elements that take styles, *165*
<NOEMBED> element, elements that take styles, *165*
<NOFRAMES> element, elements that take styles, *165*
numbered lists, Form Page Wizard, 250

O

<OBJECT> element, elements that take styles, *165*
objects, DHTML effects and, 190
ODBC-compliant databases, 211–219
    Access 2000 connections, 217–219
    configuration scenarios, 212
    connection scenarios, 212–219
    networked computers, 219
    SQL Server connections, 213–217
<OL> element, elements that take styles, *165*
One of Several Options option, Form Page Wizard, 245
online resources
    commerce and security issues, 291–293
    FrontPage 2000, 13–14
<OPTGROUP> element, elements that take styles, *165*
<OPTION> element, elements that take styles, *165*
Options for Saving Results to Database dialog box, 227–230
organizing files. *See* file organization
organizing principles, navigation, 100
outlines, collapsible DHTML, 200–201
overriding styles, CSS (Cascading Style Sheets), 181

P

<P> element, elements that take styles, *165*
packets, defined, 272
padding
    Borders and Shading dialog box, 174
    cell, *143*, 152–153
Page Options dialog box
    databases, 223–225
    Import dialog box, 223–224
    See also Compatibility tab
Page Properties dialog box
    adding font effects to hyperlinks, 198–199
    copying attributes, 336–337, *338*
page templates, 324–328
    creating, 325–326
    defined, 324–325
    global versus web-specific, 325
    levels of, 326–328
Page to Include dialog box, Include Page Component, 320
Page Transitions dialog box, 194–197
    See also DHTML (Dynamic HTML)
Painter. *See* Format Painter
Paragraph dialog box, Indents and Spacing tab, 172
paragraph fields
    Form Page Wizard, 246–247
    See also scrolling text boxes
payment processors, commerce and security issues, 290–291
PDG Shopping Cart, commerce and security issues, 286, *287*
Personal Information option, Form Page Wizard, 242–244
PGP (Pretty Good Privacy), defined, 272
phone numbers, validating, 256–257
Picture toolbar, 77
    creating hotspots on image maps, *88*
    See also graphics
pixels
    defined, 51
    See also anti-aliasing
planning Web sites, 25
    navigation and, 98–99
PNG graphics format, 45–46
point size, fonts, 343
polygonal hotspots, 89
Position dialog box, Modify Style dialog box, 177
Preview view, editing pages and, 8
previewing effects, DHTML (Dynamic HTML), 190–191
privacy, 241

See also commerce and
    security issues
private servers, ISPs comparison,
    297–302
properties
    Form Properties dialog box,
        227–230
    Hover Button Properties dialog
        box, 78–79
    Navigation Bar Properties dialog
        box, 38–39
    table, 142, *143*
    Text Box Properties dialog box,
        256–258
    theme, 2
    themes and element definitions,
        20, *21*
proxy servers, defined, 272
public-key encryption, defined, 272
Publish Status command, Site
    Summary reports, 124–125
publishing Web sites, 294–311
    final considerations before,
        372–374
    FTP (File Transfer Protocol),
        297, 304
    hit counters, 306–307
    HTTP (Hypertext Transfer
        Protocol), 297
    ISPs, 296–297
    ISPs versus private servers,
        297–302
    local hard drives, 308–309
    locations of files, 308–311
    mapping local drives to remote
        servers, 309–311
    overview, 295
    preventing pages from being
        published, 124–125
    server extensions, 303–304
    server software, 302–304
    SSL (Secure-Sockets Layer),
        297, 308
    terminology, 296–297
    testing, 372–374
    Unix servers, 305–306
    Windows NT servers, 307, 309–310
    without server extensions,
        11–12, 304
    WPP (Web Presence Provider),
        297, 299–302, 305–306

Q

questions
    frequently asked. *See* FAQs
    multiple-choice, 258, *259*, 266
    Yes/No, 266

R

radio buttons
    forms and, 259–261
    mapping columns to form
        fields, 221
rectangular hotspots, 89
Refer-it.com, affiliate programs and
    commercial advertising, 280
relational databases, 205–206
Remove Effect button, DHTML
    (Dynamic HTML), 197
replacing text and graphics globally,
    329–338
    copying attributes, 336–337, *338*
    HTML, 330–336
    logo example, 331–332
    overview, 329–330
    Replace dialog box, *335*
    sizing graphics, 333–336
reports, troubleshooting Web sites, 362
Reports view, graphics and download
    time, 57–58
resampling graphics, 62–64
    versus cropping, 64
    versus resizing, 62
resolution options, graphics, 68–69, *70*
resources
    commerce and security issues,
        291–293
    FrontPage 2000, 13–14

results
  Database Results Wizard, 230–235
  Options for Saving Results to
    Database dialog box, 227–230
review status, teams and, 369–370
rows, colored, 152
rules, tables and borders and, 149–150

S

<S> element, elements that take
  styles, *166*
SAFE-AUDIT, affiliate programs and
  commercial advertising, 281
SalesCart, commerce and security
  issues, 287
<SAMP> element, elements that take
  styles, *166*
saving graphics from themes, 343–344
scaling images, HTML and, 66
<SCRIPT> element, elements that take
  styles, *166*
scripting
  CGI, 251–252, 274
  JavaScript, 191
scrolling text boxes
  forms, 267, *268*
  mapping columns to form
    fields, 222
  See also paragraph fields
Secure Sockets Layer. See SSL
SecuredForm, commerce and security
  issues, 289
security
  defined, 272
  See also commerce and
    security issues
<SELECT> element, elements that take
  styles, *166*
Select Picture dialog box, themes and
  banners, 32
server extensions
  active graphics and, 23
  publishing pages without, 11–12
  publishing Web sites with,
    303–304
  publishing Web sites without, 304
  See also FrontPage extensions;
    include files
server software, 302–304
Server-Side Includes (SSI), Include Page
  Component and, 321–324
server-side processing, importing Web
  sites into FrontPage 2000, 360–361
server/browser interaction, forms and,
  238–239
servers
  mapping local drives to remote,
    309–311
  Unix, 305–306
  Windows NT, 307
Service Providers, Internet. See ISPs
shading, Borders and Shading dialog
  box, 174
shading text, DHTML (Dynamic
  HTML), 192–193
shared borders, 315–320
  adding content to, 317–318
  All Pages option, 316
  browser compatibility issues, 7
  defined, 315
  FrontPage extensions and, 320
  Hidden Directories option, 318–319
  include files and, 13
  Include Page Component
    comparison, 320, 324
  individual page options, 316–317
  navigation, 104–105
  Navigation Bar Properties dialog
    box, *6*
  navigation bars outside of without
    graphics, 38
  with navigation bars without
    graphics, 37–38
  reasons for, 315
  Shared Borders dialog box, 7, *316*
  templates and, 314
  ways to use, 315–316
ShopSite, commerce and security
  issues, 288

site maps
- creating, 114–115
- navigation and, 99–103

Site Summary reports, 120–125
- broken hyperlinks, 120–121
- overview, 120
- Publish Status command, 124–125
- Slow Pages report, 121–123

Sitecash, affiliate programs and commercial advertising, 281

sites. *See* Web sites

sizing
- graphics, 333–336
- thumbnails, 346–347

slicing graphics, 54–57
- Slice tool, 56, *57*

Slow Pages report, Site Summary reports, 121–123

<SMALL> element, elements that take styles, *166*

source control, teams and, 371–372

spacing between cells, *143*, 148

<SPAN> element, elements that take styles, *166*

splash pages, navigation and, 103

SQL Server connections, ODBC-compliant databases, 213–217

SSI (Server-Side Includes), Include Page Component and, 321–324

SSL (Secure Sockets Layer)
- defined, 272
- publishing Web sites and, 297, 308

StoreFront E-Commerce, commerce and security issues, 288–289, *290*

storyboarding, navigation and, 100

<STRIKETHROUGH> element, elements that take styles, *166*

<STRONG> element, elements that take styles, *166*

<STYLE> element, elements that take styles, *166*

Style dialog box, 168–178
- Borders and Shading dialog box, 173–174
- Bullets and Numbering dialog box, 175–176
- Character Spacing tab, 171
- creating element classes, 178
- Font dialog box, 170–172
- modifying element styles, 169–172
- New Style dialog box, 178
- Position dialog box, 177
- removing formatting from text, 36
- themes and, 27–28

style sheets, 179–180
- advantages of, 40
- applying styles to elements, 181–182
- borders alternatives, 146–147
- browser limitations and, 183
- cascading (CSS), 180–181
- defined, 179
- locations of styles, 179
- reasons for, 179
- tables and, 182
- themes comparison, 40
- *See also* themes

styles, 156–183
- attributes, 167–178
- classes of, 180
- defined, 158
- elements that take, *160–167*
- Font dialog box, 170–172
- graphics and, 49
- heading, 159–160
- inheritance and, 168
- locations of, 179
- overriding in sheets, 181
- overview, 157–158
- sheets. *See* style sheets
- Style dialog box, 168–178
- templates, 158

<SUB> element, elements that take styles, *166*

subfolders, navigation and, 116, *117*

summary reports. *See* Site Summary reports

<SUP> element, elements that take styles, *166*

Index

swapping graphics
    changing images when pointing, 77–80
    DHTML (Dynamic HTML), 191–192
switchboard, adding tables to Access 2000 databases, 207–208
symbols, navigation, 109, *110*

T

<TABLE> element, elements that take styles, *166*
table of contents, navigation, 113–114
table properties, borders and, 142, *143*
Table Properties dialog box
    colored rows and columns, 152
    partial borders, 148–152
    setting borders, 144–148
tables, 126–154
    adding to Access 2000 databases, 207–208
    aligning text in cells, 154
    borders, 142–148
    cell padding, *143*, 152–153
    cell spacing, *143*, 148
    colored rows and columns, 152
    Convert Text to Table dialog box, 137–138
    creating, 133–142
    creating graphics with, 139–141
    Draw Table tool, 134–137, 141–142
    formatting, 139–142
    formatting text and, 130–131, 138
    graphics in as alternative to image maps, 95
    graphics and, 54–57, 70, *71*, *72*
    graphics of text in as alternative to image maps, 94
    inheritance, 135
    Insert Table dialog box, 133–134
    Insert Table tool, 134
    overview, 127
    partial borders, 148–152
    reasons to use, 128–131
    rules, 149–150
    sliced graphics and, 54–57
    spacing between cells, *143*, 148
    structure of, 132
    style sheets and, 182
    Table menu, 133–134
    text formatting and, 130–131, 138, 153–154
    themes and formatting text, 131
    tiling graphics, 139
    when to use, 128–131
Task Manager, teams and, 363
tasks, 367–371
    See also teams
Tasks view, teams and, 367, *368*, 370
<TD> element, elements that take styles, *166*
teams, 363–372
    Assigned To report, 368–369
    categorizing files, 365–367
    Checkout Status option, 372
    defining users, 364
    file organization, 364–367
    marking tasks complete, 371
    Master Category List, 365
    New Task dialog box, *367*
    review status, 369–370
    source control, 371–372
    Task Manager, 363
    tasks, 367–371
    Tasks view, 367, *368*, 370
templates, 314–315
    CSS (Cascading Style Sheets) and, 315
    Include Page Component, 314
    page, 324–328
    shared borders and, 314
    style, 158
    See also themes
testing
    before publishing Web sites, 372–374
    layout, 352
text
    aligning in cells, 154
    as alternative to image maps, 94

associating with hotspots, 90–91
color in tables, 153–154
Convert Text to Table dialog box,
  137–138
formatting. *See* formatting text
graphics of in tables as alternative
  to image maps, 94
image maps and, 85
navigation button, 10–11
removing formatting from, 36
replacing globally, 329–338
tables and formatting,
  130–131, 138
See also fonts
Text Box Properties dialog box,
  validating data, 256–258
text boxes, scrolling. *See* scrolling
  text boxes
text files, database results as, 210
text input boxes
  Form Page Wizard, 249–250
  mapping columns to form fields,
    219–220
text links, navigation and, 107–108
text in tables, as alternative to image
  maps, 94
text-only navigation bars, image maps
  and, 87
<TEXTAREA> element, elements that
  take styles, *167*
<TFOOT> element, elements that take
  styles, *167*
<TH> element, elements that take
  styles, *167*
That Patchwork Place, navigation and,
  107–108
<THEAD> element, elements that take
  styles, *167*
themes, 16–40
  active graphics, 22–23
  banners and, 30–33
  choosing, 20–22
  colors and, 28–30
  creating, 39–40
  designing, 2–5

editing, *5*
element definitions, 20, *21*
fonts and, 26–30
formatting text and, 131
graphics and, 36–38
heading colors, 34
installing additional, 3–5
modifying, 26–40
More Colors dialog box, 30
multiple, 24–26
Navigation Bar Properties dialog
  box, 38–39
navigation buttons and, 33–34
overview, 17–18
properties, 2
reasons for, 19–20
removing formatting from text, 36
saving graphics from, 343–344
Select Picture dialog box, 32
shared borders with navigation
  bars, 37–38
Style dialog box, 27–28
style sheets comparison, 40
See also style sheets; templates
thumbnails, 345–347
  Auto Thumbnail command,
    345–346
  overview, 345–346
  sizing, 346–347
  See also graphics
tiling graphics, 67–68, 139
  backgrounds and, 67
  preventing, 68
<TITLE> element, elements that take
  styles, *167*
TLS (Transport Layer Security),
  defined, 272
toolbars, DHTML (Dynamic HTML),
  188–189, 190
<TR> element, elements that take
  styles, *167*
transitions, Page Transitions dialog box,
  194–197
transparency, GIF graphics format, 47

Index

Transport Layer Security (TLS), defined, 272
troubleshooting Web sites, 361–363
    mirror sites, 363
    reports, 362
    tools, 361–362
<TT> element, elements that take styles, *167*
typefaces. *See* fonts
typographical marks, graphics and, 49

U

<U> element, elements that take styles, *167*
<UL> element, elements that take styles, *167*
Unix servers, publishing Web sites, 305–306
URLs, automatically redirecting, 360

V

validating data, 255–258
    names, 257
    overview, 255–256
    phone numbers, 256–257
    Text Box Properties dialog box, 256–258
    zip codes, 257–258
    See also Form Page Wizard; forms
ValueClick, affiliate programs and commercial advertising, 282, *283*
<VAR> element, elements that take styles, *167*
vertical rules, graphics and, 67
virus scanning software, commerce and security issues, 274

W

Web Settings dialog box, databases, 225–226
Web sites
    commerce and security issues, 270–293
    content and, 35
    Database Results Wizard, 230–235
    development hazards, 35
    graphics, 42–80, 348
    "hacker-proofing," 273–274
    importing into FrontPage 2000, 357–361
    managing. *See* managing Web sites
    mapping, 99–100
    mirror sites, 363
    navigating. *See* navigation
    optimizing download times, 58–60, 70, *71, 72*
    planning, 25
    privacy, 241
    publishing. *See* publishing Web sites
    Site Summary reports, 120–125
    Slow Pages report, 121–123
    structure of, 98–100
    teams and, 363–372
    troubleshooting, 361–363
    ways to use images on, 53–74
web-specific page templates, global page templates comparison, 325
WEFT (Web Embedding Font Tool), 342
white space, graphics and, 50
Width property, described, *143*
Windows NT servers, publishing Web sites, 307, 309–310
World-Wide Web Consortium Security Resources, commerce and security issues, 292–293
WPP (Web Presence Provider)
    publishing Web sites, 297, 299–302, 305–306
    Unix servers and, 305–306

Y

Yes/No questions, forms and, 266

Z

zero length, Allow Zero Length property, 222
zip codes, validating, 257–258

Have all your questions been answered?

To **speak to the support experts** who handle more than one million technical issues every month, call **Stream's** Microsoft® FrontPage® answer line! Trained specialists will answer your Microsoft® FrontPage® questions including creating tables, forms and image maps, and publishing your site.

1-800-477-7613 $29.95 per problem (Charge to a major credit card.)

1-900-555-2007 $29.95 per problem (Charge to your phone bill.)

Visit our web site at www.stream.com.

Stream

We help people use technology!